ONE TO

Bilingual Dictionary

LMQLPCRØCNF

English-Farsi
Farsi-English
Dictionary

Compiled by
Maryam Zamankhani

STAR Foreign Language BOOKS

© Publishers

ISBN : 978 1 908357 57 1

First Edition	:	2011
Second	:	2012
Third Edition	:	2014
Fourth Edition	:	2017
Fifth Edition	:	2018

Published by

STAR Foreign Language BOOKS

a unit of
ibs BOOKS (UK)

56, Langland Crescent
Stanmore HA7 1NG, U.K.
info@starbooksuk.com
www.starbooksuk.com

Printed in India at
Star Print-O-Bind, New Delhi-110 020

About this Dictionary

Developments in science and technology today have narrowed down distances between countries, and have made the world a small place. A person living thousands of miles away can learn and understand the culture and lifestyle of another country with ease and without travelling to that country. Languages play an important role as facilitators of communication in this respect.

To promote such an understanding, STAR **Foreign Language** BOOKS has planned to bring out a series of bilingual dictionaries in which important English words have been translated into other languages, with Roman transliteration in case of languages that have different scripts. This is a humble attempt to bring people of the word closer through the medium of language, thus making communication easy and convenient.

Under this series of *one-to-one dictionaries*, we have published almost 50 languages, the list of which has been given in the opening pages. These have all been compiled and edited by teachers and scholars of the relative languages.

Bilingual Dictionaries in this Series

English-Afrikaans / Afrikaans-English	Abraham Venter
English-Albanian / Albanian-English	Theodhora Blushi
English-Amharic / Amharic-English	Girun Asanke
English-Arabic / Arabic-English	Rania-al-Qass
English-Bengali / Bengali-English	Amit Majumdar
English-Bosnian / Bosnian-English	Boris Kazanegra
English-Bulgarian / Bulgarian-English	Vladka Kocheshkova
English-Cantonese / Cantonese-English	Nisa Yang
English-Chinese (Mandarin) / Chinese (Mandarin)-Eng	Y. Shang & R. Yao
English-Croatian / Croatain-English	Vesna Kazanegra
English-Czech / Czech-English	Jindriska Poulova
English-Dari / Dari-English	Amir Khan
English-Dutch / Dutch-English	Lisanne Vogel
English-Estonian / Estonian-English	Lana Haleta
English-Farsi / Farsi-English	Maryam Zaman Khani
English-French / French-English	Aurélie Colin
English-Gujarati / Gujarati-English	Sujata Basaria
English-German / German-English	Bicskei Hedwig
English-Greek / Greek-English	Lina Stergiou
English-Hindi / Hindi-English	Sudhakar Chaturvedi
English-Hungarian / Hungarian-English	Lucy Mallows
English-Italian / Italian-English	Eni Lamllari
English-Korean / Korean-English	Mihee Song
English-Latvian / Latvian-English	Julija Baranovska
English-Levantine Arabic / Levantine Arabic-English	Ayman Khalaf
English-Lithuanian / Lithuanian-English	Regina Kazakeviciute
English-Nepali / Nepali-English	Anil Mandal
English-Norwegian / Norwegian-English	Samuele Narcisi
English-Pashto / Pashto-English	Amir Khan
English-Polish / Polish-English	Magdalena Herok
English-Portuguese / Portuguese-English	Dina Teresa
English-Punjabi / Punjabi-English	Teja Singh Chatwal
English-Romanian / Romanian-English	Georgeta Laura Dutulescu
English-Russian / Russian-English	Katerina Volobuyeva
English-Serbian / Serbian-English	Vesna Kazanegra
English-Sinhalese / Sinhalese-English	Naseer Salahudeen
English-Slovak / Slovak-English	Zuzana Horvathova
English-Slovenian / Slovenian-English	Tanja Turk
English-Somali / Somali-English	Ali Mohamud Omer
English-Spanish / Spanish-English	Cristina Rodriguez
English-Swedish / Swedish-English	Madelene Axelsson
English-Tagalog / Tagalog-English	Jefferson Bantayan
English-Tamil / Tamil-English	Sandhya Mahadevan
English-Thai / Thai-English	Suwan Kaewkongpan
English-Turkish / Turkish-English	Nagme Yazgin
English-Ukrainian / Ukrainian-English	Katerina Volobuyeva
English-Urdu / Urdu-English	S. A. Rahman
English-Vietnamese / Vietnamese-English	Hoa Hoang
English-Yoruba / Yoruba-English	O. A. Temitope

More languages in print

STAR Foreign Language BOOKS

ENGLISH-FARSI

A

a *art* يكي yeki
abandon *v* ترك گفتن tark goftan
abandonment *n* ترك tark
abbey *n* دير deir
abbreviate *v* خلاصه کردن kholase kardan
abbreviation *n* اختصار ekhtesar
abdicate *v* واگذار کردن vagozar kardan
abdication *n* استعفا estefa
abdomen *n* شکم shekam
abdominal *adj* شکمي shekami
abduct *v* ربودن roboodan
abduction *n* ربايش robaiesh
aberration *n* خبط khabt
abide by *v* فرمان بردن farman bordan
ability *n* توانايي tavanaee
ablaze *adj* سوزان soozan
able *adj* توانا tavana
abnormal *adj* غيرعادی gheire addi
abnormality *n* نابه هنجاري na be hanjari
aboard *adv* روي rooye
abolish *v* برانداختن barandakhtan
abominable *adj* مکروه makrooh
abort *v* سقط کردن seght kardan
abortion *n* جنين سقط seghte janin
abound *v* فراوان بودن faravan boodan

about *pre* درباره darbarehe
above *pre* بالا balla
abridge *v* کوتاه کردن kootah kardan
abruptly *adv* به تندي be tondi
absence *n* غيبت gheibat
absent *adj* غايب ghaieb
absolute *adj* مطلق motlagh
absolve *v* آمرزيدن amorzidan
absorb *v* جذب کردن jazb kardan
abstain *v* پرهيز کردن parhiz kardan
abstinence *n* پرهيز parhiz
abstract *adj* خلاصه kholase
absurd *adj* پوچ pooch
abundance *n* فراواني faravani
abundant *adj* بسيار besyar
abuse *v* سو استفاده کردن soo estefade kardan
abusive *adj* ناسزاوار na sezavar
abyss *n* بسيار عميق besyar amigh
academic *adj* دانشگاهي daneshgahi
academy *n* فرهنگستان farhangestan
accelerate *v* تسريع کردن tasri kardan
accelerator *n* شتاب دهنده shetab dahande
accent *n* تلفظ talaffoz
acceptable *adj* قابل قبول ghabele ghabool
acceptance *n* پذيرش paziresh
access *n* دسترس dastras
accessible *adj* دسترس در dar dastras

accessory *n* الوازم‌يدكي lavazem yadaki

accident *n* حادثه hadese

accidental *adj* تصادفي tasadofy

acclaim *v* ادعاكردن eddea kardan

acclimatize *v* خوگرفتن khoo gereftan

accommodate *v* جادادن ja dadan

accompany *v* همراهي كردن hamrahi kardan

accomplice *n* همدست hamdast

accomplish *v* انجام‌دادن anjam dadan

accord *n* سازگاري sazegary

according to *pre* مطابق motabeghe

accordion *n* آكوردئون akardeon

account *n* حساب hesab

accountable *adj* قابل‌محاسبه ghabele mohasebe

accountant *n* حسابدار hesabdar

accreditation *n* اعتبارگذاری e'etebar-gozari

accumulate *v* انباشتن anbashtan

accumulation *n* جمع‌آوري jam avary

accuracy *n* درستي dorosty

accurate *adj* درست dorost

accusation *n* اتهام etteham

accuse *v* متهم‌كردن mottaham kardan

accustom *v* عادت‌كردن adat kardan

ace *n* تك‌خال tak khal

ache *n* درد dard

achieve *v* دست‌يافتن dast yaftan

achievement *n* دست‌يابي dast yabi

acid *n* ترش torsh

acidity *n* ترشي torshy

acknowledge *v* قدرداني‌كردن ghadrdany kardan

acorn *n* مازو mazoo

acoustic *adj* صوتي sowti

acquaint *v* آشناكردن ashna kardan

acquaintance *n* آشنايى ashnaei

acquire *v* بدست‌آوردن be dast avardan

acquisition *n* فراگيري faragiry

acquit *v* برطرف‌كردن bartaraf kardan

acquittal *n* روسفيدي roo sefidy

acre *n* جريب jerib

acrobat *n* بازبند band baz

across *pre* سرتاسر sar-ta-sar

act *v* عمل‌كردن amal kardan

action *n* عمل amal

activate *v* فعال‌كردن fa'al kardan

activation *n* فعال‌سازي fa'al sazy

active *adj* فعال fa'al

activity *n* فعاليت fa'aliat

actor *n* بازيگرمرد bazigar e mard

actress *n* بازيگرزن bazigar e zan

actual *adj* واقعى vaghei

actualization *n* واقعيت‌دادن vagheiat dadan

actually *adv* درواقع dar vaghe

acute adj تيز tiz

adamant *adj* يكدنده yekdande

adapt *v* سازگاركردن sazegar kardan

adaptable *adj* قابل‌توافق ghabel e tavafogh

adaptation *n* سازگاري sazegary

adapter *n* وفق‌دهنده vefgh dahande

add *v* افزودن afzoodan

addict *adj* معتاد mo'tad

addiction *n* اعتياد e'etiyad

addition *n* اضافه ezafe

additional *adj* اضافى ezafi

additive *n* افزودنى afzoudani

address *v* درست کردن dorost kardan

address *n* نشانى neshani

addressee *n* مخاطب mokhatab

adequate *adj* مناسب monaseb

adhere *v* چسبيدن chasbidan

adhesive *adj* چسبنده chasbande

adjacent *adj* مجاور mojaver

adjective *n* صفت sefat

adjoin *v* پيوستن peyvastan

adjoining *adj* نزديک nazdik

adjust *v* تنظيم کردن tanzim kardan

adjustable *adj* قابل‌تنظيم ghebel e tanzim

adjustment *n* انطباق entebagh

administer *v* اداره کردن edare kardan

admirable *adj* پسنديده pasandideh

admiral *n* درياسالار dayasallar

admiration *n* حيرت heirat

admire *v* پسندکردن pasand kardan

admirer *n* تحسين‌کننده tahsin konandeh

admissible *adj* پذيرفتنى paziroftany

admission *n* پذيرش paziresh

admit *v* پذيرفتن paziroftan

admittance *n* قبول ghabool

admonish *v* نصيحت کردن nasihat kardan

admonition *n* سرزنش‌دوستانه sarzanesh e doostane

adolescence *n* بلوغ booloogh

adolescent *n* بالغ balegh

adopt *v* قبول‌کردن ghabool kardan

adoption *n* اختيار ekhtiar

adoptive *adj* انتخابى entekhabi

adorable *adj* پرستش قابل ghabel e parastesh

adoration *n* ستايش setayesh

adore *v* پرستش parastesh

adorn *v* زيباکردن ziba kardan

adrenaline *n* آدرنالين adrenalin

adrift *adv* دستخوش‌طوفان dastkhosh e toofan

adulation *n* چاپلوسى chaplousi

adult *n* بالغ balegh

adulterate *v* تقلبى‌ساختن taghallobi sakhtan

adultery *n* زنا zena

advance *v* پيشرفت کردن pishraft kardan

advancement *n* پيشرفت pishraft

advantage *n* فايده fayedeh

advantageous *adj* سودمند soodmand

advent *n* ظهور zohour

adventure *n* حادثه hadeseh

adventurer *n* ماجراجو majara joo

adverb *n* قيد gheid

adversary *n* دشمن doshman

adverse *adj* مخالف mokhalef

adversity *n* بدبختي badbakhty

advertise *v* تبليغ كردن tabligh kardan

advice *v* راهنمايي كردن rahnamaei kardan

advisable *adj* قابل هدايت ghabel e hedaiat

advise *n* راهنمايي rahnamaei

adviser *n* راهنما rahnama

advocate *v* دفاع كردن defa kardan

aesthetic *adj* وابسته به زيبايي vabaste be zibaei

affable *adj* مهربان mehraban

affair *n* كار kar

affect *v* اثر كردن بر asar kardan

affection *n* مهرباني mehrabany

affectionate *adj* مهربان mehraban

affiliate *v* پيوستن peyvastan

affiliation *n* وابستگي vabastegi

affinity *n* نزديكي nazdiki

affirm *v* اظهار كردن ezhar kardan

affirmative *adj* مثبت mosbat

affix *v* چسبانيدن chasbanidan

afflict *v* آزردن azordan

affliction *n* رنج ranj

affluence *n* فراواني faravany

affluent *adj* فراوان faravan

affront *v* آشكارا توهين كردن ashkara tohin kardan

afloat *adv* شناور shenavar

afraid *adj* هراسان harasan

afresh *adv* دوباره dobareh

after *pre* از پس pas az

afternoon *n* عصر asr

afterwards *adv* پس از آن pas az aan

again *adv* دگربار degar bar

against *pre* دربرابر dar barabar

age *n* سن sen

agency *n* نمايندگي namayandegi

agenda *n* جلسه دستور dastour-e jaleseh

agent *n* پيشكار pishkar

aggregate *v* جمع شدن jame' shodan

aggravate *v* بدتر كردن badtar kardan

aggravation *n* سختي sakhti

aggression *n* تجاوز tajavoz

aggressive *adj* پرخاشگر parkhashgar

aggressor *n* متجاوز motejavez

aghast *adj* مبهوت mabhoot

agile *adj* چابك chabok

agitator *n* آشوبگر ashoobgar

agnostic *n* بي خدا bi-khoda

agnosticism *n* بي خدايي bi-khoda'ei

agonize *v* عذاب دادن azab dadan

agony *n* درد dard

agree *v* خوشنود كردن khoshnood kardan

agreement *n* سازش sazesh

agriculture *n* زراعت zera'at

ahead *pre* پيش pish

aid *n* كمك komak

aide *n* اجودان تيمسار Azhoudan-e Timsar

ailing *adj* ناخوش na khosh

ailment *n* درد dard

aim *v* نشانه گرفتن neshaneh gereftan

aimless *adj* بی مقصد bi maghsad

air *n* هوا hava

air force *n* نیروی‌هوایی nirooye havaei

aircraft *n* هواپیما havapeyma

airfare *n* بهای‌بلیط‌هواپیما Bahay-e billit-e Havapeyma

airfield *n* پایگاه‌هوایی paygah-e hava'ei

airline *n* خط‌هوایی khat-e hava'ei

airliner *n* هواپیمای‌مسافربری havapeimaie mosafer bary

airmail *n* پست‌هوایی post e havaei

airplane *n* هواپیما havapeima

airport *n* فرودگاه foroodgah

airspace *n* فضای هوایی fazaie havaei

airstrip *n* باندفرودگاه band e foroodgah

airtight *adj* محفوظ‌ازهوا mahfooz az hava

aisle *n* راهرو rahrow

ajar *adj* نیم باز nim baz

alarm *n* هشدار hoshdar

alarm clock *n* ساعت‌شماطه‌ای soat e shammatei

alarming *adj* ترساننده tarsanandeh

alcoholic *adj* میخواره meykhareh

alcoholism *n* میخوارگی meikharegi

alert *n* بزنگ گوش goosh be zang

alfalfa *n* یونجه yonje

algae *n* برگ و ساقه بدون گیاه giah e bedoon e saghe va barg

algebra *n* جبر jabr

alien *n* بیگانه bigane

alight *adv* سوزان soozan

align *v* ردیف کردن radif kardan

alignment *n* تنظیم tanzim

alike *adj* مانندهم manand e ham

alive *adj* زنده zende

all *adj* همگی hamegi

all right *adv* صحیح sahih

allegation *n* اظهار ezhar

allege *v* اقامه کردن eghame kardan

allegedly *adv* ظاهرآ zaheran

allegiance *n* تابعیت tabeiat

allergic *adj* حساسیت‌زا hasasiyat-za

allergy *n* حساسیت hassasiat

alleviate *v* سبک کردن sabok kardan

alleviation *n* تسکین taskin

alley *n* کوچه kooche

alliance *n* اتحاد ettehad

allied *adj* پیوسته peivaste

alligator *n* نهنگ nahang

allocate *v* اختصاص دادن ekhtesas dadan

allot *v* تخصیص دادن takhsis dadan

allotment *n* پخش pakhsh

allow *v* رخصت‌دادن rokhsat dadan

allowance *n* پاداش padash

alloy *n* عیار aya'r

allure *v* شیفتن shiftan

alluring *adj* فریبنده faribande

allusion *n* گریز goriz

ally *v* پیوستن peivastan

ally *n* هم‌پیمان ham peiman

almanac *n* سالنامه salname

almighty *adj* قادرمطلق ghader e motlagh

almond *n* بادام badam

almost *adv* تقریبا taghriban

alms *n* صدقه sadaghe

alone *adj* تنها tanha

along *pre* پیش pish

alongside *pre* درکنار dar kenar

aloof *adj* دور door

aloud *adv* بلند boland

alphabet *n* الفبا alefba

already *adv* پیش‌ازاین pish az in

alright *adv* بسیارخوب besiar khoob

also *adv* نیز niz

altar *n* قربانگاه ghorbangah

alter *v* تغییردادن taghir dadan

alteration *n* دگرگونی degargoony

altercation *n* ستیزه setizeh

alternate *v* متناوب‌کردن motenaveb kardan

alternative *adj* تناوبی tanavoby

although *c* اگرچه agar che

altitude *n* بلندی bolandi

altogether *adj* روی‌هم‌رفته rooie ham rafte

altruism *n* بشردوستی bashar doosty

aluminium *n* آلومینیوم aluminium

always *adv* همواره hamvareh

amass *v* گردآوردن gerd avardan

amateur *adj* اماتور amator

amaze *v* ساختن متحیر motehaiier sakhtan

amazement *n* حیرت heirat

amazing *adj* متحیرکننده motehaiier konande

ambassador *n* سفیر safir

ambiguity *n* ابهام ebham

ambiguous *adj* مبهم mobham

ambition *n* بلندهمتی boland hemmaty

ambivalent *adj* دمدمی damdami

ambulance *n* آمبولانس amboulance

ambush *v* کمین‌کردن kamin kardan

ameliorate *v* بهترکردن behtar kardan

amenable *adj* رام‌شدنی ram shodani

amend *v* ترمیم‌کردن tarmim kardan

amendment n ترمیم tarmim

amenities *n* مطبوعیت matbou'eiyat

amiable *adj* شیرین shirin

amicable *adj* موافق movafegh

amid *pre* درمیان dar mian

ammonia *n* محلول‌یابخار‌آمونیاک mahlool ya bokhar e amoniak

ammunition *n* مهمات mohemmat

amnesia *n* فراموشی faramooshy

amnesty *n* گذشت gozasht

amok *adj* مجنون majnoon

among *pre* درزمره dar zomrehe

amoral *adj* غیراخلاقی gheir e akhlaghy

amorphous *adj* بی‌شکل bi shekl

amount *n* مبلغ mablagh

amphibious *adj* خاکی‌وآبی khaky va abi

amphitheatre *n* سالن salon

ample *adj* فراخ farakh

amplifier *n* تقويت كننده taghviat
konande

amplify *v* بزرگ كردن bozorg
kardan

amputate *v* بريدن boridan

amputation *n* قطع عضوي از بدن
ghate'e ozvi az badan

amuse *v* سرگرم كردن sargarm
kardan

amusement *n* سرگرمي sargarmy

amusing *adj* سرگرم كننده sargarm
konandeh

an art يك yek

analogous *adj* قابل قياس ghabel e
ghias

analogy *n* قياس ghias

analysis *n* تجزيه و تحليل tajziyeh
va tahlil

analyze *v* تحليل كردن tahlil kardan

anarchist *n* هرج و مرج طلب harj o
marj talab

anarchy *n* بي قانوني bi ghanoony

anatomy *n* تشريح tashrih

ancestor *n* جد jadd

ancestral *a*dj اجدادي ajdady

anchor *n* لنگر langar

anchovy *n* ماهي كولي mahi-kouli

ancient *adj* قديمي ghadimi

and *c* و va

anecdote *n* حكايت hekayat

anaemia *n* كم خوني kam khoony

anaemic *adj* كم خون kam khoon

anaesthesia *n* بيهوشي bi hooshy

anew *adv* از نو az no

angel *n* فرشته fereshteh

angelic *adj* فرشته اي fereshtei

anger *n* بر اشفتگي bar ashoftegi

angle *n* گوشه gooshe

Anglican *adj* وابسته به كليساي
انگليس vabaste be kelisaye
engelis

angrily *adv* از روي خشم az rooie
khashm

angry *adj* اوقات تلخ oghat e talkh

anguish *n* دلتنگي deltangi

angular *adj* زاويه دار zavieh dar

animal *n* جانور janevar

animate *v* زندگي بخشيدن zendegi
bakhshidan

animation *n* جان بخشي jan
bakhshy

animosity *n* دشمني doshmany

ankle *n* قوزك ghoozak

annexation *n* پيوست peivast

annihilate *v* نابود كردن nabood
kardan

annihilation *n* نابودي naboodi

anniversary *n* سوگواري ساليانه
soogvary e saliane

annotated *adj* حاشيه نويسي
hashiyeh-nevisi

announce *v* آگهي دادن agahy
dadan

announcement *n* آگهي agahy

announcer *n* گوينده gooiande

annoy *v* دلخور كردن delkhor
kardan

annoying *adj* رنجش آور ranj avar

annual *adj* ساليانه saliyaneh

annually *adv* سال به سال sal be sal

annul *v* لغو كردن laghv kardan

annulment *n* فسخ faskh

anoint v روغن‌مالي‌كردن roghan mali kardan

anonymity n گمنامي gomnamy

anonymous adj بي‌نام bi nam

another adj ديگر digar

answer v پاسخ‌دادن pasokh dadan

answer n جواب javab

ant n مورچه moorche

antagonize v مخالف‌كردن mokhalefat kardan

antelope n بزكوهي boz e koohy

antenna n آنتن anten

anthem n سرود sorood

anthropology n انسان‌شناسي ensan shenasy

anticipate v سبقت‌جستن sebghat jostan

anticipation n پيشدستي pishdasti

antidote n پادزهر pad-zahr

antipathy n انزجار enzejar

antiquated adj متروك matrouk

antique adj كهنه kohneh

antiquity n عتيق‌عهد ahd-e' atigh

anvil n سندان sendan

anxiety n اضطراب ezterab

anxious adj دلواپس del va pas

any adj هر har

anybody pro هركسي har-kasi

anyone pro هركس har kas

apart adv جدا joda

apartment n آپارتمان aparteman

apathy n خون‌سردي khoun sardi

ape n ميمون meymoon

aperitif n پيش‌غذا pish-ghaza

apex n نوك nok

aphrodisiac adj برانگيزنده‌جنسي barangizandeh-e jensi

apiece adv هرچيز har-chiz

apocalypse n مكاشفه mokashefeh

apologize v پوزش‌خواستن pouzesh-khastan

apology n پوزش‌خواهي pouzesh-khahi

apostle n رسول rasoul

apostolic adj رسالتي resalati

apostrophe n رسالت resalat

appal v ترساندن tarsandan

appalling adj ترسناك tarsnak

apparently adv ظاهرا zaheran

apparition n ظهور zohour

appeal n التماس eltemas

appeal v درخواست darkhast

appealing adj جذاب jazzab

appear v ظاهرشدن zahershodan

appearance n ظاهر zaher

appease v آرام‌كردن aram kardan

appendicitis n روده آماس amase' roudeh

appendix n ضميمه zamimeh

appetite n اشتها eshteha

appetizer n پيش‌غذا pish-ghaza

applaud v تحسين‌كردن tahsin kardan

applause n تشويق‌وتمجيد tashvigh va tamjid

apple n سيب sib

appliance n اسباب asbab

applicable adj قابل‌اجراء ghabele ejra

applicant n درخواست‌دهنده darkhast dahandeh

application n كاربرد karbord

apply v درخواست‌دادن darkhast dadan

appoint *v* تعیین کردن ta'yin kardan	**architect** *n* معمار me'mar
appointment *n* تعیین ta'yin	**architecture** *n* معماري me'mari
appraisal *n* ارزیابی arzyabi	**archive** *n* بایگانی baygani
appraise *v* ارزیابی کردن arzyabi kardan	**arctic** *adj* قطب شمالی ghotbe' shomali
appreciate *n* قدردانی کردن ghadrdani kardan	**ardent** *adj* گرم garm
	ardently *adv* باشوق bashowgh
appreciation *n* قدردانی ghadrdani	**ardour** *n* گرمي garmi
apprehensive *adj* بیمناک bimnak	**arduous** *adj* دشوار doshvar
	area *n* مساحت masahat
apprentice *n* شاگرد shagerd	**arena** *n* پهنه pahneh
approach *v* نزدیک شدن nazdik shodan	**argue** *v* بحث کردن bahs kardan
	argument *n* نشانوند neshanvand
approachable *adj* نزدیک شدني nazdik shodani	**arid** *adj* خشک khoshk
appropriate *adj* درخور dar-khor	**arise** *iv* برخاستن barkhastan
approval *n* تصویب tasvib	**aristocracy** *n* حکومت اشرافي hokoumat-e ashrafi
approve *v* تصویب کردن tasvib kardan	**aristocrat** *adj* نجیب زاده najibzadeh
apricot *n* زردآلو zard'aloo	
April *n* آوریل avril	**arm** *n* بازو bazoo
apron *n* پیش بند pishband	**arm** *v* مسلح کردن mosallah kardan
aptitude *n* استعداد este'dad	
aquarium *n* آبزیدان abzidan	**armaments** *n* سلاح selah
aquatic *adj* آبزي abzi	**armchair** *n* صندلی دسته دار sandaliye dastehdar
Arabic *adj* تازي tazi	
arable *adj* قابل کشتکاري ghabele keshtkari	**armed** *adj* مسلح mosallah kardan
arbiter *n* حکم hokm	**armistice** *n* متارکه ءجنگ motarekehe jang
arbitrary *adj* اختیاري ekhtiyari	**armour** *n* زره zereh
arc *n* قوس ghows	**armpit** *n* بغل baghal
arch *n* کمان kaman	**army** *n* ارتش artesh
archaeology *n* باستان شناسي bastan-shenasi	**aroma** *n* مادهءعطري madeye atri
	aromatic *adj* خوشبو khoshboo
archaic *adj* کهنه kohneh	**around** *pro* گرداگرد gerdagerd
archbishop *n* اسقف اعظم osghof-e a'azam	**arouse** *v* بیدار کردن bidarkardan

arrange *v* آراستن arastan

arrangement *n* ترتيب tartib

array *n* صف saff

arrest *n* توقيف towghif

arrest *v* توقيف كردن towghif kardan

arrival *n* ورود vorood

arrive *v* واردشدن varedshodan

arrogance *n* گردنفرازي gardanfarazi

arrogant *adj* گردنفراز gardanfaraz

arrow *n* تير tir

arsenal *n* قورخانه ghourkhaneh

arsenic *n* اکسيدارسنيک oxid arsenik

arson *n* آتش‌زني atashzani

arsonist *n* کسي که ايجادحريق کند kasi ke eijad-e harigh konad

art *n* هنر honar

artery *n* شريان shariyan

arthritis *n* ورم‌مفاصل varame mafasel

artichoke *n* انگنار angenar

article *n* کالا kala

articulate *v* شمرده‌سخن‌گفتن shomordeh sokhan goftan

articulation *n* بند band

artefact *n* مصنوع masnoo'

artificial *adj* ساختگي sakhtegi

artillery *n* توپخانه toupkhaneh

artisan *n* صنعتگر san'atgar

artist *n* هنرور honarvar

artistic *adj* هنرمندانه honarmandaneh

artwork *n* اثرهنری asare' honari

as *c* بطوريکه betowrike'

as *adv* مثال mesal

ascend *v* فرازيدن farazidan

ascendancy *n* فراز faraze' badan

ascertain *v* معلوم‌کردن ma'loom kardan

ascetic *adj* زاهد zahed

ash *n* خاکستر khakestar

ashamed *adj* شرمسار sharmsar

ashore *adv* درکنار dar kenar

ashtray *n* زيرسيگاری zirsigari

aside *adv* به‌يک‌طرف be yek taraf

aside from *adv* از قطع‌نظر ghate' nazar az

ask *v* پرسيدن porsidan

asleep *adj* خواب khab

asparagus *n* مارچوبه marchoubeh

aspect *n* نمود aspect

asphalt *n* قير ghir

asphyxiate *v* خفه‌کردن khafeh kardan

asphyxiation *n* خفقان khafaghan

aspiration *n* دم‌زني dam zani

aspire *v* ارزوداشتن arezoo dashtan

aspirin *n* آسپرين aspirin

ass *n* خر khar

assailant *n* حمله‌کننده hamleh konandeh

assassin *n* آدمکش adamkosh

assassinate *v* کشتن koshtan

assault *v* تجاوزياحمله‌کردن tajavoz ya hamleh kardan

assemble *v* هم‌گذاردن ham gozardan

assembly *n* هم‌گذاري ham gozari

assert *v* دفاع‌کردن‌از defa' kardan

assertion *n* تاکید ta'kid

assess *v* تشخیص دادن tashkhis dadan

assessment *n* تشخیص tashkhis

asset *n* چیزباارزش chiz-e ba arzesh

assign *v* واگذارکردن vagozar kardan

assignment *n* گمارش gomaresh

assimilate *v* یکسان کردن yeksan kardan

assimilation *n* جذبوترکیبغذا (دربدن) jazb va tarkib-e ghaza

assist *v* یاری کردن yari kardan

assistance *n* دستیاري rastyari

associate *v* آمیزش کردن amizesh kardan

association *n* شرکت sherkat

assorted *adj* جورشده joor shodeh

assortment *n* ترتیب tartib

assume *v* فرض کردن farz kardan

assumption *n* فرض farz

assurance *n* پشتگرمي poshtgarmi

assure *v* اطمینان دادن etminan dadan

asterisk *n* نشان ستاره neshan-e setareh

asteroid *n* ستارک setarak

asthma *n* نفس تنگي tangiye nafas

asthmatic *adj* آسمي a'smi

astonish کردن متحیرکردن motehayyer kardan

astonishing *adj* شگفت آور shegeft avar

astound *v* گیج کردن gij kardan

astounding *adj* گیج gij

astray *adj* گمراه gomrah

astrologer *n* منجم monajjem

astrology *n* علماحکامنجوم elme' ahkam-e nojoum

astronaut *n* فضانورد fazanavard

astronomer *n* ستارهشناس setareh shenas

astronomical *adj* نجومي nojoumi

astronomy *n* هیئت hey'at

astute *adj* زیرک zirak

asylum *n* پناهگاه panahgah

at *pre* بسوي besooye

atheism *n* خدا وجود انکار enkare' vojoode' khoda

atheist *n* منکرخدا monkere' khoda

athlete *n* ورزشکار varzeshkar

athletic *adj* ورزشي varzeshi

atmosphere *n* آتموسفر atmosfer

atmospheric *adj* هوایي hava'ei

atom *n* اتم atom

atomic *adj* اتمي atomi

atonement *n* کفاره kaffareh

atonement *v* کفارهدادن kaffareh dadan

atrocious *adj* باشرارتبيپایان ba shararat-e bi-payan

atrocity *n* سبعیت sabo'eiyat

attach *v* الصاق کردن elsagh kardan

attached *adj* پیوسته peyvasteh

attachment *n* الصاق elsagh

attack *n* آفند a'fand

attack *v* حملهکردنبر hamleh kardan bar

attacker *n* ضارب zareb

attain *v* دستیافتن dast yaftan

attainable *adj* نائلشدني na'el shodani

attempt v کوشش کردن kooshesh kardan

attend v توجه کردن tavajoh kardan

attendance n توجه tavajoh

attendant n سرپرست sarparast

attention n توجه tavajjoh

attentive adj مواظب movazeb

attic n اطاق زیرشیروانی otaghe zir shirvani

attitude n گرایش gerayesh

attorney n وکیل vakil

attract v جلب کردن jalb kardan

attraction n کشش keshesh

attractive adj کشنده keshandeh

attribute v نسبت دادن nesbat dadan

auction n حراج harraj

auctioneer n دلال حراج dallale' harraj

audacious adj پروا بی bi parva

audacity n بی باکی bi baki

audible adj شنیدنی shanidani

audience n ملاقات رسمی molaghat-e rasmi

audiovisual adj دیداری-شنیداری didari-shenidari

auditorium n تالار کنفرانس talare' konferans

augment v تکمیل کردن takmil kardan

August n اوت oot

aunt n عمه ammeh

aura n رایحه rayeheh

austere n سخت sakht

austerity n سختی sakhti

authentic adj صحیح sahih

authenticate v اعتبار دادن etebar dadan

authenticity n اعتبار etebar

author n مصنف monsef

authoritarian adj طرفدار استبداد tarafdare' estebdad

authority n قدرت ghodrat

authorization n اجازه ejazeh

authorize v اجازه دادن ejazeh dadan

auto n خودرو khodroo

autograph n دستخط مصنف dastkhat-e mosannef

automate v خودکار کردن khodkar kardan

automatic adj غیرارادی gheyre eradi

automobile n خودرو khodroo

autonomous adj خودگردان khodgardan

autonomy n خودگرانی khodgardani

autopsy n کالبدشکافی kalbad-shekafi

autumn n پائیز pa'eiz

auxiliary n امدادی emdadi

avail v سودمندبودن soodmand boodan

availability n قابلیت استفاده ghabeliyate' estefadeh

available adj دردسترس dar dastras

avalanche n بهمن bahman

avarice n زیاده جوئی ziyadeh-joo'ei

avaricious adj حریص haris

avenge v کینه جوئی کردن kine' jo'ei kardan

avenue *n* خيابان khiyaban

average *n* متوسط motevaset

aversion *n* بيزاري bizari

avert *v* برگرداندن bargardandan

aviation *n* هواپيمايي havapeyma'ei

aviator *n* هوانورد havanavard

avid *adj* حريص haris

avidly *adv* حريصانه harisaneh

avocado *n* آوكادو avokado

avoid *v* دوري كردن از douri kardan

avoidable *adj* پرهيز كردني parhiz kardani

await *v* منتظر بودن montazer boudan

awake *adj* بيدار bidar

awake *iv* بيدار شدن bidar shodan

awakening *n* بيداري bidari

award *n* جايزه jayezeh

award *v* مقرر داشتن mogharar da'shtan

aware *adj* آگاه agah

awareness *n* آگاهي agahi

away *adv* دور dour

awe *n* هيبت heybat

awesome *adj* وحشت آور vahshat-avar

awful *adj* ترسناك tarsnak

awfully *adv* به طور ترسناك betowre tarsnak

awkward *adj* زشت zesht

awning *n* پناه panah

axe *n* تبر tabar

axis *n* محور mehvar

axle *n* محور mehvar

B

baby *n* بچه bacheh

babysitter *n* دايه dayeh

bachelor *n* مردبي زن marde' bi-zan

back *adv* عقب به be aghab

back *n* پشت سر poshte' sar

back *v* پشت كردن posht kardan

back down *v* از ادعاصرف نظر كردن az edde'a' sarfenazar kardan

back up *v* كردن تهيه پشتيبان poshtiban tahiyeh kardan

backbone *n* پشت تيرهء tireye posht

backfire *v* نتيجه معكوس natijehe ma'koos

background *n* زمينه zamineh

backing *n* پشت بند poshtband

backlash *n* پس زني pas zani

backlog n ناتمام كار kare' na-tamam

backpack *n* كوله پشتي kooleh poshti

backroom *n* پشتي poshti

backup *n* پشتيبان poshtiban

backward *adj* عقب افتاده aghab oftadeh

backwards *adv* پشت به be posht

backyard *n* حياط خلوت hayat khalvat

bacon *n* گوشت خوك gooshte' khook

bacteria *n* باكتري bakteri

bad *adj* بد bad

badge *n* نشان neshan

badly *adv* بد طور به betowre' bad

baffle v گمراه‌کردن gomrah kardan

bag n کیسه kisseh

baggage n مسافر بنهء و بار bar-o-bonehe mosafer

baggy adj بادکرده bad kardeh

bail n توقیف towghif

bailiff n ناظر nazer

bait n دانه daneh

bake v پختن pokhtan

baker n نانوا nanva

bakery n نانوایی nanva'ei

balance v برابرکردن barabar kardan

balance n ترازو tarazoo

balcony n ایوان eiyvan

bald adj طاس tas

bale n عدل adl

ball n گلوله golooleh

ballad n شعرافسانه‌ای shere' afsaneh'ei

ballerina n رقاصه raghaseh

ballet n بالت balet

balloon n بالون baloon

ballot n ورقه‌رای varaghehe ra'ey

ballroom n سالن‌رقص saloone raghs

balm n مرهم marham

balmy adj خوشبو khoshboo

bamboo n خیزران kheyzaran

ban v قدغن‌کردن ghadghan

ban n لعن la'n

banal adj پیش‌پاافتاده pishepa oftadeh

banality n ابتذال ebtezal

banana n موز mowz

band n باند band

bandage n باندپیچی band pichi

bandit n سارق‌مسلح sareghe' mosalah

banish v تبعیدکردن tab'eid kardan

bank n بانک bank

bankrupt v ورشکست‌کردن varshekast kardan

bankrupt adj ورشکسته varshekasteh

bankruptcy n ورشکستگی varshekastegi

banner n پرچم parcham

banquet n مهمانی mehmani

baptism n تعمید ta'mid

baptismal adj وابسته‌به‌غسل‌تعمید vabasteh be ghosle' ta'mid

baptize v تعمیددادن ta'mid dadan

bar v مانع‌شدن mane' shodan

bar n میله milleh

barbarian v.ه بیگانه biganeh

barbaric adj وحشی vahshi

barbarism n وحشیگری vahshigari

barbecue n بریانی beryanni

barber n سلمانی salmani

bare adj لخت lokht

barefoot adj پابرهنه pa berahneh

barely adv به‌طورعریان betowre' oryan

bargain n سودا sowda

barge n کرجی karji

baritone adj صدای‌بین‌بم‌وزیر sedaye beine bam va zir

bark n پوست‌درخت pooste derakht

bark *v* وغ وغ کردن vagh vagh kardan

barley *n* جو jow

barmaid *n* گارسون garson

barman *n* مردي که پشت بار کار مي کند mardi ke poshte bar kar mikonad

barn *n* انبارغله anbare' ghalleh

barometer *n* هواسنج haza sanj

baron *n* شخص مهم وبرجسته shakhse mohem va barjasteh

barracks *n* سربازخانه sarbazkhaneh

barrage *n* سدبندي sadd-bandi

barrel *n* بشکه boshkeh

barren *adj* نازا naza

barricade *n* مانع mane'

barrier *n* حصار hesar

barring *p* جز به bejoz

barrio *n* حومه شهر hoomehe shahr

barter *v* پاياپاي معامله کردن payapay mo'ameleh kardan

base *n* بن bon

baseball *n* بال بيس بازي basebal

basement *n* زيرزمين zirzamin

bashful *adj* رو کم kamroo

basic *adj* پايه اي paye'ei

basically *adv* به طور اساسی betowre' asasi

basics *n* اصول osoul

basis *n* اساس asas

basket *n* زنبيل zanbil

basketball *n* بسكتبال basketbal

bastard *n* حرامزاده haramzadeh

bat *n* چوب choob

batch *n* دسته daste

bath *n* گرمابه garmabe

bathe *v* شستشو کردن shodtoshoo kardan

bathrobe *n* حوله حمام howlehe hamam

bathroom *n* حمام hammam

bathtub *n* وان حمام vane hammam

baton *n* عصا يا چوپ صاحب منصبان asa ya choobe saheb mansaban

battalion *n* گردان gordan

batter *v* خرد کردن khord kardan

battered *adj* شده خرد khord shodeh

battery *n* باتري battery

battle *v* جنگ کردن jang kardan

battle *n* رزم razm

battleship *n* نبردناو nabarde nav

bawl *n* گريه gerye

bay *n* کهير kahir

bayonet *n* سرنيزه sar neize

bazaar *n* بازار bazar

be *iv* داشتن وجود vojood dashtan

be born *v* زاييده شدن za'eideh shodan

beach *n* ساحل sahel

beacon *n* چراغ دريايي cheraghe darya'ei

beak *n* منقار menghar

beam *n* پرتو parto

bean n باقلا baghala

bear *iv* بردن bordan

bearable *adj* تحمل پذير tahammol pazir

beard *n* ريش rish

bearded *adj* ريشو rishoo

bearer *n* حامل hamel

beast *n* چهارپا chaharpa

beat *iv* تپیدن tapidan

beaten *adj* کوبیده koobide

beating *n* ضرب zarb

beautiful *adj* زیبا ziba

beauty *n* زیبایی ziba'ei

beaver *n* سگ‌آبی sagg-e abbi

because *c* زیرا zira

because of *p* بواسطه bevasteh

beckon *v* اشاره‌کردن eshareh kardan

become *iv* شدن shodan

bed *n* بستر bastar

bedding *n* تختخواب‌وملافه takhtekhab va malafeh

bedridden *adj* بستری bastari

bedroom *n* اتاق‌خواب otaghe khab

bedspread *n* چادرشب‌رختخواب chador shab-e rakhtekhab

bee *n* زنبورعسل zanboore' asal

beef *n* گوشت‌گاو goosht-e gav

beehive *n* کندو kandoo

beer *n* آبجو abjoo

beet *n* چغندر choghondar

beetle *n* سوسک sousk

before *adv* از پیش pishaz

beforehand *adv* پیش pish

befriend *v* دوستانه‌رفتارکردن doostaneh raftar kardan

beg *v* خواهش‌کردن khahesh kardan

beggar *n* گدا gada

begin *iv* آغازکردن aghaz kardan

beginner *n* مبتدی mobtadi

beginning *n* آغاز aghaz

behave *v* رفتارکردن raftar kardan

behaviour *n* رفتار raftar

behead *v* سربریدن sar boridan

behind *pre* پشت‌سر poshte' sar

behold *iv* دیدن didan

being *v* افریده afarideh

belated *adj* دیرشده dir shodeh

belief *n* باور bavar

believable *adj* باورکردنی bavar kardani

believe *v* باورکردن bavar kardan

believer *n* باایمان ba eiman

belittle *v* کسی‌راکوچک‌کردن kasi ra kouchek kardan

bell *n* زنگ‌زنگوله zang-e zangoleh

bell pepper *n* پیجر peyjer

belligerent *adj* متحارب motehareb

belly *n* شکم shekam

belong *v* تعلق‌داشتن ta'aloogh dashtan

belongings *n* دارایی dara'ei

beloved *v* محبوب mahboob

below *adv* پائین pa'ein

belt *n* کمربند kamarband

bench *n* نیمکت nimkat

bend *iv* خم‌کردن kham kardan

beneath *pre* درزیر dar zir

benediction *n* دعای‌خیر do'aye kheyr

beneficial *adj* سودمند soudmand

benefit *n* منفعت manfa'at

benevolent *adj* کریم karim

benign *adj* مهربان mehraban

bereavement *n* محرومیت mahroomiyat

beret *n* کلاه‌بره kollahe bere

berserk *adj* دیوانه divaneh

berth *n* خوابگاه کشتی khabgah-e kashti

beseech *iv* بودن چیزی جستجوی در dar jostojooye chizi boodan

beset *iv* احاطه‌کردن ehateh kardan

beside *pre* درکنار dar kenar

besides *pre* گذشته‌ازاین gozashteh az in

besiege *iv* محاصره‌کردن mohasereh kardan

best *adj* بهترین behtarin

best man *n* ساقدوش‌داماد saghdoosh-e damad

bestial *adj* حیوانی heyvani

bestiality *n* جانورخویی janevar-khoo'ei

bestow *v* بخشیدن bakhshidan

bet *n* شرط shart

bet *iv* بستن شرط shart bastan

betray *v* کردن تسلیم taslim kardan

betrayal *n* خیانت khiyanat

better *adj* بهتر behtar

between *pre* دربین dar beyn

beverage *n* مشروب mashroob

beware *v* زنهاردادن zenhar dadan

bewildered *adj* گیج‌شده gij shodeh

beyond *adv* انسوی a'n-sooye

bias *n* طرفداری tarafdari

bible *n* کتاب‌مقدس ketabe moghadas

biblical *adj* مطابق کتاب‌مقدس motabeghe ketabe moghadas

bibliography *n* تاریخچه کتب tarikhche kotob

bicycle *n* دوچرخه do-charkheh

bid *iv* امرکردن amr kardan

bid *n* مزایده mozayedeh

bifocals *n* دارای‌دوکانون daraye do-kanoon

big *adj* بزرگ bozorg

bigamy *n* دوزن‌داری do-zan dari

bigot *adj* متعصب mote'aseb

bigotry *n* تعصب ta'asob

bike *n* دوچرخه do-charkheh

bikini *n* لباس‌شنای‌زنانه‌دوتکه lebase shenaye zananeh do-tikeh

bilateral *adj* دوطرفه do-tarafeh

bilingual *adj* دوزبانی do-zabani

bill *n* صورت‌حساب sourate hesab

billfold *n* کیف‌جیبی‌اسکناس kif-e jibiye eskenas

billiards *n* بیلیارد biliyard

billion *adj* بیلیون bilion

billionaire *n* میلیاردر miliyarder

bin *n* صندوقچه sandoughcheh

bind *iv* بستن bastan

binding *adj* الزام‌اور elzam-avar

binoculars *n* دوچشمی do-chashmi

biography *n* زیست‌نامه zistnameh

biological *adj* میکربی mikrobi

biology *n* زیست‌شناسی zistshenasi

bird *n* پرنده parandeh

birth *n* زایش zayesh

birthday *n* زادروز zad-rooz

biscuit *n* كلوچه‌خشك kolouchehe khoshk

bishop *n* اسقف osghof

bison *n* گاومیش‌کوهاندار gavmishe kowhandar

bit *n* ذره zarreh

bitch *n* ماده‌سگ maddeh sag

bite *n* گاز gaz

bite *iv* گازگرفتن gaz gereftan

biting *n* گزنده gazandeh

bitter *adj* تلخ talkh

bitterly *adv* تلخي به be talkhi

bitterness *n* تلخي talkhi

bizarre *adj* عجیب‌وغریب ajjib-o-gharib

black *adj* سیاه siyah

blackberry *n* توت‌سیاه toote siyah

blackboard *n* تخته‌سیاه takhteh siyah

blackmail *n* تهدید tahdid

blackout *n* سیاهی siyahi

blacksmith *n* آهنگر ahangar

bladder *n* کیسه kiseh

blade *n* تیغه tigheh

blame *n* اشتباه eshtebah

blame *v* مقصردانستن moghaser danestan

blameless *adj* بی‌گناه bi-gonah

bland *adj* ملایم molayem

blank *adj* سفید safid

blanket *n* پتو patoo

blaspheme *v* کفرگویی‌کردن kofr-goo'ei kardan

blasphemy *n* کفر kofr

blast *n* وزش vazesh

blast off *n* پرواز parvaz

blaze *n* شعله sho'leh

blazer *n* اعلام‌کننده e'elam konandeh

bleach *v* سفیدکردن safid kardan

bleach *n* سفیدکننده safid konandeh

bleak *n* بی‌حفاظ bi hefaz

bleed *iv* خون‌آمدن‌از khoon amadan az

blemish *n* نقص naghs

blend *v* امیختن amikhtan

blend *n* ترکیب tarkib

blender *n* ماشین‌مخلوط‌کن mashine makhloot-kon

bless *v* قدیس‌کردن gheddis kardan

blessed *adj* مبارک mobarak

blessing *n* برکت barakat

blind *adj* کور koor

blind *v* کورکردن koor kardan

blindfold *n* چشم‌بسته chash basteh

blindly *adv* کورکورانه koorkooraneh

blindness *n* کوري koori

blink *v* چشمک‌زدن chashmak zadan

bliss *n* خوشي khoshi

blissful *adj* خوش khosh

blister *n* تاول taval

blizzard *n* کولاک koulak

bloated *adj* پف‌کرده pof kardeh

block *n* قطعه ghat'eh

blockade *n* راه‌بندان rah bandan

blockage *n* محاصره mohasereh

blond *adj* بور boor

blood *n* خون khoon

bloodthirsty *adj* سفاک saffak	**body** *n* جسد jasad
bloody *adj* خوني khooni	**bodyguard** *n* گاردمخصوص gard-e makhsous
bloom *v* شکوفه کردن shekoofeh kardan	**bogus** *adj* ساختگي sakhtegi
blossom *v* گل دادن gol dadan	**boil** *v* جوشاندن joushandan
blot *n* لک lak	**boiler** *n* دیگ بخار digg-e bokhar
blouse *n* پیراهن گشاد pirahan-e goshad	**bold** *adj* شجاع shoja'e
blow *n* دمیدن هوا damidan-e hava	**boldness** *n* تهور tahavor
blow *iv* وزیدن vazidan	**bolt** *n* پیچ pich
blow out *iv* ترکیدن tarkidan	**bomb** *n* بمب bomb
blow up *iv* منفجر کردن monfajer kardan	**bomber** *n* بمب افکن bobmafkan
blowout *n* ترکیدن دراثرفشار tarkidan dar asare feshar	**bombshell** *n* بمب bomb
	bond *n* قید gheyd
blue *adj* ابي abi	**bondage** *n* بندگي bandeggi
blueprint *adj* نقشه پیش ساخته naghshehe pish-sakhteh	**bone** *n* استخوان ostokhan
bluff *v* توپ زدن toop zadan	**bonfire** *n* آتش بزرگ atash-e bozorg
blunder *n* اشتباه بزرگ eshtebahe bozorg	**bonus** *n* انعام an'am
blunt *adj* کند kond	**book** *n* کتاب ketab
bluntly *adv* بي پرده bi-pardeh	**bookcase** *n* قفسه کتاب ghafasehe ketab
bluntness *n* کندی kondi	**bookkeeper** *n* دفتردار daftar dar
blur *v* لک کردن lak kardan	**bookkeeping** *n* دفترداري daftar dari
blurred *adj* لکه lakkeh	**booklet** *n* کتاب کوچک ketab-e kouchak
blurry *adv* محو mahv	**bookseller** *n* کتابفروش ketabforoosh
blush *v* سرخ شدن sorkh shodan	**bookstore** *n* کتابفروشي ketabforooshi
blush *n* سرخي خجلت sorkhiye khejlat	**boom** *n* غرش ghorresh
boar *n* گراز نر goraz-e nar	**boost** *v* بالا بردن bala bordan
board *n* تخته takhteh siyah	**boot** *n* چکمه chakmeh
boast *v* بالیدن balidan	**booth** *n* اطاقک otaghak
boat *n* کشتي کوچک kashtiye kouchak	**booty** *n* غنیمت ghanimat
bobcat *n* گربه وحشي gorbehe vahshi	**booze** *n* مشروب الکلي mashroob-e alkoli

border n سرحد sar hadd

bored adj خسته khasteh

boredom n ملالت malalat

boring adj خسته‌کننده khasteh konandeh

born adj زائیده‌شده za'eideh shodeh

borough n دهکده dehkadeh

borrow v قرض گرفتن gharz gereftan

bosom n آغوش aghoosh

boss n رئیس re'eis

bossy adj دارای‌برجستگی daraye barjastegi

botch v خراب کردن kharab-kardan

both adj هردو har-do

bother v دردسردادن dardesar dadan

bothersome adj پردردسر por dardesar

bottle n بطری botri

bottled adj دربطری‌ریخته‌شده dar botri rikhteh shodeh

bottleneck n تنگنا tangna

bottom n ته tah

bottomless adj بدون‌ته bedoon-e' tah

bough n شاخه shakheh

boulder n تخته‌سنگ takhteh sang

boulevard n بولوار boulvar

bounce v پریدن paridan

boundary n مرز marz

boundless adj بی‌پایان bi-payan

bouquet n دسته‌گل dasteh gol

bourgeois adj سوداگر sowdagar

boutique n دکان dokkan

bow n تعظیم ta'zim

bow v خم‌شدن kham shodan

bowels n روده roudeh

bowl n کاسه kaseh

box n جعبه ja'beh

box office n باجه‌بلیط‌فروشی bajjeh bilit foroushi

boxer n مشت‌زن moshtzan

boxing n مشت‌زنی moshtzani

boy n پسربچه pesar bacheh

boycott n تحریم tahrim

boyfriend n دوست‌پسر douste pesar

boyhood n بچگی bachegi

bra n پستان‌بند pestan band

bracelet n دست‌بند dast band

bracket n قلاب ghollab

brag v لاف‌زدن lafzan

braid n قیطان gheytan

brain n مغز maghz

brainwash v شستشوی‌مغزی‌دادن shostoshoye maghzi dadan

brake n بیشه bisheh

bran n سبوس saboos

branch n شاخه shakheh

brand n مارک mark

brand-new adj کاملانو kamelan now

brash n اشغال eshghal

brash adj گستاخ gostakh

brassiere n سینه‌بند sineh band

brat adj بچه‌لوس bachehe loos

brave adj دلاور delavar

bravery n دلیری deliri

brawl n دادوبیداد dad-o-bidad

breach n نقض‌عهد naghz-e ahd

bread *n* نان nan

breadth *n* پهنا pahna

break *iv* شکستن shekastan

break away *v* جداکردن joda kardan

break down *v* فروریختن forou-rikhtan

break in *v* درمیان‌صحبت‌کسی‌دویدن dar miyane sohbate kasi davidan

break up *v* تفکیک‌کردن tafkik kardan

breakable *adj* شکستنی shekastani

breakdown *n* تفکیک tafkik

breakfast *n* صبحانه sobhaneh

breakthrough *n* شکافتن shekaftan

breast *n* پستان pestan

breath *n* دم dam

breathe *v* دم‌زدن dam zadan

breathing *n* دم‌زنی dam zani

breathtaking *adj* مهیج mohayyej

breed *iv* پروردن parvardan

breed *n* فرزند farzand

breeze *n* بادشمال bad-e shomal

brethren *n* برادر baradar

brevity *n* کوتاهی koutahi

brew *v* دم‌کردن dam kardan

brewery *n* آبجوسازي abjo sazi

bribe *v* رشوه‌دادن roshveh dadan

bribery *n* رشوه roshveh

brick *n* آجر ajor

bricklayer *n* آجرچین ajor chin

bridal *adj* جشن‌عروسی jashn-e' aroosi

bride *n* عروس aroos

bridegroom *n* داماد damad

bridesmaid *n* ندیمه‌عروس nadimehe aroos

bridge *n* پل pol

bridle *n* افسار afsar

brief *v* خلاصه‌کردن kholaseh kardan

brief *adj* کوتاه koutah

briefcase *n* کیف‌اسناد kiffe asnad

briefing *n* توجیه‌کردن towjih kardan

briefly *adv* بطورخلاصه betowre' kholaseh

briefs *n* مختصر mokhtasar

brigade *n* تیپ tip

bright *adj* تابناک tabnak

brighten *v* روشن‌کردن rowshan kardan

brightness *n* روشني rowshani

brilliant *adj* تابان taban

bring *iv* آوردن avardan

bring back *v* برگرداندن bargardandan

bring down *v* به‌زمین‌انداختن "حریف" be zamin andakhtan

bring up *v* پرورش‌دادن parvaresh dadan

brink *n* لب lab

brisk *adj* سرزنده sarzendeh

brittle *adj* ترد tord

broad *adj* پهن pahn

broadcast *n* داده‌پراکني dadeh parakani

broadcast *v* منتشرکردن montasher kardan

broadcaster *n* گوینده(رادیویا تلویزیون) gooyandeh

broaden v پهن کردن pahn kardan

broadly adv به طور وسیع betoowr-e' vasi'e

broadminded adj روشنفکر rowshanfekr

broccoli n بروکلی berokli

brochure n جزوه jozveh

broil v (روی آتش) سرخ کردن sorkh kardan

broiler n جوشاننده jooshannandeh

broken-down adj از پای در آمده az pay dar amadeh

bronchitis n برنشیت boronshit

bronze n مفرغ mefragh

brooch n سنجاق سینه sanjagh sineh

broom n جاروب jaroub

broomstick n دسته جاروب dasteh jaroub

broth n آبگوشت abgoosht

brothel n فاحشه خانه fahesheh khaneh

brother n برادر baradar

brotherhood n برادری baradari

brown adj قهوه ای ghahve'ei

browse v چریدن charidan

browser n مرورگر morourgar

bruise n کبود شدگی kaboudshodegi

brunch n ناشتا و ناهار باهم nashta va nahar ba ham

brunette adj سبزه sabzeh

brush n لیف lif

brush v مسواک زدن mesvak zadan

brush aside v کنار گذاشتن kenargozashtan

brush up v باقلم و رنگ کردن ba ghalam-moo rang kardan

brutal adj بی رحم bi-rahm

brutality n توحش tavahoosh

bubble n حباب hobab

bubble gum n آدامس باد کنکی adamse badkonaki

buck n جنس نر حیوانات jense' nare' heyvanat

bucket n سطل satl

buckle n سگک sagak

buckle up v بستن کمربند ایمنی bastane' kamarbande' eimeni

bud n جوانه javaneh

buddy n پر شکوفه por-shekoufeh

budget n بودجه boudjeh

buffalo n گاو وحشی gave' vahshi

buffoon n لوده lowdeh

bug n اشکال eshkal

build iv ساختن sakhtan

builder n سازنده sazandeh

building n ساختمان sakhteman

build-up v ساختن تدریجی sakhtane' tadriji

bulb n لامپ lamp

bulge n برآمدگی bara'madegi

bulk n توده toodeh

bulky adj بزرگ bozorg

bull n نر گاو gave' nar

bullet n گلوله golouleh

bulletin n آگهی نامه رسمی agahi-namehe rasmi

bullfight n گاوبازی gav bazi

bullfighter n گاوباز gav baz

bully adj قلدر gholdor

bulwark n خاکریز khakriz

bum *n* مفت‌خور moft-khor

bump *n* دست‌اندازجاده dast-andaz

bump into *v* باضربه‌زدن ba zarbeh zadan

bumper *n* سپراتومبیل separe' automobil

bumpy *adj* ناهموار na-hamvar

bun *n* یاکماج komaj

bunch *n* خوشه khousheh

bundle *n* بقچه boghcheh

bunker *n* پناهگاه panahgah

bunker *n* مخزن makhzan

buoy *n* شناور shenavar

burden *n* بار bar

burdensome *adj* گرانبار geranbar

bureau *n* دفتر daftar

bureaucracy *n* حکومت‌اداری hokoumate' edari

bureaucrat *n* مامورادارى ma'moure' edari

burglar *n* دزد dozd

burglarize *v* شبانه‌دزدیدن shabaneh dozdidan

burglary *n* دزدي dozdi

burial *n* دفن dafn

burly *adj* تنومند tanoumand

burn *iv* سوزاندن souzandan

burp *v* آروغ‌زدن arough-zadan

burrow *n* سوراخ‌زیرزمینى sourakhe' zirzamini

burst *iv* ترکیدن tarkidan

bury *v* دفن‌کردن dafn kardan

bus *n* اتوبوس autoboos

bush *n* بوته booteh

business *n* تجارت tejarat

businessman *n* تاجر tajer

bust *n* بالاتنه balataneh

busy *adj* مشغول mashghoul

but *c* ولي vali

butcher *n* قصاب ghasab

butchery *n* قصابى ghasabi

butler *n* ناظر nazer

butter *n* کره kareh

butterfly *n* پروانه parvaneh

button *n* تکمه tokmeh

buy *iv* خریدن kharidan

buyer *n* خریدار kharidar

buzz *n* وزوز vezvez

buzz *v* وزوزکردن vezvez kardan

buzzer *n* زنگ‌اخبار zang-e' akhbar

by *p* ازنزدیک az nazdik

bye *e* خداحافظ khodahafez

bygones *adj* ایام‌گذشته ayyame' gozashteh

bypass *n* گذرگاه gozargah

by-product *n* فرآورده‌فرعى faravardeh-e far'ee

bystander *n* تماشاگر tamashagar

C

ab *n* تاکسى taxi

cabbage *n* کلم kalam

cabin *n* اطاق‌کوچک otaghe' kouchak

cabinet *n* قفسه ghafaseh

cable *n* کابل kabl

cactus *n* انجیرهندي anjire' hendi

cadaver *n* لاشه lasheh

cafe *n* كافه kafe'

cafeteria *n* تريا teria

caffeine *n* كافئين kafe'ein

cage *n* قفس ghafaseh

cake *n* كيك keyk

calamity *n* بلا bala

calculate *v* حساب كردن hesab kardan

calculation *n* محاسبه mohasebeh

calculator *n* حسابگر hesabgar

calendar *n* سالنامه salnameh

calf *n* گوساله goosaleh

calibre *n* قطر گلوله ghotr-e' golooleh

call *n* بانگ bang

call *v* فراخواندن fara khandan

call off *v* منحرف كردن monharef kardan

calling *n* فرياد faryad

callous *adj* بي عاطفه bi-atefeh

calm *adj* اسوده asoudeh

calmness *n* آرامش aramesh

calorie *n* كالرى karori

camel *n* شتر shotor

camera *n* دوربين dourbin

camouflage *v* مخفي كردن makhfi kardan

camp *n* اردو ordou

campaign *v* جنگيدن jangidan

campaign *n* حمله hamleh

campsite *n* محل اردو mahale' ordou

can *iv* قادر بودن ghader boudan

can *n* قوطي حلبى ghouti halabi

canal *n* آبراه abrah

canary *n* قناري ghanari

cancel *v* فسخ كردن faskh kardan

cancellation *n* فسخ faskh

cancer *n* سرطان saratan

candid *adj* بي تزوير bi-tazvir

candidacy *n* داوطلبي davtalabi

candidate *n* داوطلب davtalab

candies *n* شيريني shirini

candle *n* شمع sham'e

candour *n* سفيدي safidi

cane *n* نى ney

canned *adj* كنسرو شده konserv shodeh

cannibal *n* آدمخوار adam khar

cannon *n* استوانه ostovaneh

canoe *n* قايق باريك ghayeghe' barik

cantaloupe *n* گرمك garmak

canteen *n* قمقمه ghomghomeh

canvas *n* كرباس karbas

canyon *n* دربند darband

cap *n* طاق tagh

capability *n* قابليت ghabeliyat

capable *adj* توانا tavana

capacity *n* گنجايش gonjayesh

cape *n* شنل shenel

capital *n* پايتخت paytakht

capital letter *n* حرف بزرگ harf-e bozorg

capitalism *n* سرمايه داري sarmaye'h dari

capitalize *v* با حروف درشت نوشتن ba harf-e bozorg neveshtan

capitulate *v* تسليم شدن taslim shodan

capsize *v* واژگون كردن vazhgoon kardan

capsule *n* پوشش poushesh
captain *n* سروان sarvan
captivate *v* شیفتن shiftan
captive *n* اسیر asir
captivity *n* اسارت esarat
capture *v* اسیرکردن asir kardan
capture *n* دستگیری dastgiri
car *n* اتومبیل otomobil
caramel *n* قندسوخته ghande' soukhteh
carat *n* قیراط ghirat
caravan *n* کاروان karavan
carburettor *n* کابوراتور karbourator
card *n* کارت kart
cardboard *n* مقوا moghava
cardiac *adj* وابسته‌به‌قلب vabasteh be ghalb
cardigan *n* ژاکت‌کش‌باف‌پشمی zhakete' pashmi
cardiology *n* قلب‌شناسی ghalbshenasi
care *v* پرواداشتن parva dashtan
care *n* تیمار timar
care about *v* تیمارکردن timar kardan
care for *v* غم‌خوردن gham khordan
career *n* حرفه herfeh
carefree *adj* سبکبار sabokbar
careful *adj* بادقت ba deghat
careless *adj* بی‌دقت bi deghat
carelessness *n* بی‌مبالاتی bi mobalati
caress *v* درآغوش‌کشیدن dar aghoush keshidan
caress *n* نوازش navazesh

caretaker *n* سرپرست sarparast
cargo *n* محموله mahmouleh
caricature *n* کاریکاتور karikatoor
carnage *n* کشتار koshtar
carnal *adj* جسمانی jesmani
carnation *n* میخک‌صدپر mikhak-e sad-par
carol *n* چهچه chahchahe'
carpenter *n* درودگر doroudgar
carpentry *n* درودگری doroudgari
carpet *n* فرش farsh
carriage *n* کالسکه kaleskeh
carrot *n* هویج havij
carry *v* بردن bordan
carry on *v* ادامه‌دادن edameh dadan
carry out *v* انجام‌دادن anjam dadan
cart *n* ارابه arrabeh
cartoon *n* کاریکاتور karikator
cartridge *n* کارتریج kartrij
carve *v* حک‌کردن hakk kardan
cascade *n* آبشار abshar
case *n* سرگذشت sargozasht
cash *n* نقد naghd
cashier *n* صندوقدار sandoughdar
cashmere *n* شال‌کشمیری shalle' keshmiri
casino *n* کازینو kazino
casket *n* جعبه‌کوچک ja'beh kouchak
casserole *n* غذای‌ازگوشت‌وآرد ghaza'ei az goosht va ard
cast *iv* قالب‌گیری ghaleb giri
castaway *n* مردود mardood
castle *n* دژ dezh

casual *adj* اتفاقي etefaghi

casualty *n* تلفات talafat

cat *n* گربه gorbeh

cataclysm *n* سیل‌بزرگ seile' bozorg

catalogue *n* فهرست fehrest

cataract *n* آبشاربزرگ abshare' bozorg

catastrophe *n* بلای‌ناگهانی balaye' nagahani

catch *iv* گرفتن gereftan

catechism *n* پرسش‌نامه‌مذهبي porsesh-namehe' mazhabi

category *n* دسته dasteh

cater *v* آذوقه‌رساندن azougheh rasandan

caterpillar *n* کرم‌صدپا kerme' sad-pa

cathedral *n* کلیسای‌جامع kelisaye' jame'e

catholic *adj* کاتولیک katoulik

Catholicism *n* اصول‌مذهب‌کاتولیکي osoul-e mazhabe' katoliki

cattle *n* گله‌گاو gallehe gav

cauliflower *n* گل‌کلم gol kalam

cause *n* سبب sabab

caution *n* احتیاط ehtiyat

cautious *adj* هوشیار houshyar

cavalry *n* سواره‌نظام savareh nezam

cave *n* غار gha'r

cavern *n* غار gha'r

cavity *n* گودال gowdal

cease *v* ایستادن eistadan

ceasefire *n* آتش‌بس atash bas

ceaselessly *adv* پیوسته peyvasteh

cedar *n* سدر sedr

ceiling *n* سقف saghf

celebrate *v* جشن‌گرفتن jashn gereftan

celebration *n* جشن jashn

celebrity *adj* شهرت shohrat

celery *n* کرفس karafs

celestial *adj* الهي elahi

cell *n* یاخته yakhteh

cellar *n* زیرزمین zir-zamin

cement *n* سیمان siman

cemetery *n* گورستان gourestan

censorship *n* سانسورعقاید sansore' aghayed

censure *v* سرزنش‌کردن sarzanesh kartdan

census *n* سرشماري sar-shomari

cent *n* درصد dar sad

centenary *n* صدساله sad-saleh

centre *n* مرکز markaz

central *adj* مرکزي markazi

centralize *v* دادن‌تمرکز tamarkoz dadan

century *n* سده saddeh

ceramic *n* سرامیک seramik

cereal *n* غله ghalleh

cerebral *adj* مخي mokhi

ceremony *n* تشریفات tashrifat

certain *adj* معین moein

certainty *n* امرمسلم amre' mosallam

certificate *n* گواهینامه govahinameh

certify *v* تصدیق‌کردن tasdigh kardan

chain *n* زنجیر zanjir

chain *v* زنجیر‌کردن zanjir kardan

chainsaw *n* دندانگیر dandan gir

chair *n* صندلی sandali

chairman *n* فرنشین far neshin

chalet *n* کلبه‌ییلاقی kolbehe' ye'laqi

chalk *n* گچ gach

chalkboard *n* تخته‌سیاه takhte' siyah

challenge *v* به‌مبارزه‌طلبیدن be mobarezeh talabidan

challenge *n* طلب‌حق hagh talab

challenging *adj* چالش‌انگیز chalesh angiz

chamber *n* اتاق otagh

champion *n* پهلوان pahlavan

chance *n* بخت bakht

chancellor *n* صدراعظم sadre' a'azam

chandelier *n* چلچراغ chelcheragh

change *n* تغییر taghyier

change *v* عوض‌کردن avaz kardan

channel *n* کانال kanal

chant *n* سرود soroud

chaos *n* هرج‌ومرج harj-o-marj

chaotic *adj* پرهرج‌ومرج por harj-o-marj

chapel n کلیسای‌کوچک kelisay-e kouchak

chaplain *n* دین‌یار dinyar

chapter *n* فصل(کتاب) fasl

character *n* منش manesh

charade *n* نوعی‌معما no'ei moamma

charcoal *n* زغال‌چوب zoghale' choub

charcoaled *adj* ذغالی zoghali

charge *n* تصدی tasadi

charge *v* عهده‌دارکردن ohde'dar kardan

charisma *n* عطیه‌الهی attiyehe elahi

charitable *adj* دستگیر dastgir

charity *n* دستگیری dastgiri

charlatan *n* بازحقه hoghehbaz

charm *n* افسون afsoun

charm *v* افسون‌کردن afsoun kardan

charming *adj* فریبا fariba

charred *adj* سوخته soukhteh

chart *n* نمودار nemoudar

charter n فرمان farman

chase *n* تعقیب ta'ghib

chase *v* تعقیب‌کردن ta'ghib kardan

chase away *v* رانده‌شدن randeh shodan

chasm *n* شکاف shekaf

chastise *v* تنبیه‌کردن tanbih kardan

chastity *n* عفت‌وعصمت effat va esmat

chat *v* گپ‌زدن gap zadan

chateau *n* قلعه ghal'eh

chatter *v* تندتندحرف‌زدن tondtond harf zadan

chauffeur *n* شوفر shoufer

cheap *adj* ارزان arzan

cheer up *v* تشویق‌شدن tashvigh shodan

cheat *v* دادن‌فریب farib dadan

cheater *n* زننده‌گول goul zanandeh

check *n* مقابله moghabeleh

check *v* مقابله‌کردن moghabeleh kardan

check *in* v وارد شدن varedshodan

cheque book *n* دفترچه چک daftarchehe chek

checkmate *n* شهمات کردن shahmat kardan

cheek *n* گونه gooneh

cheekbone *n* استخوان گونه ostokhane' gooneh

cheer *n* خوشی khoshi

cheer *v* دلخوشی دادن delkhoshi dadan

cheerful *adj* بشاش bashash

cheers *n* به سلامتی besalamati

cheese *n* پنیر panir

chef *n* سرآشپز sarashpaz

chemical *adj* شیمیایی shimiya'ei

chemistry *n* شیمی shimi

cherish *v* گرامی داشتن gerami dashtan

cherry *n* گیلاس gilas

chess *n* شطرنج shatranj

chest *n* صندوق sandoughdar

chestnut *n* بلوط شاه shahbaloot

chew *v* جویدن javidan

chic *adj* شیک shik

chick *n* جوجه joujeh

chicken *n* جوجه مرغ joujeh morgh

chicken pox *n* آبله مرغان ableh morghan

chide *v* سرزنش کردن sarzanesh kardan

chief *n* رئیس re'eis

chiefly *adv* مخصوصا makhsousan

child *n* بچه bacheh

childhood *n* بچگی bachegi

childish *n* بچگانه bacheganeh

childless *adj* بی بچه bi bacheh

children *n* بچه ها bachehha

chill *v* سرد کردن sard kardan

chill *n* سرما sarma

chilly *adj* سرد sard

chime *n* سنج senj

chime *v* صدای سنج ایجاد کردن sedaye senj eijad kardan

chimney *n* دودکش doudkesh

chimpanzee *n* میمون meymoun

chin *n* چانه chaneh

chip *n* ژتن zheton

chisel *n* اسکنه eskeneh

chocolate *n* شکلات shokolat

choice *n* پسند pasand

choir *n* دسته سرایندگان dastehe' sorayandegan

choke *v* خفه کردن khafeh kardan

cholera *n* وبا vaba

cholesterol *n* کلسترول kolestrol

choose *iv* گزیدن gazidan

choosy *adj* گزینگر gozingar

chop *v* ریزریز کردن rizriz kardan

chopper *n* ساطور satour

christen *v* نام گذاری کردن (هنگام تعمید) namgozari kardan

christening *n* مراسم تعمید maraseme' ta'mid

Christian *adj* مسیحی masihi

Christianity *n* مسیحیت masihiyat

Christmas *n* عید میلاد مسیح eide' milade' masih

chronic *adj* دیرینه dirineh

chubby *adj* چاق chagh

chuckle *v* بادهان‌بسته‌خندیدن ba dahane' basteh khandidan

chunk *n* کنده kondeh

church *n* کلیسا kelissa

chute *n* شیب‌تندرودخانه shibe' tonde roudkhaneh

cider *n* شراب‌سیب sharab-e sib

cigar *n* سیگار sigar

cigarette *n* سیگارت sigaret

cinder *n* زغال‌نیم‌سوز zoghale' nimsouz

cinema *n* سینما sinema

circle *n* دایره dayereh

circuit *n* مدار madar

circulate *v* بخشنامه‌کردن bakhshnameh kardan

circulation *n* گردش gardesh

circumcise *v* ختنه‌کردن khatneh kardan

circumcision *n* ختنه khatneh

circumstance *n* چگونگی chegoonegi

circus *n* سیرک sirk

cistern *n* آب‌انبار abanbar

citizen *n* تابع tabe'e

citizenship *n* شهروندان shahrvandan

city *n* شهر shahr

city hall *n* شهرداری shahrdari

civic *adj* شهري shahri

civil *adj* غیر نظامي gheyre' nezami

civilization *n* تمدن tamadon

civilize *v* متمدن‌کردن motemaden kardan

claim *n* ادعا edde'a

claim *v* ادعاکردن edde'a kardan

clam *n* صدف sadaf

clamour *v* غریوکشیدن ghariv keshidan

clamp *n* گیره gireh

clan *n* خاندان khanedan

clandestine *adj* مخفي makhfi

clap *v* کف‌زدن kafzadan

clarification *n* روشني rowshani

clarify *v* روشن‌کردن rowshan kardan

clarinet *n* قره‌نی ghare'ney

clarity *n* وضوح vozouh

clash *v* برخورد barkhord

class *n* ردیف radif

classic *adj* باستاني bastani

classify *v* دسته‌بندي‌کردن dasteh bandi kardan

classroom *n* کلاس kelas

classy *adj* ارشد arshad

clause *n* شرط shart

claw *n* چنگ chang

claw *v* چنگ‌زدن changzadan

clay *n* خاک‌رس khake ros

clean *adj* پاک pak

clean *v* تمیزکردن tamiz kardan

clean-cut *adj* روشن rowshan

cleaner *n* جارو jaroo

cleaning *n* شستشو shostoshoo

cleanliness *n* پاکیزگي pakizegi

cleanse *v* پاک کردن pak kardan

cleanser *n* ماده‌تمیزکننده padehe' tamiz-konandeh

clear *adj* آشکار ashkar

clearance *n* اختیار ekhtiyar

clear-cut *adj* روشن rowshan

clearly *adv* اشکارا ashkara

clemency *n* بخشايندگي bakhshayandegi

clench *v* پرچ‌كردن parch kardan

clergy *n* مردروحاني marde' roohani

cleric *n* كشيش keshish

clerical *adj* دفتري daftari

clerk *n* منشي monshi

clever *adj* ناقلا naghola

click *v* ضربه‌زدن zarbeh zadan

client *n* موكل movakel

clientele *n* ارباب‌رجوع arbabe' rojo'e

cliff *n* تخته‌سنگ takhteh sang

climate *n* آب‌وهوا ab-o-hava

climatic *adj* آب‌وهوائي ab-o-hava'ei

climatic *adj* آب‌وهوائي ab-o-hava'ei

climax *n* اوج owj

climb *v* بالارفتن balaraftan

climber *n* بالارونده balaravandeh

climbing *n* صعود so'oud

cling *iv* چسبيدن chasbidan

clinic *n* درمانگاه darmangah

clip *v* كوتاه‌كردن koutah kardan

clipping *n* تكه tekkeh

cloak *n* ردا rada

clock *n* ساعت sa'at

clog *v* سنگين‌كردن sangin kardan

cloister *n* راهرو rahrow

clone *v* توليدمثل‌غيرجنسي towlide' mesle' gheyre jensi

close *v* بستن bastani

close *adj* تنگ tang

close to *pre* نزديك‌به nazdik be

closed *adj* محصور mahsour

closely *adv* دقت‌به be deghat

closet *n* صندوق‌خانه sandoughkhaneh

closure *n* خاتمه khatameh

clot *n* توده toudeh

cloth *n* پارچه parcheh

clothe *v* پوشاندن poushandan

clothes *n* لباس lebas

clothing *n* روكش roukesh

cloud *n* ابر abr

cloudless *adj* بي‌ابر biabr

cloudy *adj* ابري abri

clown *n* لوده lowdeh

club *n* چماق chomagh

clue *n* گلوله‌نخ gouloulehe nakh

clumsiness *n* زشتي zeshti

clumsy *adj* بدتركيب badtarkib

cluster *n* خوشه khousheh

cluster *v* دسته‌كردن dasteh kardan

clutch *n* كلاج kelaj

coach *n* كالسكه kaleskeh

coach *v* معلمي‌كردن mo'alemi kardan

coagulate *v* بستن bastani

coagulation *n* انعقاد en'eghad

coal *n* زغال‌سنگ zoghalsang

coalition *n* ائتلاف e'etelaf

coarse *adj* زبر zebr

coast *n* ساحل sahel

coastal *adj* ساحلي saheli

coastline *n* خط‌ساحلي khate' saheli

coat *n* كت kot

cobblestone *n* قلوه‌سنگ gholvehsang

cobweb *n* تارعنكبوت tare'ankabout

cocaine *n* كوكائين koka'ein

cockpit *n* اطاقک‌خلبان otaghake' khalaban

cockroach *n* سوسك sousk

cocktail *n* كوكتل koktel

cocky *adj* ازخودراضي az-khod razi

cocoa *n* كاكائو kaka'ou

coconut *n* نارگيل nargil

cod *n* كيسه kiseh

code *n* نظام‌نامه nezamnameh

coerce *v* به‌زوروادارکردن bezour vadar kardan

coercion *n* اجبار ejbar

coexist *v* باهم‌زيستن bahamzistan

coffee *n* قهوه ghahveh

coffin *n* تابوت tabout

cog *n* دندانه dandaneh

cogent *adj* متقاعدکننده motegha'ed konnandeh

cognac *n* كنياک koniak

cohabit *v* باهم‌زندگي‌کردن(زن‌ومرد) baham zendegi kardan

coherent *adj* منسجم monsajem

cohesion *n* پيوستگي peyvastegi

coin *n* سكه sekkeh

coincide *v* همزمان‌بودن hamzaman boudan

coincidence *n* انطباق entebagh

cold *adj* سرما sarma

cold-blooded *adj* خونسرد khounsard

coldly *adv* سردی‌به be sardi

coldness *n* سردي sardi

coleslaw *n* سالادکلم salade' kalam

colic *n* قولنج ghoulanj

collaborate *v* همدستي‌کردن hamdasti kardan

collaborator *n* همدست hamdast

collapse *v* فروريختن forourikhtan

collar *n* يقه yagheh

collarbone *n* ترقوه targhoveh

collateral *adj* پهلوبه‌پهلو pahloo be pahloo

colleague *n* هم‌كار hamkar

collect *v* جمع‌آوري‌کردن jam'e avari kardan

collection *n* جمع‌آوري jam'e avari

college *n* كالج kalej

collide *v* تصادم‌کردن tasadom kardan

collision *n* تصادم tasadom

cologne *n* كلن kolon

colon *n* مقعد megh'ad

colonel *n* سرهنگ sarhang

colonial *adj* مستعمراتي mosta'merati

colonize *v* مستعمره‌کردن mosta'mereh kardan

colony *n* مستعمره mosta'mereh

colour *n* رنگ rang

colourful *adj* رنگارنگ rangarang

colossal *adj* بسياربزرگ besyar bozorg

colt *n* كره‌اسب koreh-asb

column *n* ستون sotoun

columnist *n* مقاله‌نويس maghaleh-nevis

coma *n* اغماء eghma

comb *n* شانه shaneh

comb *v* شانه‌کردن shaneh kardan

combat *n* پیکار peykar

combat *v* مبارزه‌کردن mobarezeh kardan

combatant *n* جنگ‌آور jangavar

combination *n* ترکیب tarkib

combine *v* باهم‌پیوستن baham peyvastan

combustible *n* سوختنی soukhtani

combustion *n* سوخت soukht

come *iv* آمدن amadan

come about *v* اتفاق‌افتادن ettefaghoftadan

come across *v* برخوردن‌به barkhordan-be

come back *v* بازگشتن bazgashtan

come down *v* سقوط soghout

come forward *v* جلوآمدن jelow amadan

come in *v* بفرمائید befarma'eid

come out *v* آشکارشدن ashkar shodan

comeback *n* حاضرجوابی hazerjavabi

comedian *n* کمدین komedian

comedy *n* کمدی komedi

comet *n* ستاره‌دنباله‌دار setareh donbalehdar

comfort *n* راحتی rahati

comfortable *adj* راحت rahat

comical *adj* خنده‌آور khandehavar

comma *n* ویرگول virgool

command *v* فرمان‌دادن farman dadan

commander *n* فرمانده farmandeh

commando *n* کماندو komando

commence *v* آغازکردن aghaz kardan

commend *v* ستودن sotodan

comment *v* تفسیرنوشتن tafsir neveshtan

comment *n* توضیح towzih

commerce *n* تجارت tejarat

commercial *adj* تجاری tejari

commission *n* ماموریت ma'mouriat

commit *v* سپردن sepordan

commitment *n* سرسپردگی sarsepordegi

committee *n* هیئت heyat

common *adj* مشترک moshtarak

commonly *adv* به‌طورعادی be towre' addi

commotion *n* آشوب ashoub

communicate *v* گفتگوکردن goft-o-goo kardan

communion *n* مشارکت mosharekat

communism *n* اصول‌اشتراکی osoule' eshteraki

communist *adj* کمونیست komonist

community *n* انجمن anjoman

commute *v* تبدیل‌کردن tabdil kardan

compact *adj* جمع‌وجور jam'-o-joor

companion *n* همدم hamdam

company *n* شرکت sherkat

comparable *adj* قابل‌مقایسه ghabele' moghayeseh

comparative *adj* تطبیقی tatbighi

compare *v* مقایسه کردن moghayeseh kardan

comparison *n* مقایسه moghayeseh

compass *n* گرد gard

compassion *n* دلسوزي delsouzi

compatible *adj* سازگار sazgar

compatriot *n* هم‌ميهن ham-mihan

compel *v* مجبور کردن majbour kardan

compelling *adj* اجباری ejbari

compensate *v* تاوان‌دادن tavan dadan

compete *v* رقابت کردن reghabat kardan

competence *n* صلاحيت salahiyyat

competent *adj* لايق layegh

competition *n* مسابقه mosabegheh

competitive *adj* مسابقه‌اي mosabeghe'ei

competitor *n* رقيب raghib

compile *v* گردآوردن gerd avardan

complain *v* شکايت کردن shekayat kardan

complaint *n* شکايت shekayat

complement *n* متمم motamem

complete *adj* کامل kamel

complete *v* کامل کردن kamel kardan

completion *n* اتمام etmam

complex *adj* پيچيده pichideh

complexion *n* رنگ‌چهره range' chehreh

complexity *n* پيچيدگي pichidegi

compliance *n* قبول ghaboul

complicate *v* پيچيده کردن pichideh kardan

complication *n* پيچيدگي pichidegi

complicity *n* شريک‌جرم sharike' jorm

compliment *n* تعارف ta'arof

comply *v* موافقت کردن movafeghat kardan

component *n* اجزاء ajza'e

compose *v* سرودن soroudan

composer *n* سراينده sarayandeh

composition *n* ترکيب tarkib

composure *n* آرامش aramesh

compound *n* محوطه mohavateh

comprehend *v* دريافتن daryaftan

compress *v* متراکم کردن moterakem kardan

compression *n* تراکم tarakom

comprise *v* دربرداشتن darbar dashtan

compromise *n* مصالحه mosaleheh

compromise *v* مصالحه کردن mosaleheh kardan

compulsion *n* اجبار ejbar

compulsive *adj* اجباري ejbari

compulsory *adj* اجباري ejbari

computer *n* رايانه rayaneh

comrade *n* رفيق rafigh

conceal *v* کردن kardan

concede *v* واگذار کردن vagozar kardan

conceited *adj* خودپسندی khodpasandi

conceive *v* درک کردن dark kardan

concentrate *v* متمرکز کردن motemarkez kardan

concentric *adj* هم‌مرکز ham markaz

concept *n* مفهوم mofhoum

concern *n* ربط rabt

concern *v* مربوطبودنبه marbout boodan be

concerning *pre* درباره dar barehe

concert *n* سازوآواز saz-o-avaz

concession *n* اعطاء e'eta

concierge *n* نگهبان negahban

conciliate *v* ساکتکردن saket kardan

conciliatory *adj* مصالحه mosaleheh

concise *adj* مختصر mokhtasar

conclude *v* بهپایانرساندن be payan rasandan

conclusion *n* پایان payan

concoct *v* درستکردن dorost kardan

concoction *n* ترکیب tarkib

concourse *n* گروه gorrouh

concrete *adj* واقعی vaghe'ei

concur *v* موافقتکردن movafeghat kardan

concussion *n* تصادم tasadom

condemn *v* محکومکردن mahkoom kardan

condense *v* متراکمکردن moterakem kardan

condescend *v* تمکینکردن tamkin kardan

condiment *n* ادویه adviyeh

condition *n* شرط shart

conditional *adj* شرطی sharti

condolence *n* همدردي hamdardi

condone *v* چشمپوشيکردناز chashmpooshi kardan az

condor *n* شاهرخ shahrokh

conducive *adj* موجبشونده mowjebshavandeh

conduct *n* رفتار raftar

conductor *n* هادي hadi

cone *n* مخروط makhroot

confer *v* مشورتکردن mashverat kardan

conference *n* مشاوره moshavereh

confess *v* اقرارکردن eghrar kardan

confession *n* اقرار eghrar kardan

confidant *adj* رازدار raz dar

confide *v* سپردن sopordan

confidence *n* اطمينان etminan

confident *adj* مطمئن motma'en

confidential *adj* محرمانه mahramaneh

confine *v* محدودکردن mahdoud kardan

confinement *n* تحديد tahdid

confines *n* مرز marz

confirm *v* تاييدکردن ta'yed kardan

confirmation *n* تاييد ta'yed

confiscate *v* ضبطکردن zabt kardan

confiscation *n* توقيف towghif

conflict *n* ستيزه setizeh

conform *v* همنواييکردن hamnava'ei kardan

conformist *n* همنوا ham nava

conformist *adj* همنوا hamnava

conformity *n* انطباق entebagh

confound *v* پريشانکردن parishan kardan

confront *v* روبروشدنبا rooberooshodan ba

confuse *v* گيجکردن gij kardan

confusing adj مغشوش‌شدن maghshoosh

confusion n گيجي giji

congested adj درهم‌فشرده darham feshordeh

congestion n ازدحام ezdeham

congratulate v تبريک‌گفتن tabrik goftan

congregate v جمع‌شدن jam'e shodan

congress n همايش hamayesh

conjecture n گمان goman

conjugal adj نکاحي nekahi

conjugate v صرف‌کردن sarf kardan

conjunction n عطف atf

connect v پيوستن peyvastan

connection n پيوستگي peyvastegi

conquer v پيروزي‌يافتن‌بر piroozi yaftan bar

conqueror n فاتح fateh

conquest n غلبه ghalabeh

conscience n وجدان vojdan

conscious adj هوشيار houshyar

consciously adv ازروي‌قصد az rooye ghasd

consecrate v وقف‌شده vaghf shodeh

consecration n تخصيص takhsis

consecutive adj پياپي payapey

consensus n توافق‌عام tavafoghe' a'm

consent v راضي‌شدن razi shodan

consequent adj نتيجه‌بخش natijeh bakhsh

conservation n نگهداري negahdari

conservative adj محافظه‌کار mohafezeh kar

conserve v نگهداري‌کردن negahdari kardan

consider v (به) رسيدگي‌کردن rasidegi kardan

consignment n حمل haml

consist v مرکب‌بودن‌از morakkab boudan az

consistency n ثبات sabat

consistent adj سازگار sazgar

console v دلداري‌دادن deldari dadan

consolidate v محکم‌کردن mohkam kardan

consonant n هم‌آهنگ ham ahang

consortium n کنسرسيوم konsersiyom

conspicuous adj انگشت‌نما angoshtnama

conspiracy n توطئه towte'eh

conspire v توطئه‌چيدن towte'eh chidan

constant adj استوار ostovar

constipated adj قبض‌کردن ghabz kardan

constipation n يبوست youboosat

constitution n قانون‌اساسي ghanoone' asasi

constraint n قيد gheyd

construct v ساختن sakhtan

consulate n کنسولگري konsoolgari

consult v هم‌فکري‌کردن hamfekri kardan

consultation n مشاوره moshavereh

consume v مصرف کردن masraf kardan

consumer n مصرف کننده masraf konandeh

consumption n مصرف masraf

contact n تماس tamas

contagious adj واگیر vagir

contain v محتوی بودن mohtavi boodan

container n ظرف zarf

contaminate v آلودن aloudan

contemplate v تفکر کردن tafakor kardan

contempt n تحقیر tahghir

contend v ستیزه کردن setizeh kardan

contender n برنده احتمالی barandeh' ehtemali

content adj محتوی mohtavi

contents n محتویات mohtaviat

contest n مشاجره moshajereh

contestant n ستیزه جو setizehjoo

context n زمینه zamineh

contiguous adj هم جوار hamjavar

continent n پرهیزکار parhizkar

contingency n احتمال ehtemal

continue v ادامه دادن edame dadan

contour n محیط مرئی mohite maree

contraband n کالای قاچاق kalaye ghachagh

contract v پیمان بستن payman bastan

contract n قرارداد gharardad

contraction n انقباض enghebaz

contradict v رد کردن rad kardan

contrary adj مخالف mokhalef

contrast v برابر کردن barabar kardan

contrast n هم سنجی ham sanji

contribute v اعانه دادن eane dadan

contrition n پشیمانی pashimani

control n کنترل kontorol

controversial adj مباحثه ای mobahesee

controversy n هم ستیزی ham setizi

convene v گرد آمدن gerd amadan

convenience n آسودگی asodeghi

convenient adv راحت rahat

convent n صومعه someeh

convention n عرف orf

converge v همگرا بودن hamgara bodan

conversation n گفتگو goftego

converse v صحبت کردن sohbat kardan

convert v برگرداندن bargardandan

convict v محکوم کردن mahkom kardan

convince v متقاعد کردن moteghaed kardan

convincing adj متقاعد کننده moteghaed konandeh

convoluted adj بهم پیچیده beham pichideh

convoy n قافله ghafeleh

convulsion n تشنج tashanoj

cook n آشپز ashpaz

cook v پختن pokhtan

cookie n کلوچه kolocheh

cool adj خنک khonak

coolness n خنکی khonaki

cooperate v همياري‌کردن hamyari kardan

coordinate v هماهنگ‌کردن hamahang kardan

coordinator n هماهنگ‌کننده hamahang konandeh

cop n پلیس polis

cope v برآمدن baramadan

copier n رونویس‌کننده ronevis konandeh

copper n مس mes

copter n هلیکوپتر helikopter

copy n رونوشت ronevesht

copy v کپي‌کردن kopi kardan

cord n سیم sim

cordial adj قلبي ghalbi

cordless adj بدون‌سیم bedone sim

cordon n کمربند kamarband

cordon off v پیوستن peyvastan

core n مغزودرون‌هرچیزي maghz va darone har chizi

cork n چوب‌پنبه chob panbeh

corn n غله ghaleh

corner n گوشه gosheh

cornerstone n سنگ‌گوشه sang gosheh

cornet n نوعي‌شیپور noee shaypor

coronation n تاج‌گذاري taj gozari

corporal adj بدني badani

corporation n شرکت sherkat

corpse n نعش na'esh

corpulent adj فربه farbeh

correct adj درست dorost kardan

correct v صحیح‌کردن sahih kardan

correction n تصحیح tashih

correspond v برابربودن barabar bodan

corridor n راهرو rahro

corroborate v تائیدکردن taid kardan

corrode v خوردن(اسیدوفلزات) khordan

corrupt v فاسدکردن fased kardan

corruption n فساد fesad

cosmetic n وسیله‌آرایش vasileh arayesh

cosmic adj وابسته‌به‌گیتي vabasteh be giti

cosmonaut n کیهان‌نورد keihan navard

cost iv قیمت‌داشتن ghaymat dashtan

cost n هزینه hazineh

costly adj گران geran

costume n لباس lebas

cottage n کلبه kolbeh

cotton n پنبه banbeh

couch n تخت takht

cough n سرفه sorfeh

cough v سرفه‌کردن sorfeh kardan

council n انجمن anjoman

counsel v پنددادن(به) pand dadan

counsellor n مشاور moshaver

count v شمردن shemordan

countenance n سیما sima

counter n شمارشگر shomareshgar

counterfeit v جعل‌کردن jaal kardan

counterfeit adj جعلي jaali

counterpart n نقطه‌مقابل noghteh moghabel

countess n کنتس kontes

country *n* كشور keshvar	crab *n* خرچنگ kharchang
countryman *n* هم‌ميهن ham mihan	crack *v* تركانيدن terekanidan
countryside *n* ييلاقات yeylagh	crack *n* رخنه rekhneh
county *n* بخش bakhsh	cradle *n* گهواره gahvareh
coup *n* برهم‌زدن bar ham zadan	craft *n* پيشه pisheh
couple *n* زوج zoj	craftsman *n* هنرمند honarmand
coupon *n* كوپن kopen	cramp *n* چنگه chengeh
courage *n* جرات jorat	crane *n* جرثقيل jaresaghil
courageous *adj* دلير dalir	crank *n* هندل hendel
course *n* دوره doreh	cranky *adj* بدخو bad kho
court *n* بارگاه bargah	crap *n* گندم‌سياه gandome siah
courteous *adj* باادب ba adab	crash *v* خردكردن khord kardan
courtesy *n* ادب‌ومهرباني acab va mehrabani	crash *n* سقوط soghot
courthouse *n* دادگاه dadgah	crass *adj* زمخت zomokht
courtship *n* اظهارعشق ezhar eshgh	crater *n* دهانه‌آتش‌فشان dahaneh atash feshn
courtyard *n* حياط hayat	crave *v* آرزوكردن arezo kardan
cousin *n* پسرعمويادخترعمو pesar amoo ya dokhtar amoo	crawl *v* خزيدن khazidan
cove *n* خليج‌كوچك khalij kochak	crayon *n* مدادرنگي‌مومي medad rangiye momi
covenant *n* پيمان peyman	craziness *n* ديوانگی divanegi
cover *v* پوشاندن poshandan	crazy *adj* ديوانه divaneh
cover *n* پوشش poshesh	creak *v* صداي‌غوك‌درآوردن sedaye ghok daravardan
coverage *n* پوشش poshesh	cream *n* سرشير sarshir
covert *adj* نهان nahan	crease *n* چين chin
cover up *n* پوشش poshesh	create *v* خلق‌شدن khalgh shodan
covet *v* ميل‌به‌تملك‌چيزي‌كردن meyl be tamalok e chizi kardan	creation *n* آفرينش afarinesh
	creative *adj* خالق khalegh
cow *n* گاوماده gave madeh	creativity *n* قدرت‌ابداع ghodrate ebdae
coward *adj* نامرد namard	creator *n* آفريدگار afaridegar
cowardice *n* ترسويي tarsoee	creature *n* آفريده afarideh
cowboy *n* گاوچران gavcheran	credibility *n* اعتبار etebar
cosy *adj* راحت rahat	credible *adj* معتبر moetabar
	credit *n* اعتبار etebar

creed *n* كيش kish

creepy *adj* مورمورکننده mor mor konandeh

cremate *v* خاکسترکردن khkestar kardan

crematorium *n* کوره‌سوزاندن‌آشغال koreh sozandane ashghal

crest *n* تاج taj

crevice *n* درز darz

crew *n* خدمه‌کشتی khadameh kashti

crib *n* آخور akhor

cricket *n* جیرجیرک jirjirak

crime *n* جنایت jenayat

cripple *adj* لنگ long

crisis *n* بحران bohran

crisp *adj* ترد tord

crispy *adj* ترد tord

criterion *n* ضابطه zabeteh

critic *n* نقدگر naghdgar

criticize *v* نقدادبی‌کردن naghd adabi kardan

critique *n* انتقاد فن fane enteghad

crocodile *n* تمساح temsah

crook *n* عصای‌سرکج asaye sarkaj

crooked *adj* ناراست narast

crop *n* محصول mahsol

cross *v* روبروشدن robero shodan

cross *n* صلیب salib

cross *adj* متقاطع moteghate

cross out *v* قلم‌زدن ghalam zadan

cross-eyed *adj* لوچ looch

crossfire *n* پرتاب‌بازاویه partab ba zavie

crossing *n* دوراهی dorahi

crossroads *n* تقاطع taghato

crossword *n* جدول‌کلمات jadval kalamat

crouch *v* دولاشدن dola shodan

crowbar *n* اهرم ahrom

crowd *n* جمعیت jamiat

crown *n* تاج taj

crowning *n* محدب mohadab

crucial *adj* وخیم vakhim

crucifix *n* صلیب‌عیسی salib eisa

crucify *v* برصلیب‌آویختن bar salib avikhtan

crude *adj* خام khadem

cruel *adj* بیرحم birahm

cruise *v* گشت‌زدن gasht zadan

cruise ship *n* کشتی‌تفریحی kashtie tafrihi

crumb *n* خرده‌نان khordeh nan

crumble *v* خردشدن khord shodan

crunchy *adj* جویدنی javidani

crusade *n* جنگ‌صلیبی jange salibi

crusader *n* صلیبیون salibion

crush *v* چلاندن chelandan

crust *n* کبره kebreh

crux *n* چیستان chistan

cry *v* فریادزدن faryad zadan

cry out *v* ضجه‌وفریادزدن zajeh va faryad zadan

crystal *n* بلور bolor

cub *n* بچه‌شیر bacheh shir

cube *n* مکعب mokaab

cubicle *n* اطاقک otaghak

cucumber *n* خیار khiar

cuddle *v* درآغوش‌گرفتن dar aghosh gereftan

cuff *n* سرآستین sarastin

cuff link n دگمه‌سردست dogmeh sardast

cuisine n دست‌پخت dast pokht

culminate v به‌اوج‌رسیدن beh ooj residan

culpability n قابلیت‌مجازات ghabeliat mojazat

culprit n متهم motaham

cult n آئین‌دینی aeen dini

cultivate adj کشت‌کردن kesht kardan

culture n فرهنگ farhang

cumbersome adj سنگین sangin

cunning adj زیرک zirak

cup n فنجان fenjan

cupboard n گنجه ganjeh

curable adj علاج‌پذیر alaj pazir

curator n کتابدار ketabdar

curb v محدودکردن mahdod kardan

curdle v بستن bastan

cure v شفادادن shafa dadan

cure n علاج alaj

curfew n حکومت‌نظامی hokomat nezami

curiosity n حس‌کنجکاوی hese konjkavi

curious adj کنجکاو konjkav

curl n حلقه halghe

curl v حلقه‌کردن halghe kardan

curly adj مجعد mojaad

currency n پول‌رایج pol e rayej

current adj رایج rayej

curse v نفرین‌کردن nefrin kardan

curtail v کوتاه‌کردن kotah kardan

curve n خط‌منحنی khat monhani

cushion n متکا motaka

custard n فرنی fereni

custodian n سرایدار seraydar

custody n حفاظت hefazat

custom n رسم rasm

customer n مشتری moshtari

custom-made adj سفارشی sefareshi

customs n دفترگمرک daftar e gomrok

cut n بریدگی boridegi

cut iv بریدن boridan

cut out v جداکردن‌دراثربریدن joda kardan dar asar boridan

cut back v تقلیل‌دادن taghlil dadan

cut down v خردکردن khord kardan

cute adj جذاب jazab

cutlery n کاردوچنگال kard va changal

cyanide n سم‌مهلک sam e mohlek

cycle n دور dor

cyclist n دوچرخه‌سوار docharkhe savar

cyclone n طوفان‌موسمی tofan e mosemi

cylinder n استوانه ostovaneh

cynic adj بدبین‌وعیب‌جو badbin va eyb jo

cynicism n مکتب‌کلبیون maktab e kalbion

czar n قیصر ghaysar

D

dad *n* بابا baba

dagger *n* خنجر khanjar

daily *adv* روزانه rozaneh

dairy *n* شیر بندي shir bandi

dairy farm *n* کارخانه لبنیات سازي karkhaneh labaniat sazi

daisy *n* گل مروارید gol e morvarid

dam *n* سد sad

damage *n* خسارت khesarat

damaging *adj* آسیب آور asib avar

damn *v* لعنت کردن lanat kardan

damned *adj* دوزخي dozakhi

damp *adj* نم nam

dampen *v* رطوبت پیداکردن rotobat peida kardan

dance *n* رقص raghs

dancer *n* رقاص raghas

dandruff *n* سر شوره shoreh sar

danger *n* خطر khatar

dare *v* یارابودن yara bodan

daring *adj* جسور jasoor

dark *adj* تاریک tarik

darken *v* تاریک شدن tarik shodan

darkness *n* تاریکي tariki

darling *adj* محبوب mahbob

darn *v* رفوکردن rofo kardan

dart *n* نیزه neyzeh

dashing *adj* بی پروا bi parva

data *n* مفروضات mafrozat

date *n* تاریخ tarikh

dated *adj* مورخ movarekh

daughter *n* دختر dokhtar

daunt *v* رام کردن ram kardan

daunting *adj* رام کردن ram kardan

dawn *n* فجر fajr

day *n* روز rooz

daydream *v* خیال باطل کردن khial e batel kardan

daze *v* گیج کردن gij kardan

dazed *adj* خیرگي khiregi

dazzle *v* خیره کردن khireh kardan

dazzling *adj* خیره کننده khireh konandeh

deacon *n* شماس shamas

deaconess *n* راهبه rahebeh

dead *adj* مرده mordeh

dead end *n* بست بن bon bast

deaden *v* کشتن koshtan

deadline *n* ضرب العجل zarbol ajal

deadly *adj* مهلک mohlek

deaf *adj* کر kar

deafen *v* کرکردن kar kardan

deafness *n* کري kari

deal *iv* معامله کردن moameleh kardan

deal *n* مقدار meghdar

dean *n* رئیس rais

dear *adj* عزیز aziz

dearly *adv* به طور عزیز be tore aziz

death *n* مرگ marg

death toll *n* مرگ و میر marg o mir

deathbed *n* بستر مرگ bastare marg

deathtrap *n* تله مرگ taleh marg

debase *v* کسي را پائین بردن kasi ra paeen bordan

debatable *adj* قابل بحث ghabele bahs

debate *n* مذاکرات پارلماني mozakerat parlemani

debate *v* مناظره كردن monazereh kardan

debris *n* خرده khordeh

debt *n* بدهی bedehi

debtor *n* مديون madion

debut *n* آغازكار aghaz kar

decade *n* دهه daheh

decadence *n* زوال zaval

decapitate *v* گردنزدن gardan zadan

decay *n* پوسيدگی posidegi

decay *v* فاسدشدن fased shodan

deceased *adj* مرده mordeh

deceit *n* فريب farib

deceitful *adj* فريبآميز faribamiz

deceive *v* فريفتن fariftan

December *n* دسامبر desambr

decency *n* انطباقبهمورد entebagh beh morede

decent *adj* آراسته arasteh

deception *n* نيرنگ neirang

deceptive *adj* فريبنده faribandeh

decide *v* تصميمگرفتن tasmim gereftan

decipher *v* كشفرمزنمودن kashf ramz nemodan

decision *n* عزم azm

decisive *adj* قطعی ghatee

deck *n* عرشه arsheh

declare *v* اظهارداشتن ezhar dashtan

decline *n* زوال zaval

decline *v* شيبپيداكردن shib peida kardan

decor *n* دكور dekor

decorate *v* آذينكردن azin kardan

decrease *v* آذينكردن azin kardan

decree *n* حكم hokm

decrepit *adj* سالخوردهوفرتوت salkhordeh va fartot

dedicate *v* اهداكردن ehda kardan

deduce *v* استنباطكردن estenbat kardan

deduct *v* كمكردن kam kardan

deductible *adj* كسرپذير kasr pazir

deduction *n* كسر kasr

deed *n* كردار kerdar

deem *v* پنداشتن pendashtan

deep *adj* گود gowd

deepen *v* گودكردن gowd kardan

deer *n* آهويكوهی ahoye kohi

deface *v* بدشكلكردن bad shekl kardan

defame *v* بدنامكردن bad nam kardan

defeat *v* دادنشكست shekast dadan

defect *n* كاستی kasti

defective *n* ضعيف zaif

defend *v* دفاعكردناز defa kardan az

defendant *n* مدافع modafe

defender *n* مدافع modafe

defence *n* دفاع defa

defer *v* عقبانداختن aghab andakhtan

defiance *n* مبارزهطلبی mobarezeh talabi

defiant *adj* اعتناءبی bi etena

deficiency *n* نقص naghs

deficient *adj* دارايكمبود daraye kambod

deficit *n* كمبود kambod

defile v آلوده‌کردن alodeh kardan

define v معین‌کردن moayan kardan

definite adj معین moayan

definition n تعریف tarif

deflate v (چیزی‌را)خالی‌کردن bad (chizi ra) khali kardan

deform v زشت‌کردن zesht kardan

deformity n بدشکلی badshekli

defraud v گول‌زدن gool zadan

defrost v یخ‌چیزی‌راآب‌کردن yakhe chizi ra ab kardan

defuse v خنثی‌سازی khonsa sazi

defy v به‌مبارزه‌طلبیدن be mobarezeh talabidan

degenerate v رو‌به‌انحطاط‌گذاردن ro be enhetat gozashtan

degrade v تنزل‌کردن tanazol kardan

degree n درجه darajeh

deign v لطفاپذیرفتن lotfan paziroftan

deity n خدا khoda

dejected adj پژمان pejman

delay v تاخیرکردن takhir kardan

delegate v نمایندگی‌دادن namayandegi dadan

delete v حذف‌کردن hazf kardan

deliberate adj عمدی amdi

delicacy n ظرافت zerafat

delicious adj لذیذ laziz

delight n خوشی khoshi

delight v دلشادکردن delshad kardan

delightful adj لذت‌بخش lazat bakhshidan

delinquency n تخلف takhalof

delinquent n متخلف motekhalef

deliver v آزادکردن azad kardan

delivery n تحویل tahvil

deluge n سیل sayl

delusion n فریب farib

deluxe adj تجملی tajamoli

demand v مطالبه‌کردن motalebeh kardan

demanding adj طاقت‌فرسا taghat farsa

demean n پست‌سازی past sazi

demeaning adj پست‌کردن past kardan

demeanour n رفتار raftar

demented adj دیوانه divaneh

demise n فوت fot

democracy n دموکراسی demokrasi

demolish v ویران‌کردن viran kardan

demon n اهریمن ahriman

demonstrate v اثبات‌کردن(بادلیل) esbat kardan (ba dalil)

demoralize v تضعیف‌روحیه‌کردن tazif rohieh kardan

demote v تنزل‌رتبه‌دادن tanazol rotbeh dadan

den n غار ghar

denial n رد rad

denigrate v لکه‌دارکردن lakeh dar kardan

denounce v تقبیح‌کردن taghbih kardan

denounce v علیه‌کسی‌اظهاری‌کردن alaiheh kasi ezhari kardan

dense adj متراکم motarakem

density n تراکم tarakom

dent *n* دندانه dandaneh

dent *v* دندانه‌کردن dandaneh kardan

dental *adj* وابسته‌به‌دندانسازي vabasteh be dandansazi

dentist *n* دندانساز dandansaz

deny *v* ردکردن rad kardan

deodorant *n* بوزدا boo zoda

depart *v* راهی‌شدن rahi shodan

department *n* دایره dayereh

departure *n* حرکت harekat

depend *v* وابسته‌بودن vabasteh bodan

dependent *adj* وابسته vabasteh

depict *v* نمایش‌دادن namayesh dadan

deplete *v* تهی‌کردن tohi kardan

deplore *v* دلسوزي‌کردن‌بر delsozi kardan bar

deploy *v* گسترش‌یافتن gostaresh yaftan

deployment *n* آرایش‌قشون arayeshe ghoshon

deport *v* تبعیدکردن tabid kardan

deposit *n* پول pool

depress *v* فروبردن foro bordan

depressing *adj* دلتنگ‌کردن deltang kardan

depression *n* تورفتگی to raftegi

deprive *v* بی‌بهره‌کردن bi bahreh kardan

depth *n* ژرفا jarfa

deputy *n* نماینده namayandeh

derail *v* ازخط‌خارج‌کردن az khat kharej kardan

derailment *n* ازخط‌خارج‌شدن‌ترن az khat kharej shodan teran

deranged *adj* آشفته ashofteh

derelict *adj* متروك matrok

deride *v* تمسخرکردن tamaskhor kardan

derive *v* منتج‌کردن montaj kardan

derogatory *adj* موهن mohen

descend *v* پایین‌آمدن paeen amadan

descendant *n* نسل nasl

descent *n* نسب nasab

describe *v* شرح‌دادن sharh dadan

description *n* تشریح tashrih

desecrate *v* بی‌حرمت‌کردن bi hormat kardan

desegregate *v* لغوتبعیض‌نژادي laghv tabiz nejadi

desert *n* بیابان biaban

deserted *adj* ویران viran

deserter *n* فراري farari

deserve *v* داشتن dashtan

deserving *adj* مستحق mostahagh

design *n* نقشه naghsheh

designate *v* نامزدکردن namzad kardan

desirable *adj* پسندیده pasandideh

desire *v* میل‌داشتن mail dashtan

desist *v* بازایستادن baz istadan

desk *n* میزتحریر miz tahrir

desolation *n* ویراني virani

despair *n* نومیدي nomidi

desperate *adj* بی‌امید bi omid

despicable *adj* پست past

despise *v* خوارشمردن khar shemordan

despite *c* باوجوداینکه ba vojode inkeh

despondent *adj* محزون maghzon

despot *n* حاکم‌مطلق hakem motlagh

dessert *n* دسر deser

destination *n* مقصد maghsad

destiny *n* سرنوشت sarnevesht

destitute *adj* بینوا binava

destroy *v* خراب‌کردن kharab kardan

destroyer *n* مخرب mokhreb

destruction *n* خرابی kharabi

detach *v* جداکردن joda kardan

detail *v* به‌تفصیل‌شرح‌دادن beh tafsil sharh dadan

detail *n* جزئیات joziat

detain *v* بازداشتن bazdashtan

detect *v* پیداکردن payda kardan

detective *n* کارگاه kargah

detector *n* ردیاب radyab

detention *n* بازداشت bazdasht

deter *v* بازداشتن bazdashtan

detergent *n* کننده‌پاک pak konandeh

deteriorate *v* بدترکردن badtar kardan

determine *v* تصمیم‌گرفتن tasmim gereftan

detest *v* نفرت‌کردن nefrat kardan

detonate *v* باصداترکیدن ba seda terekidan

detour *n* انحراف enheraf

detriment *n* گزند gazand

detrimental *adj* زیان‌آور zian avar

devalue *v* تنزل‌قیمت‌دادن tanazol gheymat dadan

devastate *v* ویران‌کردن viran kardan

devastating *adj* ویران‌کننده virankonandeh

develop *v* توسعه‌دادن tosee dadan

development *n* پیشرفت pishraft

deviation *n* انحراف enheraf

device *n* دستگاه dastgah

devil *n* شیطان sheytan

devise *v* تدبیرکردن tadbir kardan

devoid *adj* تهی tohi

devote *v* وقف‌کردن vaghf kardan

devotion *n* وقف vaghf

devour *v* بلعیدن balidan

devout *adj* دیندار dindar

dew *n* شبنم shabnam

diabetic *adj* مبتلابه‌مرض‌قند motala be maraz ghand

diagnose *v* تشخیص‌دادن(طب) tashkhis dadan (teb)

diagnosis *n* تشخیص tashkhis

diagonal *adj* قطری ghotri

diagram *n* شکل‌هندسی shekl hendesi

dial *n* شاخص shakhes

dial *v* شماره‌گرفتن shomareh gereftan

dialect *n* لهجه lahjeh

dialogue *n* گفتگو goftego

diameter *n* قطردایره ghotr e dayereh

diamond *n* الماس almas

diaper *n* پارچه‌قنداق parcheh ghondagh

diarrhoea *n* اسهال eshal

diary *n* دفترخاطرات‌روزانه daftar khaterat rozaneh

dice *n* طاس‌تخته‌نرد tas e takhteh nard

dictate v دیکته‌کردن dikteh kardan

dictator n دیکتاتور diktator

dictatorship n حکومت‌استبدادي hokomat estebdadi

dictionary n فرهنگ farhang

die v مردن mordan

diet n پرهیز parhiz

differ v فرق‌داشتن fargh dashtan

difference n تفاضل tafazol

difficult n مشکل moshkel

difficulty n سختي sakhti

dig iv کاوش‌کردن kavosh kardan

digest v گواریدن govaridan

digestion n هضم hazm

digit n انگشت angosht

dignity n بزرگي bozorgi

dike n خاکریز khakriz

dilapidated adj مخروبه makhrobeh

dilemma n مسئله‌غامض masaleh ghamez

diligence n کوشش‌پیوسته koshesh e peyvasteh

dilute v رقیق‌کردن raghigh kardan

dim adj تار tar

dim v تیره‌کردن tireh kardan

dime n ده‌سنتي(آمریکایي) dah senti (amrikaee)

dimension n اندازه andazeh

diminish v کم‌شدن kam shodan

dine v ناهارخوردن nahar khordan

diner n کسي‌که‌شام‌مي‌خورد kasi ke sham mikhorad

dining room n اطاق‌ناهارخوري otaghe nahar khori

dinner n شام sham

diocese n قلمرواسقف ghalamroe osghof

diploma n دانشنامه daneshnameh

diplomacy n دیپلماسي diplomasi

diplomat n سیاستمدار siasatmadar

dire adj ترسناک tarsnak

direct adj مستقیم mostaghim

direction n جهت jahat

director n مدیر modir

dirt n چرک cherk

dirt-cheap adj بسیارارزان besyar arzan

dirt-poor adj کثافت kesafat

dirty adj چرکین cherkin

disability n ناتواني natavani

disable adj ناتوان natavani

disadvantage n زیان zian

disagree v ناهم‌راي‌بودن naham ray bodan

disagreement n مخالفت mokhalef

disappear v ناپدیدشدن napadid shodan

disappoint v مایوس‌کردن mayos kardan

disapprove v ناپسندشمردن napasand shemordan

disarm v خلع‌سلاح‌کردن khale selah kardan

disaster n بدبختي badbakhti

disastrous adj مصیبت‌آمیز mosibat amiz

disband v برهم‌زدن barham zadan

disbelief n بي‌اعتقادي bi eteghadi

discard v انداختن دور dor andakhtan

discern v تشخیص‌دادن tashkhis dadan

discharge v خالی‌کردن khali kardan

disciple n شاگرد shagerd

discipline n انضباط enzebat

disclaim v ردکردن rad kardan

disclose v فاش‌کردن fash kardan

discomfort n ناراحتي narahati

disconnect v منفصل‌کردن monfasel kardan

discontinue v ادامه‌ندادن edameh nadadan

discord n ناسازگاري nasazegari

discount n تخفیف takhfif

discourage v دلسردکردن delsard kardan

discourse n مباحثه mobaheseh

discover v پی‌بردن pay bordan

discovery n کشف kashf

discredit v بی‌اعتبارساختن bi etebar sakhtan

discreet adj بااحتیاط ba ehtiat

discrepancy n اختلاف ekhtelaf

discretion n بصیرت basirat

discriminate v تبعیض‌قائل‌شدن tabiz ghael shodan

discuss v بحث‌کردن bahs kardan

discussion n بحث bahs

disdain v خوارشمردن khar shemordan

disease n ناخوشي nakhoshi

disembark v پیاده‌کردن piadeh kardan

disentangle v ازگیردرآوردن az gir daravardan

disfigure v ازشکل‌انداختن az shekl andakhtan

disgrace n رسوایي rosva'ei

disgraceful adj رسوایي‌آور rosva'ei - avar

disgruntled adj ناخوشنود nakhoshnood

disguise v تغییرقیافه‌دادن taghyier ghiyafeh dadan

disgusting adj منزجر کننده monzajer konandeh

dish n ظرف zarf

dishearten v دلسردکردن delsard kardan

dishonest adj نادرست nadorost

dishonour n ننگ nang

dishwasher n ظرفشو zarfshoo

disillusion n رهایي‌ازشیفتگي raha'ei az shiftegi

disinfect v ضدعفوني‌کردن zedde' ofouni kardan

disintegrate v خردکردن khord kardan

disk n گرده gordeh

dislike n تنفر tanafor

dislike v دوست‌نداشتن doust nadashtan

dislocate v جابجاکردن ja be ja kardan

dislodge v ازجایي‌بیرون‌کردن az jay biroun kardan

disloyal adj ناسپاس nasepas

dismal adj دلتنگ‌کننده deltang konandeh

dismantle v بی‌مصرف‌کردن bimasraf kardan

dismay *n* ترس tars

dismay *v* ترسانیدن tarsandan

dismiss *v* روانه کردن ravaneh kardan

dismissal *n* اخراج ekhraj

disobedience *n* سرپیچی sarpichi

disobedient *adj* نافرمان nafarman

disobey *v* نافرمانی کردن nafarmani kardan

disorder *n* بی‌نظم bi nazm

disoriented *adj* سرگردان sargardan

disparaging *adj* عدم‌وفق adame' vefgh

dispatch *v* اعزام کردن e'zam kardan

dispel *v* برطرف کردن bartaraf kardan

dispersal *n* پراکندگی parakandegi

disperse *v* پراکنده کردن parakandeh kardan

displace *v* جابجا کردن ja be ja kardan

display *n* نمایش namayesh

display *v* نمایش دادن namayesh dadan

displease *v* خوش‌آیند نبودن khoshayand naboudan

displeasure *n* رنجش ranjesh

disposable *adj* از دست دادنی az dast dadani

disposal *n* دسترس dastras

dispose *v* مرتب کردن moratab kardan

disprove *v* رد کردن rad kardan

dispute *n* ستیزه setizeh

disqualify *v* سلب صلاحیت کردن salbe-salahiyyat kardan

disregard *v* نادیده گرفتن nadideh gereftan

disrespect *v* بی‌احترامی کردن bi-ehterami kardan

disrupt *v* منقطع کردن monghate' kardan

disruption *n* قطع ghate'

dissatisfied *adj* ناراضی narazi

disseminate *v* تخم کاشتن tokhm kashtan

dissipate *v* پراکنده کردن parakandeh kardan

dissolution *n* تجزیه tajziyeh

dissolve *v* آب کردن ab kardan

dissuade *v* منصرف کردن monsaref kardan

distance *n* فاصله faseleh

distant *adj* دور dour

distaste *n* بی‌رغبتی bi raghbati

distinct *adj* جدا joda

distinctive *adj* مشخص moshakhas

distinguish *v* تمیز دادن tamiz dadan

distort *v* کج کردن kaj kardan

distortion *n* تحریف tahrif

distract *v* حواس پرت کردن havas part kardan

distraction *n* گیجی giji

distraught *adj* آشفته ashofteh

distress *v* مضطرب کردن moztareb kardan

distressing *adj* غم‌فزا ghamfaza

distribute *v* توزیع کردن towzi'e kardan

distribution *n* توزیع towzi'e
district *n* بخش bakhsh
distrust *v* اعتمادنداشتن e'temad
nadashtan
distrust *n* بی‌اعتمادی bi e'temadi
distrustful *adj* بدگمان badgoman
disturb *v* مختل‌کردن mokhtal
kardan
disturbance *n* اختلال ethtelal
ditch *n* خندق khandagh
dive *v* شیرجه‌رفتن shirjeh raftan
diver *n* غواص ghavas
diverse *adj* گوناگون gounagoun
diversify *v* گوناگون‌ساختن
gounagoun sakhtan
diversion *n* تفریح tafrih
divide *v* تقسیم‌کردن taghsim
kardan
divine *adj* خدایی khoda'ei
division *n* تقسیم taghsim
divorce *n* طلاق talagh
divorcee *n* بیوه biveh
divulge *v* فاش‌کردن fash kardan
dizziness *n* گیجی giji
dizzy *adj* گیج gij
do *iv* کردن kardan
docile *adj* رام ram
dock *n* بارانداز barandaz
doctor *n* پزشک pezeshk
doctrine *n* عقیده aghideh
document *n* مدرک madrak
documentary *n* مستند mostanad
dodge *v* جاخالی‌دادن ja khali
dadan
dog *n* سگ sag
doll *n* عروسک arousak

dollar *n* دلار dolar
dolphin *n* دلفین dolfin
dome *n* گنبد gonbad
domestic *adj* خانگی khanegi
domesticate *v* اهلی‌کردن ahli
kardan
dominate *v* چیره‌شدن chireh
shodan
dominion *n* سلطنت saltanat
donate *v* بخشیدن bakhshidan
donation *n* دهش dahesh
donkey *n* الاغ olagh
donor *n* دهنده dahandeh
doomed *adj* محکوم‌به‌فنا mahkoum
be fana
door *n* درب darb
doorbell *n* زنگ‌درب zange' darb
doorstep *n* پلکان pelekan
doorway *n* راهرو rahroo
dope *n* آگاهی agahi
dormitory *n* خوابگاه khabgah
dosage *n* مقدارتجویزشده‌دارو
meghdare' tajviz-shodeh
daroo
dossier *n* پرونده parvandeh
dot *n* نقطه noghteh
double *n* برابر دو do-barabar
double *v* دوبرابر کردن do-barabar
kardan
double-check *v* دوباره کنترل
kontrol-e dobareh
double-cross *v* ناروزدن naro
zadan
doubt *n* شک shak
doubt *v* شک‌داشتن shak dashtan
doubtful *adj* مشکوک mashkouk

dough *n* خمیر khamir	drawer *n* کشو kesho
dove *n* فاخته fakhteh	drawing *n* نقشه کارگاهی naghsheh kargahi
down *adv* پایین pa'ein	
downcast *adj* دل افسردگی del afsordegi	dread *v* (از) ترسیدن tarsidan
	dreadful *adj* وحشتناک vahshatnak
downfall *n* افت oft	
downhill *adv* سرازیری saraziri	dream *n* خواب khab
down payment *n* پیش شط pish shart	dream *iv* خواب دیدن khab didan
	dress *n* لباس lebas
downpour *n* بارندگی زیاد barandegi-e ziyad	dress *v* لباس پوشیدن lebas poshidan
downsize *v* زیر اندازه zire' andazeh	dried *adj* خشکیده khoshkideh
downstairs *adv* طبقه پائین tabaghehe pa'ein	drill *n* تمرین tamrin
	drill *v* زدن مته mateh zadan
down-to-earth *adj* بین واقع vaghe'bin	drink *iv* آشامیدن ashamidan
	drink *n* آشامیدنی ashamidani
downtown *n* مرکزشهر markaze shahr	drinker *n* نوشنده noshandeh
downtrodden *adj* لگدمال شده lagadmal shodeh	drip *n* چکه chekeh
	drip *v* چکیدن chekidan
dowry *n* جهیزیه jahiziyeh	drive *iv* راندن randan
doze *n* چرت chort	driver *n* محرک moharek
doze *v* (با)چرت زدن off(chort zadan	drizzle *v* ریزباریدن riz baridan
dozen *n* دوجین dojin	drop *v* ازقلم انداختن az ghalam endakhtan
draft *v* آماده کردن amadeh kardan	
draft *n* حواله havaleh	drop *n* افت oft
drag *v* کشاندن keshandan	drought *n* خشکی khoshki
dragon *n* اژدها azhdeha	drown *v* غرق کردن ghargh kardan
drain *v* آب کشیدن ab keshidan	drowsy *adj* خواب آلود khab alod
drainage *n* زیرآب زنی zir ab zani	drug *n* دارو daroo
dramatic *adj* نمایشی nemayeshi	drug *v* دوازدن dava zadan
drape *n* پرده pardeh	drugstore *n* داروخانه darokhaneh
drastic *adv* کارکن kar kon	drum *n* چلیک chalik
draw *n* قرعه کشی ghore'keshi	drunk *adl* مست mast
draw *iv* کشیدن keshidan	drunkenness *n* مستی masti
drawback *n* اشکال ashkal	dry *adj* خشك khoshk
	dry *v* خشک کردن khoshk kardan

dry cleaners n خشک‌شوئی khoshk shoe'e

dryer n ماشین‌خشک‌کنی mashin khoshk koni

dubious adj موردشک morede shak

duchess n دوشس doshes

duck n اردک ordak

duct n زیرآب‌رفتن zir'e ab raftan

due adj پرداختنی pardakhtani

duel n جنگ‌تن‌به‌تن jang tan be tan

dues n دیون dion

duke n دوک dook

dull adj کند kond

duly adv حسب‌المقرر hasb'ol mogharar

dumb adj زبان‌بسته zaban basteh

dump v خیال khial

dump n زباله zobaleh

dung n کود kod

dungeon n محبس mahbas

dupe v گول‌زدن gol zadan

duplicate v المثنی‌برداشتن almosana bardashtan

duplication n نسخه‌برداری noskheh bardari

durable adj بادوام ba davam

duration n مدت modat

during pre درمدت dar modat

dusk v تاریک‌نمودن tarik nemodan

dust n خاک khak

dusty adj گردوخاکی gard'o khaki

duty v وظیفه vazifeh

dwarf n کوتوله kotoleh

dwell iv ساکن‌بودن saken bodan

dwelling n ساکن saken

dwindle v رفته‌رفته‌کوچک‌شدن rafteh rafteh kochak shodan

dye n رنگ rang

dye v رنگ‌کردن rang kardan

dying adj مردنی mordani

dynamite n دینامیت dinamit

dynasty n سلسله selseleh

E

each adj هر har

each other adj همدیگر hamdigar

eager adj مشتاق moshtagh

eagerness n اشتیاق eshtiagh

eagle n عقاب oghab

ear n گوش gosh

earache n دردگوش dard gosh

eardrum n پرده‌گوش pardeh gosh

early adv زود zood

earmark v نشان‌کردن neshan kardan

earn v تحصیل‌کردن tahsil kardan

earnestly adv جدا joda

earnings n درآمد daramad

earphones n گوشی goshi

earring n گوشواره goshvareh

earth n خاک khak

earthquake n زمین‌لرزه zamin larzeh

earwax n جرم‌گوش jerm gosh

ease n آسانی asani

ease v راحت‌کردن rahat kardan

easel *n* سه‌پایه‌نقاشي she payeh naghashi

easily *adv* به‌آساني beh asani

east *n* خاورمشرق khavar mashregh

eastbound *adv* بسوي‌شرق be soye shargh

Easter *n* عیدپاک ayd'e pak

eastern *adj* شرقي sharghi

easterner *n* خاورنشین khavarneshin

eastward *adv* روبه‌خاور ro beh khavar

easy *adj* آسان asani

eat *iv* خوردن khordan

ebb *v* فروکش‌کردن forokesh kardan

eccentric *adj* غیرعادي ghayr e adi

echo *n* طنین tanin

eclipse *n* گرفتگي gereftegi

ecology *n* بوم‌شناسي bom shenasi

economical *adj* صرفه‌جو sarfeh jo

economize *v* صرفه‌جویي‌کردن sarfeh joe'e kardan

economy *n* اقتصاد eghtesad

ecstasy *n* وجد vajd

ecstatic *adj* نشئه‌شده nash'e shodeh

edge *n* کنار kenar

edgy *adj* دار لبه labeh dar

edible *adj* خوردني khordani

edifice *n* عمارت emarat

edit *v* ویراستن virastan

editorial *n* سرمقاله sarmaghaleh

educate *v* تربیت‌کردن tarbiat kardan

educational *adj* معارفي moarefi

effective *adj* موثر mo'aser

efficiency *n* بازده bazdeh

efficient *adj* بهره‌ور bahreh var

effigy *n* تمثال temsal

effort *n* تقلا taghala

effusive *adj* فوران‌کننده favaran konandeh

egg *n* تخم‌مرغ tokhm'e morgh

egg white *n* سفیده‌تخم‌مرغ safideh-e tokhmmorgh

egoism *n* خودپرستي khodparasti

egoist *adj* خودپرست khodparast

eight *adj* عددهشت adad-e hasht

eighteen *adj* هجده hejdah

eighth *adj* هشتمین hashtomin

eighty *adj* هشتاد hashtad

eject *v* بیرون‌انداختن biron andakhtan

elapse *v* گذشتن gozashtan

elastic *adj* قابل‌ارتجاع ghabel erteja'e

elated *adj* خورسند khorsand

elbow *n* آرنج aranj

elect *v* برگزیدن bargozidan

election *n* انتخاب entekhab

electric *adj* الکتریکي elekteriki

electrician *n* متخصص‌برق motekhases bargh

electricity *n* برق bargh

electrocute *v* بابرق‌کشتن ba bargh koshtan

electronic *adj* الکترونیکي elektroniki

elegance *n* ظرافت zerafat

elegant *adj* زیبا ziba

element *n* عنصر onsor

elemental *adj* عنصري onsori
elephant *n* فيل fil
elevate *v* بلند کردن boland kardan
elevation *n* بلندي bolandi
elevator *n* آسانسور asansor
eleven *adj* عدديازده yazdah
eleventh *adj* يازدهم yazdahom
eligible *adj* واجدشرايط vajed sharayet
eliminate *v* زدودن zododan
elk *n* گوزن شمالي gavazn shomali
elm *n* نارونقرمز narvan ghermez
eloquence *n* شيوايي shivaee
else *adv* ديگر digar
elsewhere *adv* ديگر درجاي dar jaye digar
elude *v* اجتناب کردن از ejtenab kardan az
emaciated *adj* لاغر laghar
emanate *v* ناشي شدن nashi shodan
emancipate *v* ازقيدرها کردن az gheyd raha kardan
embalm *v* موميايي کردن momiyae'e kardan
embark *v* مبدا mabda'e
embarrass *v* دست پاچه کردن dast pacheh kardan
embassy *n* سفارت خانه sefarat khaneh
embezzle *v* دزديدن dozdidan
embitter *adj* تلخ کردن talkh kardan
emblem *n* نشان neshan
embody *v* مجسم کردن mojasam kardan
emboss *v* پوشاندن poshandan
embrace *n* پذيرفتن paziroftan

embrace *v* درآغوش گرفتن dar aghosh gereftan
embroider *v* قلاب دوزي کردن gholab dozi kardan
embroidery *adj* گلدوزي goldozi
embroil *v* بهنزاع انداختن be neza'e andakhtan
embryo *n* جنين janin
emerald *n* سبز زمرد zemorod sabz
emerge *v* پديدارشدن padidar shodan
emergency *n* امرفوق‌العاده amr fogholadeh
emigrant *n* مهاجر mohajer
emigrate *v* مهاجرت کردن mohajerat kardan
emission *n* صدور sodor
emit *v* ساطع کردن sate'e kardan
emotion *n* احساسات ehsasat
empathize *v* تاکيد کردن ta'id kardan
emperor *n* امپراتور emperator
emphasis *n* تاکيد ta'kid
emphasize *v* باقوت تلفظ کردن ba ghovat talafoz kardan
empire *n* امپراتوري emperatori
employ *v* استعمال کردن estemal kardan
employee *n* کارمند karmand
employer *n* کارفرما karfarma
employment *n* بهکارگيري beh kargiri
emptiness *n* جاي تهي jaye tohi
empty *adj* تهي tohi
enable *v* تواناساختن tavana sakhtan

enchanted *adj* مجذوب majzob

encircle *v* احاطه کردن ehateh kardan

enclave *n* تحت محاصره that mohasereh

enclose *v* درمیان گذاشتن dar-mian gozashtan

enclosure *n* پیوست peyvast

encompass *v* احاطه کردن ehateh kardan

encounter *v* روبروشدن robero shodan

encounter *n* رویارویی royaroe'e

encourage *v* تشویق کردن tashvigh kardan

encroach *v* دست اندازی کردن dast andazi kardan

encyclopaedia *n* دایرةالمعارف dayerat'al ma'aref

end *n* پایان payan

end *up* *v* فرجام farjam

endanger *v* به مخاطره انداختن be mokhatereh andakhtan

endeavour *v* تلاش کردن talash kardan

ending *n* پایان payan

endless *adj* بی پایان bi payan

endorse *v* پشت نویس کردن posht nevis kardan

endorsement *n* امضا emza

endure *v* تحمل کردن tahamol kardan

enemy *n* دشمن doshman

energy *n* کارمایه karmayeh

enforce *v* اجرا کردن ejra kardan

engagement *n* نامزدی namzadi

engine *n* ماشین mashin

engineer *n* مهندس mohandes

engrave *v* قلم زدن ghalam zadan

engraving *n* حکاکی hakaki

engrossed *adj* انحصارشده enhesar shodeh

engulf *v* غوطه ور ساختن ghoteh var sakhtan

enhance *v* بالا بردن bala bordan

enjoy *v* لذت بردن lazat bordan

enjoyable *adj* لذت بخش lazat bakhsh

enjoyment *n* لذت lazat

enlarge *v* بزرگ کردن bozorg kardan

enlargement *n* توسعه tose'eh

enlighten *v* روشن فکر کردن roshan fekr kardan

enlist *v* نام نویسی کردن nam nevisi kardan

enormous *adj* بزرگ bozorg kardan

enough *adv* کافی kafi

enrage *v* خشمگین کردن khashmgin kardan

enrich *v* غنی کردن ghani kardan

enrol *v* نام نویسی کردن nam nevisi kardan

enrolment *n* نامنویسی nam nevisi

ensure *v* مطمئن ساختن motmaen sakhtan

entail *v* مستلزم بودن mostalzem bodan

entangle *v* گرفتار کردن gereftar kardan

enter *v* ثبت کردن sabt kardan

enterprise *n* عمل پرهور آمیز amal tahavor amiz

entertain v پذیرایی کردن pazirae'e kardan

entertaining adj سرگرم کننده sargarm konandeh

entertainment n پذیرایی pazirae'e

enthral v بنده کردن bandeh kardan

enthuse v احساسات را برانگیختن ehsasat ra barangikhtan

enthusiasm n شور و ذوق shor o zogh

entice v فریفتن fariftan

enticement n اغوا eghva

enticing adj کشنده koshandeh

entire adj درست dorost

entirely adv کاملا kamelan

entrance n مدخل madkhal

entreat v درخواست کردن darkhast kardan

entree n ورود vorod

entrenched adj مستحکم mostahkam

entrepreneur n کارگشا kar gosha

entrust v سپردن sepordan

entry n ثبت sabt

enumerate v هم اندازه ham-andazeh

envelope n پاکت pakat

envious adj حسود hasood

environment n محیط mohit

envisage v روبرو شدن robero shodan

envoy n فرستاده ferestadeh

envy n رشک rashk

epilepsy n بیماری صرع bimari'e sar'e

episode n حادثه ضمني hadeseh zemni

epistle n نامه nameh

epitaph n وفات نامه vafat nameh

epoch n مبداتاریخ mabda'e tarikh

equal adj هم اندازه ham andazeh

equality n مساوات mosavat

equate v برابر کردن barabar kardan

equation n معادله moadeleh

equator n خط استوا khat ostova

equilibrium n موازنه movazeneh

equip v مجهز کردن mojahaz kardan

equipment n تجهیزات tajhizat

equivalent adj هم ارز ham arz

era n مبدا mabda'e

eradicate v از ریشه کندن az risheh kandan

erase v پاک کردن pak kardan

eraser n مدادپاک کن medad pak kon

erect v راست کردن rast kardan

erect adj عمودي amodi

erotic adj شهواني shahavani

err v خطا کردن khata kardan

errand n پیغام peygham

erroneous adj نادرست nadorost

error n لغزش laghzesh

erupt v جوانه زدن javaneh zadan

eruption n جوش joosh

escalate v بالا بردن bala bordan

escalator n پله برقي peleh barghi

escape v رستن rastan

esophagus n مري meri

especially adv خصوصا khososan

espionage *n* جاسوسی jasosi

essay *n* مقاله maghaleh

essence *n* هستي hasti

establish *v* تاسیس کردن t'asis kardan

estate *n* ملک melk

esteem *v* لایق دانستن layegh danestan

estimate *v* تخمین زدن takhmin zadan

estimation *n* تخمین takhmin

estranged *adj* قهر ghahr

eternity *n* ابدیت abadiat

ethical *adj* وابسته به علم اخلاق vabasteh beh elm akhlagh

etiquette *n* علم آداب معاشرت elm adab moasherat

euphoria *n* رضامندي rezamandi

evacuate *v* خالي کردن khali kardan

evade *v* طفره زدن از tafreh zadan az

evaluate *v* ارزیابي کردن arzyabi kardan

evaporate *v* تبخیر کردن tabkhir kardan

evasion *n* طفره tafreh

evasive *adj* گریزان gorizan

eve *n* عید شب shab eyd

even *adj* عددزوج adad' e zoj

even if *c* اگرهم agar ham

evening *n* غروب ghorob

event *n* واقعه vaghe'eh

eventuality *n* امکان emkan

eventually *adv* سرانجام saranjam

ever *adv* همیشه hamisheh

everlasting *adj* جاوداني javdani

every *adj* هر har

everybody *pro* هرکس har kas

everyday *adj* هرروز har rooz

everyone *pro* همه(کس) hameh

everything *pro* همه چیز hameh chiz

evict *v* فیصله دادن feysaleh dadan

evidence *n* گواه govah

evil *n* بدي badi

evoke *v* احضارکردن ehzar kardan

evolution *n* تکامل takamol

evolve *v* بازکردن baz kardan

exact *adj* دقیق daghigh

exaggerate *v* اغراق آمیزکردن eghragh amiz kardan

exalt *v* بلند کردن boland kardan

examination *n* آزمون azmon

examine *v* امتحان کردن emtahan kardan

example *n* نمونه nemoneh

exasperate *v* خشمگین کردن khashmgin kardan

excavate *v* کاویدن kavidan

exceed *v* تجاوزکردن tajavoz kardan

excel *v* برتري داشتن بر bartari dashtan bar

excellence *n* شگرفي shegarfi

excellent *adj* عالي ali

except *p* جز joz

exception *n* استثناء estesna'e

exceptional *adj* استثنايي estesnae'e

excerpt *n* قطعه منتخب ghet'eye montakhab

excess *n* فزوني fozoni

excessive *adj* مفرط mofrat

exchange v مبادله کردن mobadeleh kardan

excite v برآشفتن barashoftan

excitement n شور shor

exciting adj مهیج mohayej

exclaim v ازروی تعجب فریادزدن az roye ta'ajob faryad zadan

exclude v محروم کردن mahrom kardan

excruciating adj مشقت بار masheghat bar

excursion n گردش gardesh

excuse n بهانه bahaneh

excuse v معذورداشتن m'azor dashtan

execute v اجرا کردن ejra kardan

executive n مجری mojri

exemplary adj شایان تقلید shayan taghlid

exempt adj معاف mo'af

exercise v عمل کردن amal kardan

exert v اعمال کردن e'emal kardan

exhaust v تهی کردن tohi kardan

exhausting adj خسته کننده khasteh konandeh

exhaustion n خستگی khastegi

exhibit v نمایش دادن namayesh dadan

exhibition n نمایش namayesh

exhort v نصیحت کردن nasihat kardan

exile n تبعید tab'ed

exile v تبعید کردن tab'ed kardan

exist v زیستن zistan

existence n هستی hasti

exit n مخرج makhraj

exodus n خروج khoroj

exonerate v تبرئه کردن tabra'e kardan

exorbitant adj گزاف gazaf

exorcist n جن گیر jen gir

exotic adj بیگانه biganeh

expand v بسط دادن bast dadan

expansion n توسعه tose'eh

expect v چشم داشتن chashm dashtan

expediency n شتاب shetab

expedient adj مقتضی moghtazi

expedition n تسریع tasri'e

expel v بیرون انداختن biron andakhtan

expend v خرج کردن kharj kardan

expenditure n برآمد baramad

expense n برآمد baramad

expensive adj گران geran

experience n آزمودگی azmodegi

experiment n آزمایش azmayesh

expert adj ماهر maher

expiration n خاتمه khatemeh

expire v سپری شدن separi shodan

explain v توضیح دادن tozih dadan

explicit adj صریح sarih

explode v محترق شدن mohtaregh shodan

exploit v به کار انداختن beh kar andakhtan

exploit n رفتار raftar

explore v سیاحت کردن siahat kardan

explorer n جستجوگر jostejogar

explosion n انفجار enfejar

explosive adj منفجر شونده monfajer shavandeh

exploitation *n* مهمات mohemat

export *v* صادرکردن sader kardan

expose *v* بی‌پناه‌گذاشتن bi panah gozashtan

express *n* سریع‌السیر sari o seyr

expression *n* بیان bayan

expressly *adv* صریحا sarihan

expropriate *v* سلب‌مالکیت‌کردن salb malekiat kardan

expulsion *n* اخراج ekhraj

exquisite *adj* نفیس nafis

extend *v* توسعه‌دادن tose'eh dadan

extension *n* اضافی ezafi

exterior *adj* بیرونی bironi

exterminate *v* برانداختن barandakhtan

external *adj* بیرونی bironi

extinct *adj* معدوم ma'edom

extinguish *v* خاموش‌کردن khamosh kardan

extortion *n* اخذبه‌زوروعنف akhz beh zor va onf

extra *adv* اضافی ezafi

extract *v* استخراج‌کردن estekhraj kardan

extradition *n* استردادمجرمین esterdad e mojremin

extravagant *adj* عجیب ajib

extreme *adj* بینهایت binahayat

extremities *n* افراطکاری efratkari

extroverted *adj* برون boron gara

eye *n* چشم chashm

eyebrow *n* ابرو abro

eye-catching *adj* چشم‌گیر chashm gir

eyeglasses *n* عینک‌فنری eynak fanari

eyelash *n* مژه mozheh

eyelid *n* پلک pelk

eye-opener *n* چیزشگفت‌آور chiz'e shegeft avar

eyesight *n* دید did

F

fable *n* افسانه afsaneh

fabric *n* محصول mahsol

fabricate *v* ساختن sakhtan

fabulous *adj* افسانه‌ای afsaneh'ee

face *n* صورت sorat

facet *n* صورت‌کوچک sorat kochak

facilitate *v* آسان‌کردن asan kardan

fact *n* واقعیت vagheiyat

factor *n* عامل amel

factory *n* کارخانه karkhaneh

factual *adj* حقیقت‌امری haghight e amri

faculty *n* استادان‌دانشکده ostadan daneshkadeh

fad *n* مدزودگذر mod zodgozar

fade *v* محوکردن mahv kardan

fail *v* خراب‌شدن kharab shodan

failure *n* درمانگی darmangi

faint *v* ضعف‌کردن zaf kardan

faint *adj* ضعیف zaif

faint *n* غش ghash

faith *n* ایمان iman

faithful *adj* باوفا ba vafa

fake *adj* جعلی ja'eli

fake *v* حلقه‌کردن halgheh kardan

fall n ائیز paiz
fall iv افتادن oftadan
fall back v تغییرموضع‌دادن taghire mozo'e dadan
fall behind v عقب‌افتادن aghab oftadan
fall down v افتادن oftadan
fall through v به‌نتیجه‌نرسیدن beh natijeh naresidan
fallacy n سفسطه safsateh
fallout n ریزش‌اتمی rizesh atomi
falsehood n کذب kezb
falsify v تحریف‌کردن tahrif kardan
falter v گیرکردن gir kardan
fame n شهرت shohrat
familiar adj آشنا ashna
family n خاندان khandan
famine n قحطی ghahti
famous adj مشهور mashhor
fan n بادبزن bad bezan
fanatic adj شخص‌متعصب shakhs'e moteaseb
fancy adj تجملی tajamoli
fang n دندان‌ناب dandan nab
fantastic adj خیالی khiyali
fantasy n قوه‌مخیله ghoveh mokhayaleh
far adv دور door
faraway adj خیلی‌دور khayli door
farce n نمایش‌خنده‌آور namayeshe khandeh avar
fare n کرایه kerayeh
farewell n بدرود bedrood
farm n مزرعه mazraeh
farmer n کشاورز keshavarz

fascinate v مجذوب‌کردن majzoob kardan
fashion n سبک sabk
fashionable adj شیک shik
fast adj تند tond
fasten v بستن bastan
fat n چربی charbi
fat adj فربه farbeh
fatal adj کشنده koshandeh
fate n سرنوشت sarnevesht
fateful adj مهم mohem
father n پدر pedar
fatherhood n پدري pedari
father-in-law n پدرشوهر pedar shohar
fathom v اندازه‌گرفتن andazeh gereftan
fatigue n خستگی khastegi
fatten v چاق‌کردن chagh kardan
fatty adj چرب charb
faucet n شیرآب shir'e ab
fault n کاستی kasti
faulty adj معیوب ma'eyob
favour n توجه tavajoh
favourable adj مساعد mosaed
favourite adj مطلوب matlob
fear n ترس tars
fearful adj ترسان tarsan
feasible adj امکان‌پذیر emkan pazir
feast n مهمانی mehmani
feat n کاربرجسته kar barjasteh
feather n پر par
feature n خصیصه khasiseh
February n فوریه fevriyeh
fed up adj خسته‌شدن khasteh shodan

federal *adj* فدرال federal

fee *n* مزد mozd

feeble *adj* ضعيف zaif

feed *iv* خوراندن khorandan

feedback *n* فيدبک feedbak

feel *iv* احساس کردن ehsas kardan

feelings *n* احساسات ehsasat

feet *n* پايه payeh

feign *v* وانمودکردن vanemod kardan

fellow *n* مرد mard

fellowship *n* رفاقت refaghat

felon *adj* گناهکار gonahkar

felony *n* بزه bezeh

female *n* جنس‌ماده jens'e madeh

feminine *adj* جنس‌زن jens'e zan

fence *n* حصار hesar

fencing *n* شمشيربازي shamshir bazi

fend *v* دفع‌کردن daf'e kardan

fender *n* حايل hayel

ferment *v* ترش‌شدن torsh shodan

fern *n* سرخس sarakhs

ferocious *adj* وحشي vahshi

ferocity *n* درنده‌خويي darandeh khoee

ferry *n* گذرگاه gozargah

fertile *adj* حاصلخيز haselkhiz

fertility *n* حاصلخيزي haselkhizi

fertilize *v* بارورکردن barvar kardan

fervent *adj* باحرارت ba hararat

fester *v* چرک‌کردن cherk kardan

festivity *n* بزم bazm

foetus *n* جنين janin

feud *n* دشمني doshmani

fever *n* تب tab

feverish *adj* تب‌دار tab dar

few *adj* معدود ma'edod

fiancé *n* نامزد(مرد) namzad

fibre *n* رشته reshteh

fickle *adj* دمدمي damdami

fiction *n* افسانه afsaneh

fictitious *adj* جعلي ja'eli

fiddle *n* ويولن violon

fidelity *n* وفاداري vafadari

field *n* ميدان meydan

fierce *adj* درنده darandeh

fiery *adj* آتشين atashin

fifteen *adj* پانزده panzdah

fifth *adj* پنجم panjom

fifty *adj* پنجاه panjah

fifty-fifty *adv* پنجاه پنجاه panjah-panjah

fig *n* انجير anjir

fight *n* جنگ jang kardan

fight *iv* جنگ‌کردن jang kardan

fighter *n* رزمنده razmandeh

figure *n* شکل shekl

figure out *v* کشف‌کردن kashf kardan

file *v* درپرونده‌گذاشتن dar parvandeh gozashtan

file *n* سوهان sohan

fill *v* پرکردن pour kardan

film *n* فيلم film

filter *n* صافي safi

fin *n* بال‌ماهي bal'e mahi

final *adj* آخرين akharin

finalize *v* به‌پايان‌رساندن beh payan resandan

finance v تهیه‌پول‌کردن tahiyeyeh pool kardan

find iv یافتن yaftan

fine n جریمه jarimeh

fine v جریمه‌کردن jarimeh kardan

fine adv خوب khob

fine adj نازک nazouk

fine print n نکات‌ریز nokat-e riz

finger n انگشت angousht

fingernail n ناخن nakhon

fingerprint n اثرانگشت asar'e angosht

fingertip n نوک‌انگشت nok angsht

finish v کامل‌کردن kamel kardan

fire n شلیک‌تیر shelik tir

fire v شلیک‌کردن shelik kardan

firearm n اسلحه‌گرم aslaheh garm

firecracker n ترقه taragheh

firefighter n آتش‌نشان atash neshan

fireman n مامورآتش‌نشانی ma'emor atash neshani

fireplace n اجاق ojagh

firewood n هیزم hizoum

fireworks n آتش‌بازي atash bazi

firm n بنگاه bongah

firm adj محکم mohkam

firmness n ثبات‌واستحکام sobat va estehkam

first adj مقدم moghadam

first aid n کمکهای‌اولیه komakhaye avaliyeh

fish n ماهي mahi

fisherman n ماهی‌گیر mahi gir

fishy adj مثل‌ماهي mesl'e mahi

fist n مشت mosht

fit v اندازه‌بودن andazeh bodan

fitness n مناسبت monasebat

fitting adj مناسب monaseb

five adj عددپنج adad'e panj

fix v درست‌کردن dorost kardan

fjord n آبدره abdareh

flag n پرچم parcham

flagpole n تیرپرچم tir parcham

flagship n کشتي‌حامل‌پرچم keshti hamel'e parcham

flamboyant adj شعله‌دار sho'eleh dar

flame n شعله sho'eleh

flammable adj قابل‌اشتعال ghabel eshteal

flank n پهلو pahlo

flare n روشنایي‌خیره‌کننده roshana'eye khireh konanadeh

flare-up v هیجان hayajan

flash n تلالو tala'elou

flashlight n نوربرق‌آساوزودگذر noor bargh asa va zood gozar

flashy adj درخشاني derakhshani

flask n قمقمه ghomghomeh

flat adj پهن pahn

flat n قسمت‌پهن ghesmat e pahn

flatten v پهن‌کردن pahn kardan

flatter v چاپلوسي‌کردن chaplosi kardan

flattery n چاپلوسي chaplosi

flavour n مزه‌وبو mazeh va boo

flaw n درز darz

flawless adj بی‌عیب bi eyb

flea n کک kak

flee iv گریختن gorikhtan

fleece *n* خواب‌پارچه khab'e parcheh

fleet *n* ناوگان navgan

flesh *n* گوشت gosht

flex *v* خم‌کردن kham kardan

flexible *adj* خم‌شو kham sho

flick *n* تلنگر talangor

flier *n* آگهی‌روی‌کاغذکوچک agahi roye kagaz koochak

flight *n* گریز goriz

flimsy *adj* سست sost

flip *v* تلنگرزدن talangor zadan

flirt *v* لاس‌زدن las zadan

float *v* شناورشدن shenavar shodan

flock *n* گله galeh

flog *v* شلاق‌زدن shalagh zadan

flood *v* غرق‌کردن ghargh kardan

floodgate *n* سیل‌گیر sayl gir

flooding *n* سیل sayl

floor *n* کف‌زمین kaf'e zamin

flop *n* صدای‌تلپ sedaye telep

floral *adj* گلدار goldar

flour *n* آرد ard

flourish *v* رشدکردن roushd kardan

flow *v* جاری‌بودن jari bodan

flown *n* گردش gardesh

flower *n* گل gol

flowerpot *n* گلدان‌کوزه‌ای goldan kozehee

flu *n* آنفلوانزا anfolanza

fluctuate *v* نوسان‌داشتن navasan dashtan

fluently *adv* روان ravan

fluid *n* روان ravan

flunk *v* شکست‌خوردن(درامتحانات) shekast khordan

flush *v* بهیجان‌آمدن beh hayajan amadan

flute *n* فلوت foulot

flutter *v* بال‌بال‌زدن bal bal zadan

fly *iv* پروازدادن parvaz dadan

foam *n* کف kaf

focus *n* کانون kanoon

foe *n* دشمن doshman

fog *n* مه meh

foggy *adj* مه‌آلود meh alood

foil *v* بی‌اثرکردن bi asar kardan

fold *v* تاکردن ta kardan

folder *n* پوشه posheh

folk *n* مردم mardom

folks *n* قوم‌وخویش ghom o khish

folksy *adj* مشرب‌خوش khosh mashrab

follow *v* پیروی‌کردن‌از peyravi kardan az

follower *n* دنبال‌گر donbalgar

folly *n* نابخردی nabekhradi

foment *v* برانگیختن barangikhtan

fond *adj* علاقمند alaghmand

fondle *v* نوازش‌کردن navazesh kardan

fondness *n* علاقه alagheh

food *n* خوراک khorak

foodstuff *n* ماده‌غذایی madeh ghazaee

fool *v* گول‌زدن gol zadan

fool *adj* نادان nadan

foolishness *n* نادانی nadani

foot *n* پا pa

football n بازي‌فوتبال baziye
footbal

footnote n تبصره tabsareh

footprint n پا جاي jaye pa

footstep n پا جاي jaye pa

footwear n کفش kafsh

for pre برای baraye

forbid iv قدغن‌کردن ghadeghan
kardan

force n زور zoor

forceful adj قوي ghavi

forcibly adv به‌زور beh zoor

forecast iv پیش‌بینی‌کردن pish bini
kardan

foreground n پیش‌زمینه pish
zamineh

forehead n پیشانی pishani

foreign adj بیگانه biganeh

foreigner n بیگانه biganeh

foreman n سرکارگر sar kargar

foresee iv قبلاتهیه‌دیدن ghablan
tahiyeh didan

foreshadow v ازپیش‌خبردادن az
pish khabar dadan

foresight n پیش‌بینی pish bini

forest n جنگل jangal

foretaste n آزمایش‌قبلی azmayesh
ghabli

foretell v پیشگویی‌کردن pishgoee
kardan

forever adv برای‌همیشه baraye
hamisheh

forewarn v ازپیش‌اخطارکردن az
pish ekhtar kardan

foreword n پیش‌گفتار pish goftar

forfeit v خطاکردن khata kardan

forge v جعل‌کردن jal kardan

forgery n جعل‌اسناد jal e asnad

forget v فراموش‌کردن faramoosh
kardan

forgivable adj بخشایش قابل
ghabel'e bakhshayesh

forgive v بخشیدن bakhshidan

forgiveness n بخشش bakhshesh

fork n چنگال changal

form n ورقه varagheh

formal adj رسمی rasmi

formality n رسمیت rasmiat

formalize v رسمی‌کردن rasmi
kardan

format n قطع ghat'e

formation n آرایش arayesh

former adj تشکیل‌دهنده tashkil
dahandeh

formerly adv پیشتر pishtar

formidable adj ترسناک tarsnak

formula n فرمول formol

forsake iv ول‌کردن vel kardan

fort n سنگر sangar

forthcoming adj نزدیک nazdik

forthright adj رک rouk

fortify v مستحکم‌کردن mostahkam
kardan

fortitude n پایمردي paymardi

fortress n استحکامات‌نظامی
estehkamat nezami

fortunate adj خوشبخت
khoshbakht

fortune n بخت‌واقبال bakht va
eghbal

forty adj چهل chehel

forward adv به‌جلو beh jelo

fossil n سنگواره sangvareh

foster *v* غذادادن ghaza dadan	**freezer** *n* یخچال‌خیلی‌سرد yakhchal khayli sard
foul *adj* ناپاک na pak	**freezing** *adj* خنک khonak
foundation *n* پایه payeh	**freight** *n* کرایه kerayeh
founder *n* موسس moases	**French** *adj* فرانسوي faransavi
fountain *n* منبع manba	**frenetic** *adj* آتشي atashi
four *adj* چهار chahar	**frenzy** *n* دیوانگي‌آني divanegiye ani
fourteen *adj* چهارده chahardah	**frequency** *n* فرکانس ferekans
fourth *adj* چهارمین chaharumin	
fox *n* روباه robah	**frequent** *adj* تکرارشونده tekrar shavandeh
fraction *n* کسر kasr	**fresh** *adj* تروتازه tar o tazeh
fracture *n* شکستگي shekastegi	**freshness** *n* طراوت taravat
fragile *adj* شکننده shekanandeh	**friar** *n* راهب‌صومعه raheb some'eh
fragment *n* پاره pareh	**friction** *n* سایش sayesh
fragrance *n* بوي‌خوش boye khosh	**Friday** *n* جمعه jomeh
fragrant *adj* خوشبو khosh bo	**fried** *adj* سرخ‌کرده sorkh kardan
frail *adj* نازک nazouk	**friend** *n* دوست doost
frame *n* قاب ghab	**friendship** *n* دوستي doosti
framework *n* استخوان‌بندي ostokhan bandi	**fries** *n* سیب‌زمیني‌سرخ‌کرده sib zamini sorkh kardaeh
franchise *n* امتیاز emtiaz	**frigate** *n* فرقت ferghet
frank *adj* گو رك rouk go	**fright** *n* ترس‌ناگهاني tars nagahani
frankly *adv* رک‌وپوست‌کنده rouk va post kandeh	**frighten** *v* به‌وحشت‌انداختن beh vahshat andakhtan
frankness *n* رک‌گوئي rouk goee	**frightening** *adj* ترسناک tarsnak
frantic *adj* بي‌عقل bi aghl	**frigid** *adj* بسیارسرد besyar sard
fraternal *adj* دوستانه dostaneh	**frivolous** *adj* سبک‌رفتار sabk raftar
fraternity *n* برادري baradari	
fraud *n* فریب farib	**frog** *n* وزغ vazagh
fraudulent *adj* کلاه‌بردار kolah bardar	**from** *pre* از az
freckle *n* لکه lakeh	**frontier** *n* مرز marz
free *adj* آزاد azad	**frost** *n* ژاله zhaleh
free *v* آزادکردن azad kardan	**frostbite** *n* سرمازدگي sarma zadegi
freedom *n* آزادي azadi	
freeway *n* بزرگراه bozorgrah	**frown** *v* اخم‌کردن akhm kardan
freeze *iv* یخ‌بستن yakh bastan	

frugal adj صرفه‌جو sarfeh joo
frugality n صرفه‌جويي sarfeh joee
fruit n ميوه miveh
fruitful adj ميوه‌دار miveh dar
frustrate v خنثي‌كردن khonsa kardan
fry v سرخ‌كردن sorkh kardan
frying pan n ماهي‌تابه mahitabeh
fuel n سوخت sookht
fugitive n فراري farari
fulfil v انجام‌دادن anjam dadan
fulfilment n تكميل takmil
full adj پر pour
fume n دود dood
fumigate v بخاردادن bokhar dadan
fun n شوخي shokhi
function n تابع tab'e
fund n وجه vajh
fundamental adj بنيادي bonyadi
funds n وجوه voujoh
funeral n مراسم‌دفن marasem dafn
fungus n گياه‌قارچي giyah gharchi
funny adj خنده‌دار khandeh dar
fur n خز khaz
furious adj عصباني asabani
furiously adv باحالت‌غضب ba halat e ghazab
furnace n كوره koreh
furnish v مبله‌كردن mobleh kardan
furnishings n اثاثيه asasiyeh
furniture n اثاثه asaseh
furore n ديوانگي divanegi
furrow n مزرعه‌شخم‌زده mazraeh shokhm zadeh

further adv بيشتر bishtar
furthermore adv بعلاوه bealaveh
fury n غضب ghazab
fuse n فتيله‌موادمنفجره fetileh mavad monfajereh
fusion n ذوب zob
fuss n هوي و هاي hay o hoy
futile adj بيهوده bihodeh
future n آينده ayandeh
fuzzy adj كركي korki

G

gadget n آلت‌كوچك alat kochak
gag v دهان‌بندبستن dahan band bastan
gag n شيرين‌كاري shirin kari
gaily adv باخوشحالي ba khoshhali
gain v بدست‌آوردن be dast avardan
gain n سود sood
galaxy n كهكشان kahkeshan
gale n تندباد tond bad
gall bladder n كيسه‌صفرا kiseh safra
gallant adj دلاور delavar
gallery n گالري galeri
gallon n گالن galon
gallop v چهارنعل‌رفتن chahar na'el raftan
gallows n دار dar
galvanize v آب‌فلزي‌دادن ab felezi dadan

gamble v قمار کردن ghomar kardan	**gem** n گوهر gohar
game n بازي bazi	**gender** n جنس jens
gang n دسته dasteh	**gene** n ژن zhen
gangrene n قانقاریا ghangharia	**genealogy** n شجرهنامه shajareh nameh
gangster n اوباش obash	**general** n عام am
gap n شکاف shekaf	**generalize** v بهطورعامگفتن beh tore am goftan
garage n گاراژ garaj	**generate** v تولیدکردن tolid kardan
garbage n روده rodeh	**generation** n تولیدنیرو tolid niroo
garden n باغ bagh	**generator** n مولد movaled
gardener n باغبان baghban	**generic** adj جنسي jensi
gargle v غرغرهکردن gher ghereh kardan	**generosity** n بخشش bakhshesh
garland n گلچینادبي golchin adabi	**genetic** adj پیدایشي peydayeshi
garlic n سیر sir	**genius** n نابغه nabegheh
garment n جامه jameh	**genocide** n کشتاردستهجمعي koshtar dasteh jamee
garnish v آرایشدادن arayesh dadan	**genteel** adj اصیل asil
garrison n پادگان padegan	**gentle** adj نجیب najib
gas n گاز gaz	**gentleman** n آقا agha
gasoline n بنزین benzin	**gentleness** n ملایمت molayemat
gasp v نفسنفسزدن nafas nafas zadan	**genuflect** v زانوخمکردن zanoo kham kardan
gastric adj معدي me'edi	**genuine** n نبوغ nobogh
gate n دروازه darvazeh	**geography** n جغرافیا joghrafia
gather v گردآوريکردن gerd avari kardan	**geology** n زمینشناسي zamin shenasi
gathering n گردآوري gerd avari	**geometry** n علمهندسه elm hendeseh
gauge v پیمانهکردن peymaneh kardan	**geranium** n شمعدانيعطري shamdaniye atri
gay adj خوش khosh	**germ** n میکروب mikrob
gaze v خیرهنگاهکردن khireh negah kardan	**German** adj آلماني almani
gear n دنده dandeh	**germinate** v جوانهزدن javaneh zadan
gelatine n دلمه doulmeh	**gerund** n اسممصدر esm masdar

gestation *n* حاملگی hamelegi

gesticulate *v* باسرودست اشاره کردن
ba sar va dast eshareh kardan

gesture *n* اشاره eshareh

get *iv* بدست آوردن be dast avardan

get along *v* گذران کردن gozaran
kardan

get away *v* برو boro

get back *v* دوباره بدست آوردن
dobareh bedast avardan

get by *v* نگهداري کردن negah dari
kardan

get down *v* پیاده شدن piyadeh
shodan

get in *v* جمع آوری کردن jam avari
kardan

get out *v* بیرون رفتن biron raftan

get over *v* فایق امدن بر fayegh
amadan bar

get together *v* فراهم آوردن
faraham avardan

get up *v* درست شدن dorust shodan

geyser *n* آبفشان abfeshan

ghastly *adj* ترسناک tarsnak

ghost *n* شبح shabah

giant *n* آدم غول پیکر adam'e ghol
peykar

gift *n* بخشش bakhshesh

gifted *adj* بااستعداد ba estedad

gigantic *adj* غول پیکر ghol peykar

giggle *v* باخنده اظهار داشتن ba
khandeh ezhar dashtan

gimmick *n* حیله hileh

gin *n* ماشین پنبه پاک کنی mashin
panbeh pak koni

ginger *n* زنجبیل zanjebil

giraffe *n* زرافه zarafeh

girl *n* دختر dokhtar

girlfriend *n* دوست دختر dost
dokhtar

give *iv* واگذار کردن vagozar
kardan

giveaway *v* بخشیدن bakhshidan

glacier *n* یخ رود yakh e rood

glad *adj* خرسند khorsand

gladiator *n* گلادیاتور geladiator

glamorous *adj* فریبنده faribandeh

glance *n* برانداز barandaz

glance *v* برانداز کردن barandaz
kardan

gland *n* غده ghodeh

glare *n* درخشندگی زیاد
derakhshandegiye ziad

glass *n* شیشه shisheh

glasses *n* عینک eynak

glassware *n* شیشه آلات shisheh
alat

gleam *v* نور دادن noor dadan

gleam *n* نور ضعیف noor zaif

glide *v* سرخوردن sar khordan

glimmer *n* نور کم noor kam

glimpse *v* برق نگاه bargh'e negah

glimpse *v* به یک نظر دیدن beh yek
nazar didan

glitter *v* براق شدن baragh shodan

globe *n* کره koreh

globule *n* جسم کوچک کروي jesm
e kochak e koravi

gloom *n* تاریکی tariki

gloomy *adj* تاریک tariki

glorify *v* جلال دادن jalal dadan

glorious *adj* مجلل mojalal

glory *n* جلال jalal

gloss *n* جلا jala

glossy *adj* جلادار jala dar

glove *n* دستکش dast kesh

glow *v* تابیدن tabidan

glucose *n* گلوکز golokoz

glue *n* چسب chasb

glue *v* چسباندن chasbandan

glut *n* پرخوري por khori

glutton *adj* شکم‌پرست shekam parast

gnaw *v* خاییدن khaeedan

go *iv* گشتن gashtan

go back *v* برگشتن bargashtan

go down *v* غروب کردن ghorob kardan

go in *v* بی‌ملاحظگي کردن bimolahezegi kardan

go out *v* خاموش‌شدن khamosh shodan

go over *v* به‌آن‌سورفتن beh an soo raftan

go through *v* مرور کردن moror kardan

go up *v* رفتن بالا bala raftan

goad *v* تحریک کردن tahrik kardan

goal *n* مقصد maghsad

goalkeeper *n* دروازه‌بان‌فوتبال darvazeh ban football

goat *n* بز boz

God *n* خدا khoda

goddess *n* الهه elaheh

gold *n* طلا tala

golden *adj* طلایي talaee

golf *n* گلف golf

golfer *n* باز گلف golf baz

gondola *n* قایق ghayegh

gonorrhoea *n* سوزنک sozanak

good *adj* نیک nik

good-looking *adj* خوشگل khoshgel

goodness *n* خوبي khobi

goods *n* کالا kala

goodwill *n* نیت حسن hosn niyat

goof *v* اشتباه کردن eshtebah kardan

goof *n* کودن kodan

goose *n* غاز ghar

gorge *n* گلو galo

gorgeous *adj* دار نمایش namayesh dar

gorilla *n* نسناس nasnas

gory *adj* خوني khoni

gospel *n* انجیل enjil

gossip *n* اساس بي شایعات shayeat bi asas

gossip *v* دادن اساس بي شایعات shayeat bi asas dadan

gout *n* نقرس neghres

govern *v* کردن حکومت hokomat kardan

government *n* دولت dolat

governor *n* فرماندار farmandar

gown *n* زنانه بلند جامه jameh boland zananeh

grab *v* ربودن robodan

grace *n* فیض fayz

graceful *adj* دلپذیر delpazir

gracious *adj* دهنده توفیق towfigh dahandeh

grade *n* درجه darajeh

gradual *adj* آهسته ahesteh

graduate *v* فارغ‌التحصیل‌شدن faregh-ul-tahsil shodan

graft *n* پیوند peyvand

graft *v* پیوندزدن peyvand zadan

grain *n* دانه daneh

gram *n* نخود nokhod

grammar *n* دستورزبان dastour-e zaban

grand *adj* مجلل mojallal

grand total *n* کل جمع jam'e kol

grandchild *n* نوه naveh

granddad *n* (درزبان)پدربزرگ (کودکان) pedar bozorg

grandfather *n* پدربزرگ pedar bozorg

grandiose *adj* بزرگ‌نما bozorg nama

grandmother *n* مادربزرگ madar bozorg

grandpa *n* پدربزرگ pedar bozorg

grandparents *n* پدربزرگ‌ومادر بزرگ pedar bozorg va madar bozorg

grandson *n* نوه naveh

grandstand *n* حضار hozzar

granite *n* سنگ‌خارا sang-e khara

grant *n* اهداء ehda

grant *v* دادن dadan

grape *n* انگور angour

grapefruit *n* گریپ‌فروت grapeforout

grapevine *n* درخت‌انگور derakht-e angoor

graphic *adj* ترسیمی tarsimi

grasp *n* اخذ akhz

grasp *v* گیرآوردن gir-avardan

grass *n* علف alaf

grasshopper *n* ملخ malakh

grateful *adj* سپاسگزار sepasgozar

gratify *v* خشنودکردن khoshnood kardan

gratitude *n* قدردانی ghdrdani

gratuity *n* پاداش padash

gravely *adv* سخت sakht

graveyard *n* قبرستان ghabrestan

gravitate *v* گرویدن gheravidan

gravity *n* سنگینی sangini

gravy *n* آبگوشت abgosht

grey *adj* خاکستری khakestari

greyish *adj* متمایل‌به‌خاکستری motemayel beh khakestari

graze *v* چراندن cherandan

grease *n* روغن‌اتومبیل roghan otomobil

grease *v* روغن‌زدن roghan zadan

greasy *adj* روغنی roghani

great *adj* بزرگ bozorg

greatness *n* بزرگی bozorgi

greed *n* آز az

greedy *adj* حریص haris

Greek *adj* یونانی yonani

green *adj* سبز sabz

green bean *n* لوبیای‌سبز lobia sabz

greenhouse *n* گرم‌خانه garm khaneh

greet *v* درودگفتن dorod goftan

greetings *n* احترام ehteram

grenade *n* نارنجک narenjak

greyhound *n* تازی tazi

grief *n* غم gham

grievance *n* شکایت shekayat

grieve *v* غمگین‌کردن ghamgin kardan

grill *v* بریان‌کردن beryan kardan

grill n سیخ‌شبکه‌ای sikh shabakehee

grim adj ترسناک tarsnak

grimace n ادااوصول ada osol

grime n دوده dodeh

grind iv سائیدن saeedan

grip n زکام zokam

grip v نهرکندن nahr kandan

gripe n شکایت shekayat

grisly adj مهیب mahib

groan n ناله naleh

groan v ناله‌کردن naleh kardan

groceries n عطار attar

groom v تیمارکردن timar kardan

groove n شیار shiyar

gross adj عمده omdeh

grotesque adj غریب gharib

grotto n غار ghar

grouchy adj بدخلق bad kholgh

ground n زمین zamin

groundless adj بی‌اساس bi asas

grounds n تفاله tofaleh

groundwork n زمینه zamineh

group n گروه goroh

grow iv رستن rostan

growl v غرغرکردن ghor ghor kardan

grown-up n آدم‌بالغ adam-e balegh

growth n رشد roushd

grudge n بی‌میلی bi mayli

gruesome adj مخوف makhof

grumble v غرغرکردن ghor ghor kardan

grumpy adj بدخلق badkholgh

guarantee v ضمانت‌کردن zemanat kardan

guaranty n ضمانت zemanat kardan

guard n نگهبان negahban

guardian n نگهبان negahban

guerrilla n پارتیزان partizan

guess v حدس‌زدن hads zadan

guest n مهمان mehman

guide n راهنما rahnamaee kardan

guide v راهنمایی‌کردن rahnamaee kardan

guidelines n راهبرد rahbord

guild n دسته dasteh

guillotine n گیوتین giyotin

guilt n تقصیر taghsir

guilty adj گناهکار gonahkar

guise n ظاهر zaher

guitar n عود oud

gulf n خلیج khalij

gum n لثه‌دندان laseh dandan

gun n تفنگ tofang

gunfire n تیراندازی tirandazi

gunman n تفنگدار tofangdar

gunpowder n باروت barot

gunshot n تیراندازی tir andazi

gust n تندباد tond bad

gusto n ذوق zogh

gut n روده rodeh

gutter n آب‌رو ab-e ro

guy n شخص shakhs

guzzle v بلعیدن balidan

gymnasium n ورزشگاه varzeshgah

gynaecology n دانش‌امراض‌زنانه danesh-e amraz-e zananeh

gypsy n کولی koli

H

habit *n* عادت adat

habitable *adj* مسكونى maskoni

habitual *adj* معتاد mo'etad

haggle *v* چانه‌زدن chaneh zadan

hail *n* سلام salam

hail *v* سلام‌كردن salam kardan

hair *n* مو moo

hairbrush *n* برس‌موي‌سر bores-e moye sar

haircut *n* سلمانى salmani

hairdo *n* آرايش‌موي‌زنان arayesh-e moye zanan

hairdresser *n* آرايشگرمو arayeshgar-e moo

hairpiece *n* كلاه‌گيس kolah gis

hairy *adj* پرمو pour moo

half *n* نيم nim

hall *n* سرسرا sarsara

hallucinate *v* هذيان‌گفتن hazian goftan

hallway *n* تالارورودي talar-e vorodi

halt *v* مكث‌كردن maks kardan

ham *n* گوشتران gosht-e ran

hamburger *n* همبرگر hamberger

hamlet *n* دهكده dehkadeh

hammer *n* چكش chakosh

hammock *n* ننو nano

hand *n* دست dast

handbag *n* كيف‌دستى kif dasti

handbook *n* كتاب‌دستى ketab dasti

handcuffs *n* دست‌بندآهنين dast band-e ahanin

handful *adj* يك‌مشت yek mosht

handgun *n* تفنگ‌دستى tofang dasti

handicap *n* امتيازبه‌ضعيف emtiaz beh zaif

handkerchief *n* دستمال dastmal

handle *n* دسته dasteh

handle *v* گذاشتن‌دستگيره gozashtan-e dastgireh

handmade *adj* مصنوع‌دست masno-e dast

handout *n* نوبت‌بازي nobat-e bazi

handsome *adj* دلپذير delpazir

handy *adj* دستي dasti

hang *iv* آويختن avikhtan

hanger *n* اعلام‌كننده e'elam konandeh

happen *v* اتفاق‌افتادن etefagh oftadan

happiness *n* خوشحالي khoshhali

happy *adj* خوش khosh

harass *v* عاجزكردن ajez kardan

harassment *n* ستوه sotoh

harbour *n* لنگرگاه langar gah

hard *adj* سخت sakht

harden *v* سخت‌كردن sakht kardan

hardly *adv* سخت sakht

hardship *n* سختي sakhti

hardware *n* سخت‌افزار sakht afzar

hardwood *n* چوب‌سفت chob-e seft

hare *n* خرگوش khargosh

harem *n* اندرون andaroon

harlot *n* هرزه harzeh

harm *n* آسيب asib resandan

harm v آسیب‌رساندن(به) asib resandan

harmful adj مضر mozer

harmless adj بی‌ضرر bi zarar

harmony n تطبیق tatbigh

harp n چنگ chang

harpoon n نیزه nayzeh

harsh adj تند tond

harvest n خرمن kharman

hassle v جرو‌بحث jar-o bahs

haste n عجله ajaleh

hasten v شتاباندن shetabandan

hasten v شتاباندن shetabandan

hasty adj عجول ajol

hat n کلاه kolah gis

hatchet n تبرکوچک tabar-e kochak

hate v نفرت‌داشتن‌از nefrat dashtan az

hateful adj منفور manfoor

hatred n دشمنی doshmani

haughty adj مغرور maghror

haul v کشیدن keshidan

haunt v زیادرفت‌وآمدکردن ziad raft-o amad kardan

have iv دارابودن dara bodan

have to v مجبوربودن majbor bodan

haven n بندرگاه bandargah

havoc n خرابی kharabi

hawk n باز baz

howl n زوزه zouzeh

hay n علف‌خشک alaf-e khoshk

haystack n کومه‌علف‌خشک komeh alaf-e khoshk

hazard n قمار ghomar

hazardous adj پرخطر pour khatar

haze n مه‌کم meh-e kam

hazelnut n فندق fandogh

hazy adj مه‌دار meh dar

he pro او(آن‌مرد) ou

head n سر sar

headache n سردرد sardard

heading n عنوان onvan

head-on adv شاخ‌به‌شاخ shakh beh shakh

headphones n گوشی‌هدفون goshi-e hedfon

headquarters n مرکزفرماندهی markaz-e farmandehi

headway n پیشرفت pishraft

heal v شفادادن shafa dadan

healer n شفادهنده shafa dahandeh

health n تندرستی tandorosti

healthy adj سالم salem

heap n توده todeh

heap v توده‌کردن todeh kardan

hear iv شنیدن shenidan

hearsay n شایعه shye'eh

heart n قلب ghalb

heartbeat n ضربان‌قلب zaraban-e ghalb

heartburn n دردیاسوزش‌قلب dard ya sozesh-e ghalb

hearten v دل‌دادن del dadan

hearth n اجاق ojagh

hearty adj قلبی ghalbi

heat v گرم‌کردن garm kardan

heat n گرما garma

heater n چراغ‌خوراک‌پزی cheragh-e khorak pazi

heathen n کافر kafer

heaven n بهشت behesht

heavenly *adj* آسماني asemani
heaviness *n* سنگيني sangini
heavy *adj* سنگين sangini
hectic *adj* بيقرار bigharar
heed *v* (به)اعتناكردن etena kardan
heel *n* پاشنه pashneh
height *n* بلندي bolandi
heighten *v* بلندكردن boland kardan
heinous *adj* زشت zesht
heir *n* وارث vares
heiress *n* وارثه vareseh
heist *n* دزدي dozdi
helicopter *n* هليكوپتر helikopter
hell *n* دوزخ dozakh
hello *e* سلام salam
helm *n* سكان sokan
helmet *n* خود khod
help *n* كمك komak
help *v* كمك كردن komak kardan
helper *n* يار yar
helpful *adj* مفيد mofid
helpless *adj* بيچاره bichareh
hem *n* صاف كردن سينه saf kardan-e sineh
hemisphere *n* نيم كره nim koreh
haemorrhage *n* خون روي khon-e roy
hen *n* مرغ morgh
hence *adv* ازاين رو az in roo
her *adj* مال آن زن mal-e an zan
herald *n* پيشرو pishrou
herb *n* گياه giyah
here *adv* اينجا inja
hereafter *adv* ازاين پس az in pas

hereby *adv* بدين وسيله bedin vasileh
hereditary *adj* ارثي ersi
heresy *n* كفر kofr
heretic *adj* بدعت گذار bed'at gozar
heritage *n* ميراث miras
hermetic *adj* وابسته به هرمس مصري vabasteh beh hermes-e mesri
hermit *n* زاهدگوشه نشين zahed-e gosheh neshin
hernia *n* فتق fatgh
hero *n* قهرمان ghahraman
heroic *adj* قهرمان وار ghahreman var
heroin *n* هروئين heroin
heroism *n* گردي gardi
hers *pro* مال آن زن male an zan
hesitant *adj* دودل do del
hesitate *v* تامل كردن ta'amol kardan
hiccup *n* سكسكه seksekeh
hide *iv* پنهان كردن panhan kardan
hideout *n* اختفا ekhtefa
hierarchy *n* سلسله مراتب selseleh marateb
high *adj* بلند boland
highlight *n* پررنگ por rang
highly *adv* عالى alli
Highness *n* بلندمقام boland magham
highway *n* شاهراه shahrah
hijack *n* ربودن هواپيما roboudan-e havapeyma
hijack *v* هواپيماربايي havapeyma roba'ei
hijacker *n* هواپيماربا havapeyma roba

hike v مبلغرابالابردن mablagh ra bala bordan

hilarious adj خندهدار khandehdar

hill n تپه tappeh

hillside n دامنه damaneh

hilltop n بالایتپه balay-e tappeh

hilly adj پرازتپه por az tappeh

hilt n دسته dasteh

hinder v عقبانداختن aghab andakhtan

hindrance n پاگیري pagiri

hindsight n ادراک edrak

hinge n لولا lowla

hinge v لولازدن lowla zadan

hint n اشاره eshareh

hip n کفل kafal

hire v کرایهکردن kerayeh kardan

his adj مالآنمرد mal-e an mard

his pro مردانه mardaneh

Hispanic adj اسپانیولی espaniyouli

hiss v هیسکردن hiss kardan

historian n تاریخنویس tarikhnevis

history n تاریخ tarikhnevis

hit n اصابت esabat

hit iv زدن zadan

hive n کندو kandoo

hoard v احتکارکردن ehtekar kardan

hoarse adj خشن khashen

hoax n شوخيفریبآمیز shoukhiye farib-amiz

hobby n اسبکوچکاندام asb-e kouchak andam

hog n خوک khouk

hoist v بالابردن bala bordan

hold iv گرفتن gereftan

hold-up n راهزني rahzani

hole n سوراخ sourakh

holiday n تعطیل ta'til

holiness n تقدس taghados

hollow adj توخالی tookhali

holocaust n عامقتل ghatl-e 'am

holy adj مقدس moghadas

homage n تجلیل tajlil

home n خانه khaneh

homeland n خانهپدری khaneh-e pedari

homeless adj دربدر dar be dar

homely adj خودماني khodemani

homemade adj خانگي khanegi

homesick adj دلتنگ deltang

hometown n ولایت velayat

homework n مشق mashgh

homicide n آدمکشی adamkoshi

homosexual adj همجنسباز hamjensbaz

honest adj صادق sadegh

honesty n درستکاري dorostkari

honey n انگبین angabin

honeymoon n ماهعسل mah-e asal

honk v بوق boogh

honour n احترام ehteram

hood n باشلق bashlagh

hoof n سم sam

hook n قلاب ghollab

hooligan n اوباش owbash

hop v لیلیکردن leyley kardan

hope n امید omid

hopeless adj نومید nowmid

horizon n افق ofogh

horizontal adj افقي ofoghi

hormone n هورمون hormon

horn *n* شاخ shakh beh shakh

hornet *n* زنبورسرخ zanbour-e sorkh

horrendous *adj* دهشتناک dehshatnak

horrible *adj* مخوف makhoof

horrify *v* ترساندن tarsandan

horror *n* ترس tars

horse *n* اسب asb

hose *n* جوراب jourab

hospital *n* بيمارستان bimarestan

hospitality *n* مهمان‌نوازي mehman-navazi

hospitalize *v* بستري‌كردن bastari kardan

host *n* ميزباني mizbani

hostage *n* گرو geroo

hostess *n* زن‌ميزبان zan-e mizban

hostile *adj* دشمن doshmani

hostility *n* عداوت adavat

hot *adj* گرم garm

hotel *n* هتل hotel

hound *n* سگ‌شكاري sag-e shekari

hour *n* ساعت sa'at

hourly *adv* ساعتى sa'ati

house *n* خانه khaneh

household *n* خانواده khanevadeh

housekeeper *n* خانه‌دار khaneh-dar

housewife *n* كدبانو kadbanoo

housework *n* كارهاى‌خانه karhay-e khaneh

hover *v* پرپرزدن parpar zadan

how *adv* چگونه chegooneh

however *c* به‌هرحال be har hall

howl *v* زوزه‌كشيدن zouzeh keshidan

huddle *v* روي‌هم‌ريختن rooye'ham rikhtan

hug *n* آغوش aghoush

hug *v* درآغوش‌گرفتن dar aghoush gereftan

huge *adj* سترگ setorg

hull *n* پوست poust

hum *v* وزوزكردن vezvez kardan

human *adj* انسانى ensani

human being *n* آدمى adami

humanities *n* علوم‌انسانى olum-e ensani

humankind *n* نوع‌انسان no'e' ensan

humble *adj* زبون zaboon

humbly *adv* فروتنانه foroutananeh

humid *n* مرطوب martoub

humidity *n* رطوبت rotoubat

humiliate *v* پست‌كردن past kardan

humility *n* فروتنى foroutani

humour *n* خيال khiyal

humorous *adj* فكاهى fokahi

hump *n* قوز ghooz

hunch *n* قوز ghooz

hunchback *n* پشت‌قوز posht ghooz

hunched *adj* قوزى ghoozi

hundred *adj* صد sad

hunger *n* گرسنگى gorosnegi

hungry *adj* گرسنه gorosneh

hunt *v* شكاركردن shekar kardan

hunter *n* شكارچى shekarchi

hunting *n* شكار shekar

hurdle *n* مانع man'e

hurl *v* پرتاب‌كردن partab kardan

hurricane *n* تندباد tond bad

hurry *v* شتاب کردن shetab kardan

hurt *iv* آزار رساندن azar rasandan

hurt *adj* مجروح majrooh

husband *n* شوهر showhar

hush *v* خاموش کردن khamoosh kardan

husky *adj* پوست‌دار postdar

hut *n* کلبه kolbeh

hydrogen *n* هیدروژن hidrojen

hyena *n* کفتار kaftar

hygiene *n* علم‌بهداشت elm-e behdasht

hymn *n* سرودروحانی soroud-e rouhani

hyphen *n* خط‌تیره khat-e tireh

hypnotize *v* هیپنوتیزم کردن hipnotizm kardan

hypocrisy *n* ریا riya

hypothesis *n* فرض farz

hysteria *n* تشنج tashanoj

I *pro* اول‌شخص‌مفرد aval shakhs-e mofrad

ice *n* یخ yakh

ice cream *n* بستنی bastani

ice cube *n* قالب‌یخ ghalebe yakh

ice skate *v* روی‌یخ‌اسکی کردن roye yakh eski kardan

iceberg *n* توده‌یخ‌غلتان todeh yakhe ghaltan

icebox *n* یخچال yakhchal

ice-cold *adj* فوق‌العاده‌سرد fogh-oladeh sard

icon *n* شمایل shamayel

icy *adj* یخی yakhi

idea *n* اندیشه andishe

ideal *adj* ایده‌آل ideh al

identical *adj* یکی yeki

identify *v* شناختن shenakhtan

identity *n* هویت hoviyat

ideology *n* آرزوهای‌باطنی arezohaye bateni

idiom *n* لهجه lahjeh

idiot *n* آدم‌سفیه‌واحمق adam-e safih va ahmagh

idiotic *adj* ابلهانه ablahaneh

idle *adj* بیکار bikar

idol *n* بت bout

idolatry *n* بت‌پرست bout parast

if *c* اگر agar

ignite *v* آتش‌زدن atash zadan

ignore *v* تجاهل کردن tajahol kardan

ill *adj* ناخوش na khoush

illegal *adj* نامشروع na mashro'e

illegible *adj* ناخوانا na khana

illegitimate *adj* حرامزاده haram zadeh

illicit *adj* ممنوع mamno'e

illiterate *adj* بی‌سواد bi savad

illness *n* مرض maraz

illogical *adj* غیرمنطقی ghayr-e manteghi

illuminate *v* روشن‌ساختن roshan sakhtan

illusion *n* فریب farib

illustrate *v* توضیح‌دادن tozih dadan

illustrious adj برجسته barjasteh

image n مجسمه mojasameh

imagination n پندار pendar

imagine v تصورکردن tasavour kardan

imbalance n عدمتعادل adam-e taadoul

imitate v تقلیدکردن taghlid kardan

immaculate adj معصوم ma'esom

immature adj نابالغ nabalegh

immaturity n نارسی narasi

immense adj بی‌اندازه bi andazeh

immensity n زیادي ziadi

immerse v فروبردن foro bordan

immersion n غسل ghosl

immigrant n مهاجر mohajer

immigrate v مهاجرت کردن(به‌کشور دیگر) mohajerat kardan

immigration n مهاجرت mohajerat

imminent adj قریب‌الوقوع gharib-olvogho

immobile adj بی‌جنبش bi jonbesh

immobilize v ثابت‌کردن sabet kardan

immoral adj بدسیرت bad sirat

immorality n بداخلاقي bad akhlaghi

immortal adj ابدي abadi

immortality n ابدیت abadiyat

immune adj مصون masoon

immunity n مصونیت masoniat

immunize v مصونیت‌دارکردن masoniat dar kardan

immutable adj تغییرناپذیر tagh'eer napazir

impact n ضربت zarbat

impair v خراب‌کردن kharab kardan

impartial adj بی‌طرف bi taraf

impatience n بی‌تابي bi tabi

impeccable adj بی‌عیب‌ونقص bi eyb-o naghs

impediment n مانع man'e

impending adj قریب‌الوقوع gharib-olvogho

imperfection n نقص naghs

imperial adj پادشاهی padeshahi

imperialism n حکومت‌امپراتوري hokomat-e emperatori

impersonal adj غیرشخصي ghayr-e shakhsi

impertinence n جسارت jesarat

impertinent adj گستاخ gostakh

implacable adj سنگدل sangdel

implant v جاي‌دادن jay dadan

implement v انجام‌دادن anjam dadan

implicate v دلالت‌کردن‌بر delalat kardan bar

implicit adj ضمني zemni

implore v درخواست‌کردن‌از darkhast kardan az

imply v دلالت‌کردن delalat kardan

impolite adj بی‌تربیت bi tarbiyat

import v واردکردن vared kardan

importance n اهمیت ahamiyat

importation n ورود vorod

impose v تحمیل‌کردن tahmil kardan

imposing adj تحمیل‌کننده tahmil konandeh

imposition n تحمیل tahmil

impossibility *n* امکان‌ناپذيري emkan napaziri

impossible *adj* غیرممکن ghayr-e momken

impotent *adj* (ناتوان‌جنسی) عنین anin

impound *v* توقیف‌کردن toghif kardan

impractical *adj* غیرعملي ghayr-e amali

imprecise *adj* غیردقیق ghayr-e daghigh

impress *v* تحت‌تاثیرقراردادن that-e tasir gharar dadan

impressive *adj* موثر moasser

imprint *n* تحت‌عنوان that-e onvan

imprison *v* به‌زندان‌افکندن beh zendan afkandan

improbable *adj* غیرمحتمل gheyr-e mohtamel

impromptu *adv* بالبداهه belbedahe'

improper *adj* ناشایسته nashayesteh

improve *v* بهترکردن behtar kardan

improvement *n* بهبود behbod

improvise *v* فی‌البداهه‌ساختن fel bedaheh sakhtan

impulse *n* تپش tapesh

impulsive *adj* عمل‌بدون‌فکر amal-e bedon-e fekr

impunity *n* بخشودگي bakhshodegi

impure *adj* ناخالص na khales

in depth *adv* عمیقا amighan

inability *n* ناتواني na tavani

inaccessible *adj* خارج‌ازدسترس kharej az dastras

inaccurate *adj* غیردقیق gheyr-e daghigh

inadequate *adj* ناکافي na kafi

inadmissible *adj* ناروا na rava

inappropriate *adj* بیجا bi ja

inasmuch as *c* به‌درجه‌اي‌که beh darajeh 'ee keh

inaugurate *v* گشودن goshodan

incapable *adj* عاجز ajez

incapacitate *v* ناقابل‌ساختن naghabel sakhtan

incarcerate *v* زنداني‌کردن zendani kardan

incense *n* بخورخوشبو bokhor-e khoshboo

incentive *n* انگیزه angizeh

inception *n* آغاز aghaz

incessant *adj* لاینقطع la yanghat'e

inch *n* اینچ inch

incident *n* واقعه vaghe'eh

incidentally *adv* ضمنا zemnan

incision *n* شکاف shekaf

incite *v* انگیختن angikhtan

incitement *n* تحریک tahrik

incline *v* خم‌کردن kham kardan

include *v* دربرداشتن dar bar dashtan

incoherent *adj* متناقض motenaghez

income *n* درآمد daramad

incoming *adj* واردشونده vared shavandeh

incomplete *adj* ناتمام natamam

inconsistent *adj* متناقض motenaghez

incontinence n ناپرهیزکاري na parhizkari

incorporate v بهم‌پیوستن beham peyvastan

incorrect adj نادرست na dourost

incorrigible adj اصلاح‌ناپذیر eslah napazir

increase v افزودن afzodan

incredible adj باورنکردني bavar nakardani

increment n نمو nemov

incur v متحمل‌شدن motehamel shodan

incurable adj علاج‌ناپذیر alaj napazir

indecency n بي‌نزاكتي bi nezakati

indecision n بي‌تصميمي bi tasmimi

indecisive adj دودل do-del

indeed adv بهراستي beh rasti

indefinite adv نامحدود na mahdood

indemnify v تاوان‌دادن tavan dadan

indemnity n تاوان tavan

index n راهنما rahnama

indicate v نشان‌دادن neshan dadan

indifference n خونسردي khonsardi

indifferent adj خونسرد khonsard

indigent adj تهیدست tohidast

indigestion n سوءهاضمه so'e hazemeh

indirect adj غیرمستقيم ghayr-e mostaghim

indiscreet adj فاقدحس‌تشخیص faghed-e hes-e tashkhis

indivisible adj غیرقابل‌تقسيم ghayr-e ghabel-e taghsim

indoor adv خانگي khanegi

induce v القاءکردن elgha'e kardan

indulge v مخالفت‌نکردن mokhalefat nakardan

indulgent adj بخشنده bakhshandeh

industrious adj ماهر maher

industry n صنعت sanat

ineffective adj بي‌اثر bi asar

inefficient adj كم‌بازده kam bazdeh

inept adj بي‌عرضه bi orzeh

inequality n نابرابري na barabari

inevitable adj ناچار na char

inexpensive adj ارزان arzan

inexperience adj بي‌تجربه bi tajrobeh

inexplicable adj غیرقابل‌توضيح ghayr-e ghabel-e tozih

infallible adj لغزش‌ناپذیر laghzesh napazir

infamous adj رسوا rosva

infancy n كودكي koodaki

infant n كودك koodak

infantry n پیاده‌نظام piyadeh nezam

infect v آلوده‌کردن aloodeh kardan

infection n عفونت oufoonat

infectious adj واگیر vagir

infer v استنتاج‌کردن estentaj kardan

inferior adj پست past

inferno n دوزخ dozakh

infested adj مزاحم mozahem

infidelity *n* كفر koufr

infiltrate *v* تراوش کردن taravoush kardan

infinite *adj* بیکران bikaran

infirmary *n* درمانگاه darmangah

inflammation *n* آماس amas

inflate *v* باد کردن bad kardan

inflexible *adj* سخت sakht

inflict *v* ضربت وارد آوردن zarbat vared avardan

influence *n* نفوذ noufoz

influential *adj* دارای نفوذ و قدرت daraye noufoz va ghodrat

influenza *n* آنفلوانزا anfolanza

influx *n* نفوذ nofoz

inform *v* آگاهی دادن agahi dadan

informal *adj* غیر صوری gheyr-e soori

informality *n* غیر رسمی بودن ghayr-e rasmi

information *n* اطلاع etela

infraction *n* نقش naghsh

infrequent *adj* کم kam

infuriate *v* آتشی کردن atashi kardan

infusion *n* دم کرده dam kardeh

ingest *v* به شکم فرو بردن beh shekam foro bordan

ingrained *adj* دیرینه dirineh

ingratiate *v* خودشیرینی کردن khod shirini kardan

ingratitude *n* ناسپاسی nasepasi

ingredient *n* جزء joz'e

inhabit *v* ساکن شدن(در) saken shodan

inhale *v* تنفس کردن tanafous kardan

inherit *v* به میراث بردن beh miras bordan

inheritance *n* ارث rers

inhibit *v* منع کردن man'e kardan

inhuman *adj* بی عاطفه bi atefeh

initial *adj* نخستین nakhostin

initials *n* مخفف mokhafaf

initiate *v* راه انداختن rah andakhtan

initiative *n* ابتکار ebtekar

inject *v* تزریق کردن tazrigh kardan

injection *n* تزریق tazrigh

injure *v* آسیب زدن(به) asib zadan

injury *n* آسیب asib

injustice *n* بی عدالتی bi edalati

ink *n* مرکب morakab

inkling *n* اشاره eshareh

inland *adv* درون کشور daron-e keshvar

in-laws *n* خوانده khandeh

inmate *n* مقیم moghim

inn *n* مسافرخانه mosafer khaneh

inner *adj* درونی darooni

innocent *adj* بی گناه bi gonah

innuendo *n* معنی ma'eni

innumerable *adj* بی شمار bi shomar

inpatient *adj* بیمار بستری bimar-e bastari

input *n* خرج kharj

inquire *v* پرسش کردن porsesh kardan

inquiry *n* تحقیق tahghigh

inquisition *n* استنطاق estentagh

insane *adj* دیوانه divaneh

insanity *n* دیوانگی divanegi

inscription n نوشته neveshteh

insect n حشره hashareh

insecurity n ناامنی na amni

inseparable adj جدانشدنی joda nashodani

insert v درج‌کردن darj kardan

inside adj تو too

inside pre درون daron-e keshvar

inside out adv عوضی avazi

insignificant adj ناچیز nachiz

insincerity n عدم‌صمیمیت adam-e samimiyat

insinuate v تلقین‌کردن talghin kardan

insipid adj بی‌مزه bi mazeh

insist v اصرارورزیدن esrar varzidan

insistence n اصرار esrar

insolent adj گستاخ gostakh

insoluble adj حل‌نشدنی hal nashodani

insomnia n بی‌خوابی(غیرعادی) bi khabi

inspect v سرکشی‌کردن sarkeshi kardan

inspiration n دم dam

install v کارگذاشتن kar gozashtan

instalment n قسط ghest

instance n لحظه lahzeh

instant n دم dam

instantly adv فورا foran

instead adv درعوض dar avaz

instigate v برانگیختن barangikhtan

instil v چکاندن chekandan

institution n تاسیس‌قضایی tasis-e ghazaee

instruct v آموختن‌به amokhtan beh

instructor n آموزگار amozgar

insufficient adj نارسا narasa

insulate v جداکردن joda kardan

insult v توهین‌کردن‌به tohin kardan beh

insurance n بیمه bimeh

insure v بیمه‌کردن bimeh kardan

insurgency n قیام ghiyam

insurrection n طغیان toghyan

intact adj دست‌نخورده dast nakhordeh

integrate v تمام‌کردن tamam kardan

integrity n تمامیت tamamiyat

intelligent adj باهوش bahosh

intend v قصدداشتن ghasd dashtan

intense adj زیاد ziad

intensify v سخت‌کردن sakht kardan

intensity n شدت shedat

intention n قصد ghasd

intercede v پادرمیانی‌کردن padarmiyani kardan

intercept v بریدن boridan

interchange v مبادله‌کردن mobadeleh kardan

interest n تنزیل tanzil

interested adj دلبسته delbasteh

interesting adj دلچسب delchasb

interfere v دخالت‌کردن dekhalat kardan

interim adv فی‌مابین fi ma beyn

interior adj درونی daroni

intermediary n میانجی miyanji

intern v داخل‌شدن‌در dakhel shodan dar

interpret v تفسیرکردن tafsir kardan

interrogate v بازپرسی کردن bazporsi kardan

interrupt v گسیختن gosikhtan

interval n فاصله faseleh

intervene v درمیان آمدن dar miyan amadan

interview n (برای گفتگو) دیدار didar

intestine n امعاء ema'e

intimacy n صمیمیت samimiyat

intimate adj صمیمی samimy

intimidate v ترساندن tarsandan

intolerable adj تحمل ناپذیر tahamol napazir

intolerance n نابردباری na bordbari

intoxicated adj مست mast

intravenous adj موجود در سیاه رگ mojod dar siyah rag

intrepid adj دلیر dalir

intricate adj بغرنج boghranj

intrigue n توطئه tote'eh

intriguing adj توطئه کردن tote'eh kardan

intrinsic adj ذاتی zati

introduce v معرفی کردن moarefi kardan

introvert adj درونگرا daroongara

intrude v سرزده آمدن sarzadeh amadan

inundate v سیل زده کردن sayl zadeh kardan

invade v تاخت و تاز کردن در akht-o taz kardan dar

invader n تاخت و تازگر takht-o tazgar

invalid n پوچ pooch

invasion n تاخت و تاز takht-o taz

invent v اختراع کردن ekhtera kardan

invention n اختراع ekhtera

inventory n دفتر دارایی daftar-e daraee

invest v گذاردن gozardan

investigate v رسیدگی کردن residegi kardan

investment n سرمایه گذاری sarmaye gozari

invincible adj شکست ناپذیر shekast napazir

invisible adj مخفی makhfi

invite v دعوت کردن davat kardan

invoice n صورت حساب sorat hesab

invoke v دعا کردن به doa kardan beh

involve v گرفتار کردن gereftar kardan

involved v درگیر dargir

involvement n درگیری dargiri

inwards adv امعاء و احشاء ama'e va ahsha'e

iron v اتو کردن outo kardan

iron n آهن ahan

irony n طعنه ta'eneh

irrational adj ناگویا nagoya

irrefutable adj تکذیب ناپذیر takzib napazir

irregular adj بی قاعده bi ghaedeh

irrelevant adj نامربوط namarbot

irreparable adj جبران ناپذیر jobran napazir

irresistible adj غیر قابل مقاومت geyr-e ghabel-e moghavemat

irreversible *adj* تغییرناپذیر taghir napazir

irrigate *v* آبیاری کردن abyari kardan

irritate *v* عصبانی کردن asabani kardan

irritating *adj* برانگیزنده bar'angizandeh

island *n* جزیره jazireh

isle *n* جزیره jazireh

isolate *v* مجزاکردن mojaza kardan

issue *n* پخش pakhsh

italics *adj* ایتالیک etalik

itch *v* خارش کردن kharesh kardan

itchiness *n* احساس خارش ehsas-e kharesh

item *n* فقره faghareh

itemize *v* جزءبهجزءنوشتن joz beh joz neveshtan

itinerary *n* برنامهسفر barnamehe safa

J

jackal *n* شغال shoghal

jacket *n* ژاکت zhaket

jackpot *n* برندهتمامپولها barandehe tamame' poolha

jaguar *n* پلنگ خالدار palang-e khaldar

jail *v* حبس کردن habs kardan

jail *n* زندان zendanban

jailer *n* زندانبان zendanban

jam *n* مربا moraba

janitor *n* دربان darban

January *n* ژانویه zhanviyeh

Japan *n* ژاپن zhapon

Japanese *adj* ژاپنی zhaponi

jar *n* کوزهدهنگشاد kouzeh dahan-goshad

jasmine *n* یاسمن yasaman

jaw *n* فک fak

jealous *adj* حسود hasood

jealousy *n* رشک rashk

jeans *n* جین jin

jeopardize *v* بهخطرانداختن be khatar andakhtan

jerk *adj* احمق ahmagh

jerk *n* تکان takan

jersey *n* کشباف keshbaf

Jew *n* جهود johood

jewel *n* گوهر gowhar

jeweller *n* جواهرساز javahersaz

jewellery store *n* جواهرفروشی javaher foroush

Jewish *adj* یهودی yahoodiyat

job *n* کار kar

jobless *adj* بیکار bikar

join *v* ملحقکردن molhagh kardan

joint *n* محلاتصال mahalle' etesal

jointly *adv* اهم aham

joke *n* شوخی shoukhi

joke *v* شوخیکردن shoukhi kardan

jokingly *adv* بهشوخی be shoukhi

jolly *adj* سرکیف sare keif

jolt *n* تکان takan

jolt *v* تکاندادن takan dadan

journal *n* روزنامه rooznemeh

journalist *n* روزنامهنگار rooznemehnegar

journey *n* سفر safar

jovial *adv* خوشگذران khoshgozaran

joy *n* خوشی khoshi

joyful *adj* شاد shad

joyfully *adv* باخوشی ba khoshi

jubilant *adj* هلهلهشادمانه helhelehe shadmaneh

Judaism *n* یهودیت yahoodiyat

judge *n* قاضی ghazi

judgment *n* داوري davari

judicious *adj* داراي قضاوت سلیم daraye ghazavate' sahih

jug *n* کوزه koozeh

juggler *n* شعبده باز sho'badehbaz

juice *n* آب میوه abmiveh

juicy adj آبدار abdar

July *n* ژوئیه zho'eiyeh

jump *n* پرش paresh

jump *v* جستن jastan

jumpy *adj* جهنده jahandeh

junction *n* پیوندگاه peyvandgah

June *n* ژوئن zho'an

junior *adj* اصغر asghar

junk *n* نی ney

jury *n* هیئت منصفه hey'at monsefeh

just *adj* عادل ade'l

justice *n* داد dad

justify *v* هم تراز کردن hamtaraz kardan

justly *adv* حقا" haghan

juvenile *n* نوجوان now javan

juvenile *adj* نوجوانی now javani

K

kangaroo *n* کانگورو kangoro

karate *n* کاراته karateh

keep *iv* نگاه داشتن negah dashtan

keep down *v* بلندنشدن boland nashodan

keep off *v* دورشدن dour shodan

keep on *v* ادامه دادن edameh dadan

keep up *v* خوب نگاه داشتن khoub negah dashtan

keg *n* چلیک chelik

kennel *n* لانه سگ lanehe sag

kettle *n* کتري ketri

key *n* کلید kilid

key ring *n* حلقه کلید halghehe kelid

keyboard *n* صفحه کلید safheh kilid

kick *v* لگد زدن lagad zadan

kickback *n* بازپرداخت baz pardakht

kickoff *n* دور کردن door kardan

kid *n* بزغاله bozghaleh

kidnap *v* بچه دزدي کردن bacheh dozdi kardan

kidnapper *n* دزد dozd

kidney *n* گرده gardeh

kidney bean *n* لوبیاقرمز loobiya ghermez

kill *v* کشتن koshtan

killer *n* آدم کش adamkosh

killing *n* قتل ghatl

kilogram *n* کیلوگرم kiloogeram

kilometre *n* کیلومتر kiloometr

kilowatt *n* کیلووات kiloovat	**labourer** *n* کارگر kargar
kind *adj* مهربان mehrabani	**labyrinth** *n* دخمه dakhmeh
kindle *v* روشن‌شدن rowshan shodan	**lace** *n* پرسوراخ por sourakh
kindly *adv* دلپذیر delpazir	**lack** *n* احتیاج ehtiyaj
kindness *n* مهربانی mehrabani	**lack** *v* نبودن naboudan
king *n* پادشاه padeshahi	**lad** *n* بچه پسر pesar bacheh
kingdom *n* پادشاهی padeshahi	**ladder** *n* نردبان nardeban
kiosk *n* دکه dakeh	**lady** *n* بانو banoo
kiss *n* بوسه bouseh	**lagoon** *n* مرداب mordab
kiss *v* بوسیدن boosidan	**lake** *n* دریاچه daryacheh
kitchen *n* آشپزخانه ashpazkhaneh	**lamb** *n* بره barreh
kite *n* بادبادک badbadak	**lame** *adj* لنگ lang
kitten *n* بچه‌گربه bacheh gorbeh	**lament** *v* تاسف‌خوردن ta'asof khordan
knee *n* زانو zanoo	**lament** *n* سوگواری sougvari
kneecap *n* کاسه‌زانو kasehe' zanoo	**lamp** *n* لامپ lamp
kneel *iv* زانوزدن zanoo zadan	**lampshade** *n* حباب hobab
knife *n* چاقو chaghoo	**land** *v* به‌خشکی‌آمدن be khoshki amadan
knight *n* اسب‌درشطرنج asb (dar shatranj)	**land** *n* زمین zamin
knit *v* بافتن baftan	**landfill** *n* ورودبه‌خشکی voroud be khoshki
knob *n* دستگیره dastgireh	**landing** *n* به‌زمین‌نشستن be zamin neshastan
knock *v* کوبیدن koubidan	
knock *n* مشت mosht	**landlady** *n* زن‌مهمانخانه‌دار zane' mehmankhanehdar
knot *n* گره gereh	
know *iv* دانستن danestan	**landlocked** *adj* محاط‌درخشکی mahat dar khoshki
know-how *n* فوت‌وفن foot-o-fan	
knowingly *adv* دانسته danesteh	**landlord** *n* مالک malek
knowledge *n* بصیرت basirat	**landscape** *n* دورنما dournama
	lane *n* کوچه koucheh
	language *n* زبان zaban
L	**languish** *v* بیحال‌شدن bihal shodan
	lantern *n* فانوس fanous
lab *n* آزمایشگاه azmayeshgah	**lap** *n* لباس دامن damane' lebas
label *n* برچسب barchasb	

lapse v سپري‌شدن separi shodan

lapse n نسيان nesyan

larceny n دستبرد dastbord

lard n چربي‌خوک charbiye khouk

large adj وسيع vasi'e

lark n خوشي khoshi

larynx n ناي خشک khoshk-nay

laser n ليزر leyzer

lash v شلاق‌خوردن shalagh khordan

last adj اخر akhar

last v دوام‌داشتن davam dashtan

last name n فاميلى famili

lasting adj ديرپاي dirpay

latch n جفت cheft

late adv دير dir

lately adv اخيرا akhir

later adv ديرتر dirtar

lateral adj پهلويي pahloo'ei

latest adj دير dir

lather n کف‌صابون kaf saboon

latter adj آخر akher

latter n آخري akheri

laugh v خنديدن khandidan

laugh n صداي‌خنده sedaye' khandeh

laughable adj خنده‌دار khandeh dar

laughter n خنده khandeh

launch v به‌آب‌انداختن‌کشتي be ab andakhtan-e kashti

laundry n رختشوي‌خانه rakhtshoy khaneh

lavatory n دستشويي dastsho'ei

lavish adj فراوان faravan

law n قانون ghanoon

law-abiding adj پيروقانون peyrowe ghanoon

lawful adj قانوني ghanooni

lawmaker n قانون‌گزار ghanoon gozar

lawn n چمن chaman

lawsuit n مرافعه morafeh

lawyer n وكيل vakil

lax adj لخت lokht

lay iv خواباندن khabandan

lay n داستان‌منظوم dastan-e manzoom

lay off v متوقف‌ساختن motevaghef sakhtan

layout n طرح‌بندي tarh bandi

laziness n تنبلي tanbali

lazy adj تنبل tanbal

lead iv سوق‌دادن sowgh dadan

leader n سردسته sar-dasteh

leadership n رهبري rahbari

leaf n برگ barg

leaflet n بروشور boroushoor

league n اتحاديه etehadiyyeh

leak v تراوش‌کردن taravosh kardan

leak n رخنه rakhneh

leakage n تراوش taravosh

lean iv تكيه‌کردن takiyeh kardan

lean adj لاغر laghar

leaning n تكيه takiyeh

leap n جست‌وخيز jast-o-khiz

leap iv جستن jastan

leap year n سال‌کبيسه sal-e kabiseh

learn iv آموختن amoukhtan

learned adj دانا dana

lease *n* اجاره ejareh

lease *v* اجاره‌دادن ejareh dadan

leash *n* افسارسگ afsar-e sag

least *adj* کوچکترین kouchektarin

leather *n* چرم charm

leave *iv* باقي‌گذاردن baghi gozardan

lecture *n* سخنراني sokhanrani

ledger *n* معین moein

leech *n* زالو zaloo

leftovers *n* پس‌مانده pas mandeh

leg *n* پایه payeh

legal *adj* قانوني ghanooni

legalize *v* قانوني‌کردن ghanooni kardan

legend *n* افسانه afsaneh

legion *n* لژیون lezhiyon

legislate *v* قانون‌وضع‌کردن ghanoon vaz'e kardan

legislation *n* وضع‌قانون vaz'e ghanoon

legislature *n* مقننه moghananeh

legitimate *adj* حلال‌زاده halal zadeh

leisure *n* تن‌آسايي tan asaye

lemon *n* لیمو limoo

lemonade *n* لیموناد limoonad

lend *iv* قرض‌دادن gharz dadan

length *n* طول tool

lengthen *v* درازکردن deraz kardan

lengthy *adj* طویل tavil

leniency *n* نرمي narmi

lenient *adj* بامدارا ba modara

Lent *n* صیام siyam

lentil *n* عدس adas

leopard *n* پلنگ palang

leper *n* خوره khoreh

leprosy *n* جذام jozam

less *adj* کهتر kehtar

lessen *v* کمترکردن kamtar kardan

lesson *n* درس dars

let *iv* گذاشتن gozashtan

let go *v* رهاکردن raha kardan

let in *v* اجازه‌دخول‌دادن ejazehe voroud dadan

let out *v* اجازه‌خروج‌دادن ejazehe khorouj dadan

lethal *adj* کشنده koshandeh

letter *n* حرف harf

lettuce *n* کاهو kahoo

leukaemia *n* سرطان‌خون saratan-e khoun

level *n* سطح sat-h

lever *n* اهرم ahrom

leverage *n* به‌کاربردناهرم bekar bordan-e ahrom

levy *n* وضع‌مالیات vaz'e maliyat

lewd *adj* هرزه harzeh

liability *n* مسئولیت mas'ouliyat

liable *adj* مسئول mas'oul

liaison *n* رابطه‌نامشروع rabetehe' na-mashro'e

liar *adj* دروغگو gorooghgoo

libel *n* تهمت tohmat

liberate *v* آزادکردن azad kardan

liberation *n* نجات nejat

liberty *n* آزادي azadi

librarian *n* کتابدار ketabdar

library *n* کتابخانه ktebkhabeh

license *n* اجازه ejazeh

lick *v* لیسیدن lisidan

lid *n* سرپوش sarpoosh

lie *iv* خوابیدن khabidan

lie *n* دروغ dorough

lie *v* دروغ گفتن dorough goftan

lieutenant *n* ستوان setvan

life *n* جان jan

lifeguard *n* نگهبان negahban

lifeless *adj* مرده mordeh

lifestyle *n* طرززندگی tarz-e zendegi

lifetime *adv* عمر omr

lift *v* بلندکردن boland kardan

ligament *n* پیوند peyvand

light *iv* آشکارکردن ashkar kardan

light *adj* ضعیف za'eif

light *n* فروغ forough

lighter *n* فندک fandak

lighthouse *n* فانوس دریایی fanouse' darya'ei

lightly *adv* به سبکی be saboki

lightning *n* آذرخش azarakhsh

lightweight *n* سبک وزن sabok vazn

likable *adj* دوست داشتنی doust dashtani

like *v* دوست داشتن doust dashtan

like *pre* شبیه shabih

likelihood *n* احتمال ehtemal

likely *adv* محتمل mohtamal

liken *v* مانندکردن manand kardan

likeness *n* شباهت shabahat

likewise *adv* به همچنین be-hamchenin

lily *n* سوسن سفید sousane' safid

limb *n* عضو ozv

lime *n* لیموترش limoo-torsh

limestone *n* سنگ آهک sang ahak

limit *n* حد hadd

limitation *n* محدودیت mahdoudiyat

limp *v* شلیدن shalidan

line *n* خط khat

line up *v* به خط شدن be khat shodan

linen *n* کتان katan

linger *v* درنگ کردن derang kardan

lingerie *n* لباس زیر lebase' zir

lining *n* آستر astar

link *v* به هم پیوستن beham peyvastan

link *n* پیوند peyvand

lion *n* شیر shir

lip *n* لب lab

liqueur *n* لیکور likour

liquid *n* مایع maye'

liquidate *v* تسویه کردن tasviyeh kardan

liquor *n* مشروب mashroob

list *n* فهرست fehrest

list *v* فهرست کردن fehrest kardan

listen *v* شنیدن shanidan

listener *n* مستمع mostame'

litany *n* دعا do'a

litre *n* لیتر litr

literally *adv* لفظ به لفظ lafz be lafz

literate *adj* باسواد ba savad

literature *n* ادبیات adabiyat

litigate *v* طرح دعوی کردن tarhe' da'vi kardan

litigation *n* دعوی قضایی da'viye ghaza'ei

litter *n* تخت‌روان takht-e ravan

little *adj* کم kam

liturgy *n* آئین‌نماز a'eine' namaz

live *v* زندگی کردن zendegi kardan

livelihood *n* وسیله‌معاش vasilehe' mo'ash

lively *adj* باروح ba rooh

liver *n* جگر jegar

livestock *n* چارپایان‌اهلی da'm

livid *adj* کبود kabood

living room *n* اتاق‌نشیمن otaghe neshiman

lizard *n* مارمولک marmoulak

load *n* بار bar

load *v* پرکردن‌تفنگ por kardane' tofang

loaded *adj* مست mast

loaf *n* قرص‌نان ghors-e nan

loan *v* عاریه‌دادن ariyeh dadan

loan *n* وام vam

loathe *v* نفرت‌داشتن‌از nafrat dashtan az

lobby *n* راهرو rahroo

lobster *n* خرچنگ‌دریایی kharchange' darya'ei

locate *v* مکان‌یابی کردن makanyabi kardan

lock *n* قفل ghofl

lock *v* قفل‌کردن ghofl kardan

locksmith *n* قفل‌ساز ghoflsaz

locust *n* اقاقیا aghaghiya

lodging *n* منزل manzel

lofty *adj* ارجمند arjmand

log *n* کنده kondeh

logic *n* منطق mantegh

logical *adj* منطقی manteghi

logically *adv* منطقا" manteghan

loin *n* کمر kamar

loiter *v* درنگ کردن derang kardan

lone *adj* تنها tanha

loneliness *n* تنهائی tanha'ei

lonely *adv* به‌تنهایی be tanha'ei

loner *adj* گوشه‌گیر goushehgir

lonesome *adj* تنهاوبی‌کس tanha va bikas

long *adj* دراز deraz

longing *n* اشتیاق eshtiyagh

longitude *n* درازا deraza

look *n* نگاه negah

look *v* نگاه‌کردن negah kardan

look after *v* مراقب‌بودن moragheb boudan

look at *v* نگاه‌کردن negah kardan

look down *v* بانگاه‌ازروبردن ba negah az roo bordan

look for *v* نگران‌بودن negaran boudan

look into *v* رسیدگی‌کردن rasidegi kardan

look out *v* مواظب‌بودن movazeb boudan

looks *n* ظاهر zaher

loom *v* متلاطم‌شدن(دریا) motelatem shodan

loop *n* حلقه halgheh

loophole *n* سوراخ‌سنگر sourakhe sangar

loose *v* رهاکردن raha kardan

loose *adj* شل shol

loosen *v* شل‌کردن shol kardan

loot *v* غارت‌کردن gharat kardan

lord *n* صاحب saheb

lose *iv* گم‌کردن gom kardan
loser *n* بازنده bazandeh
loss *n* باخت bakht
lot *n* بسيار besyar
lotion *n* شستشو shostoshoo
lottery *n* قرعه‌کشي ghor'eh keshi
loud *adj* بلندآوا boland ava
loudly *adv* باصداى‌بلند basedaye boland
loudspeaker *n* بلندگو bolandgoo
lounge *n* محل‌استراحت mahalle esterahat
louse *n* شپش shepesh
lousy *adj* کثيف kasif
lovable *adj* دوست‌داشتني doustdashtani
love *v* دوست‌داشتن ashegh shodan
love *n* مهر mehr
lovely *adj* دوست‌داشتني doust dashtan
lover *n* عاشق ashegh
low *adj* پست past
lower *adj* پست‌تر pasttar
lowly *adj* خوار khar
loyal *adj* باوفا ba vafa
loyalty *n* وفاداري vafadari
lubricate *v* روغن‌زدن rowghanzadan
lubrication *n* روغن‌زني rowghanzani
lucid *adj* شفاف shafaf
luck *n* شانس shans
luckily *adv* خوشبختانه khoshbakhtaneh
lucky *adj* خوش‌اقبال khosheghbal
lucrative *adj* سودمند soudmand

luggage *n* توشه tousheh
lukewarm *adj* ولرم velarm
lull *n* آرامش aramesh
lumber *n* تخته takhteh
lumberyard *n* محوطه‌تيرفروشي mohavatehe' tir foroushi
luminous *adj* درخشان dorakhshan
lump *n* قلنبه gholonbeh
lunacy *n* ديوانگي divanegi
lunatic *adj* ديوانه divaneh
lunch *adj* ناهار nahar
lung *n* ضربت zarbat
lure *v* اغواکردن eghva kardan
lurk *v* کمين‌کردن kamin kardan
lust *v* شهوت‌داشتن shahvat dashtan
lust *v* هوس havas
luxurious *adj* خوش‌گذران khoshgozaran
luxury *n* خوش‌گذراني khoshgozarani
lynch *v* زجرکش‌کردن zajrkosh kardan

M

machine *n* ماشين mashin
machine gun *n* مسلسل mosalsal
mad *adj* ديوانه divaneh
madam *n* بانو banoo
madly *adv* ديوانه‌وار divanehvar
madman *n* مردديوانه mard-e divaneh

madness *n* ديوانگي divanegi

magazine *n* مجله majalleh

magic *n* جادو jadou

magical *adj* جادويي jadou'ei

magician *n* جادوگر jadougar

magistrate *n* دادرس dadrad

magnet *n* آهن‌ربا ahan-roba

magnetic *adj* آهن‌ربايي ahan-roba'ei

magnetism *n* كشش keshesh

magnificent *adj* باشكوه ba-shokouh

magnify *v* بزرگ كردن bozorg-kardan

magnitude *n* شكوه shokouh

maid *n* دختر پيشخدمت dokhtar-e pishkhedmat

maiden *n* دوشيزه doushizeh

mail *n* پست post

mail *v* پست كردن post kardan

mailbox *n* صندوق پست sandoughe posti

mailman *n* نامه‌رسان namehrasan

maim *v* معيوب كردن ma'youb kardan

main *adj* عمده omdeh

mainland *n* قاره gharreh

mainly *adv* اساسا "asa'san

maintain *v* نگهداري كردن negahdari kardan

majestic *adj* شاهانه shahaneh

majesty *n* اعليحضرت a'alahazrat

major *n* ارشد arshad

majority *n* اكثريت aksariyat

make *iv* ساختن sakhtan

make up *v* درست كردن dorost kardan

makeup *n* توالت towalet

malaria *n* مالاريا malariya

male *n* مذكر mozakar

malevolent *adj* بدخواه bad-khah

malfunction *v* بدعمل كردن bad amal kardan

malice *n* عناد e'nad

malignancy *n* بدخواهي bad khahi

malignant *adj* بدخيم bad khim

mall *n* تفرجگاه tafarojgah

malnutrition *n* سوءتغذيه so'e' taghziyeh

man *n* انسان ensan

manage *v* اداره كردن edareh kardan

manageable *adj* كنترل قابل ghabele kontrol

manager *n* مدير modir

mandate *n* حكم hokm

mandatory *n* اجبارى ejbari

manoeuvre *n* تمرين نظامي tamrine nezami

manger *n* آخور a'akhor

mangle *v* له كردن leh kardan

manhunt *n* تعقيب جنايتكاران ta'ghibe jenayatkaran

maniac *adj* مجنون majnoon

manifest *v* معلوم كردن ma'eloom kardan

manifesto *n* بيانيه bayaniyah

manipulate *v* اداره كردن edareh kardan

mankind *n* نوع بشر now'e' bashar

manliness *n* مردانگي mardanegi

manner *n* روش ravesh

mannerism *n* سبک‌شخصی sabke shakhsi

manners *n* آداب a'dab

manpower *n* نیروی‌انسانی nirouye ensani

mansion *n* عمارت‌بزرگ emarat-e bozorg

manslaughter *n* قتل‌نفس ghatl-e nafs

mantel *n* طاقچه taghcheh

mantelpiece *n* طاقچه‌بالابخاری taghchehe balaye bokhari

manual *adj* دستی dasti

manual *n* نظامنامه nezamnameh

manually *adv* به‌صورت‌دستی besourate dasti

manufacture *v* تولیدکردن towlid kardan

manure *n* کود koud

manuscript *n* دست‌خط dastkhat

many *adj* زیاد ziyad

map *n* نقشه naghsheh

marble *n* مرمر marmar

march *v* راه‌پیمایی‌کردن rahpeyma'ei kardan

March *n* مارس mars

mare *n* مادیان madiyan

margin *n* حاشیه hashiyeh

marginal *adj* حاشیه‌ای hashiye'ei

marinate *v* تردکردن tord kardan

marine *adj* دریایی darya'ei

marital *adj* تاهل ta'ahol

mark *n* علامت alamat

mark *v* علامت‌گذاردن alamat gozardan

marker *n* علامتگذاری alamatgozari

market *n* بازار bazar

marksman *n* گیرنشانه neshanehgir

marmalade *n* مربا morabba

marriage *n* ازدواج ezdevaj

married *adj* متاهل mote'ahel

marrow *n* مغز maghz

marry *v* ازدواج‌کردن ezdevaj kardan

Mars *n* مریخ merrikh

marshal *n* ارتشبد arteshbod

martial law *n* حکومت‌نظامی hokoumat nezami

martyr *n* شهید shahid

martyrdom *n* شهادت shahadat

marvel *n* شگفت shegeft

marvellous *adj* حیرت‌آور heyratavar

Marxist *n* پیرومارکس peyrowe Marks

marzipan *n* شیرینی‌بادامی shirini'e badami

mascara *n* ریمل rimel

masculine *adj* مذکر mozakar

mash *v* لاس‌زدن las zadan

mask *n* نقاب neghab

masochism *n* مازوخیسم mazokhism

mason *n* بنا banna

mass *n* توده toodeh

Mass *n* عشای‌ربانی eshay-e rabbani

massacre *n* کشتار koshtar

massage *n* ماساژ masazh

masseur *n* ماساژدهنده masazh-dahandeh

masseuse *n* دخترماساجور dokhtare masazhor

massive *adj* کلان kalan

mast *n* تیر tir

master *n* ارباب arbab

masterpiece *n* شاهکار shahkar

mat *n* پادري pa'dari

match *v* جوربودن jour boudan

match *n* کبریت kebrit

mate *n* جفت joft

material *n* جنس jens

materialism *n* مادهپرستي madeh-parasti

maternal *adj* مادرانه madaraneh

maternity *n* زایشگاه zayeshgah

math *n* حساب hesab

matriculate *v* نامنویسي کردن na'mnevisi kardan

matrimony *n* زناشویي zanashoo'ei

matter *n* ذات za't

mattress *n* تشک toshak

mature *adj* بالغ balegh

maturity *n* بلوغ bolough

maul *v* لهکردن leh kardan

maxim *n* پند pand

maximum *adj* حداکثر hadde' aksar

may *iv* امکانداشتن emkan dashtan

May *n* مه mei

maybe *adv* شاید shayad

mayhem *n* ضربوشتم zarbo-shatm

mayonnaise *n* مایونز mayonez

mayor *n* شهردار shahrdar

maze *n* هذیان hazyan

meadow *n* علفزار alafzar

meagre *adj* لاغر laghar

meal *n* غذا ghaza

mean *adj* پستفطرت past-fetrat

mean *iv* قصد داشتن ghasd dashtan

meaning *n* معني ma'ni

meaningful *adj* پرمعني por-ma'ni

meaningless *adj* بيمعني bi-ma'ni

means *n* توانایی tavana'ei

meanwhile *adv* ضمنا zemnan

measles *n* سرخک sorkhak

measure *v* سنجدین sanjidan

measurement *n* سنجش sanjesh

meat *n* گوشت gousht

meatball *n* کوفته koufteh

mechanic *n* مکانیک mekanik

mechanism *n* مکانیکي mekaniki

mechanize *v* ماشیني کردن mashini kardan

medal *n* نشان neshan

medallion *n* مدالبزرگ medal-e bozorg

meddle *v* فضوليکردن fozouli-kardan

mediate *v* وساطتکردن vesatat kardan

mediator *n* میانجي miyanji

medication *n* تجویزدوا tajviz-e darou

medicinal *adj* دارویي darou'ei

medicine *n* دارو darou

medieval *adj* قرونوسطي ghoroone vosta

mediocre *adj* میانحال miyanhaal

mediocrity *n* میانگین miyangin

meditate *v* تفکرکردن tafakor kardan

meditation *n* تعمق ta'amoogh

medium *adj* متوسط motevaset

meek *adj* بردبار bordbaar

meekness *n* فروتني foroutani

meet *iv* مواجه‌شدن movajeh shodan

meeting *n* همایش hamayesh

melancholy *n* مالیخولیا malikhouliya

mellow *adj* رسیده resideh

mellow *v* نرم‌کردن narm kardan

melodic *adj* خوش‌آهنگ khosh a'hang

melody *n* آهنگ‌شیرین a'hange shirin

melon *n* هندوانه hendavaneh

melt *v* آب‌شدن a'ab shodan

member *n* عضو ozv

membership *n* عضویت ozviyat

membrane *n* پوست poust

memento *n* خاطره khatereh

memo *n* یادداشت yad dasht

memoirs *n* سرگذشت sargozasht

memorable *adj* یادآوردني yad avardani

memorize *v* بخاطرسپردن bekhater sepordan

memory *n* حافظه hafezeh

men *n* مردان mardan

menace *n* تهدید tahdid

mend *v* تعمیرکردن ta'mir kardan

meningitis *n* مننژیت menenzhit

menopause *n* یائسگي ya'esegi

menstruation *n* قاعدگي gha'edegi

mental *adj* مغزي maghzi

mentality *n* روحیه rohiyeh

mentally *adv* روحا" rouhan

mention *n* تذکر tazakor

mention *v* ذکرکردن zekr kardan

menu *n* صورت‌غذا sourat-e ghaza

merchandise *n* کالا kala

merchant *n* بازرگان bazargan

merciful *adj* بخشنده bakhshandeh

merciless *adj* بیرحم bi-rahm

mercury *n* عطارد otarod

mercy *n* رحم rahm

merely *adv* فقط faghat

merge *v* ترکیب‌کردن tarkib kardan

merger *n* امتزاج emtezaj

merit *n* شایستگي shayestegi

mermaid *n* حوري‌دریایي houri darya'ei

merrily *adv* به‌خوشي be khoshi

merry *adj* شاد shad

mesh *n* سوراخ sourakh

mesmerize *v* هیپنوتیزم‌کردن hipnotizm kardan

mess *n* یک‌ظرف‌غذا yek zarfe ghaza

message *n* پیام payam

messenger *n* پیام‌آور payam -avar

Messiah *n* مسیح‌موعود masih-e mowoud

messy *adj* شلوغ sholough

metal *n* فلز felez

metallic *adj* فلزي felezi

metaphor *n* کنایه kenayeh

meteor *n* شهاب shahab

meter *n* متر metr

method *n* شیوه shiveh

methodical *adj* اسلوب‌دار osloub dar

meticulous *adj* باریک‌بین barik-bin

metric *adj* متری metri

metropolis *n* کلان‌شهر kalanshahr

mice *n* موش‌ها moushha

microbe *n* میکرب mikrob

microphone *n* میکروفن mikrofon

microscope *n* ذره‌بین zare-bin

microwave *n* میکروویو mikeowave

midair *n* معلق mo'allagh

midday *n* نیمروز nimrooz

middle *n* وسط vasat

middleman *n* دلال dallal

midget *n* ریزاندام riz-andam

midnight *n* نیمه‌شب nimeh-shab

midsummer *n* چله‌تابستان chelehe-tabestan

midwife *n* قابله ghabeleh

mighty *adj* مقتدر moghtader

migraine *n* میگرن migren

migrant *n* مهاجر mohajer

migrate *v* مهاجرت‌کردن mohajerat kardan

mild *adj* ملایم molayem

mildly *adv* به‌نرمی be-narmi

mile *n* میل(1609.35متر) mill

mileage *n* سنجش‌برحسب‌میل sanjesh bar hasb-e mill

militant *adj* ستیزگر setizegar

milk *n* شیر shir

milkman *n* شیرفروش shirforoush

milky *adj* شیری shiri

mill *n* آسیاب a'asiyab

millennium *n* هزاره hezareh

milligram *n* یک‌هزارم‌گرم yek-hezarome-geram

millilitre *n* یک‌هزارم‌لیتر yek-hezarome-litr

million *n* میلیون million

millionaire *adj* میلیونر millioner

mime *v* تقلیددرآوردن taghlid dar avardan

mince *v* ریزریزکردن rizriz kardan

mincemeat *n* گوشت‌قیمه‌شده gousht-e ghimeh shodeh

mind *n* فکر fekr

mind *v* مراقب‌بودن moragheb boudan

mindful *adj* متفکر motefaker

mindless *adj* بی‌فکر bifekr

mine *v* استخراج‌کردن estekhtaj kardan

mine *pro* مال‌من ma'le'man

mine *n* معدن ma'dan

minefield *n* میدان‌مین meydane min

miner *n* مین‌گذار min-gozar

mineral *n* آب‌معدنی a'be' ma'dani

mingle *v* آمیختن amikhtan

miniature *n* مینیاتور miniyator

minimum *n* حداقل hadde' aghal

miniskirt *n* دامن‌کوتاه damane koutah

minister *n* وزیر vazir

ministry *n* وزارتخانه vezaratkhaneh

minor *adj* صغیر saghir

minority *n* اقلیت aghaliat

mint *n* نعناع na'na

minus *adj* منها menha
minute *n* دقیقه daghigheh
miracle *n* معجزه mo'ejezeh
miraculous *adj* معجزه‌آسا mo'ejeze asa
mirage *n* سراب sarab
mirror *n* آئینه a'eineh
misbehave *v* بدرفتاری کردن badraftari kardan
miscalculate *v* پیش‌بینی‌غلط کردن pishbini-ghalat
miscarriage *n* عدم‌توفیق adam-e towfigh
mischief *n* شیطنت sheytanat
mischievous *adj* بدجنس bad-jens
misconduct *n* بدرفتاری badraftari
misconstrue *v* بدتعبیر کردن badta'bir kardan
misdemeanour *n* بزه bezeh
miser *n* خسیس khasis
miserable *adj* تیره‌روز tireh-rooz
misery *n* بدبختی badbakhti
misfit *adj* ناجور najour
misfortune *n* بدشانسی badshansi
misgiving *n* شبهه shobheh
misguided *adj* بدراهنمایی‌شده badrahnama'ei shodeh
misinterpret *v* به‌غلط‌تفسیر کردن beghalat-tafsir kardan
misjudge *v* بدداوری کردن bad-davari kardan
mislead *v* به‌اشتباه‌انداختن be-eshtebah andakhtan
mismanage *v* بداداره کردن bad-edareh kardan
misplace *v* گم کردن gomkardan
misprint *n* غلط چاپی ghalate-chapi

miss *n* دوشیزه doushizeh
miss *v* نداشتن nadashtan
missile *n* موشک moushak
missing *adj* مفقود mafghoud
mission *n* ماموریت ma'mouriat
missionary *n* مبلغ‌مذهبی mobaleghe maz-habi
mist *n* غبار ghobar
mistake *n* اشتباه eshtebah
mistake *iv* اشتباه کردن eshtebah kardan
mistaken *adj* اشتباهی eshtebahi
mister *n* آقا a'gha
mistreat *v* دشنام‌دادن doshnam dadan
mistreatment *n* بدرفتاری badraftari
mistress *n* معشوقه ma'shougheh
mistrust *n* بدگمانی badgomani
misty *adj* مبهم mobham
misuse *n* سوءاستفاده so'e'estefadeh
mitigate *v* تسکین دادن taskin dadan
mix *v* آمیختن amikhtan
mix *n* مخلوط makhloot
mixed-up *adj* مغشوش maghshoush
mixture *n* آمیزه amizeh
moan *n* زاری zari
moan *v* زاری کردن zari kardan
mob *v* ازدحام کردن ezdeham kardan
mob *n* انبوه‌مردم anbouh-e mardom
mobile *adj* متحرک moteharek
mobilize *v* بسیج کردن basij kardan

mock *v* استهزاءکردن estehza' kardan

mockery *n* استهزاء estehza

mode *n* رسم rasm

model *n* نمونه nemouneh

moderate *v* تعدیل کردن ta'dil kardan

modern *adj* امروزي emrouzi

modernize *v* امروزي کردن emrouzi kardan

modest *adj* فروتن foroutani

modesty *n* فروتني foroutani

modify *v* اصلاح کردن eslah kardan

moisten *v* مرطوب شدن martoub shodan

moisture *n* رطوبت،نم rotoubat

molar *n* دندان آسیاب dandane-asiyab

mould *v* قالب زدن ghaleb zadan

mole *n* خال khal

molecule *n* مولکول moulkool

molest *v* معترض شدن mo'tarez shodan

mom *n* مادر madar

moment *n* هنگام hangam

momentarily *adv* دم به دم dam-be-dam

momentous *adj* خطیر khatir

monarch *n* سلطان soltan

monarchy *n* رژیم سلطنتي rezhime saltanati

monastery *n* صومعه soume'eh

monastic *adj* رهباني rahbani

Monday *n* دوشنبه doshanbeh

money *n* پول pool

money order *n* حواله havaleh

monk *n* راهب raheb

monkey *n* میمون meymoon

monogamy *n* تک همسري tak hamsari

monologue *n* تک گويي takgou'ei

monopolize *v* انحصاري کردن enhesari kardan

monotonous *adj* یکنواخت yeknavakht

monotony *n* یکنواختي yeknavakhti

monsoon *n* موسمي باد bad-e' mowsemi

monster *n* هیولا hayoula

monstrous *adj* غول پیکر ghoulpeykar

month *n* ماه mah

monthly *adv* ماهانه mahaneh

monument *n* بنای یادبود banaye yadboud

monumental *adj* یادگاري yadgari

mood *n* حالت ha'lat

moody *adj* عبوس aboos

moon *n* ماه mah

moor *v* لنگر انداختن langar andakhtan

mop *v* پاک کردن pak kardan

moral *adj* اخلاقي akhlaghi

morality *n* اخلاق akhlagh

more *adj* بیش bish

moreover *adv* بعلاوه be-alaveh

morning *n* صبح sobh

moron *adj* کودن kowdan

morphine *n* مرفین morfin

morsel *n* لقمه loghmeh

mortal *adj* فاني fa'ni

mortality *n* مرگ و میر marg-o-mir

mortar *n* هاون ha'van

mortgage *n* رهن rahn

mortify *v* رنجاندن ranjandan

mortuary *n* مردهشويخانه morde'shoye-khaneh

mosaic *n* موزائيک mouzaeik

mosque *n* مسجد masjed

mosquito *n* پشه pashsheh

most *adj* بيشترين bishtarin

mostly *adv* بيشتر bishtar

motel *n* مهمانخانه mehmankhaneh

moth *n* بيد bid

mother *n* مادر ma'dar

motherhood *n* مادري ma'dari

mother-in-law *n* مادرزن ma'dar-zan

motion *n* جنبش jonbesh

motionless *adj* بيحركت bi-harkat

motivate *v* تحريک کردن tahrik kardan

motive *n* انگيزه angizeh

motor *n* موتور motor

motorcycle *n* موتورسيکلت motorsiklet

motorist *n* ماشينسوار mashin-savar

motto *n* حکمت hekmat

mount *v* صعودکردن so'oud kardan

mount *n* کوه kooh

mountain *n* کوهستان koohestan

mountainous *adj* کوهستانی koohestani

mourn *v* سوگواریکردن sougvari kardan

mourning *n* سوگواری sougvari

mouse *n* موش moosh

mouth *n* دهان daha'n

move *v* حرکتدادن harkat dadan

move back *v* عقبکشيدن aghab keshidan

move forward *v* جلوکشيدن jelow keshidan

move out *v* حرکتکنيد harkat konid

move up *v* تکانخوردن taka'n khordan

movement *n* حرکت harkat

movie *n* سينما sinema

mow *v* چيدن chidan

much *adv* بسيار besyar

mud *n* لجن lajan

muddy *adj* گلآلود gela'lood

muffle *v* ساکتکردن saket kardan

muffler *n* صداخفهکن seda'khafehkon

mug *v* کتکزدن kotak zadan

mug *n* ليوان livan

mugger *n* دزدخيابانی dozde'khiabani

mugging *n* دهنکجی dahankaji

mule *n* قاطر ghater

multiple *adj* مضاعف moza'af

multiply *v* تکثيرکردن taksir kardan

multitude *n* بسياری besyari

mumble *v* منمنکردن menmenkardan

mummy *n* موميا moumiya

mumps *n* اوريون oriyoon

munch *v* جويدن javidan

munitions *n* مهمات mohemma't

murder *n* قتل ghatl

murderer *n* قاتل ghatel

murky *adj* تیره tireh

murmur *n* زمزمه zamzameh

murmur *v* زمزمه‌کردن zamzameh kardan

muscle *n* ماهیچه ma'hicheh

muse *v* اندیشه‌کردن andisheh kardan

muse *n* شگفت shegeft

museum *n* موزه moozeh

mushroom *n* قارچ gharch

music *n* موزیک moozik

musical *adj* موزیکال moosikal

musician *n* نوازنده navazandeh

Muslim *n* مسلمان mosalma'n

must *iv* باید bayad

moustache *n* سبیل sibil

mustard *n* خردل khardal

muster *v* احضارکردن ehzar kardan

mutate *v* تغییردادن taghyir dadan

mute *adj* گنگ gong

mutilate *v* اخته‌کردن akhteh kardan

mutiny *n* سرکشی sarkeshi

mutually *adv* متقابلا moteghabelan

muzzle *n* پوزه pouzeh

muzzle *v* پوزه‌بندزدن pouzehband zadan

my *adj* متعلق‌به‌من mote'alegh be man

myopic *adj* نزدیک‌بین nazdikbin

myself *pro* خودم khodam

mysterious *adj* مرموز marmooz

mystery *n* رمز ramz

mystic *adj* رمزی ramzi

mystify *v* رمزی‌کردن ramzi kardan

myth *n* اسطوره ostoureh

N

nag *v* نق‌زدن negh zadan

nagging *adj* عیب‌جویی eibjoo'ei

nail *n* ناخن nakhon

naive *adj* ریا بی biriya

naked *adj* برهنه berahneh

name *n* اسم esm

namely *adv* بنام bena'm

nanny *n* پرستاربچه parastare bacheh

nap *n* چرت chort

napkin *n* دستمال dastma'l

narcotic *n* مخدر mokhader

narrate *v* نقالی‌کردن naghali kardan

narrow *adj* باریک barik

nasty *adj* زننده zanandeh

nation *n* ملت mellat

national *adj* ملی melli

nationality *n* ملیت melliyat

nationalize *v* ملی‌کردن melli kardan

native *adj* بومی boomi

natural *adj* طبیعی tabi'ei

naturally *adv* طبعا "tab'an

naughty *adj* شریر sharir

nausea *n* دل‌آشوب del-a'shoub

nave *n* سالن salon

navel *n* ناف na'f

navigate v هدایت کردن(هواپیما و غیره) hedayat kardan

navy n نیروی دریایی niroye darya'ei

near pre نزدیک nazdik

nearby adj همین اطراف hamin atra'f

nearly adv تقریبا taghriban

nearsighted adj نزدیک بین nazdikbin

neat adj شسته ورفته shosteh-rofteh

neatly adv ازروی سلیقه az roye'saligheh

necessary adj ضروری zarouri

necessitate v ایجاب کردن eijab kardan

necessity n ضرورت zaroorat

neck n گردن gardan

necklace n گردن بند gardanband

necktie n کراوات keravat

nectarine n شلیل shalil

need n نیاز niyaz

need v نیازداشتن niyaz dashtan

needle n سوزن soozan

needless adj بی نیاز bi-niyaz

needy adj نیازمند niyazmand

negative adj منفی manfi

neglect n اهمال ehma'l

neglect v غفلت کردن ghaflat kardan

negligence n غفلت ghaflat

negligent adj بی دقت bi-deghat

negotiate v مذاکره کردن mozakereh kardan

neighbour n همسایه hamsaye'

neighbourhood n همسایگی hamsaye'gi

neither adj هیچیک hichyek

nephew n پسربرادر pesar-e baradar

nerve n عصب asab

nervous adj عصبانی asabani

nest n آشیانه a'shiyaneh

net n خالص khales

network n شبکه shabakeh

neurotic adj عصبی asabi

neutral adj بی طرف bi-taraf

neutralize v خنثی کردن khonsa kardan

never adv هرگز hargez

new adj جدید jadid

newborn n نوزاد nowza'd

newcomer n تازه وارد tazehvared

newly adv به تازگی be-tazegi

newlywed adj تازه عروس tazeh-aroos

news n اخبار akhbar

newscast n اخباررادیو akhbare radiyo

newsletter n خبرنامه khabarnameh

newspaper n روزنامه rooznameh

newsstand n روزنامه فروشی rooznameh forooshi

next adj بعدی na'di

nice adj نازنین na'zanin

nicely adv به خوبی be-khoubi

nickel n ورشو varshow

nickname n لقب laghab

nicotine n نیکوتین nikotin

niece n دختربرادریاخواهر dokhtar-e baradar

night n شب shab

nightfall n شبانگاه shabangah

nightgown n لباس شب lebas-e shab

nightingale n بلبل bolbol

nightmare n كابوس kaboos

nine adj نه noh

nineteen adj نوزده noozdah

ninety adj نود navad

ninth adj نهمين nohomin

nip v گاز گرفتن ga'z gereftan

nip n نيشگون nishgoon

nipple n نوک پستان nok-e pestan

nitrogen n نيتروژن nitrozhen

no one pro هيچکس hich-kas

nobility n اصالت esa'lat

noble adj اصيل asil

nobody pro هيچ کس hich-kas

nocturnal adj شبانه shabaneh

nod v سرتکان دادن sartakan dadan

noise n سروصدا saro-seda

noisily adv باسروصدا ba saro-seda

noisy adj شلوغ sholoogh

nominate v کانديدکردن kandid kardan

none pre به هيچ وجه be hich vajh

nonetheless c بااينحال ba in ha'l

nonsense n مزخرف mozakhraf

non-smoker n غيرسيگاری gheyre-sigari

non-stop adv يکسره yeksareh

noodle n رشته فرنگي reshteh-farangi

noon n ظهر zohr

nor c نه اين ونه آن na-in-o-na-'an

norm n هنجار hanja'r

normal adj معمولي ma'mouli

normalize v طبيعي کردن tabi'ei kardan

normally adv معمولا ma'moulan

north n شمال shomal

northeast n شمال شرقي shomal-e sharghi

northern adj شمالي shomali

northerner adj اهل شمال ahle'shomal

nose n بيني bini

nosedive adv غوطهور ghoutehvar

nostalgia n احساس غربت ehsas-e ghorbat

nostril n سوراخ بيني sourakhe bini

nosy adj فضول fozool

not adv نه خير na-kheyr

notable adj جالب توجه jalebe tavajoh

notably adv برجسته barjasteh

notary n دفتراسنادرسمي daftare asnade rasmi

notation n ثبت sabt

note v ثبت کردن sabt kardan

notebook n دفتريادداشت daftare yad'dasht

nothing n هيچ hich

notice n اعلان e'elan

notice v ملاحظه کردن molahezeh kardan

noticeable adj قابل ملاحظه ghabele molahezeh

notification n اخطار ekhta'r

notify v اخطارکردن ekhta'r kardan

notion n تصور tasavor

notorious adj بدنام badnam

noun n اسم esm

nourish v خوراک‌دادن khorak dadan

nourishment n خوراک khorak

novel n رمان roma'n

novelist n رمان‌نویس roma'n-nevis

novelty n تازگي taze'gi

November n نوامبر novambre

novice n تازه‌کار tazeh-kar

now adv اکنون aknoon

nowadays adv امروزه emroozeh

nowhere adv جا هیچ hich-ja

nuance n فرق‌جزیي farghe joz'ei

nuclear adj هسته‌اي haste'ei

nude adj عریان oryan

nudist n طرفدار‌برهنگي tarafdar-e berahnegi

nudity n برهنگي berahnegi

nuisance n آزار a'za'r

null adj پوچ pooch

nullify v لغوکردن laghv kardan

numb adj کرخت karakht

number n شماره shomareh

numbness n بی‌رگي bi-ragi

numerous adj بی‌شمار bi-shomar

nun n راهبه rahebeh

nurse n پرستار parastar

nursery n شیرخوارگاه shirkhargah

nurture v پروردن parvardan

nut n آجیل a'jil

nutrition n تغذیه taghziyeh

nutritious adj مغذي moghazi

nutty adj پرفندق porfandogh

nylon n نایلون naylon

nymph n حوري houri

O

oak n بلوط balout

oar n پارو paroo

oath n سوگند sogand

oatmeal n آردجو a'rde-jow

obedience n اطاعت eta'at

obese adj چاق chagh

obey v اطاعت‌کردن ata'at kardan

object v اعتراض‌کردن e'eteraz kardan

object n چیز chiz

objection n مخالفت mokhalefat

objective n هدف hadaf

obligate v متعهد‌کردن mote'ahed kardan

obligation n التزام elteza'm

oblige v مرهون‌ساختن marhoon sakhtan

obliged adj مرهون marhoon

oblique adj مورب movarab

obliterate v معدوم‌کردن ma'doom kardan

oblivion n نسیان nesyan

oblong adj کشیده keshideh

obnoxious adj مضر mozer

obscene adj موهن moohen

obscenity n وقاحت veghahat

obscure adj مبهم mobham

obscurity n ابهام ebham

observatory n رصدخانه rasadkhaneh

observe v مشاهده‌کردن moshahedeh kardan

obsess v آزارکردن a'zar kardan

obsession *n* وسواس vasva's	officer *n* مامور ma'mour
obsolete *adj* متروک matrook	official *adj* رسمی rasmi
obstacle *n* محظور mahzour	officiate *v* اداره‌کردن edareh kardan
obstinate *adj* سرسخت sarsakht	
obstruct *v* مسدودکردن masdoud kardan	offset *v* جبران‌کردن jobran kardan
	offspring *n* مبدا mabd'a
obstruction *n* انسداد ensedad	often *adv* بسی basi
obtain *v* گرفتن gereftan	oil *n* نفت naft
obvious *adj* آشکار a'shka'r	oilfield *n* منطقه‌نفتخیز mantaghehe naftkhiz
occasion *n* موقعیت mowghe'eiyat	
occupation *n* اشغال eshghal	ointment *n* پماد poma'd
occupy *v* اشغال‌کردن eshghal kardan	okay *adv* بسیارخوب besyarkhoub
	old *adj* پیر pir
occur *v* رخ‌دادن rokh dadan	old age *n* پیری piri
ocean *n* اقیانوس oghiyanous	old-fashioned *adj* ازمدافتاده azmodoftadeh
October *n* ماه‌اکتبر oktobr	
octopus *n* پا هشت hashtpa	olive *n* زیتون zeytoon
odd *adj* فرد fard	Olympics *n* المپیک olampik
oddity *n* غرابت gherabat	omelette *n* املت omlet
odds *n* فرق fargh	omen *n* پیشگویی pishgoo'ei
odious *adj* نفرت‌انگیز nafratangiz	ominous *adj* شوم shoom
odometer *n* کیلومترشمار kiloometrshomar	omission *n* حذف hazf
	omit *v* حذف‌کردن hazf kardan
odour *n* بو boo	on *pre* بالای balaye'
odyssey *n* قطعه‌منظوم‌رزمی ghate'he manzoome razmi	once *adv* دفعتا daf'atan
	once *c* یک‌مرتبه yek martabeh
of *pre* از az	one *adj* یک yek
off *adv* قطع ghate'	oneself *p* خودشخص khode shakhs
offend *v* صدمه‌زدن sadameh zadan	
offence *n* هجوم hojoum	onetime *adv* یکوقتی yekvaghti
offensive *adj* متجاوز motejavez	ongoing *adj* مداوم modavem
offer *n* پیشنهاد pishnahad	onion *n* پیاز piyaz
offer *v* پیشنهادکردن pishnahad dadan	onlooker *n* مراقب moragheb
	onlooker *n* ناظر na'zer
offering *n* پیشکش pishkesh	only *adv* فقط faghat
office *n* دفتر daftar	onset *n* تاخت‌وتاز takht-o-taz

onslaught *n* يورش youresh
onwards *adv* به‌طرف‌جلو betarafejeloo
opaque *adj* مات ma'at
open *adj* باز ba'z
open *v* گشودن goshoudan
open-ended *adj* بی‌انتها bi-enteha
opening *n* دهانه dahaneh
openly *adv* آشكارا a'shkara'
open-minded *adj* روشنفكر rowshanfekr
openness *n* آشكارى a'shkari
opera *n* اپرا opera
operate *v* عمل كردن amal kardan
operation *n* عمل amal
opinion *n* نظر nazar
opinionated *adj* خودسر khodsar
opium *n* تریاک tarya'k
opponent *n* خصم khasm
opportune *adj* به جا be-ja
opportunity *n* فرصت forsat
oppose *v* مصاف دادن masa'f dadan
opposite *adj* ضد zedd
opposition *n* ضدیت zeddiyat
oppress *v* ستم كردن setam kardan
oppression *n* بیداد bidad
opt *v* برگزیدن bargozidan
optical *adj* نوری nouri
optician *n* عینک‌ساز einaksa'z
optimism *n* خوش‌بینی khoshbini
optimistic *adj* خوش‌بینانه khoshbinaneh
option *n* انتخاب entekhab
optional *adj* انتخابی entekhabi
opulence *n* توانگری tavangari
or *c* یا ya

oral *adj* شفاهی shafahi
orally *adv* شفاها" shafahan
orange *n* پرتقال porteghal
orangutan *n* بوزینه boozineh
orbit *n* مدار mada'r
orchard *n* شكوفه‌زار shekoufeh-zar
orchestra *n* اركستر orkestr
orchid *n* ارغوانی arghavani
ordain *v* وضع كردن vaz'e kardan
ordeal *n* شاق sha'gh
order *n* دستور dastour
ordinarily *adv* معمولا" ma'moulan
ordinary *adj* معمولی ma'mouli
ordination *n* انتصاب entesab
ore *n* سنگ‌معدن sange'ma'dan
organ *n* اندام andam
organism *n* اندامگان andamgan
organist *n* نوازنده‌ارگ navazandehe org
organization *n* تشكیلات tashkila't
organize *v* سازمان دادن sazeman dadan
orient *n* خاور kha'var
oriental *adj* شرقی sharghi
orientation *n* گرایش gera'yesh
oriented *adj* متمایل به motemayel-be
origin *n* منشا mansha'e
original *adj* اصیل asil
originate *v* سرچشمه‌گرفتن sarchashmeh gereftan
ornament *n* زیور zivar
ornamental *adj* تزیینی taz'eini
ornate *v* مزین mozayan
orphan *n* یتیم yatim

orphanage *n* پرورشگاه parvareshgah

orthodox *adj* مطابق‌مرسوم motabeghe marsoom

ostentatious *adj* متظاهر moteza'her

ostrich *n* شترمرغ shotormorgh

other *adj* دیگری digari

otherwise *adv* وگرنه vagarne'

otter *n* سموردریایی samoure darya'ei

ought to *iv* بایست bayest

ounce *n* اونس onse

our *adj* ما مال ma'le' ma'

ours *pro* مال‌خودمان ma'le' khodeman

oust *v* اخراج‌کردن ekhraj kardan

ouster *n* اخراج ekhraj

out *adv* حذف‌شده hazf shodeh

outbreak *n* شیوع shiyo'e

outburst *n* فوران favaran

outcast *adj* مطرود matrood

outcome *n* نتیجه natijeh

outcry *n* غریو ghariv

outdated *adj* منسوخ mansoukh

outdo *v* شکست‌دادن shekast dadan

outdoors *adv* درهوای‌آزاد dar havaye 'azad

outer *adj* بیرونی birouni

outfit *n* سازوبرگ saz-o-barg

outgoing *adj* صادرشونده sader shavandeh

outgrow *v* بزرگ‌ترشدن‌از bozorgtar shodan az

outing *n* تفرج tafaroj

outlast *v* بیشترطول‌کشیدن bishtar toolkeshidan

outlaw *v* ممنوع‌کردن mamnoo'e kardan

outlet *n* پریز periz

outline *n* طرح‌کلی tarhe' kolli

outlive *v* بیشتردوام‌آوردن bishtar dava'm avardan

outlook *n* چشم‌انداز chashmanda'z

outmoded *adj* غیرمتداول gheyre' motedavel

outnumber *v* افزون‌بودن‌بر afzoon boodan bar

outpatient *n* بیمارسرپایی‌بیمارستان bima're' sarpa'ei

outperform *v* کارخارق‌العاده kar-e khareghol'adeh

outpouring *n* بیرون‌ریز biroonriz

output *n* خروجی khorooji

outrage *n* تخطی takhati

outrageous *adj* ظالمانه za'le'maneh

outright *adj* آشکار a'shka'r

outrun *v* پیش‌افتادن pishoftadan

outset *n* ابتدا ebteda'

outshine *v* تحت‌الشعاع‌قراردادن tahtulsho'a gharardadan

outside *adv* بیرون biroun

outsider *n* خارجی khareji

outskirts *n* پیرامون pira'moon

outspoken *adj* رک rokk

outstanding *adj* برجسته barjasteh

outstretched *adj* مبسوط mabsout

outward *adj* بیرونی birooni

outweigh *v* مهمتربودن‌از mohemtar boudan-az

oval *adj* بیضی beyzi

ovary *n* تخمدان tokhmda'n

ovation n شادي‌وسرورعمومي shadi va soroure omoumi

oven n اجاق ojagh

over ore روی rouye'

overall adv به‌طوركلی betowre' kolli

overbearing adj طاقت‌فرسا taghatfarsa'

overboard adv روي‌كشتي rouye kashti

overcast adj ابري‌وتيره abri va tireh

overcharge v غلوكردن gholov kardan

overcoat n پالتو paltow

overcome v غلبه‌يافتن ghalabeh yaftan

overcrowded adj پرجمعيت por-jam'eiyat

overdo v به‌حدافراطرساندن be-hadde' efrat rasandan

overdose n داروي‌بيش‌ازحد darouye bish-az-hadd

overdue adj سررسيده sarrasideh

overestimate v دست‌بالاگرفتن daste' ba'la' gereftan

overflow v طغيان‌كردن toghyan kardan

overhaul v تعمیراساسی ta'mir-e asasi

overload v زيادبار‌كردن ziyad ba'r kardan

overlook v مشرف‌بودن moshref boudan

overnight adv درمدت‌شب dar moddate' shab

overpower v فتح‌كردن ghalabeh kardan

overrate v زيادبرآوردكردن ziyad baravard kardan

override v باطل‌ساختن ba'telsakhtan

override v پايمال‌كردن payma'l kardan

overrule v كنارگذاشتن kenar gozashtan

overrun v تاراج‌كردن ta'raj kardan

overseas adv ماوراءدريا ma'vara'e' bahar

oversee v سركشي‌كردن sarkeshi kardan

oversight n سهو sahv

overstep v ازحدتجاوزكردن az had taja'voz kardan

overtake v ردشدن‌از radshodan-az

overthrow v برانداختن baranda'khtan

overtime adv بيش‌ازوقت‌معين bishazvaghte' mo'ayan

overturn v واژگون‌كردن vazhgoun kardan

overview n بازبيني ba'zbini

overweight adj چاق cha'gh

overwhelm v غوطه‌ورساختن ghoutehvar sa'khtan

owe v مديون‌بودن madyoun boudan

owing to adv به‌علت be-e'llate'

owl n جغد joghd

own v داشتن da'shtan

own adj شخصي shakhsi

owner v صاحب saheb

ownership n مالكيت ma'lekiyat

ox n گاونر gav-e nar

oxen n نره‌خر narreh-khar

oxygen *n* اكسيژن oksizhen

oyster *n* صدف خوراكي sadaf

P

pace *v* قدم زدن ghadam zadan

pace *n* گام ga'm

pacify *v* تسكين دادن taskin dadan

pack *v* بسته بندي كردن bastehbandi kardan

package *n* بسته بندی bastehbandi

pact *n* عهد ahd

pad *v* باآب و تاب گفتن ba a'b-o-tab goftan

padding *n* لفاف lafaf

paddle *v* نوازش كردن navazesh kardan

padlock *n* انسداد ensedad

pagan *adj* مشرک moshrek

page *n* صفحه safheh

pail *n* سطل satl

pain *n* درد dard

painful *adj* دردناک dardna'k

painkiller *n* آرامبخش a'rambakhsh

painless *adj* بی درد bi-dard

paint *n* رنگ rang

paint *v* رنگ كردن rang kardan

paintbrush *n* قلم مو ghalammoo

painter *n* نقاش naghash

painting *n* نقاشي naghashi

pair *n* جفت joft

pyjamas *n* شلوار گشاد shalvare goshad

pal *n* يار yar

palace *n* كاخ kakh

pale *adj* كمرنگ kamrang

palette *n* جعبه رنگ نقاشي jabeh range naghashi

palm *n* نخل nakhl

palpable *adj* قابل لمس ghabele lams

pamper *v* به ناز پروردن be naz parvardan

pamphlet *n* جزوه jozveh

pan *n* ماهي تابه mahi tabeh

pancreas *n* لوزالمعده louz-al me'deh

pander *v* جاكشي كردن ja keshi kardan

panic *n* وحشت vahshat

panorama *n* منظره manzareh

panther *n* پلنگ palang

pantry *n* آبدارخانه abdar khaneh

pants *n* تنكه tonokeh

pantyhose *n* جوراب شلواری jourab shalvari

papa *n* بابا baba

papacy *n* سمت پاپي semate Papi

papaya *n* انبه هندي anbeh-ye hendi

paper *n* كاغذ kaghaz

paper clip *n* منگنه manganeh

paperwork *n* كاغذبازي kaghaz bazi

parable *n* قياس ghiyas

parachute *n* چتر نجات chatre nejat

parade *n* رژه rezheh

paradise *n* بهشت behesht

paradox *n* بيان مغاير bayan-e moghayer

paragraph *n* پاراگراف paragraf

parakeet *n* طوطي کوچک سبزرنگ toutiye kouchake sabz rang

parallel *n* موازي movazi

paralysis *n* فلج falaj

paralyze *v* فلج کردن falaj kardan

parameters *n* پارامترهاي واقعي parametr-haye vagheie

paramount *adj* بزرگتر bozorg tar

paranoid *adj* پارانویایی paranoyayi

parasite *n* انگل angal

parcel *n* بخش bakhsh

parcel *post* n بسته پستي basteh-ye posti

parchment *n* کاغذپوست kaghaze poust

pardon *n* بخشش bakhshesh

pardon *v* بخشیدن bakhshidan

parenthesis *n* پرانتز parantez

parents *n* والدین valedayn

parish *n* شهر shahr

parishioner *n* اهل بخش ahle bakhsh

parity *n* تساوي tasavi

park *v* قرار دادن gharar dadan

park *n* گردشگاه gardeshgah

parliament *n* مجلس majles

parlour *n* اطاق نشیمن otaghe neshiman

parochial *adj* ناحیه اي nahiyehee

parrot *n* طوطي touti

parsley *n* جعفري ja'fari

parsnip *n* هویج وحشي havije vahshi

part *n* بخش bakhsh

part *v* جداشدن joda shodan

partial *adj* قسمتي ghesmati

partially *adv* اندکی andaki

participate *v* شریک شدن sharik shodan

participle *n* وجه وصفي vajhe vasfi

particle *n* حرف harf

particular *adj* مخصوص makhsous

particularly *adv* جزءبه جزء joz be joz

partisan *n* طرفدار tarafdar

partition *n* تیغه tigheh

partly *adv* چندي chandi

partner *n* شریک sharik

partnership *n* مشارکت mosharekat

partridge *n* کبک kabk

party *n* مهماني mehmani

pass *n* گذرنامه gozar nameh

pass *v* گذشتن gozashtan

pass out *v* مردن mordan

passage *n* پاساژ pasazh

passenger *n* مسافر mosaferati

passer by *n* عابر aber

passion *n* هواي نفس haveye nafs

passionate *adj* آتشي مزاج atashi mazaj

passive *adj* انفعالي enfeali

passport *n* گذرنامه gozar nameh

password *n* اسم رمز esme ramz

past *adj* گذشته gozashteh

pasta *n* اسپاگتي espageti

paste *n* چسب chasb

paste *v* چسباندن chasbandan

pasteurize *v* پاستوریزه کردن pastorizeh kardan

pastime *n*	سرگرمي	sargarmi
pastor *n*	چوپان	choupan
pastoral *adj*	شباني	shabani
pastry *n*	شيريني	shirini
pasture *n*	چراگاه	charagah
pat *n*	نوازش	navazesh
pat *v*	نوازش کردن	navazesh kardan
patch *n*	جاليز	jaliz
patch *n*	وصله	vasleh
patent *n*	پروانه	parvaneh
paternal *adj*	پدري	pedari
paternity *n*	اصليت	asliyat
path *n*	مسير	masir
pathetic *adj*	سوزناک	souznak
patience *n*	بردباري	bordbari
patient *adj*	بردبار	shakiba
patio *n*	حياط	hayat
patriarch *n*	بزرگ‌خاندان	bozorg-e khanedan
patrimony *n*	ميراث	miras
patriot *n*	ميهن‌پرست	mihan parast
patriotic *adj*	ميهن‌پرستانه	mihan parastaneh
patrol *n*	گشت	gasht
patron *n*	پشتيبان	poshtiban
patronize *v*	تشويق کردن	tashwigh kardan
pattern *n*	الگو	olgoo
pavement *n*	سنگفرش	sang farsh
pavilion *n*	غرفه‌نمايشگاه	ghorfeh-ye namayesh gah
paw *n*	پنجه	panjeh
pawnbroker *n*	بنگاه‌رهني	bongah-e rahni
pay *n*	اجرت	ojrat
pay *n*	پرداخت	pardakht
pay *iv*	پرداختن	pardakhtan
pay back *v*	پس‌دادن	pas dadan
pay off *v*	تسويه کردن	taswiyeh kardan
payable *adj*	قابل‌پرداخت	ghabele pardakht
pay check *n*	حقوق‌ماهيانه	hoghoughe mahiyaneh
payee *n*	گيرنده	girandeh
payment *n*	قسط	ghest
payroll *n*	صورت‌پرداخت	sourat pardakht
pea *n*	نخودفرنگي	nokhod farangi
peace *n*	صلح	solh
peaceful *adj*	صلح‌آميز	solh amiz
peach *n*	هلو	holoo
peacock *n*	طاووس	tavous
peak *n*	قله	gholleh
peanut *n*	بادام‌زميني	badam zamini
pear *n*	گلابي	golabi
pearl *n*	مرواريد	morvarid
peasant *n*	دهاتي	dehati
pebble *n*	سنگريزه	sang rizeh
peck *n*	سوراخ	sourakh
peck *v*	نوک‌زدن	nok zadan
peculiar *adj*	ويژه	vizheh
pedagogy *n*	تربيت	tarbiyat
pedal *n*	رکاب	rekab
pedantic *adj*	فضل‌فروشي	fazl foroushi
pedestrian *n*	پياده	piyadeh
pee *v*	ادرار کردن	edrar kardan
peel *v*	پوست‌انداختن	poust andakhtan
peep *v*	جوانه‌زدن	javaneh zadan

peephole *n* روزنه rowzaneh

peer *n* جفت joft

pelican *n* مرغ‌ماهیخوار morghe mahi khar

pellet *n* گلوله golouleh

pelvis *n* لگن‌خاصره lagane khasereh

pen *n* قلم ghalam

penal *adj* کیفری keyfari

penalize *v* جریمه‌کردن jarimeh kardan

penalty *n* کیفر keyfar

penance *n* پشیمانی pashimani

penchant *n* علاقه alagheh

pencil *n* مداد medad

pendant *n* آویز aviz

pending *adj* معلق mo'alagh

penetrate *v* رخنه‌کردن rakhneh kardan

penguin *n* پنگوئن pangouan

penicillin *n* پنی‌سیلین peni silin

peninsula *n* شبه‌جزیره shebhe jazireh

penitent *n* توبه‌کار tobeh kar

penniless *adj* بی‌پول bi poul

penny *n* شاهی shahi

pension *n* مزد mozd

pentagon *n* پنج‌ضلعی panj zelee

people *n* مردم mardom

pep *v* نیرودادن niroo dadan

pepper *n* فلفل felfel

per *pre* توسط tavassote

per cent *n* درصد darsad

perceive *v* درک‌کردن dark kardan

percentage *n* صدی‌چند sadi chand

perception *n* ادراک edrak

perennial *adj* ابدی abadi

perfect *adj* کامل kamel

perfection *n* کمال kamal

perforate *v* رسوخ‌کردن rosoukh kardan

perform *v* اجراکردن ejra kardan

performance *n* نمایش namayesh

perfume *n* عطر atr

perhaps *adv* شاید shayad

peril *n* خطر khatar

perilous *adj* خطرناک khatarnak

perimeter *n* محیط mohit

period *n* دوره doureh

perish *v* مردن mordan

perishable *adj* نابودشدنی nabood shodani

perjury *n* گواهی‌دروغ govahiye dorough

permanent *adj* پایدار paydar

permission *n* اجازه ejazeh

permit *v* اجازه‌دادن ejazeh dadan

pernicious *adj* کشنده koshandeh

perpetrate *v* مرتکب‌شدن mortakeb shodan

persecute *v* آزارکردن azar kardan

persevere *v* پشتکارداشتن poshtkar dashtan

persist *v* سماجت‌کردن semajat kardan

persistence *n* پافشاری pa feshari

person *n* شخص shakhs

personal *adj* شخصی shakhsi

personality *n* شخصیت shakhsiyat

personify *v* شخصیت‌دادن shakhsiyat dadan

personnel *n* کارکنان karkonan

perspective *n* دید did

perspiration *n* عرق‌ریزي aragh rizi

perspire *v* عرق‌کردن aragh kardan

persuade *v* وادارکردن vadar kardan

persuasion *n* تشویق tashvigh

persuasive *adj* تشویقي tashvighi

pertain *v* وابسته‌بودن vabasteh boudan

pertinent *adj* درخور dar khore

perturb *v* آشفتن ashoftan

perverse *adj* منحرف monharef

pervert *v* گمراه‌شدن gomrah shodan

pervert *adj* منحرف monharef

pessimism *n* بدبیني bad bini

pessimistic *adj* بدبین bad bin

pest *n* آفت afat

pesticide *n* ماده‌ضدآفت maddehye zede afat

pet *n* حیوان‌اهلي‌منزل heyvane ahliye manzel

petal *n* گلبرگ golbarg

petite *adj* ریزه‌اندام rizeh andam

petition *n* دادخواست dad khast

petrified *adj* مسخ‌شده maskh shodeh

petroleum *n* نفت naft

pettiness *n* خردي khordi

petty *adj* فرعي faree

pew *n* مقام magham

phantom *n* هواپیمای‌فانتوم havapeymaye fantom

pharmacist *n* داروساز darou saz

pharmacy *n* داروخانه darou khaneh

phase *n* صورت sourat

phenomenon *n* پدیده padideh

philosopher *n* فیلسوف filsouf

philosophy *n* فلسفه falsafeh

phobia *n* بیم bim

phone *n* آوا ava

phoney *adj* ساختگي sakhtegi

phosphorus *n* فسفر fosfor

photo *n* عکس ax

photocopy *n* فتوکپي fotokopi

photographer *n* عکاس akkas

phrase *n* عبارت ebarat

physical *adj* فیزیکي fiziki

physician *n* پزشک pezeshk

physics *n* فیزیک fizik

pianist *n* نوازنده‌پیانو navazandeh-ye piyano

piano *n* پیانو piyano

pick *v* چیدن chidan

pick up *v* برداشتن bardashtan

pickpocket *n* جیب‌بر jib bor

pickup *n* انتخاب entekhab

picture *n* تصویر tasvir

picturesque *adj* زیبا ziba

pie *n* آدم‌ناقلا adame naghola

piece *n* قطعه ghateh

piecemeal *adv* به‌تدریج be tadrij

pier *n* ستون sotoun

pierce *v* شکافتن shekaftan

piercing *n* تیز tiz

piety *n* پارسایي parsaee

pig *n* گراز goraz

pigeon *n* کبوتر kaboutar

pile *v* اندوختن andoukhtan

pile *n* کرک kork

pileup *v* سانحه saneheh

pilfer *v* کش‌رفتن kesh raftan

pilgrim *n* مسافر mosafer

pilgrimage *n* زیارت ziyarat

pill *n* دانه daneh

pillage *v* غارت‌کردن gharat kardan

pillar *n* ستون payeh

pillow *n* متکا motaka

pillowcase *n* روبالشی Roo-baleshi

pilot *n* رهبر rahbar

pimple *n* جوش joush

pincers *n* گازانبر gaz anbor

pinch *v* نیشگون‌گرفتن nishgoun gereftan

pine *n* کاج kaj

pineapple *n* اناناس ananas

pink *adj* صورتی sourati

pinpoint *v* بادقت‌اشاره‌کردن‌به ba deghat eshareh kardan

pint *n* واحدحجم vahede hajm

pioneer *n* پیشرو pish rou

pious *adj* پارسا parsa

pipe *n* پیپ pip

pipeline *n* لوله looleh

piracy *n* یاادبی دزدی‌هنری dozdiye honari

piranha *n* کوسه kouseh

pirate *n* دزددریایی dozde daryaee

pistol *n* هفت‌تیر haft tir

piston *n* سنبه sonbeh

pit *n* چاله chaleh

pitfall *n* دام dam

pitiful *adj* رقت‌انگیز reghat angiz

pity *n* رقت reghat

placard *n* آگهی‌دیواری agahiye divari

place *n* مکان makan

placid *adj* متین matin

plague *n* جرم jorm

plain *adj* آشکار ashkar

plain *n* جلگه jolgeh

plainly *adv* صریحا sarihan

plaintiff *n* مدعی modaee

plan *n* طرح tarh

plane *n* هواپیما havapeyma

planet *n* سیاره sayareh

plant *v* کاشتن kashtan

plant *n* گیاه giyah

plaster *v* اندودن andoudan

plaster *n* گچ gach

plastic *n* پلاستیک pelastik

plate *n* بشقاب boshghab

plateau *n* فلات falat

platform *n* سکو sakkoo

platinum *n* پلاتینی pelatini

plausible *adj* حق‌به‌جانب hagh be janeb

play *n* بازی bazi

play *v* بازی‌کردن bazi kardan

player *n* بازی‌کن bazi kon

playful *adj* بازیگوش bazi goush

playground *n* زمین‌بازي zamine bazi

plea *n* دادخواست dad khast

plead *v* عرض‌حال‌دادن arz-e hall dadan

pleasant *adj* خوش‌آیند khosh ayand

please *v* کیف‌کردن keyf kardan

pleasing *adj* بشاش bashash

pleasure *n* لذت lezzat

pleat *n* چین وشکن chin va shekan

pleated *adj* پلیسه دار peliseh dar

pledge *n* گرو gerou

pledge *v* گروگذاشتن gerou gozashtan

plentiful *adj* فراوان faravan

plenty *n* فراواني faravani

pliable *adj* قابل انعطاف ghabel-e' enetaf

pliers *n* انبردست anbor dast

plot *n* طرح tarh

plot *v* نقشه کشیدن naghsheh keshidan

plow *v* شخم زدن shokhm zadan

pluck *v* کندن kandan

plug *v* بستن bastan

plug *n* دوشاخه do shakheh

plum *n* آلو aloo

plumber *n* لوله کش looleh kesh

plumbing *n* لوله کشي looleh keshi

plump *adj* فربه farbeh

plunder *v* غارت کردن ghrat kardan

plunge *v* فروبردن forou bordan

plunge *n* گودال عمیق goudale amigh

plural *n* صیغه جمع sighehye jam'e

plus *adv* به اضافه be ezafeh

plutonium *n* پلوتونیوم pelotoniyom

pneumonia *n* التهاب ریه eltehabe riyeh

pocket *n* جیب jib

poem *n* منظومه manzoomeh

poet *n* شاعر sha'er

poetry *n* شعر she'er

poignant *adj* زننده zanandeh

point *v* اشاره کردن eshareh kardan

point *n* نقطه noghteh

pointed *adj* تیز tiz

pointless *adj* بی معني bi ma'ani

poise *n* وقار vaghar

poison *n* زهر zahr

poison *v* مسموم کردن masmoum kardan

poisoning *n* مسمومیت masmoumiyat

poisonous *adj* سمي sammi

polar *adj* قطبي ghotbi

pole *n* قطب ghotb

police *n* پاسبان pasban

policeman *n* مامور پلیس ma'moure polis

policy *n* سیاست siyasat

polio *n* فلج اطفال falaje atfal

polish *v* جلادادن jala dadan

Polish *adj* لهستاني lahestani

polite *adj* ادب adab

politeness *n* تربیت tarbiyat

politician *n* سیاستمدار siyasatmadar

politics *n* علم سیاسي elme siyasi

poll *n* راي ra'ey

pollen *n* گرده gardeh

pollute *v* آلودن aloudan

pollution *n* کثافت kesafat

polygamist *adj* مرد چندزنه marde chand zaneh

polygamy *n* چندهمسري chand hamsari

pomegranate *n* انار anar

pomp *n* شکوه shokouh

pomposity *n* آب‌وتاب ab va tab

pond *n* استخر estakhr

ponder *v* سنجیدن sanjidan

pontiff *n* پاپ pop

pool *n* استخر makhzan

poor *n* فقیر faghir

poorly *adv* بطورناچیز be toure nachiz

popcorn *n* ذرت‌بوداده zorate boo dadeh

Pope *n* خلیفه‌اعظم khalifehye a'azam

poppy *n* خشخاش khashkhash

popular *adj* محبوب mahboub

popularize *v* موردپسندعامه mourede pasande ammeh

populate *v* ساکن‌شدن saken shodan

population *n* مردم mardom

porcelain *n* چینی chini

porch *n* هشتی hashti

porcupine *n* جوجه‌تیغی joojeh tighi

pore *n* منفذ manfaz

pork *n* خوک khouk

pornography *n* نقاشی‌شهوت‌انگیز naghashiye shahvat angiz

porous *adj* متخلل motekhalkhel

port *n* بندر bandar

portable *adj* قابل‌حمل ghabele haml

porter *n* باربر bar bar

portico *n* رواق ravagh

portion *n* بخش bakhsh

portrait *n* تصویر tasvir

portray *v* مجسم‌کردن mojasam kardan

Portuguese *adj* پرتقالی porteghali

pose *n* حالت halat

pose *v* گذاردن gozardan

position *n* شغل shoghl

positive *adj* مثبت mosbat

possess *v* دارابودن dara boudan

possession *n* دارایی daraee

possibility *n* امکان emkan

possible *adj* ممکن momken

post *n* پست post

post office *n* پستخانه post khaneh

postage *n* ارسال‌پست ersale post

postcard *n* کارت‌پستال kart postal

poster *n* آگهی agahi

posterior *adj* عقبی aghabi

posterity *n* اولاد owlad

postman *n* نامه‌رسان nameh resan

postmark *n* مهرباطله‌تمبر mohre batelehye tamre

postpone *v* عقب‌انداختن aghab andakhtan

pot *n* دیگ dig

potato *n* سیب‌زمینی sib zamini

potent *adj* پرزور por zoor

potential *adj* بالقوه belghoveh

pothole *n* حفره hofreh

poultry *n* مرغ‌وخروس morgh va khorus

pound *v* آردکردن ard kardan

pound *n* لیره lireh

pour *v* پاشیدن pashidan

poverty *n* فقر faghr

powder *n* پودر poudr

power *n* قدرت ghodrat

powerful *adj* مقتدر moghtader

powerless *adj* بی‌زور bi zoor

practical *adj* عملي amali

practice *v* تمرین کردن tamrin kardan

pragmatist *adj* مصلحت گراي maslehat gerai

prairie *n* چمن chaman

praise *v* تمجید کردن tamjid kardan

praise *n* ستایش setayesh

praiseworthy *adj* ستودني sotudani

prank *n* مزاح mezah

prawn *n* میگو meygoo

pray *v* نمازخواندن namaz khandan

prayer *n* نماز namaz

preach *v* موعظه کردن mowezeh kardan

preacher *n* واعظ vaez

preamble *n* دیباچه dibacheh

precarious *adj* ناپایدار na paydar

precaution *n* پیشگیری pish giri

precede *v* مقدم بودن moghadam boudan

precedent *n* سابقه sabegheh

preceding *adj* پیشی pishi

precept *n* دستور dastur

precious *adj* گرانبها geran baha

precipice *n* پرتگاه part gah

precipitate *v* سقوط کردن soghout kardan

precise *adj* دقیق daghigh

precision *n* دقت deghat

precocious *adj* زودرس zood ras

precursor *n* منادي monadi

predecessor *n* اسبق asbagh

predict *v* پیشگوئي کردن pish gooie kardan

prediction *n* پیشگوئي pishgooie

predilection *n* تمایل قلبي tamayole ghabli

predisposed *adj* مستعد mosta'ed

predominate *v* مسلط بودن mosalat boudan

pre-empt *v* تقدم پیداکردن taghadom peyda kardan

prefabricate *v* پیش ساختن pish sakhtan

preface *n* دیباچه dibacheh

prefer *v* ترجیح دادن tarjih dadan

preference *n* برتري bartari

prefix *n* پیشوند pishvand

pregnancy *n* بارداري bardari

pregnant *adj* حامله hameleh

prehistoric *adj* ماقبل تاریخي ma ghable tarikhi

prejudice *n* تعصب ta'asob

preliminary *adj* مقدماتي moghadamati

prelude *n* مقدمه moghadameh

premature *adj* پیش رس pish ras

premeditate *v* قبلافکرچیزي راکردن ghablan fekre chizi ra kardan

premier *adj* مقدم moghadam

premise *n* فرضیه farziyeh

premises *n* مقدمات moghadamat

premonition *n* اخطار ekhtar

preoccupy *v* تصرف کردن tasarrof kardan

preparation *n* تهیه tahiyeh

prepare *v* تدارک دیدن tadarok didan

preposition *n* حرف اضافه harfe ezafeh

prerequisite *n* پیش نیاز pish niyaz

prerequisite *n* پیش‌نیاز pish niyaz

prerogative *n* امتیاز emtiyaz

prescribe *v* تجویز کردن tajviz kardan

prescription *n* تجویز tajviz

presence *n* پیشگاه pishgah

present *adj* حال hal

presentation *n* نمایش namayesh

preserve *v* نگاه‌داشتن negah dashtan

preside *v* اداره کردن edareh kardan

presidency *n* ریاست riyasat

president *n* رئیس reies

press *n* مطبوعات matbo'at

pressure *n* فشار feshar

pressure *v* فشردن feshordan

prestige *n* حیثیت heysiyat

presume *v* فرض کردن farz kardan

presumption *n* فرض farz

presuppose *v* پیش‌پنداشتن pish pendashtan

pretend *v* وانمود کردن vanemood kardan

pretence *n* تظاهر tazahor

pretension *n* وانمود vanemood

pretty *adj* قشنگ ghashang

prevail *v* چربیدن charbidan

prevalent *adj* رایج rayej

prevent *v* جلوگیری کردن jelougiri kardan

prevention *n* ممانعت momane'at

previous *adj* قبلی ghabli

previously *adv* پیشتر pishtar

prey *n* شکار shekar

price *n* قیمت gheymat

pricey *adj* قیمتی gheymati

prick *n* خار khar

prick *v* خراش دادن kharash dadan

pride *n* فخر fakhr

priest *n* کشیش keshish

priestess *n* کشیشه keshisheh

priesthood *n* کشیشی keshishi

primacy *n* برتری bartari

primarily *adv* مقدمه moghadameh

primate n پیشوا pishva

prime *adj* اولین avalin

primitive *adj* اولیه avaliyeh

prince *n* شاهزاده shah zadeh

princess *n* شاهدخت shah dokht

principal *adj* اصلی asli

principle *n* سرچشمه sar cheshmeh

print *n* چاپ chap

print *v* چاپ کردن chap kardan

printer *n* چاپگر chapgar

printing *n* چاپ chap

prior *adj* نخستین nokhostin

priority *n* اولویت owlaviyat

prism *n* منشور manshour

prison *n* زندان zendan

prisoner *n* زندانی zendani

privacy *n* خلوت khalvat

private *adj* محرمانه mahramaneh

privilege *n* امتیاز emtiyaz

prize *n* جایزه jayezeh

probability *n* احتمال ehtemal

probable *adj* احتمالی ehtemali

probe *v* کاوش کردن kavosh kardan

probing *n* کاوش kavosh

problem *n* مشکل moshkel	**profound** *adj* عميق amigh
problematic *adj* حیرت‌آور heyrat avar	**program** *n* برنامه barnameh
procedure *n* روش ravesh	**programmer** *n* برنامه‌نویس barnameh nevis
proceed *v* پیش‌رفتن pish raftan	**progress** *n* پیشرفت pishraft
proceedings *n* اقدامات eghdamat	**progress** *v* پیشرفت‌کردن pishraft kardan
proceeds *n* عایدات a'yedat	**progressive** *adj* تصاعدي tasaodi
process *v* تهیه‌کردن tahiyeh kardan	**prohibit** *v* تحریم‌کردن tahrim kardan
process *n* مرحله marhaleh	**prohibition** *n* تحریم tahrim
procession *n* ترقي taraghi	**project** *n* طرح tarh
proclaim *v* جارزدن jar zadan	**project** *v* نقشه‌کشیدن naghsheh keshidan
procrastinate *v* تعلل‌کردن ta'allol kardan	**projectile** *n* سلاح‌پرتابی selahe partabi
procure *v* به‌دست‌آوردن be dast avardan	**prologue** *n* پیش‌درآمد pish dar amad
prodigious *adj* حیرت‌آور heyrat avar	**prolong** *v* امتدادادن emtedad dadan
prodigy *n* شگفتي shegefti	**promenade** *n* گردش gardesh
produce *v* تولیدکردن towlid kardan	**promiscuous** *adj* بی‌قاعده bi gha'edeh
produce *n* محصول mahsoul	**promise** *n* پیمان peyman
product *n* حاصل hasel	**promote** *v* ترویج‌کردن tarvij kardan
production *n* عمل‌آوري amal avari	**promotion** *n* ترویج tarvij
profane *adj* کفرآمیز kofr amiz	**prompt** *adj* بی‌درنگ bi derang
profess *v* اظهارکردن ezhar kardan	**promptly** *adv* به‌فوریت be fouriyat
profession *n* پیشه pisheh	**prone** *adj* متمایل motemayel
professional *adj* ور پیشه pisheh var	**pronoun** *n* ضمیر zamir
professor *n* استاد ostad	**pronounce** *v* اداکردن ada kardan
proficient *adj* ماهر maher	**proof** *n* گواه govah
profile *n* فرم form	**propaganda** *n* تبلیغ tabligh
profit *n* فایده fayedeh	**propagate** *v* گستردن gostardan
profit *v* منفعت‌بردن manfeat bordan	**propel** *v* سوق‌دادن sough dadan
profitable *adj* مفید mofid	**propensity** *n* رغبت reghbat

proper *adj* شايسته shayesteh

properly *adv* درست dorost

property *n* مايملک mayamlak

prophecy *n* پيامبرى payambari

prophesy *v* پيام‌آوردن payam avardan

prophet *n* پيامبر payambar

proportion *n* نسبت nesbat

proposal *n* پيشنهاد pishnahad

propose *v* پيشنهادکردن pishnahad kardan

proposition *n* قضيه ghaziyeh

prose *n* نثر nasr

prosecute *v* دنبال‌کردن donbal kardan

prosecutor *n* پيگردقانونى peygarde ghanooni

prospect *n* نمود nemoud

prosper *v* کامکارشدن ka'mkar shodan

prosperity *n* شکوفائى shekoufaie

prosperous *adj* شکوفا shekoufa

prostitute *n* فاحشه fahesheh

prostitution *n* فحشاء fahsha

prostrate *adj* بخاک‌افتاده be khak oftadeh

protect *v* حمايت‌کردن hemayat kardan

protection *n* حفاظت hefazat

protest *v* اعتراض‌کردن e'teraz kardan

protest *n* واخواست va khast

protracted *adj* ممتد momtad

protrude *v* بيرون‌انداختن biroun andakhtan

proud *adj* مغرور maghrour

proudly *adv* متکبرانه motekaberaneh

prove *v* استدلال‌کردن estedlal kardan

proverb *n* مثل masal

provide *v* تهيه‌کردن tahiyeh kardan

providence *n* آينده‌نگرى ayandeh negari

providing that *c* بشرطاينکه be sharte inkeh

province *n* ولايت velayat

provision *n* قيد gheyd

provocation *n* تحريک tahrik

provoke *v* تحريک‌کردن tahrik kardan

prowl *v* پرسه‌زدن parseh zadan

prowler *n* کنجکاو konjkav

proximity *n* مجاورت mojaverat

proxy *adv* وکيل vakil

prudence *n* احتياط ehtiyat

prudent *adj* محتاط mohtat

prune *v* آراستن arastan

prune *n* آلو aloo

psychiatrist *n* روانپزشک ravan pezeshk

psychiatry *n* روانپزشکى ravan pezeshki

psychic *adj* روانى ravani

psychology *n* شناسى‌روان ravan shenas

puberty *n* رسيدگى residegi

public *adj* آشکار ashkar

publication *n* نشر nashr

publicity *n* شهرت shohrat

publicly *adv* آشکارا ashkara

publish *v* چاپ‌کردن chap kardan

publisher *n* ناشر nasher	**purchase** *n* خريداري kharidari
pudding *n* دسرفرني desere fereni	**purchase** *v* خريداري كردن kharidari kardan
puerile *adj* بچگانه bacheganeh	
puff *n* پفك pofak	**pure** *adj* خالص khales
puffy *adj* پف كردن pof kardan	**puree** *n* پوره poureh
pull *v* كشيدن keshidan	**purgatory** *n* بزرخ barzakh
pull ahead *v* جلوكشيدن jelou keshidan	**purge** *v* پاك كردن pak kardan
	purge *n* تطهير tathir
pull down *v* خراب كردن kharab kardan	**purification** *n* پالايش palayesh
pull out *v* ترك كردن tark kardan	**purify** *v* تصفيه كردن tasfiyeh kardan
pulley *n* قرقره gher ghereh	**purity** *n* خلوص kholous
pullover *n* پليور poliver	**purple** *adj* زرشكي zereshki
pulp *n* تفاله tofaleh	**purpose** *n* منظور manzour
pulpit *n* ميزفرمان mize farman	**purposely** *adv* عمدا amdan
pulsate *v* (قلب)تپيدن tapidan(ghalb)	**purse** *n* كيسه kiseh
	pursue *v* دنبال كردن donbal kardan
pulse *n* ضربه zarbeh	**pursuit** *n* پيگرد peygard
pulverize *v* نرم كردن narm kardan	**pus** *n* فساد fesad
pump *n* تلمبه tolombeh	**push** *v* هل دادن hol dadan
pump *v* تلمبه زدن tolombeh zadan	**pushy** *adj* بازور ba zoor
pumpkin *n* كدوتنبل kadou tanbal	**put** *iv* گذاردن gozardan
punch *n* سوراخ كن sourakh kon	**put aside** *v* كنار گذاشتن kenar gozashtan
punch *v* مشت زدن بر mosht zadan bar	**put away** *v* كنار گذاردن kenar gozardan
punctual *adj* خوش قول khosh ghoul	**put off** *v* سردواندن sar davandan
puncture *n* پنچر panchar	**put out** *v* تقلا كردن taghalla kardan
punish *v* ادب كردن adab kardan	**put up** *v* بسته بندي كردن basteh bandi kardan
punishable *adj* قابل مجازات ghabele mojazat	
punishment *n* گوشمالي goosh mali	**put up with** *v* آشناكردن با ashena kardan ba
pupil *n* شاگرد shagerd	**putrid** *adj* متعفن mote'afen
puppet *n* عروسك aroosak	**puzzle** *n* چيستان chistan
puppy *n* توله سگ tooleh sag	

puzzling *adj* گیج‌کننده gij konandeh

pygmy *n* کوتاه koutah

pyramid *n* هرم heram

Q

quagmire *n* مرداب mordab

quail *n* بلدرچین belderchin

quake *v* لرزیدن larzidan

qualify *v* صلاحیت‌داشتن salahiyat dashtan

quality *n* کیفیت keyfiyat

qualm *n* تردید tardid

quandary *n* حیرت heyrat

quantity *n* مقدار meghdar

quarrel *n* پرخاش parkhash

quarrel *v* ستیزه‌کردن setizeh kardan

quarry *n* شکار shekar

quarter *n* یک‌چارک yek charak

quarterly *adj* سه ماهه se mahe'

quarters n مسکن maskan

quash *v* باطل‌کردن batel kardan

queen *n* ملکه malakeh

queer *adj* خنده‌دار khandeh dar

quell *v* تسکین‌دادن taskin dadan

quench *v* خاموش‌کردن khamoush kardan

quest *n* تلاش talash

question *n* پرسش porsesh

question *v* پرسیدن porsidan

questionable *adj* مشکوک mashkouk

questionnaire *n* پرسشنامه porsesh nameh

quick *adj* تند tond

quicken *v* زنده‌کردن zendeh kardan

quickly *adv* به‌سرعت be sorat

quicksand *n* ریگ‌روان rige ravan

quiet *adj* خاموش khamush

quilt *n* بالاپوش bala poush

quit *iv* ول‌کردن vel kardan

quite *adv* کاملا kamelan

quiver *v* به‌هدف‌خوردن be hadaf khordan

quiz *v* آزمایش‌کردن azmayesh kardan

quotation *n* نقل‌قول naghle ghowl

quote *n* نشان‌نقل‌قول neshane naghle ghowl

quote *v* نقل‌قول‌کردن naghle ghowl kardan

R

rabbit *n* خرگوش khargoush

rabies *n* بیماری‌هاری bimariye hari

raccoon *n* راکون rakoun

race *n* مسابقه mosabegheh

race *v* مسابقه‌دادن mosabegheh dadan

racism *n* نژادپرستی nezhad parasti

racist *adj* نژادپرست nezhad parast

racket *n* راکت raket

radiation *n* تابش tabesh

radiator *n* رادیاتور radiyator
radical *adj* تندرو tond row
radio *n* رادیو radiyo
radish *n* تربچه torobcheh
raffle *n* لاتاري latari
raft *n* دگل dagal
rag *n* کهنه kohneh
rage *n* خشم khashm
ragged *adj* ناهموار nahamvar
rags *n* لباس مندرس lebase mondares
raid *v* هجوم آوردن hojoum avardan
raid *n* یورش yoresh
rail *n* سرزنش sarzanesh
railroad *n* راه آهن rah ahan
rain *n* باران baran
rain *v* باریدن baridan
rainbow *n* رنگین کمان rangin kaman
raincoat *n* باراني barani
rainfall *n* بارش baresh
rainstorm *n* بادوباران bad va baran
rainy *adj* پرباران por baran
raise *v* بالابردن bala bordan
raise *n* ترفیع tarfi'e
raisin *n* کشمش keshmesh
rake *n* شیار shiyar
rally *n* اجتماع مجدد ejtemae mojadad
ram *n* قوچ ghooch
ramification *n* انشعاب enshe'ab
ramp *n* سطح شیب دار sathe shib dar
rampage *n* دادوبیداد dad va bidad

rampant *adj* فراوان faravan
ranch *n* مزرعه mazra'eh
rancour *n* بدخواهي bad khahi
randomly *adv* تصادفي tasadofi
range *n* محدوده mahdoudeh
rank *n* رتبه rotbeh
ransack *v* غارت کردن gharat kardan
ransom *n* خونبها khoun baha
ransom *n* غرامت gharamat
rape *n* تجاوز جنسی tajavoze jensi
rape *v* هتک ناموس کردن hatke namous kardan
rapid *adj* چابک chabok
rapist *n* مرتکب زناي به عنف mortakebe zanaye be onf
rapport *n* سازگاري sazgari
rare *adj* نادر nader
rarely *adv* به ندرت be nodrat
rash *n* جوش joush
rash *v* جوش زدن joush zadan
raspberry *n* تمشک tameshk
rat *n* موش صحرایي moushe sahraee
rate *n* نرخ nerkh
rather *adv* سریع تر sari'e tar
ratify *v* قبول کردن ghabool kardan
ratio *n* قسمت ghesmat
ration *n* جیره jireh
ration *v* سهم دادن sahm dadan
rational *adj* عقلي aghli
rationalize *v* منطقي کردن manteghi kardan
rattle *v* وراجی کردن verraji kardan
ravage *n* تاخت وتاز takht va taz
ravage *v* ویران کردن viran kardan

rave v ديوانه‌شدن divaneh shodan

raven n كلاغ‌سياه kalaghe siyah

ravine n آبكند abkand

raw adj خام kham

ray n پرتو partow

raze v ويران‌كردن viran kardan

razor n تيغ‌صورت‌تراشي tighe sourat terashi

reach v رسيدن‌به residan be

reach n كشش keshesh

react v واكنش‌نشان‌دادن vakonesh neshan dadan

reaction n انعكاس en'ekas

read iv خواندن khandan

reader n قاري ghari

readiness n آمادگي amadegi

reading n قرائت ghara'at

ready adj آماده amadeh

real adj واقعى vaghe'ee

realism n واقع‌گرايي vaghe'e geraie

reality n حقيقت haghighat

realize v درك‌كردن dark kardan

realm n مملكت mamlekat

reap v درو‌كردن derow kardan

reappear v برگشتن bargashtan

rear v تربيت‌كردن tarbiyat kardan

rear n عقب aghab

reason v استدلال‌كردن estedlal kardan

reason n دليل dalil

reasonable adj معقول ma'aghoul

reassure v دوباره‌اطمينان‌دادن dobareh etminan dadan

rebel n شورشي shoureshi

rebel v شوريدن shouridan

rebellion n طغيان toghyan

rebirth n تجديدحيات tajdide hayat

rebuff v ردكردن rad kardan

rebuff n منع man'e

rebuild v بازساختن baz sakhtan

rebuke n گوشمالي gooshmali

rebuke v ملامت‌كردن malamat kardan

rebut v پس‌زدن pas zadan

recalcitrant adj سرسخت sar sakht

recall v به‌ياد‌آوردن be yad avardan

recant v اعتراف‌كردن e'eteraf kardan

recap v روكش‌زدن rookesh zadan

recapture v پس‌گرفتن pas gereftan

recede v كنار‌كشيدن kenar keshidan

receipt n دريافت daryaft

receive v دريافت‌كردن daryaft kardan

recent adj تازه tazeh

reception n پذيرش paziresh

receptive adj پذيرا pazira

recess n بازگشت bazgasht

recession n كسادي kesadi

recharge v ازنوپركردن az now por kardan

recipe n دستورالعمل dastowr-al amal

recital n تك‌نوازي tak navazi

recite v ازبرخواندن az bar khandan

reckless adj بي‌ملاحظه bi molahezeh

reclaim v مرمت کردن maramat kardan

recline v خم‌شدن kham shodan

recluse n زاهد zahed

recognize v شناختن shenakhtan

recollect v به‌خاطرآوردن be khater avardan

recollection n تجدیدخاطره tajdide khatereh

recommend v سفارش‌کردن sefaresh kardan

recompense n پاداش padash

reconcile v صلح‌دادن solh dadan

reconsider v تجدیدنظرکردن tajdide nazar kardan

reconstruct v احیاکردن ehya kardan

record n بایگانی baygani

record v ثبت‌کردن sabt kardan

recorder n نگارنده negarandeh

recount n شمارش‌مجدد shomareshe mojadad

recoup v تلافی‌کردن talafi kardan

recourse v متوسل‌شدن‌به motevasel shodan be

recourse n مراجعه moraje'eh

recover v ترمیم‌شدن tarmim shodan

recovery n بهبود behboud

recreate v تفریح‌کردن tafrih kardan

recreation n سرگرمی sargarmi

recruit n کارمندتازه karmande tazeh

recruit v نیروی‌تازه‌گرفتن nirooye tazeh gereftan

recruitment n استخدام estekhdam

rectangle n چهارگوش chahar goosh

rectangular adj مستطیل mostatil

rectify v تصحیح‌کردن tashih kardan

rector n پیشوا pishva

rectum n مقعد megh'ad

recuperate v حال‌آمدن hal amadan

recur v تکرارشدن tekrar shodan

recurrence n بازگشت bazgasht

recycle v استفاده‌مجدد estefadehye mojadad

red adj قرمز ghermez

red tape n فرمالیته‌اداري formalitehye edari

redden v قرمزشدن ghermez shodan

redeem v رهایی‌دادن rahaee dadan

redemption n بازخرید bazkharid

red-hot adj عصباني asabani

redo v دوباره‌انجام‌دادن dobareh anjam dadan

redouble v افزودن afzoudan

redress v جبران‌کردن jobran kardan

reduce v فتح‌کردن fath kardan

redundant adj اضافی ezafi

reed n نی ney

reef n جزیره‌نما jazireh nama

reel n حلقه halgheh

re-elect v دوباره‌گزیدن dobareh gozidan

re-enactment n تصویب‌مجددقانون tasvibe mojadade ghanoon

re-entry n ورودمجدد voroude mojadad

refer v فرستادن ferestadan

referee n داور davar

reference n ارجاع erja'e

refill v دوباره‌پر‌کردن dobareh por kardan

refinance v ازنوتجارت‌کردن az now tejarat kardan

refine v پالودن palowdan

refinery n پالایشگاه palayeshgah

reflection n بازتاب baz tab

reflex n واکنش vakonesh

reflexive adj برگشت‌به‌خود bargasht be khod

reform n بهسازي beh sazi

reform v ترمیم‌کردن tarmim kardan

refrain v خودداري‌کردن khoddari kardan

refresh v روشن‌کردن rowshan kardan

refreshing adj نیروبخش niroo bakhsh

refreshment n نوشابه nooshabeh

refrigerate v خنک‌کردن khonak kardan

refuel v سوخت‌گیري(مجدد)کردن soukht giri kardan(mojadad)

refuge v پناه‌بردن panah bordan

refugee n مهاجر mohajer

refund v پس‌دادن pas dadan

refurbish v روشن‌وتازه‌کردن rowshan va tazeh kardan

refusal n سرپیچي sarpichi

refuse n پس‌مانده pas mandeh

refuse v سرباززدن sarbaz zadan

refute v تکذیب‌کردن takzib kardan

regain v بازیافتن baz yaftan

regal adj شاهوار shahva'r

regard v ملاحظه‌کردن molahezeh kardan

regarding adv درباره darbareh

regardless adv بی‌اعتنا bi e'etena

regards n احترامات ehteramat

regeneration n باززایي baz-za'ei

regent n رئیس reyis

regime n رژیم rezhim

regiment n فوج fowj

region n سرزمین sarzamin

regional adj منطقه‌اي mantaghehee

register v نگاشتن negashtan

registration n ثبت sabt

regret v افسوس‌خوردن afsous khordan

regret n پشیماني pashimani

regrettable adj قابل‌تاسف ghabele ta'assof

regularly adv مرتبا "morataban

regulate v میزان‌کردن mizan kardan

rehabilitate v توانبخشي‌کردن tavanbakhshi kardan

rehearsal n تمرین‌نمایش tamrine namayesh

rehearse v تمرین‌کردن tamrin kardan

reign v حکمفرمابودن hokm farma boudan

reimburse v جبران‌کردن jobran kardan

rein n افسار afsa'r

rein v افسار‌کردن afsar kardan

reindeer *n* گوزن‌شمالي gavazne shomali

reinforce *v* تقويت كردن taghviyat kardan

reiterate *v* تكرار كردن tekrar kardan

reject *v* نپذيرفتن napaziroftan

rejection *n* مردودسازي mardood sazi

rejoice *v* وجدكردن vajd kardan

rejoin *v* درپاسخ‌گفتن dar pasokh goftan

rejuvenate *v* دوباره‌جوان كردن dobareh javan kardan

relapse *n* برگشت bargasht

relationship *n* خويشي khishi

relative *n* خويشاوند khishavand

relative *adj* نسبي nesbi

relax *n* راحت rahat

relax *v* شل كردن shol kardan

relay *n* بازپخش baz pakhsh

release *v* رهاكردن raha kardan

relegate *v* موكول كردن moukool kardan

relentless *adj* بيرحم bi rahm

relevant *adj* مناسب monaseb

reliable *adj* قابل‌اطمينان ghabele etminan

relic *n* عتيقه atigheh

relief *n* راحتي rahati

relieve *v* كمك كردن komak kardan

religion *n* مذهب mazhab

religious *adj* مذهبي mazhabi

relinquish *v* ترك كردن tark kardan

relish *v* لذت‌بردن از lezzat bordan az

relive *v* زندگي دوباره‌يافتن zendegiye dobareh yaftan

relocate *v* سرجاي‌خود گذاردن sare jaye khod gozardan

reluctant *adj* بي‌ميل bi meyl

reluctantly *adv* ازروي‌اكراه az rooye ekrah

rely on *v* استنادكردن‌به estenad kardan

remain *v* اقامت كردن eghamat kardan

remaining *adj* باقيمانده baghi mandeh

remains *n* جنازه jenazeh

remake *v* بازسازي كردن baz sazi kardan

remark *v* اظهار داشتن ezhar dashtan

remark *n* بيان bayan

remarkable *adj* قابل‌توجه ghabele tavajjoh

remarry *v* تجديدفراش كردن tajdide farash kardan

remedy *n* چاره chareh

remedy *v* درمان كردن darman kardan

remember *v* به‌خاطرآوردن be khater avardan

remembrance *n* يادگاري yadegari

remind *v* يادآوري كردن yadavari kardan

reminder *n* تذكر tazakkor

remission *n* آمرزش amorzesh

remit *v* بخشيدن bakhshidan

remittance *n* پرداخت pardakht

remnant *n* باقي‌مانده baghimandeh

remodel v عوض کردن avaz kardan

remorse n پشیمانی pashimani

remorseful adj نادم nadem

remote adj دوردست dour dast

removal n برداشت bardasht

remove v برطرف کردن bartaraf kardan

remunerate v تاوان‌دادن tavan dadan

renew v نوکردن now kardan

renewal n تجدید tajdid

renounce v انکارکردن enkar kardan

renovate v تعمیرکردن ta'amir kardan

renowned adj نامدار namdar

rent v اجاره‌کردن ejareh kardan

rent n کرایه kerayeh

reorganize v دوباره‌سازمان‌دادن dobareh sazman dadan

repair v تعمیرکردن ta'amir kardan

reparation n تاوان tavan

repatriate v به‌میهن‌برگشتن be mihan bargashtan

repay v پس‌دادن pas dadan

repayment n غرامت gheramat

repeal n فسخ faskh

repeal v لغوکردن laghv kardan

repeat v تکرارکردن tekrar kardan

repel v نپذیرفتن napaziroftan

repent v توبه‌کردن towbeh kardan

repentance n ندامت nedamat

repetition n تکرار tekrar

replace v جایگزین‌کردن jaygozin kardan

replay n پاسخ pasokh

replenish v دوباره‌پرکردن dobareh por kardan

replete adj تکمیل takmil

replica n المثنی al-mosana

replicate v تازدن ta zadan

reply n پاسخ pasokh

reply v پاسخ‌دادن pasokh dadan

report n گزارش enteshar

report v گزارش‌دادن gozaresh dadan

reportedly adv طبق‌اخبار tebghe akhbar

reporter n خبرنگار khabar negar

repose v آرمیدن aramidan

repose n سامان saman

represent v فهماندن fahmandan

repress v بازفشردن baz feshordan

repression n سرکوبی sar koubi

reprieve n رخصت rokhsat

reprint n چاپ‌جدید chape jadid

reprint v دوبارچاپ‌کردن dobar chap kardan

reprisal n جبران jobran

reproach v خوارکردن khar kardan

reproach n سرزنش sarzanesh

reproduce v تکثیرکردن taksir kardan

reptile n خزنده khazandeh

republic n جمهوری jomhuri

repudiate v منکرشدن monker shodan

repugnant adj زننده zanandeh

repulse v دفع‌کردن daf'e kardan

repulse n رد rad

reputation *n* شهرت shohrat	respect *n* رابطه rabeteh
request *n* تقاضا taghaza	respectful *adj* باادب ba adab
request *v* تمناکردن tamanna kardan	respective *adj* مربوطه marbouteh
require *v* لازم‌بودن lazem boudan	respiration *n* تنفس tanafos
requirement *n* احتیاج ehtiyaj	respite *n* مهلت mohlat
rescue *n* خلاصی khalasi	respond *v* پاسخ‌دادن pasokh dadan
rescue *v* رهانیدن rahanidan	response *n* واکنش vakonesh
research *v* پژوهیدن pazhouhidan	responsible *adj* مسئول mas'oul
research *n* پژوهش pazhouhesh	rest *v* آرمیدن aramidan
resemble *v* شباهت‌داشتن shabahat dashtan	rest *n* آسایش asayesh
resent *v* رنجیدن‌از ranjidan az	rest room *n* مستراح mostarah
resentment *n* خشم khashm	restaurant *n* رستوران restouran
reservation *n* ذخیره zakhireh	restful *adj* پرآسایش por asayesh
reserve *v* کنارگذاشتن kenar gozashtan	restitution *n* ارتجاع erteja'e
reservoir *n* مخزن makhzan	restless *adj* بی قرار bi gharar
reside *v* اقامت‌داشتن eghamat dashtan	restore *v* ترمیم‌کردن tarmim kardan
residence *n* اقامتگاه eghamatgah	restrain *v* مهارکردن mahar kardan
residue *n* مانده پس pas mandeh	restraint *n* نگهداری negahdari
resign *v* کناره‌گرفتن kenareh gereftan	restrict *v* محدودکردن mahdood kardan
resist *v* استقامت‌کردن esteghamat kardan	result *n* نتیجه natijeh
resistance *n* مقاومت moghavemat	resume *v* ادامه‌یافتن edameh yaftan
resolution *n* تصمیم tasmim	resumption *n* بازیافت baz yaft
resolve *v* مقررداشتن mogharar dashtan	resurface *v* روکش‌کردن roukesh kardan
resort *v* متوسل‌شدن motevasel shodan	resurrection *n* رستاخیز rastakhiz
resounding *adj* منعکس‌شدنی mon'akes shodani	retain *v* حفظ‌کردن hefz kardan
resource *n* وسیله vasileh	retaliate *v* تلافی‌کردن talafi kardan
respect *v* بزرگداشتن bozorg dashtan	retaliation *n* تلافی talafi
	retarded *adj* عقب‌مانده aghab mandeh
	retention *n* حافظه hafezeh

retire v بازنشسته‌شدن bazneshasteh shodan

retirement n بازنشستگي bazneshastegi

retract v جمع‌شدن jam'e shodan

retreat v عقب‌نشاندن aghab neshandan

retreat n عقب‌نشيني aghab neshini

retrieve v پس‌گرفتن pas gereftan

retroactive adj گذشته معطوف‌به ma'atouf be gozashteh

return n برگشت bargasht

return v مراجعت‌كردن moraje'at kardan

reunion n تجديدديدار tajdide didar

reunite v دوباره‌به‌هم‌پيوستن dobareh be ham peyvastan

reveal v فاش‌كردن fash kardan

revelation n افشاء efsha

revenge n انتقام entegham

revenge v انتقام‌كشيدن entegham keshidan

revenue n بازده bazdeh

reverence n حرمت hormat

reversal n واژگوني vazhegooni

reversible adj نقض قابل ghabele naghz

review n بازديد bazdid

review v بررسي‌كردن barresi kardan

revise v تجديدنظركردن tajdide nazar kardan

revision n بازديد bazdid

revive v زنده‌شدن zendeh shodan

revoke v لغوكردن laghv kardan

revolt n شورش shouresh

revolt v شورش‌كردن shouresh kardan

revolver v ششلول sheshlool

reward v پاداش‌دادن padash dadan

reward n مزد mozd

rheumatism n مرض‌رماتيسم maraze romatism

rhinoceros n كرگدن kargadan

rhyme n قافيه ghafiyeh

rhythm n وزن vazn

rib n دنده dandeh

ribbon n نوار navar

rice n برنج berenj

rich adj ثروتمند servatmand

rid iv خلاص‌كردن khalas kardan

riddle n چيستان chistan

ride iv سوارشدن savar shodan

ride n سواري savari

ridicule v تمسخركردن tamaskhor kardan

ridicule n ريشخند rishkhand

ridiculous adj مضحك mozhek

rifle n تفنگ tofang

right adj راست rast

right adv شايسته shayesteh

rights n حقوق hoghough

rigid adj سخت sakht

rigor n سختي sakhti

ring n حلقه halgheh

ring iv زنگ‌زدن zang zadan

ringleader n سردسته sar dasteh

rinse v باآب‌شستن ba ab shostan

riot n آشوب ashoub

riot v عياشي‌كردن ayashi kardan

ripe adj رسيده resideh

ripen v رسیده‌کردن‌یاشدن resideh kardan ya shodan

rip off n برش boresh

ripple n دارای‌سطح‌ناهموار daraye sathe na hamvar

rise iv ترقی‌کردن taraghi kardan

risk n خطراحتمالی khatare ehtemali

risk v خطرکردن khatar kardan

risky adj پرمخاطره por mokhatereh

rite n مراسم marasem

rival n رقیب raghib

rivalry n رقابت reghabat

river n رودخانه rood khaneh

road n خیابان khiyaban

roam v پرسه‌زدن parseh zadan

roar n خروش khorowsh

roar v غرش‌کردن ghorresh kardan

roast v بودادن bow dadan

roast v کباب‌کردن kabab kardan

rob v دزدیدن dozdidan

robber n دزد dozd

robbery n دزدي dozdi

robe n پوشش poushesh

robust adj قوي‌هیکل ghavi heykal

rock n سنگ sang

rocket n موشک moushak

rocky adj سنگلاخ sanglakh

rod n میله mileh

rodent n جانورجونده janevare javandeh

roll n طومار toumar

romance n افسانه afsaneh

roof n سقف saghf

room n اتاق otagh

roomy adj وسیع vasi'e

rooster n خروس khorus

root n ریشه risheh

root v ریشه‌کن‌کردن risheh kan kardan

rope n طناب tanab

rosary n تسبیح tasbih

rose n گل‌سرخ gole sorkh

rosy adj گلگون golgoon

rot v پوسیدن pousidan

rot n مهمل mahmel

rotate v چرخیدن charkhidan

rotation n چرخش charkhesh

rotten adj فاسد fased

rough adj خشن khashen

round adj گرد gerd

roundup n گردآوردن gerd avardan

rouse v به‌هم‌زدن be ham zadan

rousing adj نمایان namayan

route n مسیر masir

routine n امرعادي amre adi

row n پاروزدن paroozadan

row v ردیف radif

rowdy adj سرکش sarkesh

royal adj سلطنتي saltanati

royalty n حق‌الامتیاز hagholemtiyaz

rub v مالیدن malidan

rubber n لاستیک lastik

rubbish n آشغال ashghal

rubble n پاره‌آجر pareh ajor

ruby n یاقوت yaghoot

rudder n سکان sokkan

rude adj زمخت zomokht

rudeness n وحشیگری vahshigari

rudimentary *adj* ناقص naghes	**sack** *v* اخراج کردن یاشدن ekhraj kardan
rug *n* قالیچه ghalicheh	
ruin *n* خرابه kharabeh	**sack** *n* کیسه kiseh
ruin *v* فناکردن fana kardan	**sacrament** *n* آیین دینی aeene dini
rule *v* اداره کردن edareh kardan	**sacred** *adj* مقدس moghaddas
rule *n* قاعده gha'edeh	**sacrifice** *n* قربانی،نذر ghorbani
ruler *n* خط کش khat kesh	**sacrilege** *n* توهین به مقدسات towhin be moghadasat
rum *n* عجیب ajib	
rumble *n* شکایت shekayat	**sad** *adj* غمگین ghamgin
rumble *v* غریدن ghorridan	**sadden** *v* غمگین کردن ghamgin kardan
rumour *n* شایعه shaye'eh	
run *iv* راندن randan	**saddle** *n* گردنه gardaneh
run away *v* گریختن gorikhtan	**sadist** *n* آزارگر azar gar
run into *v* گرفتارشدن gereftar shodan	**sadness** *n* غم gham
	safe *adj* محفوظ mahfouz
run over *v* لبریزشدن labriz shodan	**safeguard** *n* حفاظ hefaz
runner *n* ولگرد velgard	**safety** *n* سلامت salamat
runway *n* مجرا majra'	**sail** *n* صید seyd
rush *v* هجوم بردن hojoom bordan	**sail** *v* صیدکردن seyd kardan
Russian *n* اهل روسیه ahle rousiyeh	**sailboat** *n* قایق صیادی ghayeghe sayyadi
rust *n* زنگ zang	
rust *v* زنگ زدن zang zadan	**sailor** *n* صیاد sayyad
rustic *adj* روستایی roostaee	**saint** *n* حضرت hazrat
rustproof *adj* ضدزنگ zede zang	**salad** *n* سالاد salad
rusty *adj* زنگ زده zang zadeh	**salary** *n* حقوق ماهانه hoghooghe mahiyaneh
ruthless *adj* بی باک bi ba	
	sale *n* حُراج haraj
	sales slip *n* صورت فروش sourat foroosh

S

sabotage *n* خرابکاری kharab kari	**salesclerk** *n* فروشنده forooshandeh
sabotage *v* خرابکاری کردن kharab kari kardan	**salesman** *n* فروشنده آقا forooshandehye agha
saboteur *n* خرابکار kharabkar	**saliva** *n* بزاق bozagh
	salmon *n* ماهی آزاد mahiye azad
	saloon *n* سالن salon

salt *n* نمک namak

salty *adj* نمکی namaki

salvation *n* رستگاری rastgari

same *adj* یکسان yeksan

sample *n* نمونه nemooneh

sanctify *v* تصدیق کردن tasdigh kardan

sanction *v* ضمانت اجرا کردن zemanat-e ejra kardan

sanction *n* فرمان farman

sanctity *n* تقدس taghaddos

sanctuary *n* حرم مطهر harame motahar

sand *n* ماسه maseh

sandal *n* صندل sandal

sandpaper *n* سنباده sonbadeh

sandwich *n* ساندویچ sandvich

sane *adj* عاقل aghel

sanity *n* سلامت عقل salamate aghl

sarcasm *n* ریشخند rish khand

sarcastic *adj* نیشدار nishdar

sardine *n* ماهیان ریز mahiyane riz

satanic *adj* شیطانی sheytani

satellite *n* ماهواره mahvareh

satire *n* طنز tanz

satisfaction *n* خرسندی khorsandi

satisfactory *adj* رضایت بخش rezayat bakhsh

satisfy *v* راضی کردن razi kardan

saturate *v* اشباع کردن eshba'e kardan

Saturday *n* شنبه shanbeh

sauce *n* چاشنی chashni

saucepan *n* ماهی تابه mahi tabeh

saucer *n* نعلبکی na'albeki

sausage *n* سوسیس sosis

savage *adj* وحشی vahshi

savagery *n* وحشیگری vahshigari

save *v* نجات دادن nejat dadan

savings *n* پس انداز pas andaz

saviour *n* ناجی naji

savour *v* مزه کردن mazeh kardan

saw *iv* اره کردن arreh kardan

saw *n* سخن sokhan

say *iv* گفتن goftan

saying *n* گفته gofteh

scaffold *n* داربست darbast

scald *v* آب پز کردن ab paz kardan

scale *n* مقیاس meghyas

scale *v* مقیاس گذاشتن meghyas gozashtan

scalp *n* جمجمه jomjomeh

scam *n* نقشه naghsheh

scandal *n* افتضاح eftezah

scandalize *v* رسوا کردن rosva kardan

scapegoat *n* کسیکه قربانی دیگران شود kasi ke ghorbaniye digaran shavad

scar *n* اثر گناه asare gonah

scarce *adj* کمیاب kamyab

scarcity *n* کمیابی kamyabi

scare *n* بیم bim

scare *v* ترساندن tarsandan

scarf *n* شال گردن shal gardan

scary *adj* ترسناک tarsnak

scatter *v* پخش کردن pakhsh kardan

scenario *n* متن سینمایی matn-e sinama'ei

scene *n* منظره manzareh

scenery *n* صحنه سازی sahneh sazi

scent *n* عطر atr

schedule *n* برنامه barnameh

schedule *v* دربرنامه‌گذاردن dar barnameh gozardan

scheme *n* برنامه barnameh

schism *n* تفرقه tafragheh

school *n* مدرسه madreseh

science *n* علم elm

scientific *adj* علمی elmi

scientist *n* دانشمند daneshmand

scissors *n* قیچی gheychi

scoff *v* تمسخر کردن tamaskhor kardan

scold *v* سرزنش کردن sarzanesh kardan

scolding *n* سرزنش sarzanesh

scooter *n* روروک rowrowak

scope *n* حوزه houzeh

scorch *v* بودادن boo dadan

score *v* حساب کردن hesab kardan

score *n* نشان neshan

scorn *v* اهانت کردن ehanat kardan

scorn *n* تمسخر tamaskhor

scorpion *n* عقرب aghrab

scoundrel *n* لات lat

scourge *n* شلاق shallagh

scout *n* پیش‌آهنگ pish ahang

scrap *n* قراضه ghorazeh

scrape *v* تراشیدن tarashidan

scratch *v* خراشیدن kharashidan

scratch *v* عقب کشیدن aghab keshidan

scream *n* جیغ jigh

scream *v* جیغ‌زدن jigh zadan

screen *n* پرده‌سینما pardehye sinema

screw *n* پیچ pich

screw *v* پیچاندن pichandan

screwdriver *n* آچارپیچ‌گوشتی achar pich gooshti

scribble *v* باشتاب‌نوشتن ba shetab neveshtan

scroll *n* طومار toumar

scrub *v* مالیدن malidan

scruples *n* بی‌دقت bi deghghat

scrupulous *adj* محتاط mohtat

scuffle *v* کشمکش کردن keshmakesh kardan

scuffle *n* نزاع neza'e

sculptor *n* پیکرتراش peykartarash

sculpture *n* مجسمه‌سازي mojasameh sazi

scuttle *v* سوراخ کردن sourakh kardan

sea *n* دریا darya

sea gull *n* مرغ‌دریایی morghe daryaye

seafood *n* غذاهاي‌دریایي ghazaye daryaye

seal n مهر mohr

seal off v مهروموم کردن mohromoum kardan

seam *n* بخیه bakhiyeh

seamless *adj* یک‌پارچه yek parcheh

search *n* تجسس tajasos

search *v* گشتن gashtan

seashore *n* ساحل‌دریا sahele darya

seasick *adj* دریازده darya zadeh

season *n* فصل fasl

seasonal *adj* فصلي fasli

seasoning *n* چاشني chashni

seat *n* نیمکت nimkat

secede v کناره‌گیری کردن kenareh giri kardan

secluded adj منزوی monzavi

seclusion n انزوا enzeva

second n ثانیه saniyeh

secondary adj کمکی komaki

secret n راز raz

secretary n رازدار raz dar

secretly adv درنهان dar nahan

sect n فرقه fergheh

section n برش boresh

sector n بخش bakhsh

secure v حفظ کردن hefz kardan

secure adj محکم mohkam

security n امنیت amniyat

sedate v موقربودن movaghar budan

sedation n تسکین taskin

seduce v گمراه کردن gomrah kardan

seduction n گمراه‌سازي gool zani

see iv دیدن didan

seed n دانه daneh

seedless adj بی‌هسته bi hasteh

seek iv طلب کردن talab kardan

seem v به‌نظر آمدن be nazar amadan

segment n مقطع maghta'e

segregate v جداکردن joda kardan

segregation n جدایي jodaee

seize v قاپیدن ghapidan

seizure n تصرف tasarof

seldom adv بسیارکم besyar kam

select v گزیدن gazidan

selection n گزینش gozinesh

self-esteem n احترام‌به‌نفس ehteram be nafs

selfish adj خودپسند khod pasand

selfishness n خودپسندي khod pasandi

sell iv فروختن foroukhtan

seller n فروشنده forushandeh

sellout n فروش forush

semblance n شباهت shabahat

semester n نیمسال nimsal

seminary n مدرسه‌علوم‌دیني madresehye ooloome dini

senate n مجلس‌سنا majlese sena

senator n سناتور senator

send iv فرستادن ferestadan

senior adj ارشد arshad

seniority n ارشدیت arshadiyat

sensation n احساس ehsas

sense n حواس‌پنجگانه havase panjganeh

senseless adj بی‌احساس bi-ehsas

sensible adj محسوس mashhoud

sensual adj هوس‌ران havas ran

sentence n حکم hokm

sentence v محکوم کردن mahkoom kardan

sentiment n نیت niyat

sentimental adj احساساتي ehsasati

sentry n نگهبان negahban

separate v جداکردن joda kardan

separate adj جداگانه jodaganeh

separation n متارکه motarekeh

September n سپتامبر septambr

sequel n دنباله donbaleh

sequence n ترتیب tartib

serenade n قطعه‌موسیقی‌عاشقانه ghet'eh mousighiye asheghaneh

serene adj ساکت saket

serenity n آرامش aramesh

sergeant n گروهبان gorouhban

series n ردیف radif

serious adj وخیم vakhim

seriousness n اهمیت ahamiyat

sermon n خطابه khatabeh

serpent n ماربزرگ mare bozorg

servant n نوکر nowkar

serve v خدمت کردن khedmat kardan

service n استخدام estekhdam

session n جلسه jalaseh

set n دستگاه dastgah

set iv مرتب کردن moratab kardan

set about v حمله کردن به hamleh kardan be

set off v جلوه دادن jelveh dadan

set out v عازم‌شدن azem shodan

set up v نصب کردن nasb kardan

setback n مانع mane'e

setting n آهنگ ahang

settle v ماندن mandan

settle down v جایگیر کردن jaygir kardan

settlement n واریز variz

settler n مقیم moghim

seven adj هفت haft

seventeen adj هفده hefdah

seventh adj هفتم haftom

seventy adj هفتاد haftad

sever v بریدن boridan

several adj چند chand

severance n جداسازی jodasazi

severity n سختی sakhti

sew v دوختن doukhtan

sewage n فاضلاب fazelab

sewer n گنداب gandab

sex n روابط‌جنسی ravabete jensi

sexuality n تمایلات‌جنسی tamayolat-e jensi

sexy adj شهوت‌انگیز shahvat angiz

shabby adj پست past

shack n کلبه kolbeh

shackle n پابند paband

shade n سایه‌بان sayeh ban

shadow n سایه sayeh

shady adj سایه‌دار sayeh dar

shake iv تکان‌دادن tekan dadan

shaky adj لرزان larzan

shallow adj سطحی sathi

shambles n کشتارگاه koshtargah

shame v خجالت‌دادن khejalat dadan

shame n شرم sharm

shameful adj ننگین nangin

shameless adj بی‌حیا bi haya

shamrock n رنگ‌سبزشبدری range sabze shabdari

shape n اندام andam

shape v شکل‌دادن shekl dadan

share v سهم‌بردن sahm bordan

share n قسمت ghesmat

shareholder n سهم‌دار sahm dar

shark n کوسه‌ماهی kouseh mahi

sharp adj تیز tiz

sharpen v تیز کردن tiz kardan

sharpener *n* مدادتراش medadtarash

shatter *v* شکستن shekastan

shave *v* تراشیدن tarashidan

shawl *n* شال shal

she *pro* آن‌دختر an dokhtar

shear *iv* چیدن‌مو chidane moo

shed *iv* انداختن andakhtan

sheep *n* گوسفند goosfand

sheets *n* اوراق owragh

shelf *n* تاقچه taghcheh

shell *n* قشر gheshr

shellfish *n* حلزون‌صدف‌دار halazoone sadaf dar

shelter *v* پناه‌دادن panah dadan

shelter *n* پناهگاه panahgah

shelves *n* قفسه‌ها ghafasehha

shepherd *n* چوپان choupan

sherry *n* شراب‌اسپانیولی sharabe espaniyoli

shield *n* پوشش pooshesh

shield *v* سپرشدن separ shodan

shift *n* نوبت‌کار noubate kar

shine *iv* تابیدن tabidan

shiny *adj* صیقلی barragh

ship *n* کشتی keshti

shipment *n* محموله mahmouleh

shipwreck *n* غرق ghargh

shipyard *n* محل‌کشتی‌سازي mahale keshti sazi

shirt *n* پیراهن pirahan

shiver *n* لرزه larzeh

shiver *v* لرزیدن larzidan

shock *v* ترساندن tarsandan

shock *n* صدمه sadameh

shocking *adj* موحش mouhesh

shoddy *adj* پست past

shoe *n* کفش kafsh

shoelace *n* بندکفش bande kafsh

shoot *iv* پرتاب‌کردن partab kardan

shop *v* خریدکردن kharid kardan

shop *n* مغازه maghazeh

shopping *n* خرید kharid

shore *n* ساحل sahel

short *adj* کوتاه koutah

shortage *n* کسري kasri

shortcoming *n* کمبود kamboud

shortcut *n* میانبر miyan bor

shorten *v* مختصرکردن mokhtasar kardan

shorthand *n* تندنویسی tond-nevisi

shortly *adj.* به‌زودی be zoodi

shorts *n* شلوارکوتاه shalvar koutah

short sighted *adj* کوتاه‌بین koutah-bin

shot *n* جرعه jor'eh

shotgun *n* تفنگ‌ساچمه‌اي tofange sachmehee

shoulder *n* کتف ketf

shout *v* فریادزدن faryad zadan

shove *v* هل‌دادن hol dadan

shovel *n* خاک‌انداز khak andaz

show *iv* نشان‌دادن neshan dadan

show off *v* خودنمایي‌کردن khodnamaee kardan

show up *v* حاضرشدن hazer shodan

showdown *n* آزمایش‌نیرو azmayeshe niroo

shower *n* دوش doush

shrapnel *n* گلوله‌نارنجکی goloolehye narenjaki

shred *n* پاره pareh

shred *v* پاره‌کردن pareh kardan

shrewd *adj* زیرک zirak

shriek *v* جیغ‌زدن jigh zadan

shrimp *n* میگو meygoo

shrine *n* زیارتگاه ziyaratgah

shrink *iv* چروک‌شدن chorook shodan

shroud *n* کفن kafan

shrub *n* بوته bouteh

shudder *n* ارتعاش erte'ash

shudder *v* لرزیدن larzidan

shuffle *v* به‌هم‌آمیختن be ham amikhtan

shun *v* گریختن gorikhtan

shut *iv* بستن bastan

shy *adj* خجالتی khejalati

shyness *n* کمرویی kamrouee

sick *adj* بیمار bimar

sicken *v* مریض‌شدن mariz shodan

sickle *n* داس das

sickness *n* بیماری bimari

sideburns *n* خط‌ریش khat-e rish

sidewalk *n* پیاده‌رو piyadehrou

siege *n* محاصره mohasereh

siege *v.* محاصره‌کردن mohasereh kardan

sigh *n* آه ah

sight *n* بینایی binaye

sightseeing *v* بازدیدنقاط‌دیدنی bazdide noghat-e didani

sign *v* امضاءکردن emza kardan

sign *n* نشان neshan

signal *n* علامت alamat

signature *n* امضاء emza

significance *n* اهمیت ahammiyat

signify *v* حاکی‌بودن‌از haki boudan az

silence *n* خاموشی khamoshi

silent *adj* بی‌صدا bi seda

silhouette *n* نیمرخ nimrokh

silk *n* ابریشم abrisham

silly *adj* نادان nadan

silver *n* نقره noghreh

silversmith *n* نقره‌ساز noghreh saz

silverware *n* ظروف‌نقره zorufe noghreh

similar *adj* همسان hamsan

similarity *n* تشابه tashaboh

simmer *v* آهسته‌جوشیدن ahesteh joushidan

simple *adj* ساده sadeh

simplicity *n* سادگی sadegi

simplify *v* ساده‌کردن sadeh kardan

simply *adv* به‌سادگی be sadegi

simultaneous *n* همزمانی hamzamani

sin *v* خطاکردن khata kardan

sin *n* گناه gonah

since *pro* از az

since *c* از....تا az ... ta

sincere *adj* صادق sadegh

sincerity *n* خلوص kholous

sinful *adj* عاصی asi

sing *iv* آوازخواندن avaz khandan

singer *n* خواننده khanandeh

single *n* مجرد mojarad

singular *adj* منفرد monfared

sinister *n* شوم shoom

sink *iv* فروبردن forou bordan

sinner *n* گناهکار gonah-kar

sip *v* چشیدن cheshidan

sip *n* مزمزه maz mazeh

sir *n* آقا agha

siren *n* حوری‌دریایی houriye daryaee

sissy *adj* بچه‌ننه bacheh-naneh

sister *n* خواهر khahar

sister-in-law *n* خواهرزن khahar zan

sit *iv* نشستن neshastan

site *n* مکان makan

sitting *n* جلسه jalaseh

situated *adj* جایگزین jay gozin

situation *n* وضعیت vaziyat

six *adj* شش shesh

sixteen *adj* شانزده shanzdah

sixth *adj* ششمین sheshomin

sixty *adj* شصت shast

sizable *adj* بزرگ bozorg

size *n* اندازه andazeh

skate *v* سرخوردن sor khordan

skate *n* کفش چرخدار kafshe charkhdar

skeleton *n* کالبد kalbod

sceptic *adj* مشکوک mashkook

sketch *v* پیش‌نویس کردن pishnevis kardan

sketch *n* طراحی کلیات tarahiye kolliyat

sketchy *adj* سردستی sar dasti

ski *v* اسکی‌بازی کردن ski bazi kardan

skill *n* مهارت maharat

skilful *adj* ماهر maher

skim *v* کف kaf

skin *v* پوست کندن poust kandan

skin *n* جلد jeld

skin-deep *adj* سطحی zaheri

skinny *adj* لاغر laghar

skip *v* تپیدن tapidan

skip *n* جست jast

skirmish *n* کشمکش keshmakesh

skirt *n* دامن daman

skull *n* جمجمه jomjomeh

sky *n* آسمان aseman

skyscraper *n* آسمان‌خراش aseman kharash

slack *n* تنبل tanbal

slam *v* بهم کوفتن beham kouftan

slander *n* تهمت tohmat

slanting *adj* اریب orib

slap *n* سیلی sili

slap *v* سیلی‌زدن sili zadan

slaughter *n* قتل‌عام ghatle am

slaughter *v* کشتارکردن koshtar kardan

slave *n* غلام gholam

slavery *n* بردگی bardeggi

slay *iv* ذبح کردن zebh kardan

sleep *n* خواب khab

sleep *iv* خوابیدن khabidan

sleeve *n* آستین astin

sleeveless *adj* بی‌آستین bi-astin

sleigh *n* درشکه doroshkeh

slender *adj* باریک barik

slice *n* برش boresh

slice *v* قاچ‌کردن ghach kardan

slide *iv* سریدن soridan

slightly *adv* کمی kami

slim *v* لاغرشدن laghar shodan

slim *adj* نازک nazok

sling *v* پرتاب کردن partab kardan

slip *v* اشتباه کردن eshtebah kardan

slip *n* گمراهی gomrahi

slippery *adj* بی ثبات bi sobat

slit *iv* چاک دادن chak dadan

slope *n* شیب shib

sloppy *adj* کثیف kasif

slot *n* چاک chak

slow *adj* یواش yavash

slowly *adv* آهسته ahesteh

slump *n* افت oft

slur *v* مطلبی را حذف کردن matlabi ra hazf kardan

sly *adj* ناقلا naghola

smack *n* سیلی sili

small *adj* کوچک kouchek

smallpox *n* آبله abeleh

smart *adj* شیرین shirin

smash *v* خرد کردن khord kardan

smell *iv* بوئیدن boo'eidan

smelly *adj* بدبو bad boo

smile *n* تبسم tabasom

smile *v* لبخند زدن labkhand zadan

smoke *v* سیگار کشیدن sigar keshidan

smoker *n* اهل دخانیات ahle dokhaniyat

smoking gun *n* تفنگ دودی tofange doudi

smooth *adj* صاف saf

smoothly *adv* به نرمی be narmi

smoothness n همواری hamvari

smother *v* خفه کردن khafeh kardan

smuggler *n* قاچاقچی ghachghi

snack *n* خوراک مختصر khorake mokhtasar

snail *n* حلزون halazoun

snake *n* مار mar

snapshot *n* عکس فوری axe fowri

snare *v* به دام انداختن be dam andakhtan

snare *n* دام dam

snatch *v* ربودن robudan

sneak *v* خود را اینهان ساختن khod ra penhan sakhtan

sneeze *v* عطسه کردن atseh kardan

sniff *v* بینی گرفتن bini gereftan

sniper *n* تیرانداز از خفا tirandaz az khafa

snitch *v* کش رفتن kesh raftan

snooze *v* چرت زدن chort zadan

snore *n* خرناس khornas

snore *v* خرو پف کردن khor va pof kardan

snow *n* برف barf

snow *v* برف آمدن barf amadan

snowfall *n* بارندگی (برف) barandegi(barf)

snowflake *n* برف دانه barfe daneh

snub *n* سرزنش sarzanesh

snub *v* سرزنش کردن sarzanesh kardan

soak *v* خیس خوردن khis khordan

so-and-so *adv.* چنین و چنان chenin va chenan

soar *v* بالا رفتن bala raftan

sob *v* گریه کردن geryeh kardan

sob *n* هق هق hegh hegh

sober *adj* هوشیار hoshyar

sociable *adj* خوش برخورد khoshbarkhord

socialism *n* جامعه گرایی jame'eh geraee

socialist adj سوسياليست socialist

society n انجمن anjoman

sock n جوراب jourab

sod n چمن chaman

soda n سودا soda

sofa n نیمکت nimkat

soft adj نرم narm

soften v نرم کردن narm kardan

softly adv بەنرمی be narmi

softness n ملایمت molayemat

soggy adj خیس khis

soil n زمین zamin

soil v کثیف کردن kasif kardan

soiled adj چرکشده cherk shodeh

solace n تسکین taskin

solar adj خورشیدی khorshidi

solder v لحیم کردن lahim kardan

soldier n سرباز sarbaz

sold-out adj کاملافروش‌رفته kamelan foroush rafteh

sole adj تنها tanha

sole n کف پا kafe pa

solely adv فقط faghat

solemn adj رسمی rasmi

solicit v التماس کردن eltemas kardan

solid adj جامد jamed

solidarity n انسجام ensejam

solitary adj تنها tanha

solitude n خلوت khalvat

soluble adj قابل‌حل ghabele hall

solution n چاره‌سازی chareh sazi

solve v حل کردن hal kardan

solvent adj قادربه‌پرداخت‌قروض ghader be pardakhte ghorouz

sombre adj تاریک tarik

some adj اندکی andaki

somebody pro یک کسی yek kasi

someday adv روزی rouzi

somehow adv بطریقی be tarighi

someone pro کسی kasi

something pro چیزی chizi

sometimes adv گاهی gahi

someway adv بەطریقی be tarighi

somewhat adv قدری ghadri

son n پسر pesar

song n سرود soroud

son-in-law n داماد damad

sonnet n غزل ghazal

soon adv بزودی be zoodi

soothe v تسکین‌دادن taskin dadan

sorcerer n ساحر saher

sorcery n افسونگری afsoungari

sore n زخم zakhm

sore adj مجروح majrouh

sorrow n غم gham

sorrowful adj محزون mahzoun

sorry adj غمگین ghamgin

sort v سواکردن sava kardan

soul n روح rouh

sound n صدا seda

sound v صداکردن seda kardan

soup n سوپ soup

sour adj ترش torsh

source n سرچشمه sarcheshmeh

south n جنوب jonub

southbound adv بسوی‌جنوب be souye jonub

southeast n جنوب‌شرق jonube shargh

southern adj جنوبی jonubi

southerner n اهل‌جنوب ahle jonub

southwest *n* جنوب‌غرب jonube gharb

souvenir *n* یادگار yadegar

sovereign *adj* مطلق motlagh

sovereignty *n* سلطه solteh

sow *iv* کاشتن kashtan

space *n* فضا faza

spacious *adj* فراخ farakh

spade *n* بیل bil

span *v* چرخیدن charkhidan

span *v* وجب‌کردن vajab kardan

Spanish *adj* اسپانیایی espaniyaee

spank *v* بادست‌به‌کفل‌زدن ba dast be kafal zadan

spanking *n* تند tond

spare *v* دریغ‌داشتن darigh dashtan

spare part *n* قطعه‌یدکی ghatehe yadaki

spark *n* جرقه jaragheh

spark *v* جرقه‌زدن jaragheh zadan

spark plug *n* شمع sham'e

sparkle *v* چشمک‌زدن cheshmak zadan

sparrow *n* گنجشک gonjeshk

sparse *adj* پراکنده parakandeh

spasm *n* تشنج‌موضعی tashannoje mowzei

speak *iv* سخن‌گفتن sokhan goftan

spear *n* نیزه neyzeh

special *adj* مخصوص makhsus

specialize *v* اختصاصی‌کردن ekhtesasi kardan

specialty *n* کالای‌ویژه kalaye vizheh

species *n* قسم ghesm

specific *adj* ویژه vizheh

specify *v* مشخص‌کردن moshakhas kardan

specimen *n* نمونه nemuneh

speck *n* خال khal

spectacle *n* تماشا tamasha

spectator *n* ناظر nazer

speculate *v* تفکرکردن tafakor kardan

speech *n* گفتار goftar

speechless *adj* لال lal

speed *n* تندی tondi

speed *iv* کامیاب‌بودن kamyab budan

speedily *adv* زود zood

speedy *adj* چابک chabok

spell *iv* املاءکردن emla kardan

spell *n* سحر sehr

spelling *n* هجی heji

spend *iv* صرف‌کردن sarf kardan

spending *n* مخارج makharej

sperm *n* نطفه notfeh

sphere *n* کره koreh

spice *n* ادویه adviyeh

spicy *adj* تند tond

spider *n* عنکبوت ankabut

spider web *n* تارعنکبوت tare ankabut

spill *iv* ریختن rikhtan

spin *iv* تنیدن tanidan

spine *n* ستون‌فقرات sotune fagharat

spinster *n* دخترترشیده dokhtare torshideh

spirit *n* جان jan

spiritual *adj* روحانی rouhani

spit *iv* تف‌انداختن tof andakhtan

spite *n* لج laj

spiteful *adj* کینه‌توز kineh touz

splash *v* ترشح کردن tarashoh kardan

splendid *adj* باشکوه ba shokuh

splendour *n* زرق‌وبرق zargh va bargh

splinter *n* تراشه tarasheh

split *iv* شکافتن shekaftan

spoil *v* ضایع‌کردن zaye' kardan

spoils *n* غنایم ghanayem

sponge *n* اسفنج esfanj

sponsor *n* ضامن zamen

spontaneity *n* ناگهانی nagahani

spontaneous *adj* بی‌اختیار bi ekhtiyar

spooky *adj* شبح‌وار shabah var

spoon *n* قاشق ghshogh

spoonful *n* قاشق یک اندازه به be andazehye yek ghashogh

sporadic *adj* تک تک tak tak

sport *n* ورزش varzesh

sporty *n* ورزشی varzeshi

spot *n* خال khal

spot *v* لکه‌دارشدن lakkeh dar shodan

spotless *adj* بی‌عیب bi eyb

spouse *n* همسر hamsar

sprain *v* پیچ‌خوردن pich khordan

sprawl *v* نشستن گشاد goshad neshastan

spray *v* پاشیدن pashidan

spread *iv* گستردن gostardan

spring *n* بهار bahar

spring *iv* جهش کردن jahesh kardan

springboard *n* تخته‌شیرجه takhtehye shirjeh

sprinkle *v* ترشح کردن tarashoh kardan

sprint *n* دوسرعت doe sorat

sprout *v* جوانه‌زدن javaneh zadan

spur *n* سیخ sikh

spur *v* مهمیززدن mahmiz zadan

spy *n* جاسوس jasus

spy *v* جاسوسی کردن jasusi kardan

squalid *adj* کثیف kasif

squander *v* تلف کردن talaf kardan

square *adj* مربع moraba'e

square *n* میدان meydan

squash *v* له‌کردن leh kardan

squeak *v* جیغ‌کشیدن jigh keshidan

squeeze *v* فشردن feshordan

stab *v* خنجرزدن khanjar zadan

stab *n* زخم‌چاقو zakhme chaghoo

stability *n* استحکام estehkam

stable *adj* محکم mohkam

stack *v* انباشتن anbashtan

stack *n* خرمن kharman

staff *n* کارمندان karmandan

stage *n* مرحله marhaleh

stagger *v* گیج‌خوردن gij khordan

staggering *adj* تلوتلوخوران telow telow khoran

stagnate *v* راکدشدن raked shodan

stagnation *n* کسادی kesadi

stain *v* چرک‌کردن cherk kardan

stain *n* لکه lakkeh

stair *n* پله pelleh

staircase *n* راه‌پله rah pelleh

stairs *n* پله‌کان pelleh kan

stale *adj* بیات bayat

stalemate *n* بن‌بست bon bast

stalk *v* خرامیدن kharamidan

stalk *n* ساق sagh

stall *n* آخور akhour

stall *v* ممانعت‌کردن moman'eat kardan

stammer *v* من‌من‌کردن men men kardan

stamp *n* مهر mohr

stamp *v* مهرزدن mohr zadan

stamp out *v* خردکردن khord kardan

stampede *n* رم ram

stand *iv* ایستادن eistadan

stand for *v* داوطلب‌بودن davtalab boudan

stand out *v* دوام‌آوردن davam avardan

stand up *v* برپاماندن bar pa mandan

standard *n* پرچم parcham

standardize *v* سنجیدن‌بامعیار sanjidane ba me'eyar

standing *adv* ثابت sabet

standpoint *n* نقطه‌نظر noghteh nazar

standstill *adj* بدون‌حرکت bedoun-e harkat

staple *v* طبقه‌بندی‌کردن tabagheh bandi kardan

staple *n* مرکزبازرگانی‌عمده markaze bazarganiye omdeh

stapler *n* ماشین‌عدل‌بندی mashine adl bandi

star *n* ستاره setareh

starch *n* آهار ahar

starchy *adj* رسمی rasmi

stare *v* خیره‌نگاه‌کردن khireh negah kardan

start *n* آغاز aghaz

start *v* آغازیدن aghazidan

startle *v* تکان‌دادن tekan dadan

startled *adj* متوحش motevahesh

starve *v* گرسنگی‌دادن gorosnegi dadan

statement *n* بیان bayan

station *n* ایستگاه istgah

stationary *adj* ساکن saken

statistic *n* آمار amar

statue *n* تندیس tandis

status *n* وضعیت vaz'eiyat

statute *n* قانون ghanoon

stay *n* توقف tavaghof

stay *v* ماندن mandan

steady *adj* محکم mohkam

steak *n* باریکه‌گوشت‌کبابی barikehye goushte kababi

steal *iv* دزدیدن dozdidan

stealthy *adj* یواشکی yavashaki

steam *n* بخار bokhar

steel *n* فولاد foulad

steep *adj* سرازیر sarazir

stem *n* ساقه sagheh

stench *n* تعفن ta'affon

step *n* گام gam

stepbrother *n* نابرادری nabaradari

step-by-step *adv* گام‌به‌گام gam be gam

stepdaughter *n* نادختری na dokhtari

stepfather *n* ناپدری na pedari

stepladder *n* نردبان‌متحرک nardebane moteharek

stepmother *n* نامادري na madari

stepsister *n* ناخواهري na khahari

stepson *n* ناپسري na pesari

sterile *adj* عقيم aghim

sterilize *v* نازاكردن naza kardan

stern *adj* سخت sakht

sternly *adv* درشتي doroshti

stew *n* نگراني negarani

stewardess *n* مهماندارهواپيما mehmandare havapeyma

stick *v* گيركردن gir kardan

stick *iv* چسبانيدن chasbanidan

stick around *v* درنگ كردن derang kardan

stick *to* *v* سرقول بودن sare ghowl boudan

stick up *v* سربرافراشتن sar bar afrashtan

sticker *n* برچسب barchasb

sticky *adj* چسبناك chasbnak

stiff *adj* سفت seft

stiffness *n* خشكى khoshki

stifle *v* خفه كردن khafeh kardan

stifling *adj* خفه كننده khafeh konandeh

still *adj* بى حركت bi harkat

still *adv* هنوز hanuz

stimulant *n* داروى محرك daruye moharrek

stimulate *v* تحريک کردن tahrik kardan

stimulus *n* محرک moharrek

sting *iv* گزيدن gazidan

sting *n* نيش nish

stingy *adj* خسيس khasis

stink *iv* بوى بددادن bouye bad dadan

stink *n* گند gand

stinking *adj* نفرت آور nefrat avar

stir *v* تكان دادن tekan dadan

stitch *v* بخيه زدن bakhiyeh zadan

stitch *n* كوك kook

stocking *n* جوراب زنانه ساقه بلند jourabe zananeh sagh boland

stockpile *v* انباشته كردن anbashteh kardan

stoic *adj* بردبار bord bar

stomach *n* معده me'edeh

stone *n* سنگ sang

stool *n* كرسى korsi

stop *v* ايستادن istadan

stop *n* توقف tavaghof

storage *n* انبار كالا anbare kala

store *v* انبار كردن anbar kardan

store *n* مغازه maghazeh

stork *n* لک لک lak lak

storm *n* كولاک koulak

stormy *adj* توفانى toofani

story *n* داستان dastan

stove *n* چماق chomagh

straight *adj* راست rast

straighten *v* راست كردن rast kardan

strain *v* زورزدن zoor zadan

strain *n* كشش keshesh

strained *adj* صاف كرده saf kardeh

strainer *n* صافى safi

strait *n* تنگه tangeh

stranded *adj* معطل mo'attel

strange *adj* ناشناس nashenas

stranger *n* بيگانه biganeh

strangle v خفه کردن khaffeh kardan

strap n تسمه tasmeh

strategy n حیله hileh

straw n کاه kah

strawberry n توت فرنگی tout farangi

stray adj آواره avareh

stray v آواره کردن avareh kardan

stream n نهر nahr

street n خیابان kheyaban

strength n نیرو niroo

strengthen v تقویت کردن taghviyat kardan

stress n فشار feshar

stretch v کشیدن keshidan

stretcher n برانکار borankar

strict adj سخت sakht

stride iv قدم زدن ghadam zadan

strife n ستیزه setizeh

strike n اصابت esabat

strike iv ضربه زدن zarbeh zadan

string n نخ nakh

stringent adj سختگیر sakhtgir

strip n باریکه، نوار barikeh

strip v برهنه کردن berahneh kardan

stripe n علامت alamat

striped adj خطدار khat dar

strive iv کوشیدن koushidan

stroke n ضربه zarbeh

stroll n قدم زدن ghadam zadan

stroll v گردش gardesh

strong adj قوی ghavi

structure n ساختمان sakhteman

struggle v تقلا کردن taghalla kardan

struggle n ستیز setiz

stubborn adj سمج semej

student n دانش آموز danesh amouz

study v مطالعه کردن motale'eh kardan

stuff v انباشتن anbashtan

stuff n ماده madeh

stuffing n چاشنی chashni

stuffy adv بدبو bad boo

stumble v سهو کردن sahv kardan

stumble n لغزش laghzesh

stun v گیج کردن gij kardan

stunning adj گیج کننده gij konandeh

stupendous adj عجیب ajib

stupid adj احمق ahmagh

stupidity n حماقت hemaghat

sturdy adj قوی هیکل ghavi heykal

stutter v لکنت داشتن loknat dashtan

style n سبک sabk

subdue v رام کردن ram kardan

subdued adj رام ram

subject v مطیع کردن moti'e kardan

subject n موضوع mowzou

sublime adj والا vala

submerge v غوطه ور ساختن ghouteh var sakhtan

submissive adj مطیع moti'e

submit v تسلیم شدن taslim shodan

subscribe v تصدیق کردن tasdigh kardan

subscription n اشتراک eshterak

subsidize v کمک خرج دادن komak kharj dadan

subsidy n کمک مالی komake mali

subsist v ماندن mandan

substance n جسم jesm

substantial adj اساسی asasi

substitute v تعویض کردن ta'aviz kardan

substitute n قائم‌مقام gha'em magham

subtitle n زیرنویس zir nevis

subtle adj زیرک zirak

subtly adv از روی زیرکی az rouye ziraki

subtract v کاستن kastan

subtraction n کاهش kahesh

suburb n حومه‌شهر houmehe shahr

subway n مترو metrow

succeed v موفق‌شدن movafagh shodan

success n موفقیت movafaghiyat

successful adj کامیاب kamyab

successor n جانشین janeshin

succulent adj شاداب shadab

succumb v تسلیم‌شدن taslim shodan

such adj چنین chenin

suck v مکیدن makidan

sucker adj مکنده makandeh

sudden adj ناگهانی nagahani

suddenly adv ناگهان nagah

sue v تقاضاکردن taghaza kardan

suffer v تحمل‌کردن tahammol kardan

suffering n رنج ranj

sufficient adj کافی kafi

suffocate n خفه‌کردن khafeh kardan

sugar n شکر shekar

suggest v پیشنهادکردن pishnahad kardan

suggestion n اشاره eshareh

suggestive adj اشاره‌کننده eshareh konandeh

suicide n خودکشی khod koshi

suit n لباس lebas

suitable adj مناسب monaseb

suitcase n چمدان chamedan

sullen adj کج‌خلق kaj kholgh

sum n حاصل‌جمع hasele jam'e

summarize v خلاصه‌کردن kholaseh kardan

summary n خلاصه kholaseh

summer n تابستان tabestan

summit n قله gholleh

summon v فراخواندن fara khandan

sumptuous adj مجلل mojalal

sun n آفتاب aftab

sunburn n آفتاب‌زدگی aftab zadegi

Sunday n یکشنبه yek shanbeh

sundown n غروب ghorub

sunglasses n عینک‌آفتابی eynake aftabi

sunny adj آفتابی aftabi

sunrise v طلوع‌کردن tolou'e kardan

sunset n مغرب maghreb

superb adj باشکوه ba shokouh

superfluous adj زیادي zeyadi

superior adj بالارتبه bala rotbeh

superiority n برتري bartari

supermarket n ابربازار abar bazar

superpower n ابرقدرت abar ghodrat

superstition *n* خرافات khorafat

supervise *v* رسیدگی کردن residegi kardan

supper *n* شام sham

supple *adj* کش‌دار kesh dar

supplier *n* فروشنده foroushandeh

supplies *n* تدارکات tadarokat

supply *v* رساندن resandan

support *v* حمایت کردن hemayat kardan

supporter *n* حامی hami

suppose *v* پنداشتن pendashtan

supposing *c* بفرض be farz

supposition *n* احتمال ehtemal

suppress *v* توقیف کردن towghif kardan

supreme *adj* عالی a'li

surcharge *n* اضافه‌بها ezafeh baha

sure *adj* یقین yaghin

surely *adv* یقینا yaghinan

surf *v* موج‌بازی کردن mouj bazi kardan

surface *n* سطح sath

surgeon *n* جراح jarrah

surgical *adv* جراحی jarrahi

surname *n* لقب laghab

surplus *n* مازاد mazad

surprise *n* شگفت shegeft

surprise *v* غافلگیر کردن ghafel gir kardan

surrender *v* سپردن sepordan

surround *v* فراگرفتن fara gereftan

surroundings *n* محیط mohit

surveillance *n* نظارت nezarat

survey *n* بازدید bazdid

survival *n* بقا bagha

survive *v* زنده‌ماندن zendeh mandan

survivor *n* بازمانده baz mandeh

susceptible *adj* حساس hassas

suspect *v* شک‌داشتن shak dashtan

suspect *adj* مظنون maznoon

suspend *v* آویزان‌شدن avizan shodan

suspense *n* معلق moallagh

suspension *n* وقفه vaghfeh

suspicion *n* بدگمانی bad gomani

sustain *v* تحمل کردن tahammol kardan

swallow *v* فورت‌دادن ghoort dadan

swamp *n* مرداب mordab

swap *v* مبادله‌کردن mobadeleh kardan

swap *n* معاوضه moavezeh

swarm *n* ازدحام ezdeham

swear *iv* قسم‌دادن ghasam dadan

sweat *n* عرق aragh

sweater *n* عرق‌گیر aragh gir

sweep *iv* جاروب‌کردن jaroo kardan

sweet *adj* شیرین shirin

sweeten *v* شیرین‌کردن shirin kardan

sweetheart *n* دلبر delbar

sweetness *n* ملاحت malahat

sweets *n* عرق‌گیر ورزشی aragh gire varzeshi

swell *iv* بادکردن bad kardan

swelling *n* تورم tavarom

swift *adj* تندرو tond row

swim *iv* شناکردن shena kardan

swimmer *n* شناگر shena gar

swindle *n* فریب farib

swindle v گول‌زدن gool zadan

swindler n کلاه‌بردار kolah bardar

swing iv تاب‌خوردن tab khordan

swing n نوسان navasan

Swiss adj سویسی sowisi

switch v راه‌گزیدن rah gozidan

switch n گزینه gozineh

swivel v چرخاندن charkhandan

swollen adj ورم‌کرده varam kardeh

sword n شمشیر shamshir

swordfish n کوسه kooseh

syllable n هجا heja

symbol n نماد nemad

symmetry n تقارن tagharon

sympathize v جانبداری‌کردن janeb dari kardan

sympathy n همدمی hamdami

symphony n سمفونی samfouni

symptom n علامت alamat

synagogue n کنیسه kaniseh

synod n شورای‌کلیسایی showraye kelisaee

synthesis n تلفیق talfigh

syphilis n سیفیلیس siflis

syringe n سرنگ sorang

syrup n شربت sharbat

system n طریقه tarigheh

T

tabernacle n خیمه kheymeh

table n میز miz

tablecloth n سفره sofreh

tablespoon n قاشق‌سوپ‌خوری ghashoghe soup khori

tablet n لوح louh

tack n رویه raviyeh

tackle v گلاویزشدن galaviz shodan

tact n نزاکت nezakat

tactful adj مبادی‌آداب mobadiye adab

tactical adj ماهرانه maheraneh

tactics n فنون fonoon

tag n برچسب barchasb

tail n دم dom

tailor n خیاط khayat

tainted adj لکه‌دارکردن lakkeh dar kardan

take iv گرفتن gereftan

take apart v اوراق‌کردن ouragh kardan

take away v حمل‌کردن haml kardan

take back v پس‌گرفتن pas gereftan

take in v پذیرفتن paziroftan

take off v جهش‌کردن jahesh kardan

take out v درآوردن daravardan

take over v تحویل‌گرفتن tahvil gereftan

tale n افسانه afsaneh

talent n استعداد stedad

talk v حرف‌زدن harf zadan

talkative adj وراج verraj

tall adj بلند boland

tame adj رام ram

tan adj قهوه‌ای‌سوخته ghahveiye soukhteh

tangent n مماس momas

tangerine *n* نارنگی narengi

tangible *adj* محسوس mahsous

tangle *n* درهم‌وبرهم dar ham va bar ham

tangle *n* درهم‌وبرهم dar ham va bar ham

tank *n* مخزن makhzan

tanker *n* نفت‌کش naft kesh

tanned *adj* برنزه boronzeh

tap *n* شیرآب shire ab

tape *n* نوارچسب navar chasb

tape recorder *n* ضبط‌صوت zabte sout

tapestry *n* قالیچه‌نما ghlicheh nama

tar *n* قیر ghir

tarantula *n* رطیل ratil

tardiness *n* دیرکرد dir kard

tardy *adv* تنبل tanbal

target *n* هدف hadaf

tariff *n* تعرفه tarefeh

tarnish *v* کدرکردن keder kardan

tart *n* هرزه‌زن zane harzeh

task *n* تکلیف taklif

taste *v* چشیدن cheshidan

taste *n* مزه mazeh

tasteful *adj* خوش‌ذوق khosh zough

tasteless *adj* بی‌مزه bi mazeh

tasty *adj* خوش‌مزه khosh mazeh

tavern *n* میخانه mey khaneh

tax *n* مالیات maliyat

tea *n* چای chai

teach *iv* تعلیم‌دادن ta'alim dadan

teacher *n* معلم moallem

team *n* گروه gorouh

teapot *n* قوری‌چای ghooriye chai

tear *iv* دریدن daridan

tear *n* گریه geryeh

tearful *adj* گریان geryan

tease *v* آزاردادن azar dadan

teaspoon *n* قاشق‌چای‌خوری ghashoghe chai khori

technical *adj* فنی fanni

technicality *n* اصطلاحات‌فنی estelahate fanni

technician *n* اهل‌فن ahle fan

technique *n* فن fann

technology *n* فن‌شناسی fan shenasi

tedious *adj* ملالت‌آور malalat avar

tedium *n* یکنواختی yek navakhti

teenager *n* نوجوان(ازده‌تا۱۹ساله) nowjavan

teeth *n* دندانها dandan-ha

telegram *n* تلگرام telegram

telepathy *n* اندیشه‌خوانی andisheh khani

telephone *n* تلفن telefon

telescope *n* دوربین‌نجومی dour bine nojoomi

televise *v* درتلویزیون‌نشان‌دادن dar televiziyon neshan dadan

television *n* تلویزیون televiziyon

tell *iv* گفتن goftan

temper *n* مزاج mazaj

temperature *n* دما dama

tempest *n* توفان toufan

temple *n* پرستشگاه parasteshgah

temporary *adj* موقتی movaghati

tempt *v* وسوسه‌کردن vasvaseh kardan

temptation *n* وسوسه vasvaseh

tempting adj هوس‌انگیز havas angiz

ten adj ده dah

tenacity n سختی sakhti

tenant n مستاجر mostajer

tendency n گرایش gerayesh

tender adj نرم narm

tenderness n دلسوزی del souzi

tennis n تنیس teniss

tenor n رویه rouyeh

tense adj عصبی‌وهیجان‌زده asabi va hayajan zadeh

tension n کشش keshesh

tent n چادر chador

tentacle n شاخک shakhak

tentative adj آزمایشی azmayeshi

tenth n دهم dahom

tenuous adj نازک nazok

tepid adj ولرم velarm

term n مدت moddat

term n واژه vazheh

terminate v خاتمه‌یافتن khatemeh yaftan

terminology n واژگان vazhegan

termite n موریانه mooriyaneh

terms n شرایط sharayet

terrace n بهارخواب bahar khab

terrain n زمینه zamineh

terrestrial adj خاکی khaki

terrible adj وحشتناک vahshat nak

terrific adj ترسناک tarsnak

terrify v ترساندن tarsandan

terrifying adj ترسناک tarsnak

territory n سرزمین sarzamin

terror n دهشت dehshat

terrorism n ایجادترس‌درمردم ijade tars dar mardom

terrorist n ارعابگر era'bgar

terrorize v باتهدیدکاری‌انجام‌دادن ba tahdid kari anjam dadan

terse adj موجز mojez

test v آزمودن azmoudan

test n آزمون azmoun

testament n وصیت‌نامه vasiyat nameh

testify v گواهی‌دادن govahi dadan

testimony n گواهی govahi

text n متن matn

textbook n کتاب‌درسی ketabe darsi

texture n بافت baft

thank v سپاسگزاری‌کردن sepas gozari kardan

thankful adj سپاسگزار sepas gozar

thanks n تشکر tashakkor

that pro آن an

thaw v گداختن godakhtan

thaw n گدازش،گرمی godazesh

theatre n تماشاخانه tamasha khaneh

theft n دزدی dozdi

theme n موضوع mowzoo

themselves pro خودشان khodeshan

then adv سپس sepas

theologian n متخصص‌الهیات motekhassese elahiyat

theology n الهیات elahiyat

theory n نظریه nazariyeh

therapy n درمان darman

there adv آنجا anja

therefore *adv* بنابراین bana bar in

thermometer *n* دماسنج dama sanj

thermostat *n* دستگاه تنظیم گرما dastgahe tanzime garma

these *adj* اینها in ha

thesis *n* پایان‌نامه payan nameh

they *pro* آنها an ha

thick *adj* ضخیم zakhim

thicken *v* کلفت کردن koloft kardan

thickness *n* کلفتی kolofti

thief *n* سارق saregh

thigh *n* ران ran

thin *adj* نازک nazok

thing *n* چیز chiz

think *iv* فکر کردن fekr kardan

thinly *adv* لاغر laghar

third *adj* سومی sevvomi

thirst *v* تشنه بودن teshneh boudan

thirsty *adj* تشنه teshneh

thirteen *adj* سیزده sizdah

thirty *adj* سی si

this *adj* این in

thorn *n* خار khar

thorny *adj* خاردار khar dar

thorough *adj* از اول تا آخر az avval ta akhar

those *adj* آنها an ha

though *c* به هر حال be har hal

thought *n* اندیشه andisheh

thoughtful *adj* اندیشمند andishmand

thousand *adj* هزار hezar

thread *v* بند کشیدن band keshidan

thread *n* نخ nakh

threat *n* تهدید tahdid

threaten *v* تهدید کردن tahdid kardan

three *adj* سه she

threshold *n* آستانه astaneh

thrifty *adj* خانه‌دار khaneh dar

thrill *v* به هیجان آوردن be hayajan avardan

thrill *n* هیجان hayajan

thrive *v* رونق یافتن rownagh yaftan

throat *n* گلو galoo

throb *n* تپش tapesh

throb *v* زدن zadan

throne *n* تخت takht

throng *n* ازدحام ezdeham

through *pre* ازمیان az miyan

throw *iv* پرت کردن part kardan

thrust *iv* فرو کردن foroo kardan

thug *n* آدم کش adam kosh

thumb *n* شست shast

thumbtack *n* پونز poonez

thunder *n* رعد ra'ad

thunderbolt *n* آذرخش azarakhsh

thunderstorm *n* توفان و صاعقه toofan va saegheh

Thursday *n* پنج‌شنبه panj shanbeh

thus *adv* بدینسان bedin san

thwart *v* عقیم گذاردن aghim gozardan

tickle *v* غلغلک دادن ghel ghelak dadan

ticklish *adj* غلغلکی ghel ghelaki

tidal wave *n* سیلاب seylab

tide *n* جذر و مد jazr va mad

tidy *adj* مرتب moratab

tie *n* کراوات keravat

tie *v* گره زدن gereh zadan

tiger *n* ببر babr

tight *adj* سفت seft

tighten *v* سفت‌کردن seft kardan

tile *n* کاشی kashi

till *adv* تا ta

till *v* کشت‌کردن kesht kardan

tilt *v* کج‌کردن kaj kardan

timber *n* چوب choob

time *n* زمان zaman

timeless *adj* نامناسب na monaseb

timely *adj* به‌موقع be moghe

times *n* ایام ayyam

timetable *n* برنامه‌کار barnamehye kar

timid *adj* کمرو kam rou

timidity *n* کمرویی kam roui

tin *n* قلع ghal'e

tiny *adj* ریز riz

tip *n* انعام anam

tiptoe *n* نوک‌پنجه noke panjeh

tired *adj* خسته khasteh

tiredness *n* خستگی khastegi

tireless *adj* خستگی‌ناپذیر khastegi na pazir

tiresome *adj* خسته‌کننده khsteh konandeh

tissue *n* بافت baft

title *n* اسم esm

to *pre* بسوی be souye

toad *n* غوک ghook

toast *v* (نان)برشته‌کردن bereshteh kardan(nan)

toaster *n* نان‌برشته‌کن nan bereshteh kon

tobacco *n* توتون toutoun

today *adv* امروز emrouz

toddler *n* کودک‌نوپا koudake nou pa

toe *n* پنجه panjeh

toenail *n* ناخن‌انگشت‌پا nakhone angoshte pa

together *adv* باهم ba ham

toil *v* زحمت‌کشیدن zahmat keshidan

toilet *n* مستراح mostarah

token *n* نشانه neshaneh

tolerable *adj* قابل‌تحمل ghabele tahammol

tolerance *n* تحمل tahammol

tolerate *v* تحمل‌کردن tahammol kardan

toll *n* عوارض avarez

tomato *n* گوجه‌فرنگی gouje farangi

tomb *n* آرامگاه aramgah

tombstone *n* سنگ‌قبر sange ghabr

tomorrow *adv* فردا farda

ton *n* تن ton

tone *n* لحن lahn

tongs *n* گیره gireh

tongue *n* زبان zaban

tonic *n* مقوی moghavvi

tonight *adv* امشب emshab

tonsil *n* لوزه louzeh

too *adv* زیاد ziyad

tool *n* ابزار abzar

tooth *n* دندان dandan

toothache *n* دندان‌درد dandan dard

toothpick *n* خلال‌دندان khalal dandan

top *n* سر sar

topic *n* موضوع mowzoo

topple *v* واژگون کردن vazhgoon kardan

torch *n* مشعل mash'al

torment *n* زجر zajr

torment *v* عذاب دادن azab dadan

torrent *n* سیل seylab

torrid *adj* سوزان souzan

torso *n* پیچ یا تاب خوردن pich ya tab khordan

tortoise *n* سنگ پشت sang posht

torture *n* شکنجه shekanjeh

torture *v* عذاب دادن azab dadan

total *adj* تام tam

totalitarian *adj* خودکامه khod kameh

totality *n* کلیت kolliyat

touch *n* لمس lams

touch *v* لمس کردن lams kardan

touchdown *n* تماس هواپیما با زمین tamase hava peyma ba zamin

touchy *adj* نازک نارنجی nazok narenji

tough *adj* محکم mohkam

toughen *v* سفت شدن seft shodan

toupee *n* کاکل یا موی مصنوعی kakol ya mooye masnoui

tour *n* گشت gasht

tourism *n* جهانگردی jahan gardi

tourist *n* جهانگرد jahan gard

tournament *n* مسابقه mosabegheh

tow *v* دنبال کشیدن donbal keshidan

tow truck *n* جرثقیل jarsaghil

towards *pre* به سوی be souye

towel *n* حوله howleh

tower *n* برج borj

town *n* شهرک shahrak

town hall *n* تالار شهرداری یا فرمانداری talare shahrdari ya farmandari

toxic *adj* سمی sammi

toxin *n* سم sam

toy *n* اسباب بازی asbab bazi

trace *n* اثر asar

track *v* دنبال کردن donbal kardan

traction *n* کشش keshesh

tractor *n* تراکتور teraktor

trade *n* بازرگانی bazargani

trade *v* مبادله کردن mobadeleh kardan

trademark *n* علامت تجارتی alamate tejari

trader *n* بازرگان bazargan

tradition *n* رسم rasm

traffic *v* تردد کردن taraddod kardan

traffic *n* عبور و مرور obour va morour

tragedy *n* مصیبت mosibat

tragic *adj* غم انگیز gham angiz

trail *n* پیشقدم pish ghadam

trail *v* دنبال کشیدن donbal keshidan

train *n* قطار ghatar

trainee *n* کارآموز kar amouz

trainer *n* مربی morabi

training *n* تعلیم ta'alim

trait *n* ویژگی vizhegi

traitor *n* خائن khaen

trajectory *n* خط سیر khatte' seyr

tram *n* تراموای teramvai

trample v پایمال کردن paymal kardan

trance n نشئه nasheh

tranquility n آرامش aramesh

tranquilize v آرام کردن aram kardan

transaction n دادوستد dad va setad

transcend v سبقت جستن sebghat jostan

transcribe v رونویسی کردن rou nevisi kardan

transfer n انتقال enteghal

transfer v انتقال دادن enteghal dadan

transform v تغییر شکل دادن taghiere shekl dadan

transfusion n تزریق tazrigh

transient adj زودگذر zood gozar

transit n عبور obour

transition n انتقال enteghal

translate v ترجمه کردن tarjomeh kardan

translator n مترجم motarjem

transmit v عبور دادن obour dadan

transparent adj شفاف shafaf

transplant v نشاکردن nesh kardan

transport v ترابری کردن tarabari kardan

trap n تله taleh

trash n آشغال ashghal

trash can n سطل آشغال satle ashghal

trashy adj مهمل mohmal

traumatic adj آسیب‌زا asib za

traumatize v معذب کردن moazzab kardan

travel v سفر کردن safar kardan

traveller n مسافر mosafer

tray n سینی sini

treacherous adj خائن kha'en

treachery n خیانت khiyanat

tread iv راه رفتن rah raftan

treason n خیانت khiyanat

treasure n گنج ganj

treasurer n صندوقدار sandogh dar

treat v رفتار کردن raftar kardan

treatment n رفتار raftar

treaty n پیمان peyman

tree n درخت derakht

tremble v لرزیدن larzidan

tremendous adj شگرف shegarf

tremor n لرزش larzesh

trend n گرایش gerayesh

trendy adj مدروز mode rouz

trespass v تجاوز کردن tajavoz kardan

trial n محاکمه mohakemeh

trials n سنجش sanjesh

triangle n مثلث mosallas

tribe n تبار tabar

tribulation n محنت mehnat

tribunal n دادگاه dadgah

tribute n ستایش setayesh

trick n حیله hileh

trick v حیله زدن hileh zadan

trickle v چکیدن chekidan

tricky adj نیرنگ‌آمیز neyrang amiz

trigger v رهاکردن raha kardan

trim v آراستن arastan

trimester *n* دوره‌سه‌ماهه dourehye seh mahe

trimmings *n* آرايش arayesh

trip *n* گردش gardesh

triple *adj* سه‌گانه she ganeh

tripod *n* سه‌پايه se payeh

triumph *n* پيروزي pirouzi

triumphant *adj* پيروز pirouz

trivia *n* ناچيز na chiz

trivial *adj* مبتذل mobtazal

trivialize *v* مبتذل‌كردن mobtazal kardan

trolley *n* گاري gari

troop *n* گروه gorouh

trophy *n* غنائم ghanaem

tropic *n* استوا ostova

tropical *adj* استوايى ostovai

trouble *n* آزار azar

troublesome *adj* پرزحمت por zahmat

trousers *n* شلوار shalvar

trout *n* قزل‌آلا ghezel ala

truce *n* آتش‌بس atash bas

truck *n* كاميون kamiyoun

trucker *n* راننده‌كاميون ranandeh kamiyoun

trump *n* صداي‌شيپور sedaye sheypour

trumpet *n* شيپور sheypour

trunk *n* تنه taneh

trust *n* اعتماد etemad

trust *v* اعتمادداشتن etemad dashtan

truth *n* راستي rasti

truthful *adj* راستگو rastgoo

try *v* كوشش‌كردن kooshesh kardan

T-shirt *n* پيراهن‌بي‌يقه pirahane bi yagheh

tub *n* وان van

tuberculosis *n* مرض‌سل maraze sel

Tuesday *n* سه‌شنبه she shanbeh

tulip *n* لاله laleh

tumble *v* جست‌وخيزكردن jasto khiz kardan

tummy *n* شكم shekam

tumour *n* غده ghddeh

tumult *n* غوغا ghowgha

tumultuous *adj* شلوغ sholoogh

tuna *n* ماهي‌تون mahiye ton

tune *n* آهنگ ahang

tune *v* ميزان‌كردن mizan kardan

tunic *n* نيام niyam

tunnel *n* تونل tounel

turbine *n* توربين tourbin

turbulence *n* آشوب ashoub

turf *n* چمن chaman

turmoil *adj* غوغا ghowgha

turn *v* تازدن ta zadan

turn *n* نوبت nowbat

turn back *v* پس‌دادن pas dadan

turn in *v* برگرداندن‌به‌انبار bar gardandan be anbar

turn off *v* خاموش‌كردن khamoosh kardan

turn on *v* روشن‌كردن roushan kardan

turn over *v* غلتاندن ghaltandan

turn up *v* ظاهرشدن zaher shodan

turnip *n* شلغم shalgham

turret *n* برج‌گردان borje gardan

turtle *n* لاك‌پشت lak posht

tusk n دندان‌درازوتیز dandane deraz va tiz

tweezers n موچین moo chin

twelfth adj دوازدهمین davazdahomin

twelve adj دوازده davazdah

twentieth adj بیستمین bistomin

twenty adj بیست bist

twice adv دوبار do bar

twilight n تاریک‌روشن tarik roushan

twin n دوقلو do gholoo

twist n پیچ pich

twist v پیچیدن pichidan

twisted adj گرد باد gerd bad

twister n چرخان charkhan

two adj دو do

tycoon n سرمایه‌داربانفوذ sarmayeh dare ba nofooz

type v طبقه‌بندی‌کردن tabagheh bandi kardan

typical adj نوعی noui

tyranny n ستمگری setamgari

tyrant n ستمگر setamgar

U

ugliness n زشتی zeshti

ugly adj زشت zesht

ulcer n زخم zakhm

ultimate adj نهایی nahai

ultimatum n اتمام‌حجت etmam hojjat

umbrella n چتر chatr

umpire n سرداور sar davar

unable adj عاجز ajez

unanimity n اتفاق‌آرا ettefagh ara

unarmed adj غیرمسلح gheire mosallah

unattached adj ناوابسته na vabasteh

unavoidable adj اجتناب‌ناپذیر ejtenab na pazir

unaware adj بی‌اطلاع bi ettela

unbearable adj تحمل‌ناپذیر tahammol na pazir

unbeatable adj شکست‌ناپذیر shekast na-pazir

unbelievable adj باورنکردنی bavar nakardani

unbiased adj بی‌غرض bi gharaz

unbroken adj رام‌نشده ram nashodeh

unbutton v گشودن‌دکمه goshoodane dokmeh

uncertain adj نامعلوم na ma'aloom

uncommon adj غیرعادی gheire addi

unconscious adj بیهوش bihoush

uncover v برهنه‌کردن berahneh kardan

undecided adj مردد moradad

undeniable adj انکارناپذیر enkar na pazir

under pre درزیر dar zir

underground adj قطارزیرزمینی ghatare zir zamini

underline v زیرچیزی‌خط‌کشیدن zire chizi khat keshidan

underneath pre زیرین zirin

understand v فهمیدن fahmidan

undertake *v* برعهده گرفتن bar ohdeh gereftan

underwear *n* لباس‌زیر lebase zir

underwrite *v* درزیرسندی‌نوشتن dar zire sanadi neveshtan

undesirable *adj* نامطلوب na matloob

undo *v* باطل‌کردن batel kardan

undress *v* برهنه شدن berahneh shodan

unearth *v* اززیرخاک‌دراوردن az zire khak dar avardan

uneasiness *n* ناراحتی narahati

uneasy *adj* بی‌ارام bi aram

uneducated *adj* بیسواد bi savad

unemployed *adj* بیکار bi kar

unemployment *n* بیکاری bi kari

unending *adj* بی‌پایان bi payan

unequal *adj* نابرابر na barabar

unequivocal *adj* غیرمبهم gheyre mobham

uneven *adj* ناهموار na hamvar

unexpected *adj* غیرمنتظره gheyre montazereh

unfailing *adj* پایدار paydar

unfair *adj* بی‌انصاف bi ensaf

unfairly *adv* غیرمنصفانه gheire monsefaneh

unfairness *n* بدی badi

unfaithful *adj* بی‌وفا bi vafa

unfamiliar *adj* ناآشنا na ashena

unfasten *v* بازکردن baz kardan

unfavourable *adj* نامساعد na mosaed

unfit *adj* ناشایسته na shayesteh

unfold *v* فاش‌کردن fash kardan

unforeseen *adj* پیش‌بینی‌نشده pish bini nashodeh

unforgettable *adj* ازیادنرفتنی az yad naraftani

unfounded *adj* بی‌اساس bi asas

unfriendly *adj* غیردوستانه gheyre doostaneh

ungrateful *adj* ناسپاس na sepas

unhappiness *n* بدبختی bad bakhti

unhappy *adj* ناکام na kam

unhealthy *adj* ناسالم na salem

unheard-of *adj* بی‌سابقه bi sabegheh

unification *n* تک‌سازی tak sazi

uniform *n* یک‌شکل yek shekl

uniformity *n* یگانگی yeganegi

unify *v* متحدکردن motahed kardan

unilateral *adj* یک‌طرفه yek tarafeh

union *n* وحدت vahdat

unique *adj* یگانه yganeh

unit *n* یکان yekan

unite *v* متحدکردن motahed kardan

unity *n* اتحاد ettehad

universal *adj* جهانی jahani

universe *n* وجود vojood

university *n* دانشگاه daneshgah

unjust *adj* غیرعادلانه gheyre adelaneh

unjustified *adj* ناحق na hagh

unknown *adj* ناشناس na shenas

unlawful *adj* نامشروع na mashrou

unleaded *adj* بی‌سرب bi sorb

unleash *v* رهاکردن raha kardan

unless *c* مگر magar

unlike *adj* بی‌شباهت bi shebahat

unlikely *adj* غیرمحتمل gheyre motehammel

unlimited *adj* نامحدود na mahdood

unload *v* خالی کردن khali kardan

unlock *v* (قفل)گشودن goshoudan(ghofl)

unlucky *adj* تیره‌بخت tireh bakht

unmarried *adj* غیرمتاهل gheyre moteahel

unmask *v* نقاب‌برداشتن neghab bardashtan

unnecessary *adj* غیرضروری gheyr-e zarouri

unnoticed *adj* موردتوجه‌قرارنگرفته mourede tavajoh gharar nagerefteh

unoccupied *adj* اشغال‌نشده eshghal nashodeh

unofficially *adv* غیررسمی gheyre rasmi

unpack *v* بازکردن baz kardan

unpleasant *adj* نامطبوع na matbou

unplug *v* کشیدن‌پریزازبرق keshidan periz az bargh

unpopular *adj* نامحبوب na mahboub

unprotected *adj* محافظت‌نشده mohafezat nashodeh

unreal *adj* تصوری tasavori

unrealistic *adj* غیرواقعی gheyre vaghei

unreasonable *adj* نابخرد na bekhrad

unrelenting *adj* بی‌امان bi aman

unreliable *adj* نامطمئن na motmaen

unrest *n* ناآرامی na arami

unsafe *adj* ناامن na amn

unspeakable *adj* ناگفتنی na goftani

unstable *adj* بی‌ثبات bi sobat

unsteady *adj* لرزان larzan

unsuccessful *adj* شکست shekast

unsuitable *adj* نامناسب na monaseb

unthinkable *adj* غیرقابل‌فکر gheyre ghabele fekr

untie *v* بازکردن baz kardan

until *adv* تا ta

untimely *adj* نابهنگام na be hengam

untouchable *adj* نجس najes

untrue *adj* خلاف khelaf

unusual *adj* غیرعادی gheyre addi

unveil *v* پرده‌برداری‌کردن pardeh bardari

unwillingly *adv* ازروی‌بی‌میلی az rouye bi meyli

unwind *v* بازکردن baz kardan

unwise *adj* نادان nadan

upbringing *n* تربیت tarbiyat

upcoming *adj* درآتیه‌نزدیک dar atiyehye nazdik

update *v* جدیدکردن jadid kardan

upgrade *v* پیشرفت‌دادن pishraft dadan

upheaval *n* تحول tahavvol

uphill *adv* دشوار doshvar

uphold *v* حمایت‌کردن hemayat kardan

upholstery *n* اثاثه‌داخلي asasiyehe dakheli

upkeep *n* نگهداري negahdari

upon *pre* برفراز bar faraze

upper *adj* فوقانى fowghani

upright *adj* راد rad

uprising *n* شورش shouresh

uproar *n* هنگامه hengameh

uproot *v* برکندن bar kandan

upset *v* واژگون کردن vazhgoun kardan

upside-down *adv* وارونه varouneh

upstairs *adv* ساختمان‌فوقاني sakhtemane foughani

uptight *adj* محکم

upwards *adv* روبه‌بالا roo be bala

urban *adj* شهري shahri

urge *n* اصرار esrar

urge *v* اصرار کردن esrar kardan

urgency *n* ميل meyl

urgent *adj* ضروري zarouri

urinate *v* ادرارکردن edrar kardan

urine *n* ادرار edrar

urn *n* کوزه kouzeh

usage *n* کاربرد karbord

use *v* مصرف کردن masraf kardan

used to *adj* عادت کردن adat kardan

useful *adj* مفيد mofid

usefulness *n* سودمندي soudmandi

useless *adj* بي‌فايده bi fayedeh

usher *n* راهنما rahnama

usual *adj* هميشگي hamishegi

usurp *v* بەزورگرفتن be zour gereftan

utensil *n* لوازم‌آشپزخانه lavazeme ashpaz khaneh

uterus *n* رحم rahem

utilize *v* استفاده کردن estefadeh kardan

utopia *n* مدينه‌فاضله madinehye fazeleh

V

vacancy *n* جاي‌خالي jaye khali

vacant *adj* خالي khali

vacate *v* تعطيل کردن ta'atil kardan

vacation *n* مرخصي گرفتن morakhasi gereftan

vaccinate *v* واکسن‌زدن vaksan zadan

vaccine *n* واکسن vaksan

vagrant *n* آدم‌آواره‌وولگرد adame avareh va velgard

vague *adj* مبهم mobham

vain *adj* باطل batel

vainly *adv* ازروي‌خودبيني az rouye khod bini

valiant *adj* شجاع shoja

valid *adj* معتبر mo'tabar

validate *v* قانوني کردن ghanouni kardan

valley *n* دره darreh

valuable *adj* باارزش ba arzesh

value *n* قيمت gheymat

valve *n* سرپوش sarpoush

vampire *n* خون‌آشام khoun asham

van *n* بارکش bar kesh

vandal *n* خرابکار kharabkar

vandalism *n* وحشيگري vahshi gari

vandalize *v* ویران‌سازی کردن viran-sazi kardan

vanish *v* ناپدیدشدن na padid shodan

vanity *n* خودبینی khod bini

vanquish *v* مغلوب‌ساختن maghloub sakhtan

vapour *n* بخار bokhar

vaporize *v* تبخیرشدن tabkhir shodan

variable *adj* بی‌قرار bi gharar

variety *n* تنوع tanavoe

various *adj* گوناگون gounagoun

varnish *v* جلادادن jala dadan

varnish *n* صیقل seyghal

vary *v* تغییردادن taghier dadan

vase *n* گلدان goldan

vast *adj* پهناور pahnavar

veal *n* گوشت گوساله goushte gousaleh

vegetable *v* سبزی کاشتن sabzi kashtan

vegetarian *v* گیاهخواری giyah-khari

vegetation *n* زندگی گیاهی zendegiye giyahi

vehicle *n* وسیله‌نقلیه vasileh-e naghliyeh

veil *n* نقاب neghab

vein *n* ورید varid

velocity *n* شتاب shetab

venerable *adj* محترم mohtaram

venerate *v* تکریم کردن takrim kardan

vengeance *n* انتقام entegham

venom *n* کینه kineh

vent *n* دریچه daricheh

ventilate *v* تهویه کردن tahviyeh kardan

ventilation *n* طرح موضوعی tarhe mouzooei

venture *v* اقدام کردن eghdam kardan

verb *n* فعل fe'el

verbally *adv* شفاها" shafahan

verdict *n* قضاوت ghezavat

verge *n* حدود hodoud

verification *n* رسیدگی residegi

verify *v* تحقیق کردن tahghigh kardan

versatile *adj* سلیس salis

verse *n* شعر she'er

version *n* تفسیر tafsir

vertebra *n* مهره mohreh

very *adv* بسیار besyar

vessel *n* آوند avand

vest *n* جلیقه jeligheh

vestige *n* ذره zarreh

veteran *n* کهنه‌کار kohneh kar

veterinarian *n* دامپزشک dam pezeshk

viaduct *n* پل راه‌آهن pole rah ahan

vibrant *adj* مرتعش mortaesh

vibrate *v* لرزیدن larzidan

vibration *n* ارتعاش erte'ash

vice *n* گناه gonah

vicinity *n* مجاورت mojaverat

vicious *adj* فاسد fased

victim *n* قربانی ghorbani

victor *n* قهرمان ghahraman

victorious *adj* فاتح fateh

victory *n* فتح fath

view *n* عقیده aghideh

viewpoint *n* دیدگاه didgah

vigil *n* شب‌زندهداري shab zendeh dari

vigour *adv* زورمند zourmand

village *n* دهکده dehkadeh

villager *n* دهاتي dehati

villain *n* تبه‌کار tabah kar

vindicate *v* توجیه‌کردن toujih kardan

vindictive *adj* کینه‌جو kineh joo

vine *n* درخت‌مو derakhte mou

vinegar *n* سرکه serkeh

vineyard *n* تاکستان takestan

violate *v* تجاوزکردن tajavoz kardan

violence *n* خشونت khoshounat

violent *adj* شدید shadid

violet *n* بنفش banafsh

violin *n* ویلن viyolon

violinist *n* ویولن‌زن viyolon zan

viper *n* شریر sharir

virgin *n* باکره bakereh

virginity *n* بکارت bekarat

virile *adj* مردانه mardaneh

virility *n* مردي mardi

virtual *adj* واقعي vaghei

virtually *adv* واقعا vaghe'an

virtue *n* پاکدامني pak damani

virtuous *adj* پاکدامن pak daman

virulent *adj* زهرآگین zahr agin

virus *n* ویروس virus

visible *adj* نمایان namayan

vision *n* دید did

visit *n* دیدار didar

visitor *n* مهمان mehman

visual *adj* دیداري didani

visualize *v* تجسم‌کردن tajassom kardan

vital *adj* حیاتي hayati

vitality *n* قدرت‌حیاتي ghodrate hayati

vitamin *n* ویتامین vitamin

vivacious *adj* مسرور masroor

vivid *adj* واضح vazeh

vocabulary *n* واژگان vazhegan

vocation *n* حرفه herfeh

vogue *n* رواج ravaj

voice *n* صوت sout

void *adj* باطل batel

volatile *adj* بخارشدني bokhar shodani

volcano *n* آتشفشان atashfeshan

volleyball *n* والیبال valiball

voltage *n* ولتاژ voltazh

volume *n* حجم hajm

volunteer *n* داوطلب davtalab

vomit *n* استفراغ estefragh

vomit *v* استفراغ‌کردن estefragh kardan

vote *n* راي ra'ei

vote *v* راي‌دادن ra'y dadan

voucher *n* سند sanad

vow *v* عهدکردن ahd kardan

vowel *n* صوتي souti

voyage *v* سفردریاکردن safare darya kardan

voyager *n* مسافر mosafer

vulgar *adj* عوامانه avamaneh

vulgarity *n* عوام avam

vulnerable *adj* آسیب‌پذیر asib pazir

vulture *n* کرکس karkas

W

wafer *n* قرص ghors

wag *v* تکان‌دادن takan dadan

wage *n* مزد mozd

wagon *n* واگن vagon

waist *n* دورکمر doure kamar

wait *v* صبرکردن sabr kardan

waiter *n* منتظر montazer

waitress *n* پیکلفت kolfat

waive *v* چشم‌پوشیدن‌از cheshm poushidan az

waiver *n* فسخ faskh

wake *iv* شب‌زنده‌داری‌کردن shab zendeh dari kardan

walk *v* راه‌رفتن rah raftan

walkout *n* اعتصاب e'etesab

wall *n* دیوار divar

wallet *n* کیف‌پول kife poul

walnut *n* گردو gerdoo

walrus *n* شیرماهی shir mahi

waltz *n* والس vals

wander *v* آواره‌بودن avareh boudan

wanderer *n* سرگردان sargardan

wane *v* کم‌شدن kam shodan

want *v* خواستن khastan

war *n* جنگ jang

ward *n* نگهبان negahban

warden *n* سرپرست sarparast

wardrobe *n* جارختی ja rakhti

warehouse *n* مخزن makhzan

warfare *n* جنگاوری jang avari

warm *adj* گرم garm

warn *v* هشداردادن hoshdar dadan

warning *n* اخطار ekhtar

warranty n تضمین tazmin

warrior *n* جنگاور jang avar

warship *n* کشتی‌جنگی keshtiye jangi

wary *adj* هشیار hoshyar

wash *v* شستن shostan

wasp *n* زنبور zanbour

waste *v* هرزدادن harz dadan

wastebasket *n* آشغال‌دان ashghal dan

watch *n* ساعت sa'at

watch *v* مراقبت‌کردن moraghebat kardan

watchmaker *n* ساعت‌ساز sa'at saz

water *n* آب ab

water *v* آب‌دادن ab dadan

waterfall *n* آبشار abshar

water *heater* n آبگرم‌کن ab garm kon

watermelon *n* هندوانه hendevaneh

watertight *adj* کیپ kip

watery *adj* آبدار abdar

watt *n* وات vat

wave *n* موج mowj

wavy *adj* پرتلاطم por talatom

wax *n* موم moom

way *n* طریق tarigh

we *pro* ما ma

weak *adj* ضعیف za'eif

weaken *v* سست‌شدن sost shodan

weakness *n* ضعف za'af

wealth *n* دارایی daraee

wealthy *adj* توانگر tavangar

weapon *n* اسلحه aslaheh

wear *iv* پوشیدن poushidan

wear n فرسايش farsayesh

weary adj كسل kesel

weather n هوا hava

weave iv بافتن baftan

web n تارعنكبوت tare ankabout

website n سايتهاي اينترنتي sayt-haye interneti

wed iv عروسي كردن arousi kardan

wedding n جشن عروسی jashne arousi

wedge n سرتيشه sar tisheh

Wednesday n چهارشنبه chahar shanbeh

weed n درازولاغر deraz va laghar

weed v علف كشيدن alaf keshidan

week n هفته hafteh

weekday adj ايام هفته ayame hafteh

weekend n آخرهفته akhare hafteh

weekly adv هفتگي haftegi

weep iv گريستن geristan

weigh v وزن كردن vazn kardan

weight n وزن vazn

weird adj خارق العاده kharegh-al adeh

welcome v خوشامدگفتن khoshamad goftan

weld v جوش دادن joosh dadan

welder n جوشكار joosh kar

welfare n آسايش asayesh

well n چشمه cheshmeh

west n مغرب maghreb

westbound adv مسافرمغرب mosafere maghreb

western adj غربی gharbi

westerner adj اهل مغرب ahle maghreb

wet adj مرطوب martoub

whale n نهنگ nahang

wharf n بارانداز bar andaz

what adj علامت استفهام alamate estefham

whatever adj هرچه har cheh

wheat n گندم gandom

wheel n چرخ charkh

wheelbarrow n چرخ دستي charkh dasti

wheelchair n صندلي چرخ دار sandaliye charkh dar

wheeze v خس خس كردن khes khes kardan

when adv وقتيكه vaghti keh

whenever adv هرزمان كه har zaman keh

where adv هركجا har koja

whereabouts n جاي تقريبي jaye taghribi

whereas c ازآنجايي كه az anjaee keh

whether c آيا a'ya

which adj كدام kodam

while c هنگامي كه hengami keh

whim n هوس havas

whine v ناليدن nalidan

whip n تازيانه taziyaneh

whip v شلاق زدن shallagh zadan

whiskers n ريش rish

whisper n نجوا najva

whisper v نجوا كردن najva kardan

whistle n سوت soot

whistle v سوت زدن soot zadan

white adj سفيد sefid

whiten v سفيد كردن sefid kardan

who *pro* چه کسی cheh kasi

whoever *pro* هرکسی که har kasi keh

whole *adj* تمام tamam

wholehearted *adj* یکدل yekdel

wholesale *n* عمده‌فروش omdeh forush

wholesome *adj* سرحال sar hal

why *adv* چرا chera

wicked *adj* شریر sharir

wickedness *n* شرارت sherarat

wide *adj* پهن pahn

widely *adv* زیاد ziyad

widen *v* عریض کردن ariz kardan

widespread *adj* گسترده gostardeh

widow *n* بیوه biveh

widower *n* مردزن‌مرده marde zan mordeh

width *n* پهنا pahna

wield *v* اداره کردن edareh kardan

wife *n* زن zan

wig *n* کلاه‌گیس kolah gis

wiggle *v* جنبیدن jonbidan

wild *adj* وحشی vahshi

wilderness *n* بیابان biyaban

wildlife *n* وحوش vohoush

will *n* وصیت vasiyat

wilfully *adv* مشتاق moshtagh

willingly *adv* ازروی‌میل az rouye meyl

willingness *n* رضایت rezayat

willow *n* بید bid

win *iv* بردن bordan

wind *n* باد bad

wind *iv* کوک کردن kook kardan

winding *adj* پیچ‌درپیچ pich dar pich

windmill *n* آسیاب‌بادی asiyabe badi

window *n* پنجره panjereh

windpipe *n* نای nay

windshield *n* شیشه‌جلواتومبیل shishehye jelowye otomobil

windy *adj* باد پر por bad

wine *n* شراب sharab

wing *n* بال bal

wink *n* چشمک cheshmak

winner *n* برنده barandeh

winter *n* زمستان zemestan

wipe *v* پاک کردن pak kardan

wire *n* سیم sim

wisdom *n* خرد kherad

wise *n* فرزانه farzaneh

wish *n* آرزو arezoo

wish *v* خواستن khastan

wit *n* مزاح mezah

witch *n* ساحره sahereh

witchcraft *n* جادوگري jadoogari

with *pre* با ba

withdraw *v* ردکردن rad kardan

withdrawal *n* کناره‌گیري kenareh giri

wither *v* پژمرده‌شدن pazhmordeh shodan

within *pre* درحدود dar hodoude

without *pre* بدون bedoone

withstand *v* مقاومت کردن با moghavemat kardan ba

witness *n* شاهد shahed

witty *adj* لطیفه‌گو latifeh goo

wizard *n* نابغه nabegheh

woes *n* آه ah...

wolf *n* گرگ gorg

woman *n* زن zan

womb *n* شکم shekam

women *n* زنان zanan

wonder *v* درشگفت‌شدن dar shegeft shodan

wonder *n* شگفت shegeft

wonderful *adj* شگرف shegarf

wood *n* چوب choob

wooden *adj* چوبی choobi

woods *n* هیزم hizom

wool *n* پشم pashm

woollen *adj* پشمی pashmi

word *n* کلمه kalameh

work *n* کار kar

workbook *n* کارنامه kar nameh

worker *n* کارگر karegar

workshop *n* کارگاه kargah

world *n* جهان jahan

worldwide *adj* جهانی jahani

worm *n* کرم kerm

worry *n* اضطراب ezterab

worry *v* نگران‌بودن negaran boudan

worse *adj* بدتر badtar

worsen *v* بدترکردن badtar kardan

worship *n* پرستش parastesh

worst *adj* بدترین badtarin

worth *n* ازرش arzesh

worthless *adj* بی‌ارزش bi arzesh

worthwhile *adj* ارزنده arzandeh

worthy *adj* شایسته shayesteh

would-be *adj* خواستار khastar

wound *n* جراحت jarahat

wound *v* مجروح‌کردن majruh kardan

wrap *v* بستن bastan

wrapping *n* لفاف lafaf

wreath *n* تاج گل taje gol

wreck *v* خراب‌کردن kharab kardan

wreckage *n* خرابی kharabi

wrench *n* آچار achar

wrestle *v* کشتی‌گرفتن koshti gereftan

wrestler *n* کشتی‌گیر koshti gir

wrestling *n* کشتی koshti

wring *iv* فشردن feshordan

wrinkle *n* آژنگ azhang

wrinkle *v* چین‌دادن chin dadan

wrinkled *adj* چین‌خورده chin khordeh

wrist *n* مچ moch

write *iv* نوشتن neveshtan

writer *n* نویسنده nevisandeh

wrong *adj* غلط ghalat

wrongful *adj* غیرقانونی gheyre ghanooni

X-mas *n* کریسمس kerismas

X-ray *n* اشعه‌ایکس asha'ehe x

yard *n* محوطه mohavateh

yarn n الیاف alyaf

yacht n کرجی karji

yawn v خمیازه‌کشیدن khamiyazeh keshidan

yawn n دهن‌دره dahan dareh

year n سال sal

yearly adv سال‌به‌سال sal be sal

yearn v آرزوکردن arezoo kardan

yeast n مخمر mokhammer

yellow adj زرد zard

yes adv بله baleh

yesterday adv دیروز dirouz

yet c ولی vali

yield n بازده bazdeh

yield v باورکردن bavar kardan

yoke n سلطه solteh

yolk n زرده‌تخم‌مرغ zardehye tokhme morgh

you pro شما shoma

young adj جوان javan

youngster n جوانک javanak

your adj مال‌شما male shoma

yours pro مال‌شما male shoma

yourself pro شخص‌شما shakhse' shoma

youth n جوانان javanan

youthful adj باطراوت ba taravat

Z

zeal n حمیت hammiyat

zealous adj مجاهد mojahed

zebra n گورخر goure khar

zero n صفر sefr

zest n مزه mazeh

zinc n روي rouy

zip code n کدپستي kode posti

zipper n زیب‌لباس zibe lebas

zone n حوزه howzeh

zoo n باغ‌وحش baghe vahsh

zoology n جانورشناسي janevar shenasi

zucchini n کدوسبز kadoo sabz

Farsi to English

آ

aeen dini *n* آئین‌دینی cult
a'eine' namaz *n* آئین‌نماز liturgy
a'eineh *n* آئینه mirror
ab *n* آب water
abanbar *n* آب‌انبار cistern
ab paz kardan *v* آب‌پزکردن scald
ab dadan *v* آب‌دادن water
ab-e ro *n* آب‌رو gutter
a'ab shodan *v* آب‌شدن melt
ab felezi dadan *v* آب‌فلزي‌دادن galvanize
ab kardan *v* آب‌کردن dissolve
ab keshidan *v* آب‌کشیدن drain
a'be' ma'dani *n* آب‌معدني mineral
abmiveh *n* آب‌میوه juice
ab va tab *n* آب‌وتاب pomposity
ab-o-hava *n* آب‌وهوا climate
ab-o-hava'ei *adj* آب‌وهوائی climatic
ab-o-hava'ei *adj* آب‌وهوائی climatic
abjoo *n* آبجو beer
abjo sazi *n* آبجوسازي brewery
abdar *adj* آبدار watery
abdar *adj* آبدار juicy
abdar khaneh *n* آبدارخانه pantry
abdareh *n* آبدره fjord
abrah *n* آبراه canal
abzi *adj* آبزي aquatic
abzidan *n* آبزیدان aquarium

abshar *n* آبشار waterfall
abshar *n* آبشار cascade
abshare' bozorg *n* آبشار بزرگ cataract
abfeshan *n* آبفشان geyser
abkand *n* آبکند ravine
ab garm kon *n* آبگرم‌کن water heater
abgoosht *n* آبگوشت broth
abgosht *n* آبگوشت gravy
abeleh *n* آبله smallpox
ableh morghan *n* آبله‌مرغان chicken pox
abyari kardan *v* آبیاري‌کردن irrigate
aparteman *n* آپارتمان apartment
atash bazi *n* آتش‌بازي fireworks
atash-e bozorg *n* آتش‌بزرگ bonfire
atash bas *n* آتش‌بس ceasefire
atash bas *n* آتش‌بس truce
atash zadan *v* آتش‌زدن ignite
atashzani *n* آتش‌زني arson
atash neshan *n* آتش‌نشان firefighter
atashfeshan *n* آتشفشان volcano
atashi *adj* آتشي frenetic
atashi kardan *v* آتشي‌کردن infuriate
atashi mazaj *adj* آتشي‌مزاج passionate
atashin *adj* آتشین fiery
atmosfer *n* آتموسفر atmosphere
ajor *n* آجر brick
ajor chin *n* آجرچین bricklayer
a'jil *n* آجیل nut

achar *n* آچار wrench

achar pich gooshti *n* آچارپیچ گوشتي screwdriver

akher *adj* آخر latter

akhare hafteh *n* آخرهفته weekend

akheri *n* آخري latter

akharin *adj* آخرین final

a'akhor *n* آخور manger

akhour *n* آخور stall

akhor *n* آخور crib

a'dab *n* آداب manners

adamse badkonaki *n* آدامس بادکنکي bubble gum

adrenalin *n* آدرنالین adrenaline

adame avareh va velgard *n* آدم آواره وولگرد vagrant

adam-e balegh *n* آدم بالغ grown-up

adam khar *n* آدم خوار cannibal

adam-e safih va ahmagh *n* آدم سفیه واحمق idiot

adam'e ghol peykar *n* آدم غول پیکر giant

adamkosh *n* آدم کش killer

adam kosh *n* آدم کش thug

adame naghola *n* آدم ناقلا pie

adamkosh *n* آدمکش assassin

adamkoshi *n* آدمکشی homicide

adami *n* آدمی human being

azarakhsh *n* آذرخش lightning

azarakhsh *n* آذرخش thunderbolt

azougheh rasandan *v* آذوقه رساندن cater

azin kardan *v* آذین کردن decorate

azin kardan *v* آذین کردن decrease

arastan *v* آراستن trim

arastan *v* آراستن arrange

arastan *v* آراستن prune

arasteh *adj* آراسته decent

aram kardan *v* آرام کردن appease

aram kardan *v* آرام کردن tranquilize

a'rambakhsh *n* آرامبخش painkiller

aramesh *n* آرامش serenity

aramesh *n* آرامش calmness

aramesh *n* آرامش composure

aramesh *n* آرامش lull

aramesh *n* آرامش tranquility

aramgah *n* آرامگاه tomb

arayesh *n* آرایش formation

arayesh dadan *v* آرایش دادن garnish

arayeshe ghoshon *n* آرایش قشون deployment

arayesh-e moye zanan *n* آرایش موی زنان hairdo

arayeshgar-e moo *n* آرایشگر مو hairdresser

arayesh *n* آرایش trimmings

ard *n* آرد flour

a'rde-jow *n* آرد جو oatmeal

ard kardan *v* آرد کردن pound

arezoo *n* آرزو wish

arezo kardan *v* آرزو کردن crave

arezoo kardan *v* آرزو کردن yearn

arezohaye bateni *n* آرزوهای باطني ideology

aramidan *v* آرمیدن repose

aramidan *v* آرمیدن rest

aranj *n* آرنج elbow

arough-zadan *v* آروغ زدن burp

az *n* آز greed
azad *adj* آزاد free
azad kardan *v* آزادکردن deliver
azad kardan *v* آزادکردن free
azad kardan *v* آزادکردن liberate
azadi *n* آزادي freedom
azadi *n* آزادي liberty
azar *n* آزار trouble
a'za'r *n* آزار nuisance
azar dadan *v* آزار دادن tease
azar rasandan *iv* آزاررساندن hurt
a'zar kardan *v* آزارکردن obsess
azar kardan *v* آزارکردن persecute
azar gar *n* آزارگر sadist
azordan *v* آزردن afflict
azmayesh *n* آزمایش experiment
azmayesh ghabli *n* آزمایش قبلي foretaste
azmayesh kardan *v* آزمایش کردن quiz
azmayeshe niroo *n* آزمایش نیرو showdown
azmayeshgah *n* آزمایشگاه lab
azmayeshi *adj* آزمایشي tentative
azmodegi *n* آزمودگي experience
azmoudan *v* آزمودن test
azmoun *n* آزمون test
azmon *n* آزمون examination
azhang *n* آژنگ wrinkle
asani *adj* آسان easy
asan kardan *v* آسان کردن facilitate
asansor *n* آسانسور elevator
asani *n* آساني ease
asayesh *n* آسایش rest
asayesh *n* آسایش welfare

aspirin *n* آسپرین aspirin
astaneh *n* آستانه threshold
astar *n* آستر lining
astin *n* آستین sleeve
aseman *n* آسمان sky
aseman kharash *n* آسمان خراش skyscraper
asemani *adj* آسماني heavenly
a'smi *adj* آسمي asthmatic
asodeghi *n* آسودگي convenience
a'asiyab *n* آسیاب mill
asiyabe badi *n* آسیاب بادي windmill
asib resandan *n* آسیب harm
asib *n* آسیب injury
asib avar *adj* آسیب آور damaging
asib pazir *adj* آسیب پذیر vulnerable
asib resandan *v* آسیب رساندن(به) harm
asib zadan *v* آسیب زدن(به) injure
ashamidan *iv* آشامیدن drink
ashamidani *n* آشامیدني drink
ashpaz *n* آشپز cook
ashpazkhaneh *n* آشپزخانه kitchen
ashghal *n* آشغال rubbish
ashghal *n* آشغال trash
ashghal dan *n* آشغال دان wastebasket
ashoftan *v* آشفتن perturb
ashofteh *adj* آشفته deranged
ashkar *adj* آشکار public
a'shka'r *adj* آشکار outright
ashkar adj آشکار plain
ashkar adj آشکار clear

a'shka'r *adj* آشكار obvious
ashkar kardan *iv* آشكاركردن light
ashkara *adv* آشكارا publicly
a'shkara' *adv* آشكارا openly
ashkara tohin kardan *v* آشكارا
توهين كردن affront
ashkar shodan *v* آشكارشدن come
out
a'shkari *n* آشكارى openness
ashna *adj* آشنا familiar
ashna kardan *v* آشناكردن
acquaint
ashena kardan ba *v* آشناكردنبا
put up with
ashnaei *n* آشنايى acquaintance
ashoub *n* آشوب commotion
ashoub *n* آشوب riot
ashoub *n* آشوب turbulence
ashoobgar *n* آشوبگر agitator
a'shiyaneh *n* آشيانه nest
aghaz *n* آغاز start
aghaz *n* آغاز beginning
aghaz *n* آغاز inception
aghaz kar *n* آغازكار debut
aghaz kardan *iv* آغازكردن begin
aghaz kardan *v* آغازكردن
commence
aghazidan *v* آغازيدن start
aghoush *n* آغوش hug
aghoosh *n* آغوش bosom
afat *n* آفت pest
aftab *n* آفتاب sun
aftab zadegi *n* آفتابزدگى sunburn
aftabi *adj* آفتابى sunny
afaridegar *n* آفريدگار creator
afarideh *n* آفريده creature

afarinesh *n* آفرينش creation
a'fand *n* آفند attack
agha *n* آقا gentleman
a'gha *n* آقا mister
agha *n* آقا sir
akardeon *n* آكوردئون accordion
agah *adj* آگاه aware
agahi *n* آگاهى awareness
agahi *n* آگاهى dope
agahi dadan *v* آگاهىدادن inform
agahy *n* آگهى announcement
agahi *n* آگهى poster
agahy dadan *v* آگهىدادن
announce
agahi roye kagaz koochak *n*
آگهىروىكاغذكوچك flier
agahi-namehe rasmi *n* آگهىنامه
رسمى bulletin
agahiye divari *n* آگهىديوارى
placard
alat kochak *n* آلتكوچك gadget
almani *adj* آلمانى German
aloo *n* آلو plum
aloo *n* آلو prune
aloudan *v* آلودن pollute
aloudan *v* آلودن contaminate
alodeh kardan *v* آلودهكردن defile
aloodeh kardan *v* آلودهكردن
infect
aluminium *n* آلومينيوم aluminum
amadegi *n* آمادگى readiness
amadeh *adj* آماده ready
amadeh kardan *v* آمادهكردن draft
amar *n* آمار statistic
amas *n* آماس inflammation
amase' roudeh *n* آماسروده
appendicitis

amboulance *n* آمبولانس
ambulance

amadan *iv* آمدن come

amorzesh *n* آمرزش remission

amorzidan *v* آمرزیدن absolve

amoukhtan *iv* آموختن learn

amokhtan beh *v* به آموختن
instruct

amozgar *n* آموزگار instructor

amikhtan *v* آمیختن mix

amikhtan *v* آمیختن mingle

amizesh kardan *v* آمیزش کردن
associate

amizeh *n* آمیزه mixture

an *pro* آن that

an dokhtar *pro* آن‌دختر she

anten *n* آنتن antenna

anja *adv* آنجا there

anfolanza *n* آنفلوانزا flu

anfolanza *n* آنفلوانزا influenza

an ha *pro* آنها they

an ha *adj* آنها those

ah *n* آه sigh

ah... *n* آه woes

ahar *n* آهار starch

ahesteh *adv* آهسته slowly

ahesteh *adj* آهسته gradual

ahesteh joushidan *v* آهسته
جوشیدن simmer

ahan *n* آهن iron

ahan-roba *n* آهن‌ربا magnet

ahan-roba'ei *adj* آهن‌ربایی
magnetic

ahang *n* آهنگ setting

ahang *n* آهنگ tune

a'hange shirin *n* آهنگ‌شیرین
melody

ahangar *n* آهنگر blacksmith

ahoye kohi *n* آهوي کوهي deer

ava *n* آوا phone

avareh *adj* آواره stray

avareh boudan *v* آواره‌بودن
wander

avareh kardan *v* آواره‌کردن stray

avaz khandan *iv* آوازخواندن sing

avardan *iv* آوردن bring

avril *n* آوریل April

avokado *n* آوکادو avocado

avand *n* آوند vessel

avikhtan *iv* آویختن hang

aviz *n* آویز pendant

avizan shodan *v* آویزان‌شدن
suspend

a'ya *c* آیا whether

ayandeh *n* آینده future

ayandeh negari *n* آینده‌نگري
providence

aeene dini *n* آیین‌دینی sacrament

۱

e'etelaf *n* ائتلاف coalition

ebteda' *n* ابتدا outset

ebtezal *n* ابتذال banality

ebtekar *n* ابتکار initiative

abadi *adj* ابدي immortal

abadi *adj* ابدي perennial

abadiyat *n* ابدیت immortality

abadiat *n* ابديت eternity
abr *n* ابر cloud
abar bazar *n* ابربازارsupermarket
abar ghodrat *n* ابرقدرت
  superpower
abro *n* ابرو eyebrow
abri *adj* ابري cloudy
abri va tireh *adj* ابريوتيره
  overcast
abrisham *n* ابريشم silk
abzar *n* ابزار tool
ablahaneh *adj* ابلهانه idiotic
ebham *n* ابهام ambiguity
ebham *n* ابهام obscurity
abi *adj* ابي blue
opera *n* اپرا opera
otagh *n* اتاق room
otagh *n* اتاق chamber
otaghe khab *n* اتاقخواب bedroom
otaghe neshiman *n* اتاقنشيمن
  living room
ettehad *n* اتحاد unity
ettehad *n* اتحاد alliance
etehadiyyeh *n* اتحاديه league
ettefaghoftadan *v* افتادن اتفاق
  come about
etefagh oftadan *v* اتفاقافتادن
  happen
ettefagh ara *n* اتفاقآراunanimity
etefaghi *adj* اتفاقي casual
atom *n* اتم atom
etmam *n* اتمام completion
etmam hojjat *n* اتمامحجت
  ultimatum
atomi *adj* اتمي atomic
ram etteham *n* اتهام accusation

outo kardan *v* اتوکردن iron
autoboos *n* اتوبوس bus
otomobil *n* اتومبيل car
asaseh *n* اثاثه furniture
asasiyehe dakheli *n* اثاثهداخلي
  upholstery
asasiyeh *n* اثاثيه furnishings
esbat kardan (ba dalil) *v* اثبات
  (دليل با)کردن demonstrate
asar *n* اثر trace
asar'e angosht *n* اثرانگشت
  fingerprint
asar kardan *v* اثرکردنبر affect
asare gonah *n* اثرگناهscar
asare' honari *n* اثرهنرى artwork
ejareh *n* اجاره lease
ejareh dadan *v* اجارهدادن lease
ejareh kardan *v* اجارهکردن rent
ejazeh *n* اجازه permission
ejazeh *n* اجازه authorization
ejazeh *n* اجازه license
ejazehe khorouj dadan *v* اجازه
  خروجدادن let out
ejazeh dadan *v* اجازهدادن
  authorize
ejazeh dadan *v* اجازهدادن permit
ejazehe voroud dadan *v* اجازه
  ادخولدادن let in
ojagh *n* اجاق oven
ojagh *n* اجاق fireplace
ojagh *n* اجاق hearth
ejbar *n* اجبار coercion
ejbar *n* اجبار compulsion
ejbari *adj* اجباري compulsive
ejbari *adj* اجباري compulsory
ejbari *adj* اجبارى compelling

ejbari *n* اجبارى mandatory

ejtemae mojadad *n* اجتماعمجدد rally

ejtenab kardan az *v* اجتنابکردن از elude

ejtenab na pazir *adj* اجتنابناپذیر unavoidable

ajdady *adj* اجدادي ancestral

ejra kardan *v* اجراکردن enforce

ejra kardan *v* اجراکردن execute

ejra kardan *v* اجراکردن perform

ojrat *n* اجرت pay

a;za'e *n* اجزاء component

Azhoudan-e Timsar *n* اجودان تیمسار aide

ehateh kardan *iv* احاطهکردن beset

ehateh kardan *v* احاطهکردن encircle

ehateh kardan *v* احاطهکردن encompass

ehteram *n* احترام greetings

ehteram *n* احترام honor

ehteram be nafs *n* احترامبهنفس self-esteem

ehteramat *n* احترامات regards

ehtekar kardan *v* احتکارکردن hoard

ehtemal *n* احتمال probability

ehtemal *n* احتمال supposition

ehtemal *n* احتمال contingency

ehtemal *n* احتمال likelihood

ehtemali *adj* احتمالي probable

ehtiyaj *n* احیاج lack

ehtiyaj *n* احیاج requirement

ehtiyat *n* احتیاط prudence

ehtiyat *n* احتیاط caution

ehsas *n* احساس sensation

ehsas-e kharesh *n* احساسخارش itchiness

ehsas-e ghorbat *n* احساسغربت nostalgia

ehsas kardan *iv* احساسکردن feel

ehsasat *n* احساسات feelings

ehsasat *n* احساسات emotion

ehsasat ra barangikhtan *v* احساساترابرانگیختن enthuse

ehsasati *adj* احساساتي sentimental

ehzar kardan *v* احضارکردن muster

ehzar kardan *v* احضارکردن evoke

ahmagh *adj* احمق stupid

ahmagh *adj* احمق jerk

ehya kardan *v* احیاکردن reconstruct

akhbar *n* اخبار news

akhbare radiyo *n* اخباررادیو newscast

ekhtera *n* اختراع invention

ekhtera kardan *v* اختراعکردن invent

ekhtesar *n* اختصار abbreviation

ekhtesas dadan *v* اختصاصدادن allocate

ekhtesasi kardan *v* اختصاصيکردن specialize

ekhtefa *n* اختفا hideout

ekhtelaf *n* اختلاف discrepancy

ethtelal *n* اختلال disturbance

akhteh kardan *v* اختهکردن mutilate

ekhtiar *n* اختیار adoption

ekhtiyar *n* اختیار clearance

ekhtiyari *adj* اختیاري arbitrary

akhz *n* اخذ grasp

akhz beh zor va onf *n* اخذبهزورو عنف extortion

akhar *adj* اخر last

ekhraj *n* اخراج dismissal

ekhraj *n* اخراج expulsion

ekhraj *n* اخراج ouster

ekhraj kardan *v* اخراج کردن oust

ekhraj kardan *v* اخراج کردن یا شدن sack

ekhta'r *n* اخطار notification

ekhtar *n* اخطار premonition

ekhtar *n* اخطار warning

ekhta'r kardan *v* اخطار کردن notify

akhlagh *n* اخلاق morality

akhlaghi *adj* اخلاقي moral

akhm kardan *v* اخم کردن frown

akhir *adv* اخیرا lately

ada kardan *v* اداکردن pronounce

ada osol *n* اداواصول grimace

edareh kardan *v* اداره کردن manage

edareh kardan *v* اداره کردن rule

edareh kardan *v* اداره کردن wield

edare kardan *v* اداره کردن administer

edareh kardan *v* اداره کردن manipulate

edareh kardan *v* اداره کردن officiate

edareh kardan *v* اداره کردن preside

edameh dadan *v* ادامه دادن carry on

edame dadan *v* ادامه دادن continue

edameh dadan *v* ادامه دادن keep on

edameh nadadan *v* ادامه ندادن discontinue

edameh yaftan *v* ادامه یافتن resume

adab *adj* ادب polite

adab kardan *v* ادب کردن punish

acab va mehrabani *n* ادبو مهربانی courtesy

adabiyat *n* ادبیات literature

edrar *n* ادرار urine

edrar kardan *v* ادرار کردن pee

edrar kardan *v* ادرار کردن urinate

edrak *n* ادراک hindsight

edrak *n* ادراک perception

edde'a *n* ادعا claim

edde'a kardan *v* ادعا کردن claim

eddea kardan *v* ادعا کردن acclaim

adviyeh *n* ادویه spice

adviyeh *n* ادویه condiment

arrabeh *n* ارابه cart

arbab *n* ارباب master

arbabe' rojo'e *n* ارباب رجوع clientele

erteja'e *n* ارتجاع restitution

artesh *n* ارتش army

arteshbod *n* ارتشبد marshal

erte'ash *n* ارتعاش shudder

erte'ash *n* ارتعاش vibration

rers *n* ارث inheritance

ersi *adj* ارثي hereditary

erja'e *n* ارجاع reference

arjmand *adj* ارجمند lofty

ordak *n* اردک duck

ordou *n* اردو camp

arzan *adj* ارزان cheap

arzan *adj* ارزان inexpensive

arzandeh *adj* ارزنده worthwhile

arezoo dashtan *v* ارزوداشتن aspire

arzyabi *n* ارزيابي appraisal

arzyabi kardan *v* ارزيابي كردن appraise

arzyabi kardan *v* ارزيابي كردن evaluate

ersale post *n* ارسال‌پست postage

arshad *n* ارشد major

arshad *adj* ارشد senior

arshad *adj* ارشد classy

arshadiyat *n* ارشديت seniority

era'bgar *n* ارعابگر terrorist

arghavani *n* ارغواني orchid

orkestr *n* اركستر orchestra

arreh kardan *iv* كردن اره saw

orib *adj* اريب slanting

az *pre* از of

az *pro* از since

az *pre* از from

az ... ta *c* از ... تا since

az edde'a' sarfenazar kardan *v* ازادعاصرفنظركردن back down

az avval ta akhar *adj* ازاول‌تاآخر thorough

az in pas *adv* ازاين‌پس hereafter

az in roo *adv* ازاين‌رو hence

az anjaee keh *c* ازآنجايي‌كه whereas

az bar khandan *v* ازبرخواندن recite

az pay dar amadeh *adj* ازپاي درآمده broken-down

az pish ekhtar kardan *v* ازپيش اخطاركردن forewarn

az pish khabar dadan *v* ازپيش خبردادن foreshadow

az jay biroun kardan *v* ازجاي بيرون كردن dislodge

az had taja'voz kardan *v* ازحد تجاوزكردن overstep

az khat kharej shodan teran *n* ازخط‌خارج‌شدن‌ترن derailment

az khat kharej kardan *v* ازخط خارج كردن derail

az-khod razi *adj* ازخودراضي cocky

az dast dadani *adj* ازدست‌دادني disposable

az rooye ekrah *adv* ازروی‌اكراه reluctantly

az rouye bi meyli *adv* ازروی‌بی ميلی unwillingly

az rouye khod bini *adv* ازروی خودبينی vainly

az roye'saligheh *adv* ازروی‌سليقه neatly

az rouye meyl *adv* ازروی‌ميل willingly

az roye ta'ajob faryad zadan *v* ازروي‌تعجب‌فريادزدن exclaim

az rooie khashm *adv* ازروي‌خشم angrily

az rouye ziraki *adv* ازروي‌زيركي subtly

az rooye ghasd *adv* ازروي‌قصد consciously

az risheh kandan *v* ازريشه‌كندن eradicate

az zire khak dar avardan *v* از زيرخاك‌دراوردن unearth

az shekl andakhtan *v* ازشكل انداختن disfigure

az ghalam endakhtan *v* ازقلم انداختن drop

az gheyd raha kardan *v* ازقیدرها کردن emancipate

az gir daravardan *v* ازگیردر آوردن disentangle

azmodoftadeh *adj* ازمدافتاده old-fashioned

az miyan *pre* ازمیان through

az nazdik *p* ازنزدیک by

az no *adv* ازنو anew

az now por kardan *v* ازنوپرکردن recharge

az now tejarat kardan *v* ازنو تجارت کردن refinance

az yad naraftani *adj* ازیادنرفتنی unforgettable

ezdeham *n* ازدحام throng

ezdeham *n* ازدحام congestion

ezdeham *n* ازدحام swarm

ezdeham kardan *v* ازدحام کردن mob

ezdevaj *n* ازدواج marriage

ezdevaj kardan *v* ازدواج کردن marry

arzesh *n* ارزش worth

azhdeha *n* اژدها dragon

esarat *n* اسارت captivity

asas *n* اساس basis

asa'san *adv* اساسا" mainly

asasi *adj* اساسی substantial

asb *n* اسب horse

asb (dar shatranj) *n* اسب در شطرنج knight

asb-e kouchak andam *n* اسب کوچک‌اندام hobby

asbab *n* اسباب appliance

asbab bazi *n* اسباب‌بازي toy

asbagh *n* اسبق predecessor

espageti *n* اسپاگتی pasta

espaniyouli *adj* اسپانیولی Hispanic

espaniyaee *adj* اسپانیایی Spanish

ostad *n* استاد professor

ostadan daneshkadeh *n* استادان دانشکده faculty

estesna'e *n* استثناء exception

estesnae'e *adj* استثنایي exceptional

estehkam *n* استحکام stability

estehkamat nezami *n* استحکامات نظامي fortress

estekhdam *n* استخدام service

estekhdam *n* استخدام recruitment

estakhr *n* استخر pond

makhzan *n* استخر pool

estekhraj kardan *v* استخراج کردن extract

estekhtaj kardan *v* استخراج کردن mine

ostokhan *n* استخوان bone

ostokhan bandi *n* استخوان‌بندي framework

ostokhane' gooneh *n* استخوان‌گونه cheekbone

estedlal kardan *v* استدلال کردن reason

estedlal kardan *v* استدلال کردن prove

esterdad e mojremin *n* استرداد مجرمین extradition

este'dad *n* استعداد aptitude

stedad *n* استعداد talent

estefa *n* استعفا abdication

estemal kardan *v* استعمال کردن employ

estefadeh kardan *v* استفاده کردن utilize

estefadehye mojadad *v* استفاده مجدد recycle

estefragh *n* استفراغ vomit

estefragh kardan *v* استفراغ کردن vomit

esteghamat kardan *v* استقامت کردن resist

estenad kardan *v* استناد کردن به rely on

estenbat kardan *v* استنباط کردن deduce

estentaj kardan *v* استنتاج کردن infer

estentagh *n* استنطاق inquisition

estehza *n* استهزاء mockery

estehza' kardan *v* استهزاء کردن mock

ostova *n* استوا tropic

ostovar *adj* استوار constant

ostovaneh *n* استوانه cannon

ostovaneh *n* استوانه cylinder

ostovai *adj* استوایی tropical

ostoureh *n* اسطوره myth

esfanj *n* اسفنج sponge

osghof *n* اسقف bishop

osghof-e a'azam *n* اسقف اعظم archbishop

eskeneh *n* اسکنه chisel

ski bazi kardan *v* اسکی بازی کردن ski

aslaheh *n* اسلحه weapon

aslaheh garm *n* اسلحه گرم firearm

osloub dar *adj* اسلوب دار methodical

esm *n* اسم name

esm *n* اسم noun

esm *n* اسم title

esme ramz *n* اسم رمز password

esm masdar *n* اسم مصدر gerund

eshal *n* اسهال diarrhea

asoudeh *adj* اسوده calm

asib za *adj* اسیب زا traumatic

asir *n* اسیر captive

asir kardan *v* اسیر کردن capture

eshareh *n* اشاره gesture

eshareh *n* اشاره hint

eshareh *n* اشاره inkling

eshareh *n* اشاره suggestion

eshareh kardan *v* اشاره کردن point

eshareh kardan *v* اشاره کردن beckon

eshareh konandeh *adj* اشاره کننده suggestive

eshba'e kardan *v* اشباع کردن saturate

eshtebah *n* اشتباه blame

eshtebah *n* اشتباه mistake

eshtebahe bozorg *n* اشتباه بزرگ blunder

eshtebah kardan *v* اشتباه کردن slip

eshtebah kardan *v* اشتباه کردن goof

eshtebah kardan *iv* اشتباه کردن mistake

eshtebahi *adj* اشتباهی mistaken

eshterak *n* اشتراک subscription

eshteha *n* اشتها appetite

eshtiagh *n* اشتیاق eagerness

eshtiyagh *n* اشتیاق longing

asha'ehe x *n* ایکس اشعه X-ray

eshghal *n* اشغال brash

eshghal *n* اشغال occupation

eshghal kardan *v* اشغال کردن occupy

eshghal nashodeh *adj* اشغال‌نشده unoccupied

ashofteh *adj* اشفته distraught

ashkara *adv* اشکارا clearly

eshkal *n* اشکال bug

ashkal *n* اشکال drawback

esabat *n* اصابت strike

esabat *n* اصابت hit

esa'lat *n* اصالت nobility

esrar *n* اصرار urge

esrar *n* اصرار insistence

esrar kardan *v* اصرارکردن urge

esrar varzidan *v* اصرارورزیدن insist

estelahate fanni *n* اصطلاحات‌فنی technicality

asghar *adj* اصغر junior

eslah kardan *v* اصلاح‌کردن modify

eslah napazir *adj* اصلاح‌ناپذیر incorrigible

asli *adj* اصلی principal

asliyat *n* اصلیت paternity

osoul *n* اصول basics

osoule' eshteraki *n* اصول‌اشتراکی communism

osoul-e mazhabe' katoliki *n* اصول‌مذهب‌کاتولیکی Catholicism

asil *adj* اصیل original

asil *adj* اصیل genteel

asil *adj* اصیل noble

ezafe *n* اضافه addition

ezafeh baha *n* اضافه‌بها surcharge

ezafi *adj* اضافی redundant

ezafi *n* اضافی extension

ezafi *adv* اضافی extra

ezafi *adj* اضافی additional

ezterab *n* اضطراب anxiety

ezterab *n* اضطراب worry

eta'at *n* اطاعت obedience

ata'at kardan *v* اطاعت‌کردن obey

otaghe zir shirvani *n* اطاق‌زیر شیروانی attic

otaghe' kouchak *n* اطاق‌کوچک cabin

otaghe nahar khori *n* اطاق‌ناهار خوری dining room

otaghe neshiman *n* اطاق‌نشیمن parlor

otaghak *n* اطاقک booth

otaghak *n* اطاقک cubicle

otaghake' khalaban *n* اطاقک‌خلبان cockpit

etela *n* اطلاع information

etminan *n* اطمینان confidence

etminan dadan *v* اطمینان‌دادن assure

ezhar *n* اظهار allegation

ezhar dashtan *v* اظهارداشتن declare

ezhar dashtan *v* اظهارداشتن remark

ezhar eshgh *n* اظهارعشق courtship

ezhar kardan *v* اظهارکردن affirm

ezhar kardan *v* اظهارکردن profess

eane dadan *v* اعانه‌دادن contribute

etebar *n* اعتبار authenticity

etebar *n* اعتبار credibility

etebar *n* اعتبار credit

etebar dadan *v* اعتباردادن authenticate

e'etebar-gozari *n* اعتبارگذاری accreditation

e'eteraz kardan *v* اعتراض کردن protest

e'eteraz kardan *v* اعتراض کردن object

e'eteraf kardan *v* اعتراف کردن recant

e'etesab *n* اعتصاب walkout

etemad *n* اعتماد trust

etemad dashtan *v* اعتمادداشتن trust

e'temad nadashtan *v* اعتمادنداشتن distrust

etena kardan *v* اعتناکردن(به)heed

e'etiyad *n* اعتیاد addiction

e'zam kardan *v* اعزام کردن dispatch

e'eta *n* اعطاء concession

e'elam konandeh *n* اعلام کننده blazer

e'elam konandeh *n* اعلام کننده hanger

e'elan *n* اعلان notice

a'alahazrat *n* اعلیحضرت majesty

e'emal kardan *v* اعمال کردنexert

eghragh amiz kardan *v* اغراق آمیز کردن exaggerate

eghma *n* اغماء coma

eghva *n* اغوا enticement

eghva kardan *v* اغواکردنlure

oft *n* افت downfall

oft *n* افت drop

oft *n* افت slump

oftadan *iv* افتادن fall

oftadan *v* افتادن fall down

eftezah *n* افتضاح scandal

efratkari *n* افراطکاری extremities

afarideh *v* افریده being

afzoodan *v* افزودن add

afzodan *v* افزودن increase

afzoudan *v* افزودن redouble

afzoudani *n* افزودنی additive

afzoon boodan bar *v* افزون بودن بر outnumber

afsa'r *n* افسار rein

afsar *n* افسار bridle

afsar-e sag *n* سگ افسار leash

afsar kardan *v* افسارکردنrein

afsaneh *n* افسانه tale

afsaneh *n* افسانه fable

afsaneh *n* افسانه fiction

afsaneh *n* افسانه legend

afsaneh *n* افسانه romance

afsaneh'ee *adj* اي افسانه fabulous

afsous khordan *v* افسوس خوردن regret

afsoun *n* افسون charm

afsoun kardan *v* افسون کردن charm

afsoungari *n* افسونگري sorcery

efsha *n* افشاء revelation

ofogh *n* افق horizon

ofoghi *adj* افقی horizontal

aghaghiya *n* اقاقیا locust

eghamat dashtan *v* اقامت داشتن reside

eghamat kardan *v* اقامت کردن remain

eghamatgah *n* اقامتگاه residence

eghame kardan *v* اقامه کردنallege

eghtesad *n* اقتصاد economy

eghdam kardan *v* اقدام کردن venture

eghdamat *n* اقدامات proceedings

eghrar kardan *n* اقرار confession

eghrar kardan *v* اقرارکردن
confess

aghaliat *n* اقلیت minority

oghiyanous *n* اقیانوس ocean

aksariyat *n* اکثریت majority

oxid arsenik *n* اکسیدارسنیک
arsenic

oksizhen *n* اکسیژن oxygen

aknoon *adv* اکنون now

agar *c* اگر if

agar ham *c* اگرهم even if

agar che *c* اگرچه although

olagh *n* الاغ donkey

elteza'm *n* التزام obligation

eltemas *n* التماس appeal

eltemas kardan *v* التماسکردن
solicit

eltehabe riyeh *n* التهابریه
pneumonia

elzam-avar *adj* الزام‌اور binding

elsagh *n* الصاق attachment

elsagh kardan *v* الصاق‌کردن attach

alefba *n* الفبا alphabet

elgha'e kardan *v* القاءکردن induce

elektroniki *adj* الکترونیکی
electronic

elekteriki *adj* الکتریکی electric

olgoo *n* الگو pattern

almas *n* الماس diamond

olampik *n* المپیک Olympics

al-mosana *n* المثنی replica

almosana bardashtan *v* المثنی
برداشتن duplicate

elaheh *n* الهه goddess

elahi *adj* الهی celestial

elahiyat *n* الهیات theology

alyaf *n* الیاف yarn

amator *adj* اماتور amateur

emperator *n* امپراتور emperor

emperatori *n* امپراتوری empire

emtahan kardan *v* امتحان‌کردن
examine

emtedad dadan *v* امتدادددادن
prolong

emtezaj *n* امتزاج merger

emtiaz *n* امتیاز franchise

emtiyaz *n* امتیاز prerogative

emtiyaz *n* امتیاز privilege

emtiaz beh zaif *n* امتیازبه‌ضعیف
handicap

emdadi *n* امدادی auxiliary

amre adi *n* امرعادی routine

amr fogholadeh *n* امرفوق‌العاده
emergency

amr kardan *iv* امرکردن bid

amre' mosallam *n* امرمسلم
certainty

emrouz *adv* امروز today

emroozeh *adv* امروزه nowadays

emrouzi *adj* امروزی modern

emrouzi kardan *v* امروزی‌کردن
modernize

emshab *adv* امشب tonight

emza *n* امضا endorsement

emza *n* امضاء signature

emza kardan *v* امضاءکردن sign

ema'e *n* امعاء intestine

ama'e va ahsha'e *adv* امعاءواحشاء
inwards

emkan *n* امکان eventuality

emkan *n* امکان possibility

emkan pazir *adj* امکان‌پذیر feasible

emkan dashtan *iv* امکان‌داشتنmay

emkan napaziri *n* امکان‌ناپذیري impossibility

emla kardan *iv* املاءکردن spell

omlet *n* املت omelette

amniyat *n* امنیت security

amikhtan *v* امیختن blend

omid *n* امید hope

anar *n* انار pomegranate

ananas *n* اناناس pineapple

anbare' ghalleh *n* انبارغله barn

anbare kala *n* انبارکالا storage

anbar kardan *v* انبارکردن store

anbashtan *v* انباشتن accumulate

anbashtan *v* انباشتن stack

anbashtan *v* انباشتن stuff

anbashteh kardan *v* انباشته‌کردن stockpile

anbor dast *n* انبردست pliers

anbeh-ye hendi *n* انبه‌هندي papaya

anbouh-e mardom *n* انبوه‌مردم mob

entekhab *n* انتخاب election

entekhab *n* انتخاب option

entekhab *n* انتخاب pickup

entekhabi *adj* انتخابي adoptive

entekhabi *adj* انتخابي optional

entesab *n* انتصاب ordination

enteghal *n* انتقال transition

enteghal *n* انتقال transfer

enteghal dadan *v* انتقال‌دادن transfer

entegham *n* انتقام revenge

entegham *n* انتقام vengeance

entegham keshidan *v* انتقام‌کشیدن revenge

anjam dadan *v* انجام‌دادن accomplish

anjam dadan *v* انجام‌دادن carry out

anjam dadan *v* انجام‌دادن fulfill

anjam dadan *v* انجام‌دادن implement

anjoman *n* انجمن society

anjoman *n* انجمن community

anjoman *n* انجمن council

anjir *n* انجیر fig

anjire' hendi *n* انجیرهندي cactus

enjil *n* انجیل gospel

enheraf *n* انحراف detour

enheraf *n* انحراف deviation

enhesar shodeh *adj* انحصارشده engrossed

enhesari kardan *v* انحصاري‌کردن monopolize

andakhtan *iv* انداختن shed

andazeh *n* اندازه dimension

andazeh *n* اندازه size

andazeh bodan *v* اندازه‌بودن fit

andazeh gereftan *v* اندازه‌گرفتن fathom

andam *n* اندام organ

andam *n* اندام shape

andamgan *n* اندامگان organism

andaroon *n* اندرون harem

andaki *adv* اندکی partially

andaki *adj* اندکي some

andoukhtan *v* اندوختن pile

andoudan *v* اندودن plaster

andishmand *adj* اندیشمند thoughtful

andishe *n* اندیشه idea

andisheh *n* اندیشه thought

andisheh khani *n* اندیشه‌خوانی telepathy

andisheh kardan *v* اندیشه‌کردن muse

enzejar *n* انزجار antipathy

enzeva *n* انزوا seclusion

ensan *n* انسان man

ensan shenasy *n* انسان‌شناسی anthropology

ensani *adj* انساني human

ensejam *n* انسجام solidarity

ensedad *n* انسداد obstruction

ensedad *n* انسداد padlock

a'n-sooye *adv* انسوی beyond

enshe'ab *n* انشعاب ramification

enzebat *n* انضباط discipline

entebagh *n* انطباق adjustment

entebagh *n* انطباق coincidence

entebagh *n* انطباق conformity

entebagh beh morede *n* انطباق‌به مورد decency

an'am *n* انعام bonus

anam *n* انعام tip

en'eghad *n* انعقاد coagulation

en'ekas *n* انعکاس reaction

enfejar *n* انفجار explosion

enfeali *adj* انفعالي passive

enghebaz *n* انقباض contraction

enkar kardan *v* انکارکردن renounce

enkar na pazir *adj* انکارناپذیر undeniable

enkare' vojoode' khoda *n* انکار وجودخدا atheism

angabin *n* انگبین honey

angosht *n* انگشت digit

angousht *n* انگشت finger

angoshtnama *adj* انگشت‌نما conspicuous

angal *n* انگل parasite

angenar *n* انگنار artichoke

angour *n* انگور grape

angikhtan *v* انگیختن incite

angizeh *n* انگیزه motive

angizeh *n* انگیزه incentive

ehanat kardan *v* اهانت‌کردن scorn

ehda kardan *v* اهداکردن dedicate

ehda *n* اهداء grant

ahrom *n* اهرم crowbar

ahrom *n* اهرم lever

ahriman *n* اهریمن demon

ahle bakhsh *n* اهل‌بخش parishioner

ahle jonub *n* اهل‌جنوب southerner

ahle dokhaniyat *n* اهل‌دخانیات smoker

ahle rousiyeh *n* اهل‌روسیه Russian

ahle'shomal *adj* اهل‌شمال northerner

ahle fan *n* اهل‌فن technician

ahle maghreb *adj* اهل‌مغرب westerner

ahli kardan *v* اهلی‌کردن domesticate

aham *adv* اهم jointly

ehma'l *n* اهمال neglect

ahamiyat *n* اهمیت seriousness

ahamiyat *n* اهمیت importance

ahammiyat *n* اهمیت significance
ou *pro* او(آن‌مرد) he
obash *n* اوباش gangster
owbash *n* اوباش hooligan
oot *n* اوت August
owj *n* اوج climax
owragh *n* اوراق sheets
ouragh kardan *v* اوراق‌کردن take apart
oriyoon *n* اوریون mumps
oghat e talkh *adj* اوقات‌تلخ angry
aval shakhs-e mofrad *pro* اول شخص‌مفرد I
owlad *n* اولاد posterity
owlaviyat *n* اولویت priority
avaliyeh *adj* اولیه primitive
avalin *adj* اولین prime
onse *n* اونس ounce
ayyam *n* ایام times
eijab kardan *v* ایجاب‌کردن necessitate
ijade tars dar mardom *n* ایجاد ترس‌درمردم terrorism
ideh al *adj* ایده‌آل ideal
eistadan iv ایستادن stand
eistadan *v* ایستادن cease
istadan *v* ایستادن stop
istgah *n* ایستگاه station
iman *n* ایمان faith
inja *adv* اینجا here
inch *n* اینچ inch
in ha *adj* اینها these
eiyvan *n* ایوان balcony
ayyame' gozashteh *adj* ایام‌گذشته bygones

ayame hafteh *adj* ایام‌هفته weekday
etalik *adj* ایتالیک italics
in *adj* این this

ba *pre* با with
ba ehtiat *adj* بااحتیاط discreet
ba adab *adj* باادب courteous
ba adab *adj* باادب respectful
ba arzesh *adj* باارزش valuable
ba estedad *adj* بااستعداد gifted
ba eiman *n* باایمان believer
ba in ha'l *c* بااینحال nonetheless
ba ab shostan *v* باآب‌شستن rinse
ba a'b-o-tab goftan *v* باآب‌وتاب گفتن pad
ba bargh koshtan *v* بابرق‌کشتن electrocute
ba tahdid kari anjam dadan *v* با تهدیدکاری‌انجام‌دادن terrorize
ba halat e ghazab *adv* باحالت غضب furiously
ba hararat *adj* باحرارت fervent
ba khandeh ezhar dashtan *v* با خنده‌اظهار داشتن giggle
ba khoshhali *adv* باخوشحالی gaily
ba dast be kafal zadan *v* بادست‌به کفل‌زدن spank
ba deghat *adj* بادقت careful
ba deghat eshareh kardan *v* با دقت‌اشاره‌کردن‌به pinpoint

ba dahane' basteh khandidan *v* بادهان‌بسته‌خندیدن chuckle

ba davam *adj* بادوام durable

ba rooh *adj* باروح lively

ba zoor *adj* بازور pushy

ba sar va dast eshareh kardan *v* باسرودست‌اشاره‌کردن gesticulate

ba saro-seda *adv* باسروصدا noisily

ba shetab neveshtan *v* باشتاب نوشتن scribble

ba shararat-e bi-payan *adj* با شرارت‌بی‌پایان atrocious

ba seda terekidan *v* باصداترکیدن detonate

basedaye boland *adv* باصدای‌بلند loudly

ba zarbeh zadan *v* باضربه‌زدن bump into

ba ghovat talafoz kardan *v* با قوت‌تلفظ‌کردن emphasize

ba negah az roo bordan *v* بانگاه‌از روبردن look down

ba vojode inkeh *c* باوجوداینکه despite

ba vafa *adj* باوفا faithful

baba *n* بابا dad

baba *n* بابا papa

battery *n* باتری battery

bajjehe bilit foroushi *n* باجه‌بلیط فروشی box office

ba harf-e bozorg neveshtan *v* باحروف‌درشت‌نوشتن capitalize

bakht *n* باخت loss

ba khoshi *adv* باخوشی joyfully

bad *n* باد wind

bad (chizi ra) khali kardan *v* باد (چیزی‌را)خالی‌کردن deflate

bad bezan *n* بادبزن fan

bad-e shomal *n* بادشمال breeze

bad kardan *v* بادکردن inflate

bad kardan *iv* بادکردن swell

bad kardeh *adj* بادکرده baggy

bad-e' mowsemi *n* بادموسمی monsoon

bad va baran *n* بادوباران rainstorm

badam *n* بادام almond

badam zamini *n* بادام‌زمینی peanut

badbadak *n* بادبادک kite

bar *n* بار burden

bar *n* بار load

bar-o-bonehe mosafer *n* باروبنهء مسافر baggage

baran *n* باران rain

bar andaz *n* بارانداز wharf

barandaz *n* بارانداز dock

barani *n* بارانی raincoat

bar bar *n* باربر porter

bardari *n* بارداری pregnancy

baresh *n* بارش rainfall

bar kesh *n* بارکش van

bargah *n* بارگاه court

barandegi(barf) *n* بارندگی(برف) snowfall

barandegi-e ziyad *n* بارندگی‌زیاد downpour

barot *n* باروت gunpowder

barvar kardan *v* بارورکردن fertilize

baridan *v* باریدن rain

barik *adj* باریک narrow

barik *adj* باریک slender

barik-bin *adj* باریک‌بین meticulous

barikeh *n* باریکه ، نوار strip

barikehye goushte kababi *n* باریکه گوشت کبابی steak

baz *n* باز hawk

ba'z *adj* باز open

baz istadan *v* بازایستادن desist

bazkharid *n* بازخرید redemption

baz-za'ei *n* بازرزایی regeneration

baz feshordan *v* بازفشردن repress

baz kardan *v* بازکردن unfasten

baz kardan *v* بازکردن evolve

baz kardan *v* بازکردن unpack

baz kardan *v* بازکردن untie

baz kardan *v* بازکردن unwind

baz yaft *n* بازیافت resumption

baz yaftan *v* بازیافتن regain

bazar *n* بازار bazaar

bazar *n* بازار market

ba'zbini *n* بازبینی overview

baz pakhsh *n* بازپخش relay

baz pardakht *n* بازپرداخت kickback

bazporsi kardan *v* بازپرسی کردن interrogate

baz tab *n* بازتاب reflection

bazdasht *n* بازداشت detention

bazdashtan *v* بازداشتن detain

bazdashtan *v* بازداشتن deter

bazdeh *n* بازده efficiency

bazdeh *n* بازده revenue

bazdeh *n* بازده yield

bazdid *n* بازدید revision

bazdid *n* بازدید survey

bazdid *n* بازدید review

bazdide noghat-e didani *v* بازدید نقاط دیدنی sightseeing

bazargan *n* بازرگان trader

bazargan *n* بازرگان merchant

bazargani *n* بازرگانی trade

baz sakhtan *v* بازساختن rebuild

baz sazi kardan *v* بازسازی کردن remake

bazgasht *n* بازگشت recess

bazgasht *n* بازگشت recurrence

bazgashtan *v* بازگشتن come back

baz mandeh *n* بازمانده survivor

bazandeh *n* بازنده loser

bazneshastegi *n* بازنشستگی retirement

bazneshasteh shodan *v* بازنشسته شدن retire

bazoo *n* بازو arm

bazi *n* بازی game

basebal *n* بال بیس بازی baseball

baziye footbal *n* بازی‌فوتبال football

bazi goush *adj* بازیگوش playful

bazi *n* بازی play

bazi kardan *v* بازی کردن play

bazi kon *n* بازی کن player

bazigar e zan *n* بازیگرزن actress

bazigar e mard *n* بازیگرمرد actor

bastan-shenasi *n* باستان‌شناسی archaeology

bastani *adj* باستانی classic

ba savad *adj* باسواد literate

ba-shokouh *adj* باشکوه magnificent

ba shokouh *adj* باشکوه splendid

ba shokouh *adj* باشكوه superb
bashlagh *n* باشلق hood
bashowgh *adv* باشوق ardently
ba taravat *adj* باطراوت youthful
batel *adj* باطل vain
batel *adj* باطل void
ba'telsakhtan *v* باطل‌ساختن override
batel kardan *v* باطل‌كردن quash
batel kardan *v* باطل‌كردن undo
bagh *n* باغ garden
baghe vahsh *n* باغ‌وحش zoo
baghban *n* باغبان gardener
baft *n* بافت tissue
baft *n* بافت texture
baftan *v* بافتن knit
baftan *iv* بافتن weave
baghala *n* باقلا bean
ba ghalam-moo rang kardan *v* باقلم‌مورنگ‌كردن brush up
baghi gozardan *iv* باقي‌گذاردن leave
baghimandeh *n* باقي‌مانده remnant
baghi mandeh *adj* باقيمانده remaining
bakteri *n* باكتري bacteria
bakereh *n* باكره virgin
bal *n* بال wing
bal bal zadan *v* بال‌بال‌زدن flutter
bal'e mahi *n* بال‌ماهي fin
balla *pre* بالا above
bala bordan *v* بالابردن raise
bala bordan *v* بالابردن boost
bala bordan *v* بالابردن enhance
bala bordan *v* بالابردن escalate
bala bordan *v* بالابردن hoist

bala rotbeh *adj* بالارتبه superior
bala raftan *v* بالارفتن go up
balaraftan *v* بالارفتن climb
bala raftan *v* بالارفتن soar
balaravandeh *n* بالارونده climber
bala poush *n* بالاپوش quilt
balataneh *n* بالاتنه bust
balaye' *pre* بالاى on
balay-e tappeh *n* بالاى‌تپه hilltop
belbedahe' *adv* بالبداهه impromptu
balet *n* بالت ballet
balegh *n* بالغ adolescent
balegh *n* بالغ adult
balegh *adj* بالغ mature
belghoveh *adj* بالقوه potential
baloon *n* بالون balloon
balidan *v* باليدن boast
ba modara *adj* بامدارا lenient
band *n* باند band
band e foroodgah *n* باندفرودگاه airstrip
band pichi *n* باندپيچى bandage
bank *n* بانک bank
bang *n* بانگ call
banoo *n* بانو lady
banoo *n* بانو madam
ba ham *adv* باهم together
baham peyvastan *v* باهم‌پيوستن combine
baham zendegi kardan *v* باهم زندگي‌كردن(زن‌ومرد) cohabit
bahamzistan *v* باهم زيستن coexist
bahosh *adj* باهوش intelligent
bavar *n* باور belief
bavar kardan *v* باوركردن believe

bavar kardan *v* باور کردن yield

bavar kardani *adj* باور کردنی believable

bavar nakardani *adj* باور نکردنی unbelievable

bavar nakardani *adj* باور نکردنی incredible

ba vafa *adj* باوفا loyal

bayad *iv* باید must

bayest *iv* بایست ought to

baygani *n* بایگانی archive

baygani *n* بایگانی record

babr *n* ببر tiger

bout *n* بت idol

bout parast *n* بت‌پرست idolatry

bacheganeh *n* بچگانه childish

bacheganeh *adj* بچگانه puerile

bachegi *n* بچگی boyhood

bachegi *n* بچگی childhood

bacheh *n* بچه baby

bacheh *n* بچه child

bacheh dozdi kardan *v* بچه‌دزدی کردن kidnap

bacheh shir *n* بچه‌شیر cub

bacheh gorbeh *n* بچه‌گربه kitten

bachehe loos *adj* بچه‌لوس brat

bacheh-naneh *adj* بچه‌ننه sissy

bachehha *n* بچه‌ها children

bahs *n* بحث discussion

bahs kardan *v* بحث کردن argue

bahs kardan *v* بحث کردن discuss

bohran *n* بحران crisis

bokhar *n* بخار steam

bokhar *n* بخار vapor

bokhar dadan *v* بخار دادن fumigate

bokhar shodani *adj* بخار شدنی volatile

bekhater sepordan *v* بخاطر سپردن memorize

be khak oftadeh *adj* بخاک‌افتاده prostrate

bakht *n* بخت chance

bakht va eghbal *n* بخت‌واقبال fortune

bakhsh *n* بخش county

bakhsh *n* بخش district

bakhsh *n* بخش parcel

bakhsh *n* بخش part

bakhsh *n* بخش portion

bakhsh *n* بخش sector

bakhshayandegi *n* بخشایندگی clemency

bakhshesh *n* بخشش pardon

bakhshesh *n* بخشش forgiveness

bakhshesh *n* بخشش generosity

bakhshesh n بخشش gift

bakhshnameh kardan *v* بخشنامه کردن circulate

bakhshandeh *adj* بخشنده indulgent

bakhshandeh *adj* بخشنده merciful

bakhshodegi *n* بخشودگی impunity

bakhshidan *v* بخشیدن bestow

bakhshidan *v* بخشیدن donate

bakhshidan *v* بخشیدن forgive

bakhshidan *v* بخشیدن giveaway

bakhshidan *v* بخشیدن pardon

bakhshidan *v* بخشیدن remit

bokhor-e khoshboo *n* بخور خوشبو incense

bakhiyeh *n* بخیه seam
bakhiyeh zadan *v* بخیه‌زدن stitch
bad *adj* بد bad
bad-edareh kardan *v* بداداره‌کردن
mismanage
badta'bir kardan *v* بدتعبیرکردن
misconstrue
bad kholgh *adj* بدخلق grouchy
bad-davari kardan *v* بدداوری
کردن misjudge
badrahnama'ei shodeh *adj* بد
راهنمایی‌شده misguided
badraftari *n* بدرفتاری misconduct
bad sirat *adj* بدسیرت immoral
bad akhlaghi *n* بداخلاقی
immorality
bad bakhti *n* بدبختی unhappiness
badbakhty *n* بدبختی adversity
badbakhti *n* بدبختی misery
badbakhti *n* بدبختی disaster
bad boo *adj* بدبو smelly
bad boo *adv* بدبو stuffy
bad bin *adj* بدبین pessimistic
badbin va eyb jo *adj* بدبین‌وعیب
جو cynic
bad bini *n* بدبینی pessimism
badtar *adj* بدتر worse
badtar kardan *v* بدترکردن
aggravate
badtar kardan *v* بدترکردن worsen
badtar kardan *v* بدترکردن
deteriorate
badtarkib *adj* بدترکیب clumsy
badtarin *adj* بدترین worst
bad-jens *adj* بدجنس mischievous
badkholgh *adj* بدخلق grumpy

bad kho *adj* بدخو cranky
bad-khah *adj* بدخواه malevolent
bad khahi *n* بدخواهی malignancy
bad khahi *n* بدخواهی rancor
bad khim *adj* بدخیم malignant
badraftari kardan *v* بدرفتاری
کردن misbehave
badraftari *n* بدرفتاری
mistreatment
bedrood *n* بدرود farewell
be dast avardan *v* بدست‌آوردن
acquire
be dast avardan *v* بدست‌آوردن
gain
be dast avardan *iv* بدست‌آوردن
get
badshansi *n* بدشانسی misfortune
bad shekl kardan *v* بدشکل‌کردن
deface
badshekli *n* بدشکلی deformity
bed'at gozar *adj* بدعت‌گذار
heretic
bad amal kardan *v* بدعمل‌کردن
malfunction
badgoman *adj* بدگمان distrustful
badgomani *n* بدگمانی mistrust
bad gomani *n* بدگمانی suspicion
badnam *adj* بدنام notorious
bad nam kardan *v* بدنام‌کردن
defame
badani *adj* بدنی corporal
bedehi *n* بدهی debt
bedoone *pre* بدون without
bedoon-e' tah *adj* بدون‌ته
bottomless
bedoun-e harkat *adj* بدون‌حرکت
standstill

bedone sim *adj* بدون‌سیم cordless
badi *n* بدي evil
bedin vasileh *adv* بدین‌وسیله hereby
bedin san *adv* بدینسان thus
badi *n* بدی unfairness
baranda'khtan *v* برانداختن overthrow
bar ohdeh gereftan *v* برعهده گرفتن undertake
bar faraze *pre* برفراز upon
barabar bodan *v* برابربودن correspond
barabar kardan *v* برابرکردن balance
barabar kardan *v* برابرکردن contrast
barabar kardan *v* برابرکردن equate
baradar *n* برادر brethren
baradar *n* برادر brother
baradari *n* برادري brotherhood
baradari *n* برادري fraternity
bar ashoftegi *n* برآشفتگی anger
baragh shodan *v* براق‌شدن glitter
barandakhtan *v* برانداختن abolish
barandakhtan *v* برانداختن exterminate
barandaz *n* برانداز glance
barandaz kardan *v* برانداز کردن glance
borankar *n* برانکار stretcher
barangikhtan *v* برانگیختن foment
barangikhtan *v* برانگیختن instigate
bar'angizandeh *adj* برانگیزنده irritating

barangizandeh-e jensi *adj* برانگیزنده‌جنسی aphrodisiac
baraye hamisheh *adv* برای‌همیشه forever
baraye *pre* برای for
barashoftan *v* برآشفتن excite
baramad *n* برآمد expenditure
baramad *n* برآمد expense
bara'madegi *n* برآمدگی bulge
baramadan *v* برآمدن cope
bar pa mandan *v* برپاماندن stand up
bartari *n* برتري preference
bartari *n* برتري primacy
bartari *n* برتري superiority
bartari dashtan bar *v* برتري‌داشتن بر excel
borj *n* برج tower
borje gardan *n* برج‌گردان turret
barjasteh *adj* برجسته illustrious
barjasteh *adv* برجسته notably
barjasteh *adj* برجسته outstanding
barchasb *n* برچسب sticker
barchasb *n* برچسب label
barchasb *n* برچسب tag
barkhastan *iv* برخاستن arise
barkhord *v* برخورد clash
barkhordan-be *v* برخوردن‌به come across
bardasht *n* برداشت removal
bardashtan *v* برداشتن pick up
bordbaar *adj* بردبار meek
shakiba *adj* بردبار patient
bord bar *adj* بردبار stoic
bordbari *n* بردباري patience
bardeggi *n* بردگي slavery

bordan *iv* بردن bear
bordan *iv* بردن win
bordan *v* بردن carry
barresi kardan *v* بررسی‌کردن review
bores-e moye sar *n* برس‌موی‌سر hairbrush
boresh *n* برش rip off
boresh *n* برش section
boresh *n* برش slice
bereshteh kardan(nan) *v* برشته کردن(نان) toast
bar salib avikhtan *v* برصلیب آویختن crucify
bartaraf kardan *v* برطرف‌کردن acquit
bartaraf kardan *v* برطرف‌کردن dispel
bartaraf kardan *v* برطرف‌کردن remove
barf *n* برف snow
barf amadan *v* برف‌آمدن snow
barfe daneh *n* برف‌دانه snowflake
bargh *n* برق electricity
bargh'e negah *v* برق‌نگاه glimpse
barakat *n* برکت blessing
bar kandan *v* برکندن uproot
barg *n* برگ leaf
bargardandan *v* برگرداندن avert
bargardandan *v* برگرداندن bring back
bargardandan *v* برگرداندن convert
bar gardandan be anbar *v* برگرداندن‌به‌انبار turn in
bargozidan *v* برگزیدن opt
bargozidan *v* برگزیدن elect

bargasht *n* برگشت relapse
bargasht *n* برگشت return
bargasht be khod *adj* برگشت‌به‌خود reflexive
bargashtan *v* برگشتن go back
bargashtan *v* برگشتن reappear
barnameh *n* برنامه program
barnameh *n* برنامه scheme
barnameh *n* برنامه schedule
barnamehe safar *n* برنامه‌سفر itinerary
barnamehye kar *n* برنامه‌کار timetable
barnameh nevis *n* برنامه‌نویس programmer·
berenj *n* برنج rice
barandeh *n* برنده winner
barandehe' ehtemali *n* برنده احتمالی contender
barandehe tamame' poolha *n* برنده‌تمام‌پول‌ها jackpot
boronzeh *adj* برنزه tanned
boronshit *n* برنشیت bronchitis
barreh *n* بره lamb
bar ham zadan *n* برهم‌زدن coup
barham zadan *v* برهم‌زدن disband
berahnegi *n* برهنگی nudity
berahneh *adj* برهنه naked
berahneh shodan *v* برهنه‌شدن undress
berahneh kardan *v* برهنه‌کردن strip
berahneh kardan *v* برهنه‌کردن uncover
boro *v* برو get away
boroushoor *n* بروشور leaflet
berokli *n* بروکلی broccoli

boron gara *adj* برون extroverted

beryan kardan *v* بریان‌کردن grill

beryanni *n* بریانی barbecue

boridegi *n* بریدگي cut

boridan *v* بریدن sever

boridan *v* بریدن amputate

boridan *iv* بریدن cut

boridan *v* بریدن intercept

boz *n* بز goat

bozagh *n* بزاق saliva

barzakh *n* بزرخ purgatory

bozorg *adj* بزرگ big

bozorg *adj* بزرگ bulky

bozorg kardan *adj* بزرگ enormous

bozorg *adj* بزرگ great

bozorg *adj* بزرگ sizable

bozorgtar shodan az *v* بزرگ‌تر شدن‌از outgrow

bozorg-e khanedan *n* بزرگ خاندان patriarch

bozorg-kardan *v* بزرگ‌کردن magnify

bozorg kardan *v* بزرگ‌کردن amplify

bozorg kardan *v* بزرگ‌کردن enlarge

bozorg nama *adj* بزرگ‌نما grandiose

bozorg tar *adj* بزرگ‌تر paramount

bozorg dashtan *v* بزرگداشتن respect

bozorgrah *n* بزرگراه freeway

bozorgi *n* بزرگي dignity

bozorgi *n* بزرگي greatness

bozghaleh *n* بزغاله kid

boz e koohy *n* بزکوهي antelope

bazm *n* بزم festivity

bezeh *n* بزه misdemeanor

bezeh *n* بزه felony

be zoodi *adv* بزودي soon

bastar *n* بستر bed

bastare marg *n* بستر مرگ deathbed

bastari *adj* بستري bedridden

bastari kardan *v* بستري‌کردن hospitalize

bastan *v* بستن plug

bastan *v* بستن wrap

bastan *iv* بستن bind

bastani *v* بستن close

bastani *v* بستن coagulate

bastan *v* بستن curdle

bastan *v* بستن fasten

bastan *iv* بستن shut

bastane' kamarbande' eimeni *v* بستن‌کمربند ایمنی buckle up

bastani *n* بستني ice cream

bastehbandi *n* بندی بسته package

bastehbandi kardan *v* بسته‌بندي کردن pack

basteh bandi kardan *v* بسته‌بندي کردن put up

basteh-ye posti *n* بسته‌پستي parcel post

bast dadan *v* بسط دادن expand

basketbal *n* بسکتبال basketball

be souye *pre* بسوی to

besooye *pre* بسوي at

be soye shargh *adv* بسوي‌شرق eastbound

be souye jonub *adv* بسوی‌جنوب southbound

basi *adv* بسي often

besyar *adv* بسيار much

besyar *adj* بسيار abundant

besyar *n* بسيار lot

besyar *adv* بسيار very

besyar arzan *adj* بسيارارزان dirt-cheap

besyar bozorg *adj* بسياربزرگ colossal

besiar khoob *adv* بسيارخوب alright

besyarkhoub *adv* بسيارخوب okay

besyar sard *adj* بسيارسرد frigid

besyar amigh *n* بسيارعميق abyss

besyar kam *adv* بسيارکم seldom

besyari *n* بسياري multitude

basij kardan *v* بسيج کردن mobilize

bashash *adj* بشاش cheerful

bashash *adj* بشاش pleasing

bashar doosty *n* بشردوستي altruism

be sharte inkeh *c* بشرطاينکه providing that

boshghab *n* بشقاب plate

boshkeh *n* بشکه barrel

basirat *n* بصيرت discretion

basirat *n* بصيرت knowledge

botri *n* بطري bottle

be tarighi *adv* بطريقي somehow

betowre' kholaseh *adv* بطور خلاصه briefly

be toure nachiz *adv* بطورناچيز poorly

betowrike' *c* بطوريکه as

na'di *adj* بعدى next

bealaveh *adv* بعلاوه furthermore

be-alaveh *adv* بعلاوه moreover

boghranj *adj* بغرنج intricate

baghal *n* بغل armpit

be farz *c* بفرض supposing

befarma'eid *v* بفرمائيد come in

bagha *n* بقا survival

boghcheh *n* بقچه bundle

bekarat *n* بکارت virginity

bala *n* بلا calamity

balaye' nagahani *n* بلاي ناگهاني catastrophe

bolbol *n* بلبل nightingale

belderchin *n* بلدرچين quail

balidan *v* بلعيدن devour

balidan *v* بلعيدن guzzle

boland *adv* بلند aloud

boland *adj* بلند high

boland *adj* بلند tall

boland ava *adj* آوا بلند loud

boland kardan *v* بلندکردن elevate

boland kardan *v* بلندکردن exalt

boland kardan *v* بلندکردن heighten

boland kardan *v* بلندکردن lift

boland magham *n* بلندمقام Highness

boland nashodan *v* بلندنشدن keep down

boland hemmaty *n* بلندهمتي ambition

bolandgoo *n* بلندگو loudspeaker

bolandi *n* بلندي altitude

bolandi *n* بلندي elevation

bolandi *n* بلندي height

baleh *adv* بله yes

bolor *n* بلور crystal
balout *n* بلوط oak
boloogh *n* بلوغ adolescence
bolough *n* بلوغ maturity
bomb *n* بمب bomb
bomb *n* بمب bombshell
bobmafkan *n* بمب افكن bomber
bon *n* بن base
bon bast *n* بست بن dead end
bon bast *n* بست بن stalemate
banna *n* بنا mason
bana bar in *adv* بنابراين therefore
bena'm *adv* بنام namely
banaye yadboud *n* بناي ياد بود monument
band *n* بند articulation
band baz *n* بند باز acrobat
band keshidan *v* بند كشيدن thread
bande kafsh *n* بند كفش shoelace
bandar *n* بندر port
bandargah *n* بندرگاه haven
bandeggi *n* بندگي bondage
bandeh kardan *v* بنده كردن enthrall
benzin *n* بنزين gasoline
banafsh *n* بنفش violet
bongah *n* بنگاه firm
bongah-e rahni *n* بنگاه رهني pawnbroker
bonyadi *adj* بنيادي fundamental
be-eshtebah andakhtan *v* به اشتباه انداختن mislead
be ezafeh *adv* به اضافه plus
be andazehye yek ghashogh *n* به اندازه يک قاشق spoonful

beh ooj residan *v* به اوج رسيدن culminate
be ab andakhtan-e kashti *v* به آب انداختن كشتي launch
beh asani *adv* به آساني easily
beh an soo raftan *v* به آن سو رفتن go over
be payan rasandan *v* به پايان رساندن conclude
beh payan resandan *v* به پايان رساندن finalize
be posht *adv* به پشت backwards
be-tazegi *adv* به تازگي newly
be tadrij *adv* به تدريج piecemeal
beh tafsil sharh dadan *v* به تفصيل شرح دادن detail
be talkhi *adv* به تلخي bitterly
be tondi *adv* به تندي abruptly
be tanha'ei *adv* به تنهايي lonely
be-ja *adj* به جا opportune
bejoz *p* به جز barring
beh jelo *adv* به جلو forward
be-hadde' efrat rasandan *v* به حد افراط رساندن overdo
be khater avardan *v* به خاطر آوردن recollect
be khater avardan *v* به خاطر آوردن remember
be khoshki amadan *v* به خشكي آمدن land
be khat shodan *v* به خط شدن line up
be khatar andakhtan *v* به خطر انداختن jeopardize
be-khoubi *adv* به خوبي nicely
be khoshi *adv* به خوشي merrily
be dam andakhtan *v* به دام انداختن snare

beh darajeh 'ee keh *c* بدرجهاي که
inasmuch as

be dast avardan *v* بدست‌آوردن
procure

be deghat *adv* بدقت‌closely

beh rasti *adv* بهراستي indeed

be zamin andakhtan *v* بزمين
"حريف"انداختن bring down

be zamin neshastan *n* بزمين
انشستنlanding

beh zendan afkandan *v* بزندان
افكندن imprison

be zoodi *adv* بزودى shortly

beh zoor *adv* بزورforcibly

be zour gereftan *v* بزورگرفتن
usurp

bezour vadar kardan *v* بزور
وادارکردن coerce

be sadegi *adv* بسادگي simply

be saboki *adv* بسبكي lightly

be sardi *adv* بسردى coldly

be sorat *adv* بسرعت quickly

besalamati *n* بسلامتيcheers

be souye *pre* بسوى towards

beh shekam foro bordan *v* به
شكم‌فروبردن ingest

be shoukhi *adv* بهشوخي jokingly

besourate dasti *adv* بصورت‌دستي
manually

betarafejeloo *adv* بهطرف‌جلو
onwards

be tarighi *adv* بهطريقي someway

betowre' asasi *adv* بهطوراساسى
basically

betowre' bad *adv* بهطوربد badly

betowre tarsnak *adv* بهطور
ترسناك awfully

be towre' addi *adv* بهطورعادي
commonly

beh tore am goftan *v* بهطورعام
گفتن generalize

betowre' oryan *adv* بهطورعريان
barely

be tore aziz *adv* بهطورعزيزdearly

betowre' kolli *adv* بهطوركلى
overall

betoowr-e' vasi'e *adv* بهطوروسيع
broadly

be aghab *adv* بهعقب back

be-e'llate' *adv* بهعلت owing to

beghalat-tafsir kardan *v* بهغلط
تفسيرکردن misinterpret

be fouriyat *adv* بهفوريت promptly

beh kar andakhtan *v* بهکارانداختن
exploit

bekar bordan-e ahrom *n* بهکار
بردناهرم leverage

beh kargiri *n* بهکارگيري
employment

be mobarezeh talabidan *v* به
مبارزه‌طلبيدن challenge

be mobarezeh talabidan *v* به
مبارزه‌طلبيدن defy

be mokhatereh andakhtan *v* به
مخاطره‌انداختن endanger

be moghe *adj* بهموقع timely

beh miras bordan *v* بهميراث‌بردن
inherit

be mihan bargashtan *v* بهميهن
برگشتن repatriate

be naz parvardan *v* بهنازپروردن
pamper

beh natijeh naresidan *v* بهنتيجه
نرسيدنfall through

be nodrat *adv* بهندرت rarely

be narmi *adv* بهنرمی smoothly
be narmi *adv* بهنرمی softly
be-narmi *adv* بهنرمي mildly
be neza'e andakhtan *v* بهنزاع
انداختن embroil
be nazar amadan *v* بهنظرآمدن
seem
be hadaf khordan *v* بههدفخوردن
quiver
be har hall *c* بههرحال however
be har hal *c* بههرحال though
be ham amikhtan *v* بههمآميختن
shuffle
be ham zadan *v* بههمزدن rouse
be-hamchenin *adv* بههمچنین
likewise
be hayajan avardan *v* بههیجان
آوردن thrill
be hich vajh *pre* بههیچوجه none
beh vahshat andakhtan *v* به
وحشتانداختن frighten
be yad avardan *v* بهیادآوردن recall
be yek taraf *adv* بهیکطرف aside
beh yek nazar didan *v* بهیکنظر
دیدن glimpse
bahar *n* بهار spring
bahar khab *n* بهارخواب terrace
bahaneh *n* بهانه excuse
Bahay-e billit-e Havapeyma *n*
بهایبلیطهواپیما airfare
behboud *n* بهبود recovery
behbod *n* بهبود improvement
behtar *adj* بهتر better
behtar kardan *v* بهترکردن
ameliorate
behtar kardan *v* بهترکردن
improve

behtarin *adj* بهترین best
bahreh var *adj* وربهره efficient
beh sazi *n* بهسازي reform
behesht *n* بهشت heaven
behesht *n* بهشت paradise
beham pichideh *adj* بهمپیچیده
convoluted
beham peyvastan *v* بهمپیوستن
incorporate
beham peyvastan *v* بهمپیوستن link
beham kouftan *v* بهمکوفتن slam
bahman *n* بهمن avalanche
beh hayajan amadan *v* بهیجان
آمدن flush
boo *n* بو odor
bow dadan *v* بودادن roast
boo dadan *v* بودادن scorch
boo zoda *n* بوزدا deodorant
boo'eidan *iv* بوئیدن smell
bevasteh *p* بواسطه because of
bouteh *n* بوته shrub
booteh *n* بوته bush
boudjeh *n* بودجه budget
boor *adj* بور blond
boozineh *n* بوزینه orangutan
bouseh *n* بوسه kiss
boosidan *v* بوسیدن kiss
boogh *v* بوق honk
boulvar *n* بولوار boulevard
bom shenasi *n* بومشناسي ecology
boomi *adj* بومي native
bouye bad dadan *iv* بويبددادن
stink
boye khosh *n* بويخوش fragrance
bi aram *adj* بیآرام uneasy
bi asas *adj* بیاساس unfounded

bi ensaf *adj* بی‌انصاف unfair

bi payan *adj* بی‌پایان unending

bi-harkat *adj* بی‌حرکت motionless

bi sabegheh *adj* بی‌سابقه
unheard-of

bi sorb *adj* بی‌سرب unleaded

bi shebahat *adj* بی‌شباهت unlike

bi eyb *adj* بی‌عیب flawless

bi-niyaz *adj* بی‌نیاز needless

bi vafa *adj* بی‌وفا unfaithful

biabr *adj* بی‌ابر cloudless

bi asar *adj* بی‌اثر ineffective

bi asar kardan *v* بی‌اثر کردن foil

bi-ehsas *adj* بی‌احساس senseless

bi ekhtiyar *adj* بی‌اختیار
spontaneous

bi arzesh *adj* بی‌ارزش worthless

bi asas *adj* بی‌اساس groundless

bi ettela *adj* بی‌اطلاع unaware

bi etebar sakhtan *v* بی‌اعتبارساختن
discredit

bi eteghadi *n* بی‌اعتقادی disbelief

bi e'temadi *n* بی‌اعتمادی distrust

bi etena *adj* بی‌اعتناء defiant

bi aman *adj* بی‌امان unrelenting

bi omid *adj* بی‌امید desperate

bi-enteha *adj* بی‌انتها open-ended

bi andazeh *adj* بی‌اندازه immense

bi bak *adj* بی‌باک ruthless

bi baki *n* بی‌باکی audacity

bi bacheh *adj* بی‌بچه childless

bi bahreh kardan *v* بی‌بهره کردن
deprive

bi-payan *adj* بی‌پایان boundless

bi payan *adj* بی‌پایان endless

bi-pardeh *adv* بی‌پرده bluntly

bi parva *adj* بی‌پروا audacious

bi parva *adj* بی‌پروا dashing

bi panah gozashtan *v* بی‌پناه
گذاشتن expose

bi poul *adj* بی‌پول penniless

bi tabi *n* بی‌تابی impatience

bi tarbiyat *adj* بی‌تربیت impolite

bi-tazvir *adj* بی‌تزویر candid

bi tasmimi *n* بی‌تصمیمی indecision

bi sobat *adj* بی‌ثبات slippery

bi sobat *adj* بی‌ثبات unstable

bi jonbesh *adj* بی‌جنبش immobile

bi hormat kardan *v* بی‌حرمت
کردن desecrate

bi hefaz *n* بی‌حفاظ bleak

bi haya *adj* بی‌حیا shameless

bi khabi *n* بی‌خوابی(عادی غیر)
insomnia

bi-dard *adj* بی‌درد painless

bi derang *adj* بی‌درنگ prompt

bi-deghat *adj* بی‌دقت negligent

bi deghat *adj* بی‌دقت careless

bi-rahm *adj* بی‌رحم brutal

bi raghbati *n* بی‌رغبتی distaste

biriya *adj* بی‌ریا naive

bi zoor *adj* بی‌زور powerless

bi savad *adj* بی‌سواد illiterate

bi shekl *adj* بی‌شکل amorphous

bi-shomar *adj* بی‌شمار numerous

bi shomar *adj* بی‌شمار
innumerable

bi seda *adj* بی‌صدا silent

bi zarar *adj* بی‌ضرر harmless

bi-taraf *adj* بی طرف neutral

bi taraf *adj* بی‌طرف impartial

bi-atefeh *adj* بی‌عاطفه callous

bi atefeh *adj* بی‌عاطفه inhuman

bi edalati *n* بی‌عدالتی injustice

bi orzeh *adj* بی‌عرضه inept

bi aghl *adj* بی‌عقل frantic

bi eyb *adj* بی‌عیب spotless

bi eyb-o naghs *adj* بی‌عیب‌ونقص impeccable

bi gharaz *adj* بی‌غرض unbiased

bi fayedeh *adj* بی‌فایده useless

bi ghaedeh *adj* بی‌قاعده irregular

bi gha'edeh *adj* بی‌قاعده promiscuous

bi ghanoony *n* بی‌قانونی anarchy

bi gharar *adj* بی‌قرار variable

bi gharar *adj* بی‌قرار restless

bi-gonah *adj* بی‌گناه blameless

bi mobalati *n* بی‌مبالاتی carelessness

bi mazeh *adj* بی‌مزه insipid

bi mazeh *adj* بی‌مزه tasteless

bimasraf kardan *v* بی‌مصرف‌کردن dismantle

bi-ma'ni *adj* بی‌معنی meaningless

bi ma'ani *adj* بی‌معنی pointless

bi maghsad *adj* بی‌مقصد aimless

bimolahezegi kardan *v* بی‌ملاحظگی‌کردن go in

bi molahezeh *adj* بی‌ملاحظه reckless

bi meyl *adj* بی‌میل reluctant

bi mayli *n* بی‌میلی grudge

bi nam *adj* بی‌نام anonymous

bi nezakati *n* بی‌نزاکتی indecency

bi nazm *n* بی‌نظم disorder

bi hasteh *adj* بی‌هسته seedless

biaban *n* بیابان desert

biyaban *n* بیابان wilderness

bayat *adj* بیات stale

bayan *n* بیان remark

bayan *n* بیان expression

bayan *n* بیان statement

bayan-e moghayer *n* بیان‌مغایر paradox

bayaniyah *n* بیانیه manifesto

bi ja *adj* بیجا inappropriate

bichareh *adj* بیچاره helpless

bihal shodan *v* بیحال‌شدن languish

bid *n* بید willow

bid *n* بید moth

bidad *n* بیداد oppression

bidar *adj* بیدار awake

bidar shodan *iv* بیدارشدن awake

bidarkardan *v* بیدارکردن arouse

bidari *n* بیداری awakening

bi rahm *adj* بیرحم relentless

birahm *adj* بیرحم cruel

bi-rahm *adj* بیرحم merciless

biroun *adv* بیرون outside

biron andakhtan *v* بیرون‌انداختن eject

biron andakhtan *v* بیرون‌انداختن expel

biroun andakhtan *v* بیرون‌انداختن protrude

biron raftan *v* بیرون‌رفتن get out

biroonriz *n* بیرون‌ریز outpouring

birouni *adj* بیرونی outer

bironi *adj* بیرونی exterior

bironi *adj* بیرونی external

birooni *adj* بیرونی outward

bizari *n* بیزاری aversion

bish *adj* بیش more

bishazvaghte' mo'ayan *adv* بيش ازوقت‌معين overtime

bishtar *adv* بيشتر further

bishtar *adv* بيشتر mostly

bishtar dava'm avardan *v* بيشتر دوام‌آوردن outlive

bishtar toolkeshidan *v* بيشترطول كشيدن outlast

bishtarin *adj* بيشترين most

bisheh *n* بيشه brake

beyzi *adj* بيضي oval

bifekr *adj* بيفكر mindless

bigharar *adj* بيقرار hectic

bikar *adj* بيكار idle

bikaran *adj* بيكران infinite

bigane *n* بيگانه alien

biganeh *n* بيگانه stranger

biganeh *n* بيگانه barbarian

biganeh *adj* بيگانه exotic

biganeh *adj* بيگانه foreign

biganeh *n* بيگانه foreigner

bi gonah *adj* بيگناه innocent

bil *n* بيل spade

biliyard *n* بيليارد billiards

bilion *adj* بيليون billion

bim *n* بيم scare

bim *n* بيم phobia

bimar *adj* بيمار sick

bimar-e bastari *adj* بيماربستری inpatient

bima're' sarpa'ei *n* بيمارسرپايي بيمارستان outpatient

bimarestan *n* بيمارستان hospital

bimari *n* بيماري sickness

bimari'e sar'e *n* بيماري‌صرع epilepsy

bimariye hari *n* بيماري‌هاري rabies

bimnak *adj* بيمناك apprehensive

bimeh *n* بيمه insurance

bimeh kardan *v* بيمه‌كردن insure

binaye *n* بينايي sight

binahayat *adj* بينهايت extreme

binava *adj* بينوا destitute

bini *n* بيني nose

bini gereftan *v* بيني‌گرفتن sniff

bihodeh *adj* بيهوده futile

bihoush *adj* بيهوش unconscious

bi hooshy *n* بيهوشي anesthesia

biveh *n* بيوه divorcee

biveh *n* بيوه widow

bi-ehterami kardan *v* بی‌احترامی كردن disrespect

bi e'etena *adv* بی‌اعتنا regardless

bi-astin *adj* بی‌آستين sleeveless

bi tajrobeh *adj* بی‌تجربه inexperience

bi harkat *adj* بی‌حركت still

bi-khoda *n* بی‌خدا agnostic

bi-khoda'ei *n* بی‌خدايی agnosticism

bi deghghat *n* بی‌دقت scruples

bi-ragi *n* بی‌رگی numbness

bikar *adj* بی‌كار jobless

bist *adj* بيست twenty

bistomin *adj* بيستمين twentieth

bi savad *adj* بيسواد uneducated

bi kar *adj* بيكار unemployed

bi kari *n* بيكاری unemployment

pa *n* پا foot

paiz *n* پائيز fall

pa'eiz *n* پائيز autumn

pa'ein *adv* پائين below

pa berahneh *adj* پابرهنه barefoot

paband *n* پابند shackle

pop *n* پاپ pontiff

padash *n* پاداش allowance

padash *n* پاداش gratuity

padash *n* پاداش recompense

padash dadan *v* پاداش دادن reward

padarmiyani kardan *v* پادرمياني کردن intercede

pa'dari *n* پادري mat

pad-zahr *n* پادزهر antidote

padeshahi *n* پادشاه king

padeshahi *adj* پادشاهی imperial

padeshahi *n* پادشاهي kingdom

padegan *n* پادگان garrison

paragraf *n* پاراگراف paragraph

parametr-haye vagheie *n* پارامترهاي واقعي parameters

paranoyayi *adj* پارانويايی paranoid

partizan *n* پارتيزان guerrilla

parcheh *n* پارچه cloth

parcheh ghondagh *n* پارچهءقنداق diaper

parsa *adj* پارسا pious

parsaee *n* پارسايي piety

pareh *n* پاره shred

pareh *n* پاره fragment

pareh ajor *n* پارهآجر rubble

pareh kardan *v* پاره کردن shred

paroo *n* پارو oar

paroozadan *n* پاروزدن row

pasazh *n* پاساژ passage

pasban *n* پاسبان police

pastorizeh kardan *v* پاستوريزه کردن pasteurize

pasokh *n* پاسخ replay

pasokh *n* پاسخ reply

pasokh dadan *v* پاسخ دادن answer

pasokh dadan *v* پاسخ دادن respond

pasokh dadan *v* پاسخ دادن reply

pashneh *n* پاشنه heel

pashidan *v* پاشيدن pour

pashidan *v* پاشيدن spray

pa feshari *n* پافشاري persistence

pak *adj* پاک clean

pak kardan *v* پاک کردن cleanse

pak kardan *v* پاک کردن erase

pak kardan *v* پاک کردن mop

pak kardan *v* پاک کردن purge

pak kardan *v* پاک کردن wipe

pak konandeh *n* پاک کننده detergent

pakat *n* پاکت envelope

pak daman *adj* پاکدامن virtuous

pak damani *n* پاکدامني virtue

pakizegi *n* پاکيزگي cleanliness

pagiri *n* پاگيري hindrance

palayesh *n* پالايش purification

palayeshgah *n* پالايشگاه refinery

paltow *n* پالتو overcoat

palowdan *v* پالودن refine

panzdah *adj* پانزده fifteen

payapay mo'ameleh kardan *v* پاياپاي معامله کردن barter

payan *n* پايان conclusion

payan *n* پایان end

payan *n* پایان ending

payan nameh *n* پایان‌نامه thesis

paydar *adj* پایدار permanent

paydar *adj* پایدار unfailing

payma'l kardan *v* پایمال‌کردن override

paymal kardan *v* پایمال‌کردن trample

paymardi *n* پایمردي fortitude

payeh *n* پایه feet

payeh *n* پایه foundation

payeh *n* پایه leg

paye'ei *adj* پایه‌اي basic

pa'ein *adv* پایین down

paeen amadan *v* پایین‌آمدن descend

paytakht *n* پایتخت capital

paygah-e hava'ei *n* پایگاه‌هوایی airfield

por talatom *adj* پرتلاطم wavy

patoo *n* پتو blanket

pokhtan *v* پختن cook

pokhtan *v* پختن bake

pakhsh *n* پخش allotment

pakhsh *n* پخش issue

pakhsh kardan *v* \scatter

pedar *n* پدر father

pedar bozorg *n* پدربزرگ grandpa

pedar bozorg *n* پدربزرگ grandfather

pedar bozorg va madar bozorg *n* پدربزرگ‌ومادربزرگ grandparents

pedar shohar *n* پدرشوهر father-in-law

pedar bozorg *n* پدربزرگ(درزبان کودکان) granddad

pedari *n* پدري fatherhood

pedari *adj* پدري paternal

padidar shodan *v* پدیدارشدن emerge

padideh *n* پدیده phenomenon

pazira *adj* پذیرا receptive

pazirae'e *n* پذیرایي entertainment

pazirae'e kardan *v* پذیرایي‌کردن entertain

paziresh *n* پذیرش reception

paziroftan *n* پذیرفتن embrace

paziroftan *v* پذیرفتن take in

paziresh *n* پذیرش admission

paziresh *n* پذیرش acceptance

paziroftan *v* پذیرفتن admit

paziroftany *adj* پذیرفتنی admissible

par *n* پر feather

pour *adj* پر full

por az tappeh *adj* پرازتپه hilly

por asayesh *adj* پرآسایش restful

por bad *adj* پرباد windy

por baran *adj* پرباران rainy

por dardesar *adj* پردردسر bothersome

por zahmat *adj* پرزحمت troublesome

por sourakh *n* پرسوراخ lace

pour kardan *v* پرکردن fill

por kardane' tofang *v* پرکردن تفنگ load

por mokhatereh *adj* پرمخاطره risky

por-ma'ni *adj* پرمعني meaningful

parakandegi n پراکندگی dispersal	pardeh bardari v پرده‌برداري کردن unveil
parakandeh adj پراکنده sparse	pardehye sinema n پرده‌سینما screen
parakandeh kardan v پراکنده کردن disperse	pardeh gosh n پرده‌گوش eardrum
parakandeh kardan v پراکنده کردن dissipate	por rang n پررنگ highlight
parantez n پرانتز parenthesis	por zoor adj پرزور potent
parpar zadan v پرپرزدن hover	parastar n پرستار nurse
part kardan iv پرت کردن throw	parastare bacheh n پرستاربچه nanny
partab ba zavie n پرتاب‌بازاویه crossfire	parastesh n پرستش worship
partab kardan v پرتاب کردن sling	parastesh v پرستش adore
partab kardan v پرتاب کردن hurl	parasteshgah n پرستشگاه temple
partab kardan iv پرتاب کردن shoot	porsesh n پرسش question
porteghal n پرتقال orange	porsesh kardan v پرسش کردن inquire
porteghali adj پرتقالی Portuguese	porsesh-namehe' mazhabi n پرسش‌نامه‌مذهبي catechism
part gah n پرتگاه precipice	porsesh nameh n پرسشنامه questionnaire
parto n پرتو beam	parseh zadan v پرسه‌زدن prowl
partow n پرتو ray	parseh zadan v پرسه‌زدن roam
por-jam'eiyat adj پرجمعیت overcrowded	porsidan v پرسیدن question
parch kardan v پرچ کردن clench	porsidan v پرسیدن ask
parcham n پرچم banner	paresh n پرش jump
parcham n پرچم flag	por-shekoufeh n پرشکوفه buddy
parcham n پرچم standard	porfandogh adj پرفندق nutty
parkhash n پرخاش quarrel	pour moo adj پرمو hairy
parkhashgar adj پرخاشگر aggressive	parandeh n پرنده bird
pour khatar adj پرخطر hazardous	por harj-o-marj adj پرهرج‌ومرج chaotic
por khori n پرخوري glut	parhiz n پرهیز abstinence
pardakht n پرداخت pay	parhiz n پرهیز diet
pardakht n پرداخت remittance	parhiz kardan v پرهیز کردن abstain
pardakhtan iv پرداختن pay	parhiz kardani adj پرهیز کردني avoidable
pardakhtani adj پرداختني due	
pardeh n پرده drape	

parhizkar *n* پرهیزکار continent

parva dashtan *v* پرواداشتن care

parvaz *n* پرواز blast off

parvaz dadan *iv* پروازدادن fly

parvaneh *n* پروانه butterfly

parvaneh *n* پروانه patent

parvardan *v* پروردن nurture

parvardan *iv* پروردن breed

parvaresh dadan *v* پرورش‌دادن bring up

parvareshgah *n* پرورشگاه orphanage

parvandeh *n* پرونده dossier

paridan *v* پریدن bounce

periz *n* پریز outlet

parishan kardan *v* پریشان‌کردن confound

pezeshk *n* پزشک physician

pezeshk *n* پزشک doctor

pejman *adj* پژمان dejected

pazhmordeh shodan *v* پژمرده‌شدن wither

pazhouhesh *n* پژوهش research

pazhouhidan *v* پژوهیدن research

pas az *pre* پس‌از after

pas az aan *adv* پس‌ازآن afterwards

pas andaz *n* پس‌انداز savings

pas dadan *v* پس‌دادن pay back

pas dadan *v* پس‌دادن turn back

pas dadan *v* پس‌دادن refund

pas dadan *v* پس‌دادن repay

pas zadan *v* پس‌زدن rebut

pas zani *n* پس‌زنی backlash

pas gereftan *v* پس‌گرفتن take back

pas gereftan *v* پس‌گرفتن recapture

pas gereftan *v* پس‌گرفتن retrieve

pas mandeh *n* پس‌مانده leftovers

pas mandeh *n* پس‌مانده refuse

pas mandeh *n* پس‌مانده residue

past *adj* پست shabby

past *adj* پست shoddy

past *adj* پست despicable

past *adj* پست inferior

past *adj* پست low

post *n* پست mail

post *n* پست post

pasttar *adj* پست‌تر lower

past sazi *n* پست‌سازی demean

past-fetrat *adj* پست‌فطرت mean

past kardan *adj* پست‌کردن demeaning

post kardan *v* پست‌کردن mail

past kardan *v* پست‌کردن humiliate

post e havaei *n* پست‌هوایی airmail

pestan *n* پستان breast

pestan band *n* پستان‌بند bra

post khaneh *n* پستخانه post office

pesar *n* پسر son

pesar bacheh *n* پسربچه boy

pesar bacheh *n* پسربچه lad

pesar-e baradar *n* پسربرادر nephew

pesar amoo ya dokhtar amoo *n* پسرعمویادخترعمو cousin

pasand *n* پسند choice

pasand kardan *v* پسندکردن admire

pasandideh *adj* پسندیده admirable

pasandideh *adj* پسندیده desirable

poshtband *n* پشت‌بند backing
poshte' sar *n* پشت‌سر back
poshte' sar *pre* پشت‌سر behind
posht ghooz *n* پشت‌قوز hunchback
posht kardan *v* پشت‌ کردن back
posht nevis kardan *v* پشت‌نویس
کردن endorse
poshtkar dashtan *v* پشتکارداشتن
persevere
poshtgarmi *n* پشتگرمی assurance
poshtiban *n* پشتیبان backup
poshtiban *n* پشتیبان patron
poshtiban tahiyeh kardan *v*
پشتیبان‌تهیه کردن back up
poshti *n* پشتی backroom
pashm *n* پشم wool
pashmi *adj* پشمی woolen
pashsheh *n* پشه mosquito
pashimani *n* پشیمانی contrition
pashimani *n* پشیمانی penance
pashimani *n* پشیمانی regret
pashimani *n* پشیمانی remorse
pof kardan *adj* پف‌ کردن puffy
pof kardeh *adj* پف‌کرده bloated
pofak *n* پفك puff
pol *n* پل bridge
pole rah ahan *n* پل‌راه‌آهن viaduct
pelatini *n* پلاتینی platinum
pelastik *n* پلاستیک plastic
pelk *n* پلک eyelid
pelekan *n* پلکان doorstep
palang *n* پلنگ leopard
palang *n* پلنگ panther
palang-e khaldar *n* پلنگ‌خالدار
jaguar
pelleh *n* پله stair

peleh barghi *n* پله‌برقی escalator
pelleh kan *n* پله‌کان stairs
pelotoniyom *n* پلوتونیوم plutonium
polis *n* پلیس cop
peliseh dar *adj* پلیسه‌دار pleated
poliver *n* پلیور pullover
poma'd *n* پماد ointment
panah *n* پناه awning
panah bordan *v* پناه‌بردن refuge
panah dadan *v* پناه‌دادن shelter
panahgah *n* پناهگاه bunker
panahgah *n* پناهگاه shelter
panahgah *n* پناهگاه asylum
banbeh *n* پنبه cotton
panj shanbeh *n* پنج‌شنبه Thursday
panj zelee *n* پنج‌ضلعی pentagon
panjah *adj* پنجاه fifty
panjah-panjah *adv* پنجاه‌پنجاه
fifty-fifty
panjereh *n* پنجره window
panjom *adj* پنجم fifth
panjeh *n* پنجه paw
panjeh *n* پنجه toe
panchar *n* پنچر puncture
pand *n* پند maxim
pand dadan *v* پندددادن(به) counsel
pendar *n* پندار imagination
pendashtan *v* پنداشتن suppose
pendashtan *v* پنداشتن deem
pangouan *n* پنگوئن penguin
panhan kardan *iv* پنهان‌ کردن hide
peni silin *n* پنی‌سیلین penicillin
panir *n* پنیر cheese
pahlo *n* پهلو flank
pahloo be pahloo *adj* پهلوبه‌پهلو
collateral

pahlavan *n* پهلوان champion
pahloo'ei *adj* پهلوي lateral
pahn *adj* پهن wide
pahn *adj* پهن broad
pahn *adj* پهن flat
pahn kardan *v* پهن کردن broaden
pahn kardan *v* پهن کردن flatten
pahna *n* پهنا breadth
pahna *n* پهنا width
pahnavar *adj* پهناور vast
pahneh *n* پهنه arena
pooch *adj* پوچ null
pooch *adj* پوچ absurd
pooch *n* پوچ invalid
poudr *n* پودر powder
poureh *n* پوره puree
pouzesh-khastan *v* پوزش‌خواستن apologize
pouzesh-khahi *n* پوزش‌خواهی apology
pouzeh *n* پوزه muzzle
pouzehband zadan *v* پوزه‌بندزدن muzzle
poust *n* پوست hull
poust *n* پوست membrane
poust andakhtan *v* پوست‌انداختن peel
postdar *adj* دار پوست husky
pooste derakht *n* پوست‌درخت bark
poust kandan *v* پوست‌کندن skin
posidegi *n* پوسیدگی decay
pousidan *v* پوسیدن rot
poushandan *v* پوشاندن clothe
poshandan *v* پوشاندن cover
poshandan *v* پوشاندن emboss

poushesh *n* پوشش capsule
poshesh *n* پوشش cover
poshesh *n* پوشش coverage
poshesh *n* پوشش cover up
poushesh *n* پوشش robe
pooshesh *n* پوشش shield
posheh *n* پوشه folder
poushidan *iv* پوشیدن wear
pool *n* پول deposit
pool *n* پول money
pol e rayej *n* پول‌رایج currency
poonez *n* پونز thumbtack
pay bordan *v* پی‌بردن discover
payapey *adj* پیاپی consecutive
piyadeh *n* پیاده pedestrian
piyadehrou *n* پیاده‌رو sidewalk
piyadeh shodan *v* پیاده‌شدن get down
piadeh kardan *v* پیاده‌کردن disembark
piyadeh nezam *n* پیاده‌نظام infantry
piyaz *n* پیاز onion
payam *n* پیام message
payam -avar *n* پیام‌آور messenger
piyano *n* پیانو piano
pip *n* پیپ pipe
pich *n* پیچ screw
pich *n* پیچ bolt
pich *n* پیچ twist
pich khordan *v* پیچ‌خوردن sprain
pich ya tab khordan *n* پیچ‌یاتاب خوردن torso
pichandan *v* پیچاندن screw
pichidegi *n* پیچیدگی complexity

pichidegi *n* پیچیدگی
complication

pichidan *v* پیچیدن twist

pichideh *adj* پیچیده complex

pichideh kardan *v* پیچیده‌کردن
complicate

payda kardan *v* پیداکردن detect

peydayeshi *adj* پیدایشی genetic

pir *adj* پیر old

pira'moon *n* پیرامون outskirts

pirahan *n* پیراهن shirt

pirahane bi yagheh *n* پیراهن‌بی‌یقه
T-shirt

pirahan-e goshad *n* پیراهن‌گشاد
blouse

peyrowe ghanoon *adj* پیروقانون
law-abiding

pirouz *adj* پیروز triumphant

pirouzi *n* پیروزي triumph

piroozi yaftan bar *v* پیروزي‌یافتن‌بر
conquer

peyravi kardan az *v* پیروي‌کردن‌از
follow

piri *n* پیري old age

pish *pre* پیش ahead

pish *pre* پیش along

pish *adv* پیش beforehand

pishaz *adv* از پیش before

pish az in *adv* پیش‌ازاین already

pishoftadan *v* پیش‌افتادن outrun

pish ahang *n* پیش‌آهنگ scout

pishband *n* بند پیش apron

pish bini nashodeh *adj* پیش‌بینی
نشده unforeseen

pish bini *n* پیش‌بینی foresight

pishbini-ghalat *v* پیش‌بینی‌غلط
کردن miscalculate

pish bini kardan *iv* پیش‌بینی‌کردن
forecast

pishepa oftadeh *adj* پیش‌پاافتاده
banal

pish pendashtan *v* پیش‌پنداشتن
presuppose

pish dar amad *n* پیش‌درآمد
prologue

pish ras *adj* پیش‌رس premature

pish raftan *v* پیش‌رفتن proceed

pish zamineh *n* پیش‌زمینه
foreground

pish-ghaza *n* پیش‌غذا appetizer

pish goftar *n* پیش‌گفتار foreword

pishnevis kardan *v* پیش‌نویس
کردن sketch

pish niyaz *n* پیش‌نیاز prerequisite

pish niyaz *n* پیش‌نیاز prerequisite

pishani *n* پیشانی forehead

pishtar *adv* پیشتر formerly

pishtar *adv* پیشتر previously

pishdasti *n* پیشدستي anticipation

pishraft *n* پیشرفت development

pishraft *n* پیشرفت headway

pishraft *n* پیشرفت progress

pishraft dadan *v* پیشرفت‌دادن
upgrade

pishraft kardan *v* پیشرفت‌کردن
progress

pishrou *n* پیشرو herald

pish ghadam *n* پیشقدم trail

pishkar *n* پیشکار agent

pishkesh *n* پیشکش offering

pishgah *n* پیشگاه presence

pishgooie *n* پیشگوئي prediction

pish gooie kardan *v* پیشگوئي
کردن predict

pishgoo'ei *n* پیشگویی omen

pishgoee kardan *v* پیشگویی کردن foretell

pish giri *n* پیشگیری precaution

pishnahad *n* پیشنهاد offer

pishnahad kardan *v* پیشنهاد کردن suggest

pishnahad dadan *v* پیشنهاد کردن offer

pishnahad kardan *v* پیشنهاد کردن propose

pisheh *n* پیشه craft

pisheh *n* پیشه profession

pisheh var *adj* پیشه ور professional

pishva *n* پیشوا primate

pishva *n* پیشوا rector

pishvand *n* پیشوند prefix

pishi *adj* پیشی preceding

peygham *n* پیغام errand

peykar *n* پیکار combat

peykartarash *n* تراش پیکر sculptor

kolfat *n* پیکلفت waitress

peygard *n* پیگرد pursuit

peyman *n* پیمان covenant

peyman *n* پیمان promise

peyman n پیمان treaty

payman bastan *v* پیمان بستن contract

peymaneh kardan *v* پیمانه کردن gauge

peivast *n* پیوست annexation

peyvast *n* پیوست enclosure

peyvastegi *n* پیوستگی cohesion

peyvastegi *n* پیوستگی connection

peyvastan *v* پیوستن adjoin

peyvastan *v* پیوستن affiliate

peivastan *v* پیوستن ally

peyvastan *v* پیوستن connect

peivaste *adj* پیوسته allied

peyvasteh *adj* پیوسته attached

peyvasteh *adv* پیوسته ceaselessly

peyvand *n* پیوند graft

peyvand *n* پیوند ligament

peyvand *n* پیوند link

peyvand zadan *v* پیوند زدن graft

peyvandgah *n* پیوندگاه junction

payam avardan *v* پیام آوردن prophesy

payambar *n* پیامبر prophet

payambari *n* پیامبری prophecy

peyjer n پیجر bell pepper

pich dar pich *adj* پیچ در پیچ winding

peyrowe Marks *n* پیرو مارکس Marxist

pish shart *n* پیش شرط down payment

pish sakhtan *v* پیش ساختن prefabricate

pish-ghaza *n* پیش غذا aperitif

pishraft *n* پیشرفت advancement

pishraft kardan *v* پیشرفت کردن advance

pish rou *n* پیشرو pioneer

pishnahad *n* پیشنهاد proposal

peygarde ghanooni *n* پیگرد قانونی prosecutor

peyvastan *v* پیوستن cordon off

ت

ta *adv* تا till

ta *adv* تا until

ta zadan *v* تازدن turn

ta kardan *v* تاکردن fold

taid kardan *v* تائیدکردن corroborate

tab khordan *iv* تاب‌خوردن swing

taban *adj* تابان brilliant

tabestan *n* تابستان summer

tabesh *n* تابش radiation

tabe'e *n* تابع citizen

tab'e *n* تابع function

tabeiat *n* تابعیت allegiance

tabnak *adj* تابناک bright

tabout *n* تابوت coffin

tabidan *iv* تابیدن shine

tabidan *v* تابیدن glow

taj *n* تاج crest

taj *n* تاج crown

taj gozari *n* تاج‌گذاري coronation

taje gol *n* تاج‌گل wreath

tajer *n* تاجر businessman

takht va taz *n* تاخت‌وتاز ravage

takht-o taz *n* تاخت‌وتاز invasion

takht-o-taz *n* تاخت‌وتاز onset

takht-o taz kardan dar *v* تاخت‌و تاز کردن‌در invade

takht-o tazgar *n* تاخت‌وتازگر invader

takhir kardan *v* تاخیرکردن delay

tar *adj* تار dim

tare'ankabout *n* تارعنکبوت cobweb

tare ankabut *n* تارعنکبوت spider web

tare ankabout *n* تارعنکبوت web

ta'raj kardan *v* تاراج‌کردن overrun

tarikh *n* تاریخ date

tarikhnevis *n* تاریخ history

tarikhnevis *n* تاریخ‌نویس historian

tarikhche kotob *n* تاریخچه کتب bibliography

tariki *n* تاریکي darkness

tarik *adj* تاریک somber

tarik *adj* تاریک dark

tariki *adj* تاریک gloomy

tarik roushan *n* تاریک‌روشن twilight

tarik shodan *v* تاریک‌شدن darken

tarik nemodan *v* تاریک‌نمودن dusk

tariki *n* تاریکي gloom

ta zadan *v* تازدن replicate

taze'gi *n* تازگي novelty

tazeh *adj* تازه recent

tazeh-aroos *adj* تازه‌عروس newlywed

tazeh-kar *n* تازه‌کار novice

tazehvared *n* تازه‌وارد newcomer

tazi *adj* تازي Arabic

tazi *n* تازي greyhound

taziyaneh *n* تازیانه whip

ta'asof khordan *v* تاسف‌خوردن lament

tasis-e ghazaee *n* تاسیس قضایي institution

t'asis kardan *v* تاسیس‌کردن establish

taghcheh *n* تاقچه shelf

takestan *n* تاکستان vineyard

taxi *n* تاکسی cab

ta'kid *n* تاکید assertion

ta'kid *n* تاکید emphasis

ta'id kardan *v* تاکیدکردن empathize

talare shahrdari ya farmandari *n* تالارشهردارییافرمانداری town hall

talare' konferans *n* تالارکنفرانس auditorium

talar-e vorodi *n* تالارورودی hallway

tam *adj* تام total

ta'amol kardan *v* تاملکردن hesitate

ta'ahol *adj* تاهل marital

tavan *n* تاوان reparation

tavan *n* تاوان indemnity

tavan dadan *v* تاواندادن remunerate

tavan dadan *v* تاواندادن compensate

tavan dadan *v* تاواندادن indemnify

taval *n* تاول blister

ta'yed *n* تایید confirmation

ta'yed kardan *v* تاییدکردن confirm

tab *n* تب fever

tab dar *adj* تبدار feverish

tabar *n* تبار tribe

tabkhir shodan *v* تبخیرشدن vaporize

tabkhir kardan *v* تبخیرکردن evaporate

tabdil kardan *v* تبدیلکردن commute

tabar *n* تبر ax

tabar-e kochak *n* تبرکوچک hatchet

tabra'e kardan *v* تبرئهکردن exonerate

tabrik goftan *v* تبریکگفتن congratulate

tabasom *n* تبسم smile

tabsareh *n* تبصره footnote

tab'ed *n* تبعید exile

tab'ed kardan *v* تبعیدکردن exile

tab'eid kardan *v* تبعیدکردن banish

tabid kardan *v* تبعیدکردن deport

tabiz ghael shodan *v* تبعیضقائل شدن discriminate

tabligh *n* تبلیغ propaganda

tabligh kardan *v* تبلیغکردن advertise

tabah kar *n* تبهکار villain

tapesh *n* تپش impulse

tapesh *n* تپش throb

tappeh *n* تپه hill

tapidan *iv* تپیدن beat

tapidan *v* تپیدن skip

tapidan(ghalb) *v* تپیدن(قلب) pulsate

tejarat *n* تجارت business

tejarat *n* تجارت commerce

tejari *adj* تجاري commercial

tajahol kardan *v* تجاهلکردن ignore

tajavoz *n* تجاوز aggression

tajavoze jensi *n* تجاوزجنسی rape

tajavoz kardan *v* تجاوزکردن trespass

tajavoz kardan *v* تجاوزکردن exceed

tajavoz kardan *v* تجاوز کردن
violate

tajavoz ya hamleh kardan *v*
تجاوزیاحمله کردن assault

tajdid *n* تجدید renewal

tajdide hayat *n* تجدیدحیات rebirth

tajdide khatereh *n* تجدیدخاطره
recollection

tajdide didar *n* تجدیددیدار
reunion

tajdide farash kardan *v* تجدید
فراش کردن remarry

tajdide nazar kardan *v* تجدیدنظر
کردن reconsider

tajdide nazar kardan *v* تجدیدنظر
کردن revise

tajziyeh *n* تجزیه dissolution

tajziyeh va tahlil *n* تجزیهوتحلیل
analysis

tajasos *n* تجسس search

tajassom kardan *v* تجسم کردن
visualize

tajlil *n* تجلیل homage

tajamoli *adj* تجملی deluxe

tajamoli *adj* تجملی fancy

tajhizat *n* تجهیزات equipment

tajviz *n* تجویز prescription

tajviz-e darou *n* تجویزدوا
medication

tajviz kardan *v* تجویز کردن
prescribe

tahtulsho'a gharardadan *v* تحت
الشعاع قرار دادن outshine

that-e tasir gharar dadan *v* تحت
تاثیر قرار دادن impress

that-e onvan *n* تحت عنوان imprint

that mohasereh *n* تحت محاصره
enclave

tahdid *n* تحدید confinement

tahrif *n* تحریف distortion

tahrif kardan *v* تحریف کردن
falsify

tahrik kardan *v* تحریک کردن
provoke

tahrik *n* تحریک provocation

tahrik *n* تحریک incitement

tahrik kardan *v* تحریک کردن
motivate

tahrik kardan *v* تحریک کردن
goad

tahrik kardan *v* تحریک کردن
stimulate

tahrim *n* تحریم boycott

tahrim *n* تحریم prohibition

tahrim kardan *v* تحریم کردن
prohibit

tahsin kardan *v* تحسین کردن
applaud

tahsin konandeh *n* تحسین کننده
admirer

tahsil kardan *v* تحصیل کردن earn

tahghir *n* تحقیر contempt

tahghigh *n* تحقیق inquiry

tahghigh kardan *v* تحقیق کردن
verify

tahlil kardan *v* تحلیل کردن
analyze

tahammol *n* تحمل tolerance

tahammol pazir *adj* تحمل پذیر
bearable

tahammol kardan *v* تحمل کردن
suffer

tahammol kardan *v* تحمل کردن
sustain

tahamol kardan *v* تحمل کردن
endure

tahammol kardan *v* تحمل کردن tolerate

tahammol na pazir *adj* تحمل ناپذیر unbearable

tahamol napazir *adj* تحمل ناپذیر intolerable

tahmil *n* تحمیل imposition

tahmil kardan *v* تحمیل کردن impose

tahmil konandeh *adj* تحمیل کننده imposing

tahavvol *n* تحول upheaval

tahvil *n* تحویل delivery

tahvil gereftan *v* تحویل گرفتن take over

takht *n* تخت couch

takht *n* تخت throne

takht-e ravan *n* تخت روان litter

takhtekhab va malafeh *n* تختخواب و ملافه bedding

takhteh siyah *n* تخته board

takhteh *n* تخته lumber

takhteh sang *n* تخته سنگ boulder

takhteh sang *n* تخته سنگ cliff

takhteh siyah *n* تخته سیاه blackboard

takhte' siyah *n* تخته سیاه chalkboard

takhtehye shirjeh *n* تخته شیرجه springboard

takhsis *n* تخصیص consecration

takhsis dadan *v* تخصیص دادن allot

takhati *n* تخطی outrage

takhfif *n* تخفیف discount

takhalof *n* تخلف delinquency

tokhm kashtan *v* تخم کاشتن disseminate

tokhm'e morgh *n* تخم مرغ egg

tokhmda'n *n* تخمدان ovary

takhmin *n* تخمین estimation

takhmin zadan *v* تخمین زدن estimate

tadarok didan *v* تدارک دیدن prepare

tadarokat *n* تدارکات supplies

tadbir kardan *v* تدبیر کردن devise

tazakor *n* تذکر mention

tazakkor *n* تذکر reminder

tar o tazeh *adj* تر و تازه fresh

tarabari kardan *v* ترابری کردن transport

tarazoo *n* ترازو balance

tarasheh *n* تراشه splinter

tarashidan *v* تراشیدن scrape

tarashidan *v* تراشیدن shave

teraktor *n* تراکتور tractor

tarakom *n* تراکم compression

tarakom *n* تراکم density

teramvai *n* تراموای tram

taravosh *n* تراوش leakage

taravoush kardan *v* تراوش کردن infiltrate

taravosh kardan *v* تراوش کردن leak

torobcheh *n* تربچه radish

tarbiyat *n* تربیت pedagogy

tarbiyat *n* تربیت politeness

tarbiyat *n* تربیت upbringing

tarbiat kardan *v* تربیت کردن educate

tarbiyat kardan *v* تربیت کردن rear

tartib *n* ترتیب arrangement

tartib *n* ترتیب assortment

tartib *n* ترتیب sequence

tarjomeh kardan *v* ترجمه‌کردن translate

tarjih dadan *v* ترجیح‌دادن prefer

tord *adj* ترد brittle

tord *adj* ترد crisp

tord *adj* ترد crispy

tord kardan *v* ترد‌کردن marinate

taraddod kardan *v* تردد‌کردن traffic

tardid *n* تردید qualm

tars *n* ترس dismay

tars *n* ترس fear

tars *n* ترس horror

tars nagahani *n* ترس‌ناگهانی fright

tarsan *adj* ترسان fearful

tarsandan *v* ترساندن shock

tarsandan *v* ترساندن terrify

tarsandan *v* ترساندن appall

tarsandan *v* ترساندن horrify

tarsandan *v* ترساندن intimidate

tarsandan *v* ترساندن scare

tarsanandeh *adj* ترساننده alarming

tarsandan *v* ترسانیدن dismay

tarsnak *adj* ترسناك scary

tarsnak *adj* ترسناک terrific

tarsnak *adj* ترسناک terrifying

tarsnak *adj* ترسناک appalling

tarsnak *adj* ترسناک awful

tarsnak *adj* ترسناک dire

tarsnak *adj* ترسناک formidable

tarsnak *adj* ترسناک frightening

tarsnak *adj* ترسناک ghastly

tarsnak *adj* ترسناک grim

tarsoee *n* ترسویی cowardice

tarsidan *v* (از) ترسیدن dread

tarsimi *adj* ترسیمی graphic

torsh *adj* ترش sour

torsh *n* ترش acid

torsh shodan *v* ترش‌شدن ferment

tarashoh kardan *v* ترشح‌کردن sprinkle

tarashoh kardan *v* ترشح‌کردن splash

torshy *n* ترشی acidity

tarfi'e *n* ترفیع raise

taragheh *n* ترقه firecracker

targhoveh *n* ترقوه collarbone

taraghi *n* ترقی procession

taraghi kardan *iv* ترقی‌کردن rise

tark *n* ترك abandonment

tark kardan *v* ترك‌کردن pull out

tark goftan *v* ترك‌گفتن abandon

tark kardan *v* ترک‌کردن relinquish

terekanidan *v* ترکانیدن crack

tarkib *n* ترکیب blend

tarkib *n* ترکیب combination

tarkib *n* ترکیب composition

tarkib *n* ترکیب concoction

tarkib kardan *v* ترکیب‌کردن merge

tarkidan *iv* ترکیدن blow out

tarkidan *iv* ترکیدن burst

tarkidan dar asare feshar *n* ترکیدن‌در‌اثر‌فشار blowout

tarmim *n* ترمیم amendment

tarmim shodan *v* ترمیم‌شدن recover

tarmim kardan *v* ترمیم‌کردن reform

tarmim kardan *v* ترمیم کردن
amend

tarmim kardan *v* ترمیم کردن
restore

tarvij *n* ترویج promotion

tarvij kardan *v* ترویج کردن
promote

tarya'k *n* تریاک opium

teria *n* تریا cafeteria

tazrigh *n* تزریق transfusion

tazrigh *n* تزریق injection

tazrigh kardan *v* تزریق کردن inject

taz'eini *adj* تزیینی ornamental

tasavi *n* تساوي parity

tasbih *n* تسبیح rosary

tasri'e *n* تسریع expedition

tasri kardan *v* تسریع کردن
accelerate

taskin *n* تسکین alleviation

taskin *n* تسکین sedation

taskin *n* تسکین solace

taskin dadan *v* تسکین دادن
mitigate

taskin dadan *v* تسکین دادن quell

taskin dadan *v* تسکین دادن soothe

taskin dadan *v* تسکین دادن pacify

taslim shodan *v* تسلیم شدن
capitulate

taslim shodan *v* تسلیم شدن submit

taslim shodan *v* تسلیم شدن
succumb

taslim kardan *v* تسلیم کردن betray

tasmeh *n* تسمه strap

tasviyeh kardan *v* تسویه کردن
liquidate

taswiyeh kardan *v* تسویه کردن pay
off

tashaboh *n* تشابه similarity

tashkhis *n* تشخیص assessment

tashkhis *n* تشخیص diagnosis

tashkhis dadan *v* تشخیص دادن
assess

tashkhis dadan *v* تشخیص دادن
discern

tashkhis dadan (teb) *v* تشخیص
(طب)دادن diagnose

tashrih *n* تشریح anatomy

tashrih *n* تشریح description

tashrifat *n* تشریفات ceremony

toshak *n* تشک mattress

tashakkor *n* تشکر thanks

tashkil dahandeh *adj* تشکیل دهنده
former

tashkila't *n* تشکیلات organization

tashanoj *n* تشنج convulsion

tashanoj *n* تشنج hysteria

tashannoje mowzei *n* تشنج موضعی
spasm

teshneh *adj* تشنه thirsty

teshneh boudan *v* تشنه بودن thirst

tashvigh *n* تشویق persuasion

tashwigh kardan *v* تشویق کردن
patronize

tashvigh kardan *v* تشویق کردن
encourage

tashvigh va tamjid *n* تشویق و
تمجید applause

tashvighi *adj* تشویقی persuasive

tashvigh shodan *v* تشویق شدن
cheer up

tasadofy *adj* تصادفي accidental

tasadofi *adv* تصادفي randomly

tasadom *n* تصادم collision

tasadom *n* تصادم concussion

tasadom kardan *v* تصادم کردن collide

tasaodi *adj* تصاعدي progressive

tashih *n* تصحیح correction

tashih kardan *v* تصحیح کردن rectify

tasadi *n* تصدي charge

tasdigh kardan *v* تصدیق کردن subscribe

tasdigh kardan *v* تصدیق کردن certify

tasdigh kardan *v* تصدیق کردن sanctify

tasarof *n* تصرف seizure

tasarrof kardan *v* تصرف کردن preoccupy

tasfiyeh kardan *v* تصفیه کردن purify

tasmim *n* تصمیم resolution

tasmim gereftan *v* تصمیم گرفتن decide

tasmim gereftan *v* تصمیم گرفتن determine

tasavor *n* تصور notion

tasavour kardan *v* تصور کردن imagine

tasavori *adj* تصوري unreal

tasvib *n* تصویب approval

tasvib kardan *v* تصویب کردن approve

tasvibe mojadade ghanoon *n* تصویب‌مجددقانون reenactment

tasvir *n* تصویر picture

tasvir *n* تصویر portrait

tazif rohieh kardan *v* تضعیف روحیه‌کردن demoralize

tazmin *n* تضمین warranty

tatbigh *n* تطبیق harmony

tatbighi *adj* تطبیقي comparative

tathir *n* تطهیر purge

tazahor *n* تظاهر pretense

ta'arof *n* تعارف compliment

ta'dil kardan *v* تعدیل کردن moderate

tarefeh *n* تعرفه tariff

tarif *n* تعریف definition

ta'asob *n* تعصب prejudice

ta'asob *n* تعصب bigotry

ta'til *n* تعطیل holiday

ta'atil kardan *v* تعطیل کردن vacate

ta'zim *n* تعظیم bow

ta'affon *n* تعفن stench

ta'ghib *n* تعقیب chase

ta'ghibe jenayatkaran *n* تعقیب جنایتکاران manhunt

ta'ghib kardan *v* تعقیب کردن chase

ta'aloogh dashtan *v* تعلق داشتن belong

ta'allol kardan *v* تعلل کردن procrastinate

ta'alim *n* تعلیم training

ta'alim dadan *iv* تعلیم‌دادن teach

ta'amoogh *n* تعمق meditation

ta'mid *n* تعمید baptism

ta'mid dadan *v* تعمیددادن baptize

ta'mir kardan *v* تعمیر کردن mend

ta'amir kardan *v* تعمیر کردن renovate

ta'amir kardan *v* تعمیر کردن repair

ta'mir-e asasi *v* تعمیر اساسی overhaul

ta'aviz kardan *v* تعویض کردن substitute

ta'yin *n* تعیین appointment

ta'yin kardan *v* تعیین کردن appoint

taghziyeh *n* تغذیه nutrition

taghyier *n* تغییر change

taghyir dadan *v* تغییر دادن mutate

taghiere shekl dadan *v* تغییر شکل دادن transform

taghyier ghiyafeh dadan *v* تغییر قیافه دادن disguise

taghire mozo'e dadan *v* تغییر موضع دادن fall back

tagh'eer napazir *adj* تغییر ناپذیر immutable

taghir napazir *adj* تغییر ناپذیر irreversible

taghir dadan *v* تغییر دادن alter

taghier dadan *v* تغییر دادن vary

tof andakhtan *iv* تف انداختن spit

tafazol *n* تفاضل difference

tofaleh *n* تفاله grounds

tofaleh *n* تفاله pulp

tafaroj *n* تفرج outing

tafarojgah *n* تفرجگاه mall

tafragheh *n* تفرقه schism

tafrih *n* تفریح diversion

tafrih kardan *v* تفریح کردن recreate

tafsir *n* تفسیر version

tafsir kardan *v* تفسیر کردن interpret

tafsir neveshtan *v* تفسیر نوشتن comment

tafakor kardan *v* تفکر کردن speculate

tafakor kardan *v* تفکر کردن contemplate

tafakor kardan *v* تفکر کردن meditate

tafkik *n* تفکیک breakdown

tafkik kardan *v* تفکیک کردن break up

tofang *n* تفنگ rifle

tofang *n* تفنگ gun

tofang dasti *n* تفنگ دستی handgun

tofange doudi *n* تفنگ دودی smoking gun

tofange sachmehee *n* تفنگ ساچمه ای shotgun

tofangdar *n* تفنگدار gunman

tagharon *n* تقارن symmetry

taghaza *n* تقاضا request

taghaza kardan *v* تقاضا کردن sue

taghato *n* تقاطع crossroads

taghbih kardan *v* تقبیح کردن denounce

taghaddos *n* تقدس sanctity

taghados *n* تقدس holiness

taghadom peyda kardan *v* تقدم پیدا کردن preempt

taghriban *adv* تقریبا almost

taghriban *adv* تقریبا nearly

taghsim *n* تقسیم division

taghsim kardan *v* تقسیم کردن divide

taghsir *n* تقصیر guilt

taghala *n* تقلا effort

taghalla kardan *v* تقلا کردن struggle

taghalla kardan *v* تقلا کردن put out

taghallobi sakhtan v تقلبی ساختن adulterate

taghlid dar avardan v تقلید در آوردن mime

taghlid kardan v تقلید کردن imitate

taghlil dadan v تقلیل دادن cut back

taghviat konande n تقویت کننده amplifier

taghviyat kardan v تقویت کردن strengthen

taghviyat kardan v تقویت کردن reinforce

tak tak adj تک تک sporadic

tak khal n تک خال ace

takgou'ei n تک گویی monologue

tak navazi n تک نوازی recital

tak hamsari n تک همسری monogamy

takamol n تکامل evolution

takan n تکان jerk

takan n تکان jolt

taka'n khordan v تکان خوردن move up

tekan dadan iv تکان دادن shake

takan dadan v تکان دادن wag

takan dadan v تکان دادن jolt

tekan dadan v تکان دادن startle

tekan dadan v تکان دادن stir

taksir kardan v تکثیر کردن multiply

taksir kardan v تکثیر کردن reproduce

takzib kardan v تکذیب کردن refute

takzib napazir adj تکذیب ناپذیر irrefutable

tekrar n تکرار repetition

tekrar shodan v تکرار شدن recur

tekrar shavandeh adj تکرار شونده frequent

tekrar kardan v تکرار کردن reiterate

tekrar kardan v تکرار کردن repeat

takrim kardan v تکریم کردن venerate

tak sazi n تکسازی unification

taklif n تکلیف task

tokmeh n تکمه button

takmil n تکمیل fulfillment

takmil adj تکمیل replete

takmil kardan v تکمیل کردن augment

tekkeh n تکه clipping

takiyeh n تکیه leaning

takiyeh kardan iv تکیه کردن lean

talash n تلاش quest

talash kardan v تلاش کردن endeavor

talafi n تلافی retaliation

talafi kardan v تلافی کردن recoup

talafi kardan v تلافی کردن retaliate

tala'elou n تلالو flash

talkh adj تلخ bitter

talkh kardan adj تلخ کردن embitter

talkhi n تلخی bitterness

talaf kardan v تلف کردن squander

talafat n تلفات casualty

talaffoz n تلفظ accent

telefon n تلفن telephone

talfigh n تلفیق synthesis

talghin kardan v تلقین کردن insinuate

telegram *n* تلگرام telegram

tolombeh *n* تلمبه pump

tolombeh zadan *v* تلمبه‌زدن pump

talangor *n* تلنگر flick

talangor zadan *v* تلنگرزدن flip

taleh *n* تله trap

taleh marg *n* تله‌مرگ deathtrap

telow telow khoran *adj* تلوتلو خوران staggering

televiziyon *n* تلویزیون television

tamas *n* تماس contact

tamase hava peyma ba zamin *n* تماس‌هواپیمابازمین touchdown

tamasha *n* تماشا spectacle

tamasha khaneh *n* تماشاخانه theater

tamashagar *n* تماشاگر bystander

tamam *adj* تمام whole

tamam kardan *v* تمام‌کردن integrate

tamamiyat *n* تمامیت integrity

tamayole ghabli *n* تمایل‌قبلی predilection

tamayolat-e jensi *n* تمایلات‌جنسی sexuality

temsal *n* تمثال effigy

tamjid kardan *v* تمجیدکردن praise

tamadon *n* تمدن civilization

tamarkoz dadan *v* تمرکز دادن centralize

tamrin *n* تمرین drill

tamrin kardan *v* تمرین‌کردن practice

tamrin kardan *v* تمرین‌کردن rehearse

tamrine nezami *n* تمرین‌نظامی maneuver

tamrine namayesh *n* تمرین‌نمایش rehearsal

temsah *n* تمساح crocodile

tamaskhor *n* تمسخر scorn

tamaskhor kardan *v* تمسخرکردن deride

tamaskhor kardan *v* تمسخرکردن ridicule

tamaskhor kardan *v* تمسخرکردن scoff

tameshk *n* تمشک raspberry

tamkin kardan *v* تمکین‌کردن condescend

tamanna kardan *v* تمناکردن request

tamiz dadan *v* تمیز دادن distinguish

tamiz kardan *v* تمیز کردن clean

ton *n* تن ton

tan asaye *n* تن‌آسایی leisure

tanavoby *adj* تناوبی alternative

tanbal *n* تنبل slack

tanbal *adv* تنبل tardy

tanbal *adj* تنبل lazy

tanbali *n* تنبلی laziness

tanbih kardan *v* تنبیه‌کردن chastise

tond *n* تند spanking

tond *adj* تند fast

tond *adj* تند harsh

tond *adj* تند quick

tond *adj* تند spicy

tond bad *n* تندباد gale

tond bad *n* تندباد gust

tond-nevisi *n* تندنویسی shorthand

tond bad *n* تندباد hurricane

tondtond harf zadan *v* تندتند حرف‌زدن chatter

tandorosti *n* تندرستي health

tond row *adj* تندرو radical

tond row *adj* تندرو swift

tondi *n* تندي speed

tandis *n* تنديس statue

tanazol rotbeh dadan *v* تنزل‌رتبه دادن demote

tanazol gheymat dadan *v* تنزل قیمت‌دادن devalue

tanazol kardan *v* تنزل‌کردن degrade

tanzil *n* تنزیل interest

tanzim *n* تنظیم alignment

tanzim kardan *v* تنظیم‌کردن adjust

tanafor *n* تنفر dislike

tanafos *n* تنفس respiration

tanafous kardan *v* تنفس‌کردن inhale

tonokeh *n* تنکه pants

tang *adj* تنگ close

tangna *n* تنگنا bottleneck

tangeh *n* تنگه strait

tangiye nafas *n* تنگي‌نفس asthma

taneh *n* تنه trunk

tanha *adj* تنها alone

tanha *adj* تنها sole

tanha *adj* تنها lone

tanha *adj* تنها solitary

tanha va bikas *adj* تنهاوبي‌کس lonesome

tanha'ei *n* تنهائي loneliness

tanavoe *n* تنوع variety

tanoumand *adj* تنومند burly

tanidan *iv* تنیدن spin

teniss *n* تنیس tennis

tah *n* ته bottom

tahdid *n* تهدید threat

tahdid *n* تهدید blackmail

tahdid *n* تهدید menace

tahdid kardan *v* تهدیدکردن threaten

tohmat *n* تهمت slander

tohmat *n* تهمت libel

tahavor *n* تهور boldness

tahviyeh kardan *v* تهویه‌کردن ventilate

tohi *adj* تهي devoid

tohi *adj* تهي empty

tohi kardan *v* تهي‌کردن deplete

tohi kardan *v* تهي‌کردن exhaust

tohidast *adj* تهیدست indigent

tahiyeh *n* تهیه preparation

tahiyeyeh pool kardan *v* تهیه‌پول کردن finance

tahiyeh kardan *v* تهیه‌کردن process

tahiyeh kardan *v* تهیه‌کردن provide

too *adj* تو inside

to raftegi *n* تورفتگي depression

tavafoghe' a'm *n* توافق‌عام consensus

towalet *n* توالت makeup

tavana *adj* توانا able

tavana *adj* توانا capable

tavana sakhtan *v* تواناساختن enable

tavana'ei *n* توانایی means

tavanaee *n* توانایی ability

tavanbakhshi kardan v توانبخشی کردن rehabilitate

tavangar adj توانگر wealthy

tavangari n توانگري opulence

tobeh kar n کار توبه penitent

towbeh kardan v توبه کردن repent

toop zadan v توپ‌زدن bluff

toupkhaneh n توپخانه artillery

toote siyah n توت‌سیاه blackberry

tout farangi n توت‌فرنگي strawberry

toutoun n توتون tobacco

tavajoh n توجه attendance

tavajjoh n توجه attention

tavajoh n توجه favor

tavajoh kardan v توجه کردن attend

towjih kardan n توجیه کردن briefing

toujih kardan v توجیه کردن vindicate

tavahoosh n توحش brutality

tookhali adj توخالی hollow

toodeh n توده bulk

toudeh n توده clot

todeh n توده heap

toodeh n توده mass

todeh kardan v توده کردن heap

todeh yakhe ghaltan n توده‌یخ غلتان iceberg

tourbin n توربین turbine

tavarom n تورم swelling

towzi'e n توزیع distribution

towzi'e kardan v توزیع کردن distribute

tavassote pre توسط per

tose'eh n توسعه enlargement

tose'eh n توسعه expansion

tosee dadan v توسعه‌دادن develop

tose'eh dadan v توسعه‌دادن extend

tousheh n توشه luggage

towzih n توضیح comment

tozih dadan v توضیح‌دادن explain

tozih dadan v توضیح‌دادن illustrate

towte'eh n توطئه conspiracy

tote'eh n توطئه intrigue

towte'eh chidan v توطئه‌چیدن conspire

tote'eh kardan adj توطئه کردن intriguing

toufan n توفان tempest

toofan va saegheh n توفان‌وصاعقه thunderstorm

toofani adj توفاني stormy

towfigh dahandeh adj توفیق‌دهنده gracious

tavaghof n توقف stay

tavaghof n توقف stop

towghif n توقیف arrest

towghif n توقیف bail

towghif n توقیف confiscation

towghif kardan v توقیف کردن arrest

toghif kardan v توقیف کردن impound

towghif kardan v توقیف کردن suppress

tooleh sag n توله‌سگ puppy

towlid kardan v تولید کردن manufacture

towlid kardan v تولید کردن produce

tolid kardan *v* تولیدکردن generate

towlide' mesle' gheyre jensi *v* تولیدمثل‌غیرجنسی clone

tolid niroo *n* تولیدنیرو generation

tounel *n* تونل tunnel

towhin be moghadasat *n* توهین‌به مقدسات sacrilege

tohin kardan beh *v* توهین‌کردن‌به insult

tip *n* تیپ brigade

tir *n* تیر arrow

tir *n* تیر mast

tirandazi *n* تیراندازي gunfire

tir andazi *n* تیراندازي gunshot

tir parcham *n* تیرپرچم flagpole

tirandaz az khafa *n* تیراندازازخفا sniper

tireh *adj* تیره murky

tireh bakht *adj* تیره‌بخت unlucky

tireh-rooz *adj* تیره‌روز miserable

tireh kardan *v* تیره‌کردن dim

tireye posht *n* تیره‌ءپشت backbone

tiz *adj* تیز acute

tiz *n* تیز piercing

tiz *adj* تیز sharp

tiz *adj* تیز pointed

tiz kardan *v* تیزکردن sharpen

tighe sourat terashi *n* تیغصورت تراشي razor

tigheh *n* تیغه blade

tigheh *n* تیغه partition

timar *n* تیمار care

timar kardan *v* تیمارکردن groom

timar kardan *v* تیمارکردن care about

sabet *adv* ثابت standing

sabet kardan *v* ثابت‌کردن immobilize

saniyeh *n* ثانیه second

sabat *n* ثبات consistency

sobat va estehkam *n* ثبات‌و استحکام firmness

sabt *n* ثبت entry

sabt *n* ثبت notation

sabt *n* ثبت registration

sabt kardan *v* ثبت‌کردن enter

sabt kardan *v* ثبت‌کردن note

sabt kardan *v* ثبت‌کردن record

servatmand *adj* ثروتمند rich

ج

ja dadan *v* جادادن accommodate

ja be ja kardan *v* جابجاکردن dislocate

ja be ja kardan *v* جابجاکردن displace

ja khali dadan *v* جاخالي‌دادن dodge

jadou *n* جادو magic

jadougar *n* جادوگر magician

jadoogari *n* جادوگري witchcraft

jadou'ei *adj* جادویی magical

jar zadan *v* جارزدن proclaim

ja rakhti *n* جارختي wardrobe

jaroo *n* جارو cleaner

jaroub *n* جاروب broom

jaroo kardan *iv* جاروب کردن sweep

jari bodan *v* جاري بودن flow

jasus *n* جاسوس spy

jasosi *n* جاسوسي espionage

jasusi kardan *v* جاسوسي کردن spy

ja keshi kardan *v* جاکشي کردن pander

jalebe tavajoh *adj* جالب توجه notable

jaliz *n* جاليز patch

jamed *adj* جامد solid

jame'eh geraee *n* جامعه گرايي socialism

jameh *n* جامه garment

jameh boland zananeh *n* جامه بلند زنانه gown

jan *n* جان life

jan *n* جان spirit

jan bakhshy *n* جان بخشي animation

janeb dari kardan *v* جانبداري کردن sympathize

janeshin *n* جانشين successor

janevar *n* جانور animal

janevare javandeh *n* جانورجونده rodent

janevar-khoo'ei *n* جانورخويي bestiality

janevar shenasi *n* جانورشناسي zoology

javdani *adj* جاوداني everlasting

jaye pa *n* جاي پا footprint

jaye pa *n* جاي پا footstep

jaye taghribi *n* جاي تقريبي whereabouts

jaye tohi *n* جاي تهي emptiness

jaye khali *n* جاي خالي vacancy

jay dadan *v* جاي دادن implant

jayezeh *n* جايزه award

jay gozin *adj* جايگزين situated

jaygozin kardan *v* جايگزين کردن replace

jayezeh *n* جايزه prize

jaygir kardan *v* جايگير کردن settle down

jabr *n* جبر algebra

jobran *n* جبران reprisal

jobran kardan *v* جبران کردن offset

jobran kardan *v* جبران کردن redress

jobran kardan *v* جبران کردن reimburse

jobran napazir *adj* جبران ناپذير irreparable

jadd *n* جد ancestor

joda *adv* جدا apart

joda *adj* جدا distinct

joda *adv* جدا earnestly

jodasazi *n* جدا سازي severance

joda shodan *v* جداشدن part

joda kardan *v* جداکردن segregate

joda kardan *v* جداکردن break away

joda kardan *v* جداکردن detach

joda kardan *v* جداکردن insulate

joda kardan *v* جداکردن separate

joda kardan dar asar boridan *v* جداکردن در اثر بريدن cut out

joda nashodani *adj* جدانشدني inseparable

jodaganeh *adj* جداگانه separate

jodaee *n* جدايي segregation

jadval kalamat n جدول کلمات crossword

jadid adj جدید new

jadid kardan v جدید کردن update

jazzab adj جذاب appealing

jazab adj جذاب cute

jozam n جذام leprosy

jazb kardan v جذب کردن absorb

jazb va tarkib-e ghaza n جذب و ترکیب غذا(دربدن) assimilation

jazr va mad n جذرومد tide

jar-o bahs v جروبحث hassle

jorat n جرات courage

jarrah n جراح surgeon

jarahat n جراحت wound

jarrahi adv جراحی surgical

jaresaghil n جرثقیل crane

jarsaghil n جرثقیل tow truck

jor'eh n جرعه shot

jaragheh n جرقه spark

jaragheh zadan v جرقه زدن spark

jorm n جرم plague

jerm gosh n جرم گوش earwax

jerib n جریب acre

jarimeh n جریمه fine

jarimeh kardan v جریمه کردن fine

jarimeh kardan v جریمه کردن penalize

joz p جز except

joz'e n جزء ingredient

joz be joz adv جزءبهجزء particularly

joz beh joz neveshtan v جزءبهجزء نوشتن itemize

joziat n جزئیات detail

jozveh n جزوه brochure

jozveh n جزوه pamphlet

jazireh n جزیره island

jazireh n جزیره isle

jazireh nama n جزیرهنما reef

jesarat n جسارت impertinence

jast n جست skip

jasto khiz kardan v جستوخیز کردن tumble

jast-o-khiz n جستوخیز leap

jostejogar n جستجوگر explorer

jastan v جستن jump

jastan iv جستن leap

jasad n جسد body

jesm n جسم substance

jesm e kochak e koravi n جسم کوچک کروی globule

jesmani adj جسمانی carnal

jasoor adj جسور daring

jashn n جشن celebration

jashne arousi n جشنعروسی wedding

jashn-e' aroosi adj جشنعروسی bridal

jashn gereftan v جشنگرفتن celebrate

ja'beh n جعبه box

jabeh range naghashi n جعبهرنگنقاشی palette

ja'beh kouchak n جعبهکوچک casket

ja'fari n جعفری parsley

jal e asnad n جعلاسناد forgery

jaal kardan v جعلکردن counterfeit

jal kardan v جعلکردن forge

ja'eli adj جعلی fake

jaali *adj* جعلی counterfeit

ja'eli *adj* جعلی fictitious

joghd *n* جغد owl

joghrafia *n* جغرافیا geography

joft *n* جفت mate

joft *n* جفت pair

joft *n* جفت peer

jegar *n* جگر liver

jala *n* جلا gloss

jala dadan *v* جلادادن polish

jala dadan *v* جلادادن varnish

jala dar *adj* جلادار glossy

jalal *n* جلال glory

jalal dadan *v* جلال‌دادن glorify

jalb kardan *v* جلب کردن attract

jeld *n* جلد skin

jalaseh *n* جلسه session

jalaseh *n* جلسه sitting

jolgeh *n* جلگه plain

jelow amadan *v* جلوآمدن come forward

jelow keshidan *v* جلوکشیدن move forward

jelou keshidan *v* جلوکشیدن pull ahead

jelougiri kardan *v* جلوگیری کردن prevent

jelveh dadan *v* جلوه‌دادن set off

jeligheh *n* جلیقه vest

jomjomeh *n* جمجمه skull

jomjomeh *n* جمجمه scalp

jam avari kardan *v* جمع‌آوری کردن get in

jam avary *n* جمع‌آوری accumulation

jam'e avari *n* جمع‌آوری collection

jam'e avari kardan *v* جمع‌آوری کردن collect

jame' shodan *v* جمع‌شدن aggregate

jam'e shodan *v* جمع‌شدن retract

jam'e shodan *v* جمع‌شدن congregate

jam'e kol *n* جمع کل grand total

jam'-o-joor *adj* جمع‌وجور compact

jomeh *n* جمعه Friday

jamiat *n* جمعیت crowd

jomhuri *n* جمهوری republic

jen gir *n* جن گیر exorcist

jenazeh *n* جنازه remains

jenayat *n* جنایت crime

jonbesh *n* جنبش motion

jonbidan *v* جنبیدن wiggle

jens *n* جنس gender

jens *n* جنس material

jens'e zan *adj* زن جنس feminine

jens'e madeh *n* جنس‌ماده female

jense' nare' heyvanat *n* جنس نرحیوانات buck

jensi *adj* جنسی generic

jang *n* جنگ war

jang kardan *n* جنگ fight

jangavar *n* جنگ آور combatant

jang tan be tan *n* جنگ‌تن‌به‌تن duel

jange salibi *n* جنگ‌صلیبی crusade

jang kardan *v* جنگ کردن battle

jang kardan *iv* جنگ کردن fight

jang avar *n* جنگاور warrior

jang avari *n* جنگاوری warfare

jangal *n* جنگل forest

jangidan *v* جنگیدن campaign	joujeh *n* جوجه chick
jonub *n* جنوب south	joojeh tighi *n* جوجه‌تیغی porcupine
jonube shargh *n* جنوب‌شرق southeast	joujeh morgh *n* جوجه‌مرغ chicken
jonube gharb *n* جنوب‌غرب southwest	jour boudan *v* جوربودن match
	joor shodeh *adj* جورشده assorted
jonubi *adj* جنوبي southern	jourab *n* جوراب sock
janin *n* جنین embryo	jourab *n* جوراب hose
janin *n* جنین fetus	jourabe zananeh sagh boland *n*
jahan *n* جهان world	جوراب‌زنانه‌ساقه‌بلند stocking
jahan gard *n* جهانگرد tourist	jourab shalvari *n* جوراب‌شلواری pantyhose
jahan gardi *n* جهانگردي tourism	
jahani *adj* جهاني worldwide	joush *n* جوش rash
jahani *adj* جهانی universal	joosh *n* جوش eruption
jahat *n* جهت direction	joush *n* جوش pimple
jahesh kardan *iv* جهش کردن spring	joosh dadan *v* جوش‌دادن weld
	joush zadan *v* جوش‌زدن rash
jahesh kardan *v* جهش کردن take off	joushandan *v* جوشاندن boil
	jooshannandeh *n* جوشاننده broiler
jahandeh *adj* جهنده jumpy	
johood *n* جهود Jew	joosh kar *n* جوشکار welder
jahiziyeh *n* جهیزیه dowry	javidan *v* جویدن chew
jow *n* جو barley	javidan *v* جویدن munch
javab *n* جواب answer	javidani *adj* جویدنی crunchy
javan *adj* جوان young	jib *n* جیب pocket
javanan *n* جوانان youth	jib bor *n* جیب‌بر pickpocket
javanak *n* جوانک youngster	jirjirak *n* جیرجیرک cricket
javaneh *n* جوانه bud	jireh *n* جیره ration
javaneh zadan *v* جوانه‌زدن peep	jigh *n* جیغ scream
javaneh zadan *v* جوانه‌زدن erupt	jigh keshidan *v* جیغ‌کشیدن squeak
javaneh zadan *v* جوانه‌زدن germinate	jigh zadan *v* جیغ‌زدن scream
	jigh zadan *v* جیغ‌زدن shriek
javaneh zadan *v* جوانه‌زدن sprout	jin *n* جین jeans
javahersaz *n* جواهرساز jeweler	
javaher foroush *n* جواهرفروشی jewelry store	

chabok *adj* چابک agile

chabok *adj* چابک rapid

chabok *adj* چابک speedy

chap *n* چاپ print

chap *n* چاپ printing

chape jadid *n* چاپ‌جدید reprint

chap kardan *v* چاپ کردن publish

chap kardan *v* چاپ کردن print

chapgar *n* چاپگر printer

chaplousi *n* چاپلوسي adulation

chaplosi *n* چاپلوسي flattery

chaplosi kardan *v* چاپلوسي کردن flatter

chador *n* چادر tent

chador shab-e rakhtekhab *n* چادرشب رختخواب bedspread

da'm *n* چارپایان‌اهلي livestock

chareh *n* چاره remedy

chareh sazi *n* چاره‌سازي solution

chashni *n* چاشني sauce

chashni *n* چاشني seasoning

chashni *n* چاشنی stuffing

chagh *adj* چاق chubby

chagh *adj* چاق obese

cha'gh *adj* چاق overweight

chagh kardan *v* چاق کردن fatten

chaghoo *n* چاقو knife

chak *n* چاک slot

chak dadan *iv* چاک‌دادن slit

chalesh angiz *adj* چالش‌انگیز challenging

chaleh *n* چاله pit

chaneh *n* چانه chin

chaneh zadan *v* چانه‌زدن haggle

chai *n* چاي tea

chatr *n* چتر umbrella

chatre nejat *n* چتر نجات parachute

chera *adv* چرا why

cheragh-e khorak pazi *n* چراغ خوراک‌پزي heater

cheraghe darya'ei *n* چراغ دریایي beacon

charagah *n* چراگاه pasture

cherandan *v* چراندن graze

charb *adj* چرب fatty

charbi *n* چربي fat

charbiye khouk *n* چربي‌خوک lard

charbidan *v* چربیدن prevail

chort *n* چرت doze

chort *n* چرت nap

chort zadan *v* چرت‌زدن snooze

chort zadan *v* چرت زدن (off) doze

charkh *n* چرخ wheel

charkh dasti *n* چرخ‌دستي wheelbarrow

charkhan *n* چرخان twister

charkhandan *v* چرخاندن swivel

charkhesh *n* چرخش rotation

charkhidan *v* چرخیدن rotate

charkhidan *v* چرخیدن span

cherk shodeh *adj* چرک‌شده soiled

cherk *n* چرک dirt

cherk kardan *v* چرک کردن stain

cherk kardan *v* چرک کردن fester

cherkin *adj* چرکین dirty

charm *n* چرم leather

chorook shodan *iv* چروک‌شدن shrink

charidan *v* چریدن browse

chasb *n* چسب glue

chasb *n* چسب paste

chasbandan *v* چسباندن glue

chasbandan *v* چسباندن paste

chasbanidan *v* چسبانیدن affix

chasbanidan *iv* چسبانیدن stick

chasbnak *adj* چسبناک sticky

chasbande *adj* چسبنده adhesive

chasbidan *v* چسبیدن adhere

chasbidan *iv* چسبیدن cling

chashm *n* چشم eye

chashmanda'z *n* انداز چشم outlook

chash basteh *n* چشم‌بسته blindfold

chashmpooshi kardan az *v* چشم پوشی کردن از condone

cheshm poushidan az *v* چشم پوشیدن از waive

chashm dashtan *v* چشم‌داشتن expect

chashm gir *adj* چشم‌گیر eye-catching

cheshmak *n* چشمک wink

chashmak zadan *v* چشمک‌زدن blink

cheshmak zadan *v* چشمک‌زدن sparkle

cheshmeh *n* چشمه well

cheshidan *v* چشیدن taste

cheshidan *v* چشیدن sip

choghondar *n* چغندر beet

cheft *n* چفت latch

chekandan *v* چکاندن instill

chakosh *n* چکش hammer

chakmeh *n* چکمه boot

chekeh *n* چکه drip

chekidan *v* چکیدن trickle

chekidan *v* چکیدن drip

chegoonegi *n* چگونگی circumstance

chegooneh *adv* چگونه how

chelandan *v* چلاندن crush

chelcheragh *n* چلچراغ chandelier

chelehe-tabestan *n* چله‌تابستان midsummer

chelik *n* چلیک keg

chalik *n* چلیک drum

chomagh *n* چماق stove

chomagh *n* چماق club

chamedan *n* چمدان suitcase

chaman *n* چمن prairie

chaman *n* چمن lawn

chaman *n* چمن turf

chaman *n* چمن sod

chand *adj* چند several

chand hamsari *n* چندهمسری polygamy

chandi *adv* چندی partly

chang *n* چنگ harp

chang *n* چنگ claw

changzadan *v* چنگ زدن claw

changal *n* چنگال fork

chengeh *n* چنگه cramp

chenin *adj* چنین such

chenin va chenan *adv* چنین و چنان so-and-so

cheh kasi *pro* چه کسی who

chahar *adj* چهار four

chahar shanbeh *n* چهارشنبه Wednesday

chahar na'el raftan *v* چهارنعل‌رفتن gallop

chaharpa *n* چهارپا beast

chahardah *adj* چهارده fourteen

chahar goosh *n* چهارگوش rectangle

chaharumin *adj* چهارمین fourth

chahchahe' *n* چهچه carol

chehel *adj* چهل forty

choob *n* چوب timber

choob *n* چوب wood

choob *n* چوب bat

chob panbeh *n* چوب‌پنبه cork

chob-e seft *n* چوب‌سفت hardwood

choobi *adj* چوبی wooden

choupan *n* چوپان shepherd

choupan *n* چوپان pastor

chidan *v* چیدن mow

chidan *v* چیدن pick

chidane moo *iv* چیدن‌مو shear

chireh shodan *v* چیره‌شدن dominate

chiz *n* چیز object

chiz *n* چیز thing

chiz-e ba arzesh *n* چیزباارزش asset

chiz'e shegeft avar *n* چیزشگفت آور eye-opener

chistan *n* چیستان puzzle

chistan *n* چیستان crux

chistan *n* چیستان riddle

chin *n* چین crease

chin dadan *v* چین‌دادن wrinkle

chin va shekan *n* چین‌وشکن pleat

chini *n* چینی porcelain

chizi *pro* چیزی something

chin khordeh *adj* چین‌خورده wrinkled

ح

hadese *n* حادثه accident

hadeseh *n* حادثه adventure

hadeseh zemni *n* حادثه‌ضمني episode

hashiyeh *n* حاشیه margin

hashiye'ei *adj* حاشیه‌ای marginal

hashiyeh-nevisi *adj* حاشیه‌نویسی annotated

hasel *n* حاصل product

hasele jam'e *n* حاصل‌جمع sum

haselkhiz *adj* حاصلخیز fertile

haselkhizi *n* حاصلخیزی fertility

hazer shodan *v* حاضرشدن show up

hazerjavabi *n* حاضرجوابی comeback

hafezeh *n* حافظه retention

hafezeh *n* حافظه memory

hakem motlagh *n* حاکم‌مطلق despot

haki boudan az *v* حاکي‌بودن‌از signify

hal *adj* حال present

hal amadan *v* حال‌آمدن recuperate

halat *n* حالت pose

ha'lat *n* حالت mood

hamel *n* حامل bearer

hamelegi *n* حاملگي gestation

hameleh *adj* حامله pregnant

hami *n* حامي supporter

hayel *n* حايل fender

hobab *n* حباب bubble

hobab *n* حباب lampshade

habs kardan *v* حبس کردن jail

hajm *n* حجم volume

hadd *n* حد limit

hadde' aghal *n* حداقل minimum

hadde' aksar *adj* حداکثر maximum

hads zadan *v* حدس زدن guess

hodoud *n* حدود verge

hazf *n* حذف omission

hazf shodeh *adv* حذف شده out

hazf kardan *v* حذف کردن delete

hazf kardan *v* حذف کردن omit

haraj *n* حراج sale

harraj *n* حراج auction

haramzadeh *n* حرامزاده bastard

haram zadeh *adj* حرامزاده illegitimate

harf *n* حرف letter

harf *n* حرف particle

harfe ezafeh *n* حرف اضافه preposition

harf-e bozorg *n* حرف بزرگ capital letter

harf zadan *v* حرف زدن talk

herfeh *n* حرفه vocation

herfeh *n* حرفه career

harekat *n* حرکت departure

harkat *n* حرکت movement

harkat dadan *v* حرکت دادن move

harkat konid *v* حرکت کنید move out

harame motahar *n* حرم مطهر sanctuary

hormat *n* حرمت reverence

haris *adj* حریص avaricious

haris *adj* حریص avid

haris *adj* حریص greedy

harisaneh *adv* حریصانه avidly

hese konjkavi *n* حس کنجکاوي curiosity

hesab *n* حساب account

hesab *n* حساب math

hesab kardan *v* حساب کردن score

hesab kardan *v* حساب کردن calculate

hesabdar *n* حسابدار accountant

hesabgar *n* حسابگر calculator

hassas *adj* حساس susceptible

hassasiat *n* حساسیت allergy

hasasiyat-za *adj* حساسیت زا allergic

hasb'ol mogharar *adv* حسب المقرر duly

hosn niyat *n* حسن نیت goodwill

hasood *adj* حسود envious

hasood *adj* حسود jealous

hashareh *n* حشره insect

hesar *n* حصار barrier

hesar *n* حصار fence

hozzar *n* حضار grandstand

hazrat *n* حضرت saint

hefaz *n* حفاظ safeguard

hefazat *n* حفاظت protection

hefazat *n* حفاظت custody

hofreh *n* حفره pothole

hefz kardan *v* حفظ کردن retain

hefz kardan *v* حفظ کردن secure

hagholemtiyaz *n* حق الامتیاز royalty

hagh be janeb *adj* حق‌به‌جانب plausible

haghan *adv* حقا" justly

hoghehbaz *n* حقه باز charlatan

hoghough *n* حقوق rights

hoghooghe mahiyaneh *n* حقوق ماهانهsalary

hoghoughe mahiyaneh *n* حقوق ماهیانهpaycheck

haghighat *n* حقیقت reality

haghight e amri *adj* حقیقت‌امری factual

hekayat *n* حکایت anecdote

hakk kardan *v* حک کردن carve

hakaki *n* حکاکی engraving

hokm *n* حکم arbiter

hokm *n* حکم decree

hokm *n* حکم mandate

hokm *n* حکم sentence

hekmat *n* حکمت motto

hokm farma boudan *v* حکمفرما بودن reign

hokoumate' edari *n* حکومت‌اداری bureaucracy

hokomat estebdadi *n* حکومت استبدادی dictatorship

hokoumat-e ashrafi *n* حکومت اشرافی aristocracy

hokomat-e emperatori *n* حکومت امپراتوری imperialism

hokomat kardan *v* حکومت کردن govern

hokoumat nezami *n* حکومت‌نظامی martial law

hokomat nezami *n* حکومت‌نظامی curfew

hal kardan *v* حل کردنsolve

hal nashodani *adj* حل‌نشدنی insoluble

halal zadeh *adj* حلال‌زاده legitimate

halazoun *n* حلزون snail

halazoone sadaf dar *n* حلزون صدف‌دار shellfish

halghe *n* حلقه curl

halgheh *n* حلقه loop

halgheh *n* حلقه reel

halgheh *n* حلقه ring

halghe kardan *v* حلقه‌کردن curl

halgheh kardan *v* حلقه‌کردن fake

halghehe kelid *n* حلقه‌کلید key ring

hemaghat *n* حماقت stupidity

hammam *n* حمام bathroom

hemayat kardan *v* حمایت کردن support

hemayat kardan *v* حمایت کردن protect

hemayat kardan *v* حمایت کردن uphold

haml *n* حمل consignment

haml kardan *v* حمل کردنtake away

hamleh *n* حمله campaign

hamleh kardan bar *v* حمله کردن بر attack

hamleh kardan be *v* حمله کردن‌به set about

hamleh konandeh *n* حمله‌کننده assailant

hammiyat *n* حمیت zeal

havas part kardan *v* حواس‌پرت کردن distract

havase panjganeh *n* حواس‌پنجگانه sense

havaleh *n* حواله draft

havaleh *n* حواله money order

houri *n* حوري nymph

houriye daryaee *n* حوري‌دريايي siren

houri darya'ei *n* حوري‌دريايي mermaid

houzeh *n* حوزه scope

howzeh *n* حوزه zone

howleh *n* حوله towel

howlehe hamam *n* حوله‌حمام bathrobe

hoomehe shahr *n* حومه‌شهرbarrio

houmehe shahr *n* حومه‌شهرsuburb

hayati *adj* حياتي vital

hayat *n* حياط courtyard

hayat *n* حياط patio

heysiyat *n* حيثيت prestige

heirat n حيرت amazement

heirat *n* حيرت admiration

heyratavar *adj* آور حيرت marvelous

heyrat avar *adj* حيرت‌آور problematic

heyrat avar *adj* حيرت‌آور prodigious

hileh *n* حيله gimmick

hileh *n* حيله strategy

hileh *n* حيله trick

hileh zadan *v* حيله‌زدن trick

heyvane ahliye manzel *n* حيوان اهلي‌منزل pet

heyvani *adj* حيواني bestial

hayat khalvat *n* حياط‌خلوت backyard

heyrat *n* حيرت quandary

khaen *n* خائن traitor

kha'en *adj* خائن treacherous

khatameh *n* خاتمه closure

khatemeh *n* خاتمه expiration

khatemeh yaftan *v* خاتمه‌يافتن terminate

khar *n* خار prick

khar *n* خار thorn

kharej az dastras *adj* خارج‌از دسترس inaccessible

khareji *n* خارجي outsider

khar dar *adj* خاردار thorny

kharesh kardan *v* خارش‌کردنitch

kharegh-al adeh *adj* خارق‌العاده weird

khatereh *n* خاطره memento

khaky va abi *adj* خاکي‌وآبي amphibious

khak *n* خاک dust

khak *n* خاک earth

khak andaz *n* خاک‌انداز shovel

khake ros *n* خاک‌رس clay

khakriz *n* خاکريز bulwark

khakriz n خاکريز dike

khakestar *n* خاکستر ash

khkestar kardan *v* خاکستر‌کردن cremate

khakestari *adj* خاکستري gray

khaki *adj* خاکي terrestrial

khal *n* خال mole

khal *n* خال speck

khal *n* خال spot

khales *n* خالص net

khales *adj* خالص pure

khalegh *adj* خالق creative

khali *adj* خالی vacant

khali kardan *v* خالی کردن unload

khali kardan *v* خالی کردن discharge

khali kardan *v* خالی کردن evacuate

kham *adj* خام raw

khadem *adj* خام crude

khamush *adj* خاموش quiet

khamosh shodan *v* خاموش شدن go out

khamoush kardan *v* خاموش کردن quench

khamoosh kardan *v* خاموش کردن turn off

khamosh kardan *v* خاموش کردن extinguish

khamoosh kardan *v* خاموش کردن hush

khamoshi *n* خاموشی silence

khanedan *n* خاندان clan

khandan *n* خاندان family

khanegi *adj* خانگی homemade

khanegi *adj* خانگی domestic

khanegi *adv* خانگی indoor

khaneh *n* خانه home

khaneh n خانه house

khaneh-e pedari *n* خانه پدری homeland

khaneh-dar *n* خانه دار housekeeper

khaneh dar *adj* خانه دار thrifty

khanevadeh *n* خانواده household

kha'var *n* خاور orient

khavar mashregh *n* خاور مشرق east

khavarneshin *n* خاورنشین easterner

khaeedan *v* خاییدن gnaw

khabarnameh *n* خبرنامه newsletter

khabar negar *n* خبرنگار reporter

khabt *n* خبط aberration

khatneh *n* ختنه circumcision

khatneh kardan *v* ختنه کردن circumcise

khejalat dadan *v* خجالت دادن shame

khejalati *adj* خجالتی shy

khoda *n* خدا deity

khoda *n* خدا God

khodahafez *e* خداحافظ bye

khoda'ei *adj* خدایی divine

khedmat kardan *v* خدمت کردن serve

khadameh kashti *n* خدمه کشتی crew

khar *n* خر ass

kharab shodan *v* خراب شدن fail

kharab kardan *v* خراب کردن pull down

kharab kardan *v* خراب کردن wreck

kharab-kardan *v* خراب کردن botch

kharab kardan *v* خراب کردن destroy

kharab kardan *v* خراب کردن impair

kharabkar *n* خرابکار saboteur

kharabkar *n* خرابکار vandal

kharab kari *n* خرابکاری sabotage

kharab kari kardan *v* خرابکاری کردن sabotage

kharabeh *n* خرابه ruin

kharabi *n* خرابی destruction

kharabi *n* خرابی havoc

kharabi *n* خرابی wreckage

kharash dadan *v* خراش دادن prick

kharashidan *v* خراشیدن scratch

khorafat *n* خرافات superstition

kharamidan *v* خرامیدن stalk

kharj *n* خرج input

kharj kardan *v* خرج کردن expend

kharchang *n* خرچنگ crab

kharchange' darya'ei *n* خرچنگ دریایی lobster

kherad *n* خرد wisdom

khord shodan *v* خرد شدن crumble

khord shodeh *adj* خرد شده battered

khord kardan *v* خرد کردن stamp out

khord kardan *v* خرد کردن batter

khord kardan *v* خرد کردن crash

khord kardan *v* خرد کردن cut down

khord kardan *v* خرد کردن disintegrate

khord kardan *v* خرد کردن smash

khardal *n* خردل mustard

khordeh *n* خرده debris

khordeh nan *n* خرده نان crumb

khordi *n* خردي pettiness

khorsand *adj* خرسند elated

khorsand *adj* خرسند glad

khorsandi *n* خرسندي satisfaction

khargoush *n* خرگوش rabbit

khargosh *n* خرگوش hare

kharman *n* خرمن harvest

kharman *n* خرمن stack

khornas *n* خرناس snore

khor va pof kardan *v* خروپف کردن snore

khoroj *n* خروج exodus

khorooji *n* خروجي output

khorus *n* خروس rooster

khorowsh *n* خروش roar

kharid *n* خرید shopping

kharid kardan *v* خرید کردن shop

kharidar *n* خریدار buyer

kharidari *n* خریداري purchase

kharidari kardan *v* خریداري کردن purchase

kharidan *iv* خریدن buy

khaz *n* خز fur

khazandeh *n* خزنده reptile

khazidan *v* خزیدن crawl

khes khes kardan *v* خس خس کردن wheeze

khesarat *n* خسارت damage

khastegi *n* خستگی tiredness

khastegi *n* خستگي exhaustion

khastegi *n* خستگي fatigue

khastegi na pazir *adj* خستگي ناپذیر tireless

khasteh *adj* خسته tired

khasteh *adj* خسته bored

khasteh shodan *adj* خسته شدن fed up

khasteh konandeh *adj* خسته کننده exhausting

khasteh konandeh *adj* خسته کننده boring

khsteh konandeh *adj* خسته‌کننده tiresome

khasis *n* خسیس miser

khasis *adj* خسیس stingy

khashkhash *n* خشخاش poppy

khoshk *adj* خشك dry

khoshk *adj* خشک arid

khoshk shoe'e *n* خشک‌شوئی dry cleaners

khoshk kardan *v* خشک‌کردن dry

khoshk-nay *n* خشک‌نای larynx

khoshki *n* خشکی stiffness

khoshki *n* خشکی drought

khoshkideh *adj* خشکیده dried

khashm *n* خشم rage

khashm *n* خشم resentment

khashmgin kardan *v* خشمگین کردن enrage

khashmgin kardan *v* خشمگین کردن exasperate

khashen *adj* خشن rough

khashen *adj* خشن hoarse

khoshnood kardan *v* خشنودکردن gratify

khoshounat *n* خشونت violence

khasm *n* خصم opponent

khososan *adv* خصوصا especially

khasiseh *n* خصیصه feature

khat *n* خط line

khat ostova *n* خط‌استوا equator

khat-e tireh *n* خط‌تیره hyphen

khat dar *adj* خط‌دار striped

khat-e rish *n* خط‌ریش sideburns

khate' saheli *n* خط‌ساحلی coastline

khatte' seyr *n* خط‌سیر trajectory

khat kesh *n* خط‌کش ruler

khat monhani *n* خط‌منحنی curve

khat-e hava'ei *n* خط‌هوایی airline

khata kardan *v* خطاکردن sin

khata kardan *v* خطاکردن err

khata kardan *v* خطاکردن forfeit

khatabeh *n* خطابه sermon

khatar *n* خطر danger

khatar *n* خطر peril

khatare ehtemali *n* خطراحتمالی risk

khatar kardan *v* خطرکردن risk

khatarnak *adj* خطرناک perilous

khatir *adj* خطیر momentous

khafaghan *n* خفقان asphyxiation

khafeh kardan *v* خفه‌کردن smother

khafeh kardan *v* خفه‌کردن stifle

khafeh kardan *n* خفه‌کردن suffocate

khafeh kardan *v* خفه‌کردن asphyxiate

khafeh kardan *v* خفه‌کردن choke

khaffeh kardan *v* خفه‌کردن strangle

khafeh konandeh *adj* خفه‌کننده stifling

khalas kardan *iv* خلاص‌کردن rid

kholaseh *n* خلاصه summary

kholase *adj* خلاصه abstract

kholase kardan *v* خلاصه‌کردن abbreviate

kholaseh kardan *v* خلاصه‌کردن brief

kholaseh kardan *v* خلاصه‌کردن summarize

khalasi *n* خلاصی rescue

khelaf *adj* خلاف untrue

khalal dandan *n* دندان خلال toothpick

khale selah kardan *v* خلع‌سلاح کردن disarm

khalgh shodan *v* خلق‌شدن create

khalvat *n* خلوت solitude

khalvat *n* خلوت privacy

kholous *n* خلوص purity

kholous *n* خلوص sincerity

khalij *n* خلیج gulf

khalij kochak *n* خلیج‌کوچک cove

khalifehye a'azam *n* خلیفه‌اعظم Pope

kham shodan *v* خم‌شدن recline

kham shodan *v* خم‌شدن bow

kham sho *adj* خم‌شو flexible

kham kardan *iv* خم‌کردن bend

kham kardan *v* خم‌کردن flex

kham kardan *v* خم‌کردن incline

khamiyazeh keshidan *v* خمیازه کشیدن yawn

khamir *n* خمیر dough

khonsa kardan *v* خنثی‌کردن frustrate

khonsa kardan *v* خنثی‌کردن neutralize

khonsa sazi *v* خنثی‌سازی defuse

khanjar *n* خنجر dagger

khanjar zadan *v* خنجرزدن stab

khandagh *n* خندق ditch

khandeh *n* خنده laughter

khandehavar *adj* خنده‌آور comical

khandeh dar *adj* خنده‌دار funny

khandehdar *adj* خنده‌دار hilarious

khandeh dar *adj* خنده‌دار laughable

khandeh dar *adj* خنده‌دار queer

khandidan *v* خندیدن laugh

khonak *adj* خنک cool

khonak *adj* خنک freezing

khonak kardan *v* خنک‌کردن refrigerate

khonaki *n* خنکی coolness

khoo gereftan *v* خو‌گرفتن acclimatize

khab *n* خواب dream

khab *n* خواب sleep

khab *adj* خواب asleep

khab alod *adj* خواب‌آلود drowsy

khab'e parcheh *n* خواب‌پارچه fleece

khab didan *iv* خواب‌دیدن dream

khabandan *iv* خواباندن lay

khabgah *n* خوابگاه dormitory

khabgah-e kashti *n* خوابگاه‌کشتی berth

khabidan *iv* خوابیدن sleep

khabidan *iv* خوابیدن lie

khar *adj* خوار lowly

khar shemordan *v* خوارشمردن despise

khar shemordan *v* خوارشمردن disdain

khar kardan *v* خوارکردن reproach

khastar *adj* خواستار would-be

khastan *v* خواستن want

khastan *v* خواستن wish

khandan *iv* خواندن read

khandeh *n* خوانده in-laws

khanandeh *n* خواننده singer

khahar *n* خواهر sister

khahar zan *n* خواهرزن sister-in-law

khahesh kardan *v* خواهش‌کردن beg

khob *adv* خوب fine

khoub negah dashtan *v* خوب‌نگاه داشتن keep up

khobi *n* خوبی goodness

khod *n* خود helmet

khod ra penhan sakhtan *v* خود رابنهان‌ساختن sneak

khodsar *adj* خودسر opinionated

khode shakhs *p* خودشخص oneself

khod shirini kardan *v* خودشیرینی کردن ingratiate

khodkar kardan *v* خودکارکردن automate

khod bini *n* خودبینی vanity

khodparast *adj* خودپرست egoist

khodparasti *n* خودپرستی egoism

khod pasand *adj* خودپسند selfish

khodpasandi *adj* خودپسندی conceited

khod pasandi *n* خودپسندی selfishness

khoddari kardan *v* خودداری کردن refrain

khodroo *n* خودرو auto

khodroo *n* خودرو automobile

khodeshan *pro* خودشان themselves

khod kameh *adj* خودکامه totalitarian

khod koshi *n* خودکشی suicide

khodgardani *n* خودگرانی autonomy

khodgardan *adj* خودگردان autonomous

khodam *pro* خودم myself

khodemani *adj* خودمانی homely

khodnamaee kardan *v* خودنمایی کردن show off

khorak *n* خوراک food

khorak *n* خوراک nourishment

khorak dadan *v* خوراک‌دادن nourish

khorake mokhtasar *n* خوراک مختصر snack

khorandan *iv* خوراندن feed

khordan *iv* خوردن eat

khordan *v* خوردن(اسیدوفلزات) corrode

khordani *adj* خوردنی edible

khorshidi *adj* خورشیدی solar

khoreh *n* خوره leper

khosh *adj* خوش blissful

khosh *adj* خوش gay

khosh *adj* خوش happy

khosheghbal *adj* خوش‌اقبال lucky

khosh a'hang *adj* خوش‌آهنگ melodic

khosh ayand *adj* خوش‌آیند pleasant

khoshayand naboudan *v* خوش آیندنبودن displease

khoshbarkhord *adj* خوش‌برخورد sociable

khoshbinaneh *adj* خوش‌بینانه optimistic

khoshbini *n* خوش‌بینی optimism

khosh zough *adj* خوش‌ذوق tasteful

khosh ghoul *adj* خوش‌قول punctual

khoshgozaran *adj* خوش‌گذران luxurious

khoshgozarani *n* خوش‌گذرانی luxury

khosh mashrab *adj* خوش‌مشرب folksy

khoshamad goftan *v* خوشامدگفتن welcome

khoshbakht *adj* خوشبخت fortunate

khoshbakhtaneh *adv* خوشبختانه luckily

khoshboo *adj* خوشبو aromatic

khoshboo *adj* خوشبو balmy

khosh bo *adj* خوشبو fragrant

khoshhali *n* خوشحالی happiness

khoshgozaran *adv* خوشگذران jovial

khoshgel *adj* خوشگل good-looking

khosh mazeh *adj* خوشمزه tasty

khoshnood kardan *v* خوشنود کردن agree

khousheh *n* خوشه bunch

khousheh *n* خوشه cluster

khoshi *n* خوشی bliss

khoshi *n* خوشی cheer

khoshi *n* خوشی delight

khoshi *n* خوشی joy

khoshi *n* خوشی lark

khouk *n* خوک hog

khouk *n* خوک pork

khoon *n* خون blood

khoun asham *n* خون‌آشام vampire

khoon amadan az *iv* خون‌آمدن‌از bleed

khon-e roy *n* خون‌روی hemorrhage

khoun sardi *n* خون‌سردی apathy

khoun baha *n* خون‌بها ransom

khounsard *adj* خونسرد cold-blooded

khonsard *adj* خونسرد indifferent

khonsardi *n* خونسردی indifference

khooni *adj* خونی bloody

khoni *adj* خونی gory

khishi *n* خویشی relationship

khishavand *n* خویشاوند relative

khiyaban *n* خیابان road

khiyaban *n* خیابان avenue

kheyaban *n* خیابان street

khiar *n* خیار cucumber

khayat *n* خیاط tailor

khial *v* خیال dump

khiyal *n* خیال humor

khial e batel kardan *v* خیال‌باطل کردن daydream

khiyali *adj* خیالی fantastic

khiyanat *n* خیانت betrayal

khiyanat *n* خیانت treachery

khiyanat *n* خیانت treason

khiregi *adj* خیرگی dazed

khireh konandeh *adj* خیره‌کننده dazzling

khireh kardan *v* خیره‌کردن dazzle

khireh negah kardan *v* خیره‌نگاه کردن stare

khireh negah kardan *v* خیره‌نگاه کردن gaze

kheyzaran *n* خیزران bamboo

khis *adj* خیس soggy

khis khordan *v* خیس‌خوردن soak

khayli door *adj* خیلی‌دور faraway

kheymeh *n* خیمه tabernacle

د

dakhel shodan dar *v* داخل‌شدن‌در intern

dad *n* داد justice

dad-o-bidad *n* دادوبیداد brawl

dad va bidad *n* دادوبیدادrampage

dad va setad *n* دادوستد transaction

dad khast *n* دادخواست petition

dad khast *n* دادخواست plea

dadrad *n* دادرس magistrate

dadgah *n* دادگاه courthouse

dadgah *n* دادگاه tribunal

dadan *v* دادن grant

dadeh parakani *n* داده‌پراکنی broadcast

dar *n* دار gallows

dara bodan *iv* دارابودن have

dara boudan *v* دارابودن possess

daraye barjastegi *adj* دارای برجستگی bossy

daraye sathe na hamvar *n* دارای سطح‌ناهموار ripple

daraye do-kanoon *n* دارای‌دو کانون bifocals

daraye ghazavate' sahih *adj* دارای‌قضاوت‌سلیم judicious

daraye kambod *adj* دارای‌کمبود deficient

daraye noufoz va ghodrat *adj* دارای‌نفوذ‌وقدرت influential

daraee *n* دارایی possession

daraee *n* دارایی wealth

dara'ei *n* دارایی belongings

darbast *n* داربست scaffold

daroo *n* دارو drug

darou *n* دارو medicine

darou khaneh *n* داروخانه pharmacy

darokhaneh *n* داروخانه drugstore

darou saz *n* داروساز pharmacist

darouye bish-az-hadd *n* داروی بیش‌از‌حد overdose

darou'ei *adj* دارویی medicinal

daruye moharrek *n* داروی‌محرک stimulant

das *n* داس sickle

dastan *n* داستان story

dastan-e manzoom *n* داستان‌منظوم lay

da'shtan *v* داشتن own

dashtan *v* داشتن deserve

dam *n* دام pitfall

dam *n* دام snare

damad *n* داماد bridegroom

damad *n* داماد son-in-law

dam pezeshk *n* دامپزشک veterinarian

daman *n* دامن skirt

damane koutah *n* دامن‌کوتاه miniskirt

damane' lebas *n* دامن‌لباس lap

damaneh *n* دامنه hillside

dana *adj* دانا learned

danestan *iv* دانستن know

danesteh *adv* دانسته knowingly

danesh-e amraz-e zananeh *n* دانش‌امراض‌زنانه gynecology

danesh amouz *n* دانش‌آموز student

daneshgah *n* دانشگاه university

daneshgahi *adj* دانشگاهی academic

daneshmand *n* دانشمند scientist

daneshnameh *n* دانشنامه diploma

daneh *n* دانه seed

daneh *n* دانه bait

daneh *n* دانه grain

daneh *n* دانه pill

davar *n* داور referee

davari *n* داوري judgment

davtalab *n* داوطلب candidate

davtalab *n* داوطلب volunteer

davtalab boudan *v* داوطلب‌بودن stand for

davtalabi *n* داوطلبي candidacy

dayereh *n* دايره circle

dayereh *n* دايره department

dayerat'al ma'aref *n* دايرةالمعارف encyclopedia

dayeh *n* دايه babysitter

dekhalat kardan *v* دخالت‌كردن interfere

dokhtar *n* دختر daughter

dokhtar *n* دختر girl

dokhtar-e baradar *n* دختربرادريا خواهرniece

dokhtar-e pishkhedmat *n* دختر پيشخدمتmaid

dokhtare torshideh *n* دخترترشيده spinster

dokhtare masazhor *n* دختر ماساجورmasseuse

dakhmeh *n* دخمه labyrinth

dar aghoush keshidan *v* درآغوش كشيدنcaress

dar bar dashtan *v* دربرداشتن include

dar barnameh gozardan *v* در برنامه‌گذاردنschedule

dar pasokh goftan *v* درپاسخ‌گفتن rejoin

dar parvandeh gozashtan *v* در پرونده‌گذاشتنfile

dar televiziyon neshan dadan *v* درتلويزيون‌نشان‌دادنtelevise

dar jostojooye chizi boodan *iv* درجستجوي‌چيزي‌بودنbeseech

dar hodoude *pre* درحدودwithin

dar dastras *adj* دردسترس accessible

dar zomrehe *pre* درزمرهamong

dar zir *pre* درزير beneath

dar zire sanadi neveshtan *v* در زيرسندي‌نوشتنunderwrite

dar avaz *adv* درعوضinstead

dar kenar *pre* دركنار alongside

dar moddate' shab *adv* درمدت شب overnight

dar miyan amadan *v* درميان‌آمدن intervene

dar miyane sohbate kasi davidan *v* درميان‌صحبت‌كسي دويدنbreak in

dar nahan *adv* درنهانsecretly

darham feshordeh *adj* درهم فشردهcongested

dar ham va bar ham *n* درهم‌وبر هم tangle

deraz *adj* دراز long

deraz kardan *v* درازكردن lengthen

deraz va laghar *n* درازولاغرweed

deraza *n* درازا longitude

dar atiyehye nazdik *adj* درآتيه نزديكupcoming

dar aghosh gereftan *v* درآغوش گرفتن cuddle

dar aghosh gereftan *v* در آغوش گرفتن embrace

dar aghoush gereftan *v* در آغوش گرفتن hug

daramad *n* در آمد earnings

daramad *n* در آمد income

daravardan *v* در آوردن take out

darb *n* درب door

darbareh *adv* درباره regarding

darbarehe *pre* درباره about

dar bareh *pre* درباره concerning

darban *n* دربان janitor

dar be dar *adj* دربدر homeless

dar barabar *pre* دربرابر against

darbar dashtan *v* دربرداشتن comprise

dar botri rikhteh shodeh *adj* دربطری ریخته شده bottled

darband *n* دربند canyon

dar beyn *pre* دربین between

darj kardan *v* درج کردن insert

dar jaye digar *adv* درجای دیگر elsewhere

darajeh *n* درجه degree

darajeh *n* درجه grade

derakht *n* درخت tree

derakht-e angoor *n* درخت انگور grapevine

derakhte mou *n* درخت مو vine

dorakhshan *adj* درخشان luminous

derakhshani *adj* درخشانی flashy

derakhshandegiye ziad *n* درخشندگی زیاد glare

darkhast *v* درخواست appeal

darkhast dadan *v* درخواست دادن apply

darkhast dahandeh *n* درخواست دهنده applicant

darkhast kardan *v* درخواست کردن entreat

darkhast kardan az *v* درخواست کردن از implore

dar-khor *adj* درخور appropriate

dar khore *adj* درخور pertinent

dard *n* درد ache

dard *n* درد pain

dard *n* درد agony

dard *n* درد ailment

dard gosh *n* درد گوش earache

dard ya sozesh-e ghalb *n* دردیا سوزش قلب heartburn

dar dastras *adj* در دسترس available

dardesar dadan *v* دردسر دادن bother

dardna'k *adj* دردناک painful

darz *n* درز crevice

darz *n* درز flaw

dar zir *pre* درزیر under

dars *n* درس lesson

dorost *adj* درست accurate

dorost kardan *adj* درست correct

dorost *adj* درست entire

dorost *adv* درست properly

dorust shodan *v* درست شدن get up

dorost kardan *v* درست کردن address

dorost kardan *v* درست کردن concoct

dorost kardan *v* درست کردن fix

dorost kardan *v* درست کردن make up

dorostkari *n* درستکاري honesty	dar ham va bar ham *n* درهمو برهم tangle
dorosty *n* درستي accuracy	dar havaye 'azad *adv* درهوايآزاد outdoors
doroshti *adv* درشتي sternly	derow kardan *v* درو کردن reap
doroshkeh *n* درشکه sleigh	darvazeh *n* دروازه gate
dar shegeft shodan *v* درشگفت شدن wonder	darvazeh ban footbal *n* دروازهبان فوتبال goalkeeper
darsad *n* درصد per cent	dar vaghe *adv* درواقع actually
dar sad *n* درصد cent	dorod goftan *v* درود گفتن greet
dark kardan *v* درک کردن realize	doroudgar *n* درودگر carpenter
dark kardan *v* درک کردن conceive	doroudgari *n* درودگري carpentry
dark kardan *v* درک کردن perceive	dorough *n* دروغ lie
dar kenar *pre* درکنار beside	dorough goftan *v* دروغ گفتن lie
dar kenar *adv* درکنار ashore	gorooghgoo *adj* دروغگو liar
dargiri *n* درگيري involvement	daron-e keshvar *pre* درون inside
dargir *v* درگير involved	daron-e keshvar *adv* درون کشور inland
darman *n* درمان therapy	daroongara *adj* درونگرا introvert
darman kardan *v* درمان کردن remedy	darooni *adj* دروني inner
darmangah *n* درمانگاه clinic	daroni *adj* دروني interior
darmangah *n* درمانگاه infirmary	darya *n* دريا sea
darmangi n درمانگي failure	daryacheh *n* درياچه lake
dar modat *pre* درمدت during	darya zadeh *adj* دريازده seasick
dar mian *pre* درميان amid	dayasallar *n* درياسالار admiral
dar-mian gozashtan *v* درميان گذاشتن enclose	daryaft *n* دريافت receipt
darandeh *adj* درنده fierce	daryaft kardan *v* دريافت کردن receive
darandeh khoee *n* درندهخويي ferocity	daryaftan *v* دريافتن comprehend
derang kardan *v* درنگ کردن linger	darya'ei *adj* دريايي marine
derang kardan *v* درنگ کردن loiter	daricheh *n* دريچه vent
derang kardan *v* درنگ کردن stick around	daridan *iv* دريدن tear
darreh *n* دره valley	darigh dashtan *v* دريغداشتن spare
	dozd *n* دزد robber
	dozd *n* دزد burglar
	dozd *n* دزد kidnapper

dozde'khiabani *n* دزدخیابانی
mugger

dozde daryaee *n* دزددریایی pirate

dozdiye honari *n* دزدی‌هنری‌یاادبی
piracy

dozdi *n* دزدی burglary

dozdi *n* دزدی heist

dozdi *n* دزدي robbery

dozdi *n* دزدي theft

dozdidan *v* دزدیدن rob

dozdidan *v* دزدیدن embezzle

dozdidan *iv* دزدیدن steal

dezh *n* دژ castle

desambr *n* دسامبر December

dast *n* دست hand

dast-andaz *n* دست‌اندازجاده bump

dast andazi kardan *v* دست‌اندازي
کردن encroach

daste' ba'la' gereftan *v* دست‌بالا
گرفتن overestimate

dast band *n* دست‌بند bracelet

dast band-e ahanin *n* دست‌بند
آهنین handcuffs

dast pacheh kardan *v* دست‌پاچه
کردن embarrass

dast pokht *n* دست‌پخت cuisine

dastkhat *n* دست‌خط manuscript

dast nakhordeh *adj* دست‌نخورده
intact

dast yabi *n* دست‌یابی achievement

dast yaftan *v* دست‌یافتن achieve

dast yaftan *v* دست‌یافتن attain

dastbord *n* دستبرد larceny

dastkhat-e mosannef *n* دست‌خط
مصنف autograph

dastkhosh e toofan *adv* دستخوش
طوفان adrift

dastras *n* دسترس access

dastras *n* دسترس disposal

dastsho'ei *n* دستشویی lavatory

dast kesh *n* دستکش glove

dastgah *n* دستگاه set

dastgah *n* دستگاه device

dastgahe tanzime garma *n*
دستگاه‌تنظیم‌گرما thermostat

dastgir *adj* دستگیر charitable

dastgireh *n* دستگیره knob

dastgiri *n* دستگیري capture

dastgiri *n* دستگیري charity

dastma'l *n* دستمال napkin

dastmal *n* دستمال handkerchief

daste *n* دسته batch

dasteh *n* دسته category

dasteh *n* دسته gang

dasteh *n* دسته guild

dasteh *n* دسته handle

dasteh *n* دسته hilt

dasteh bandi kardan *v* دسته‌بندي
کردن classify

dasteh jaroub *n* دسته‌جاروب
broomstick

dastehe' sorayandegan *n* دسته
سرایندگان choir

dasteh kardan *v* دسته‌کردن cluster

dasteh gol *n* دسته‌گل bouquet

dastour *n* دستور order

dastur *n* دستور precept

dastour-e jaleseh *n* دستورجلسه
agenda

dastour-e zaban *n* دستورزبان
grammar

dastowr-al amal *n* دستورالعمل
recipe

dasti *adj* دستی manual

dasti *adj* دستی handy

rastyari *n* دستیاری assistance

deser *n* دسر dessert

desere fereni *n* دسرفرنی pudding

doshman *n* دشمن adversary

doshman *n* دشمن enemy

doshman *n* دشمن foe

doshmani *adj* دشمن hostile

doshmany *n* دشمنی animosity

doshmani *n* دشمنی feud

doshmani *n* دشمنی hatred

doshnam dadan *v* دشنام‌دادن mistreat

doshvar *adj* دشوار arduous

doshvar *adv* دشوار uphill

do'a *n* دعا litany

doa kardan beh *v* دعاکردن‌به invoke

do'aye kheyr *n* دعای‌خیر benediction

davat kardan *v* دعوت‌کردن invite

da'viye ghaza'ei *n* دعوی‌قضایی litigation

defa *n* دفاع defense

defa kardan *v* دفاع‌کردن advocate

defa' kardan *v* دفاع‌کردن‌از assert

defa kardan az *v* دفاع‌کردن‌از defend

daftar *n* دفتر bureau

daftar *n* دفتر office

daftare asnade rasmi *n* دفتراسناد رسمی notary

daftar khaterat rozaneh *n* دفتر خاطرات‌روزانه diary

daftar-e daraee *n* دفتردارایی inventory

daftar dari *n* دفترداری bookkeeping

daftar e gomrok *n* دفترگمرک customs

daftare yad'dasht *n* دفتریادداشت notebook

daftarchehe chek *n* دفترچه‌چک checkbook

daftar dar *n* دفتردار bookkeeper

daftari *adj* دفتری clerical

daf'e kardan *v* دفع‌کردن repulse

daf'e kardan *v* دفع‌کردن fend

daf'atan *adv* دفعتا once

dafn *n* دفن burial

dafn kardan *v* دفن‌کردن bury

deghat *n* دقت precision

daghigh *adj* دقیق precise

daghigh *adj* دقیق exact

daghigheh *n* دقیقه minute

dokkan *n* دکان boutique

dakeh *n* دکه kiosk

dekor *n* دکور decor

degar bar *adv* دگربار again

degargoony *n* دگرگونی alteration

dagal *n* دگل raft

dogmeh sardast *n* دگمه‌سردست cuff link

del afsordegi *adj* دل‌افسردگی downcast

del-a'shoub *n* دل‌آشوب nausea

del dadan *v* دل‌دادن hearten

dolar *n* دلار dollar

dallal *n* دلال middleman

dallale' harraj *n* دلال‌حراج auctioneer

delalat kardan *v* دلالت‌کردن imply

delalat kardan bar v دلالت‌کردن بر implicate

delavar adj دلاور brave

delavar adj دلاور gallant

delbar n دلبر sweetheart

delbasteh adj دلبسته interested

delpazir adj دلپذیر graceful

delpazir adj دلپذیر handsome

delpazir adv دلپذیر kindly

deltang adj دلتنگ homesick

deltang kardan adj دلتنگ‌کردن depressing

deltang konandeh adj دلتنگ کننده dismal

deltangi n دلتنگی anguish

delchasb adj دلچسب interesting

delkhor kardan v دلخورکردن annoy

delkhoshi dadan v دلخوشی‌دادن cheer

deldari dadan v دلداری‌دادن console

delsard kardan v دلسردکردن discourage

delsard kardan v دلسردکردن dishearten

del souzi n دلسوزی tenderness

delsouzi n دلسوزی compassion

delsozi kardan bar v دلسوزی کردن‌بر deplore

delshad kardan v دلشادکردن delight

dolfin n دلفین dolphin

doulmeh n دلمه gelatin

del va pas adj دلواپس anxious

dalir adj دلیر courageous

dalir adj دلیر intrepid

deliri n دلیری bravery

dalil n دلیل reason

dam n دم breath

dam n دم inspiration

dam n دم instant

dom n دم tail

dam-be-dam adv دم‌به‌دم momentarily

dam zadan v دم‌زدن breathe

dam zani n دم‌زنی aspiration

dam zani n دم‌زنی breathing

dam kardan v دم‌کردن brew

dam kardeh n دم‌کرده infusion

dama n دما temperature

dama sanj n دماسنج thermometer

damdami adj دمدمی ambivalent

damdami adj دمدمی fickle

demokrasi n دموکراسی democracy

damidan-e hava n دمیدن‌هوا blow

donbal kardan v دنبال‌کردن pursue

donbal kardan v دنبال‌کردن prosecute

donbal kardan v دنبال‌کردن track

donbal keshidan v دنبال‌کشیدن tow

donbal keshidan v دنبال‌کشیدن trail

donbalgar n دنبالگر follower

donbaleh n دنباله sequel

dandan n دندان tooth

dandane-asiyab n دندان‌آسیاب molar

dandane deraz va tiz n دندان‌دراز‌وتیز tusk

dandan dard *n* دندان‌درد toothache

dandan nab *n* دندان‌ناب fang

dandansaz *n* دندانساز dentist

dandan gir *n* دندانگیرchainsaw

dandaneh *n* دندانه cog

dandaneh *n* دندانه dent

dandaneh kardan *v* دندانه‌کردن dent

dandan-ha *n* دندانها teeth

dandeh *n* دنده gear

dandeh *n* دنده rib

dah *adj* ده ten

dah senti (amrikaee) *n* ده‌سنتي (آمریکایی)dime

dehati *n* دهاتي villager

dehati *n* دهاتي peasant

daha'n *n* دهان mouth

dahan band bastan *v* دهان‌بندبستن gag

dahaneh *n* دهانه opening

dahaneh atash feshn *n* دهانه‌آتش فشان crater

dahesh *n* دهش donation

dehshat *n* دهشت terror

dehshatnak *adj* دهشتناک horrendous

dehkadeh *n* دهکده borough

dehkadeh *n* دهکده hamlet

dehkadeh *n* دهکده village

dahom *n* دهم tenth

dahan dareh *n* دهن‌دره yawn

dahankaji *n* دهن‌کجیmugging

dahandeh *n* دهنده donor

daheh *n* دهه decade

do *adj* دو two

do bar *adv* دوباهtwice

do-barabar *n* دوبرابر double

do-chashmi *n* دوچشمیbinoculars

do-zan dari *n* دوزن‌داري bigamy

doe sorat *n* دوسرعتsprint

dava zadan *v* دوازدن drug

davazdah *adj* دوازده twelve

davazdahomin *adj* دوازدهمین twelfth

davam avardan *v* دوام‌آوردنstand out

davam dashtan *v* دوام‌داشتن last

dobar chap kardan *v* دوبارچاپ کردن reprint

dobareh *adv* دوباره afresh

dobareh etminan dadan *v* دوباره اطمینان‌دادن reassure

dobareh anjam dadan *v* دوباره انجام‌دادن redo

dobareh bedast avardan *v* دوباره بدست‌آوردنget back

dobareh be ham peyvastan *v* دوباره‌به‌هم‌پیوستن reunite

dobareh por kardan *v* دوباره‌پر کردن refill

dobareh por kardan *v* دوباره‌پر کردن replenish

dobareh javan kardan *v* دوباره جوان‌کردن rejuvenate

dobareh sazman dadan *v* دوباره سازمان‌دادنreorganize

dobareh gozidan *v* دوباره‌گزیدن reelect

do-barabar kardan *v* دوبرابر کردن double

dojin *n* دوجین dozen

do-charkheh *n* دوچرخهbicycle

do-charkheh *n* دوچرخه bike

docharkhe savar *n* دوچرخه‌سوار cyclist

doukhtan *v* دوختن sew

dood *n* دود fume

doudkesh *n* دودکش chimney

do del *adj* دودل hesitant

do-del *adj* دودل indecisive

dodeh *n* دوده grime

door *adj* دور aloof

dour *adv* دور away

door *adv* دور far

dor *n* دور cycle

dour *adj* دور distant

dor andakhtan *v* دورانداختن discard

dour dast *adj* دوردست remote

dour shodan *v* دورشدن keep off

doure kamar *n* دورکمر waist

dorahi *n* دوراهی crossing

dourbin *n* دوربین camera

dour bine nojoomi *n* دوربین‌نجومی telescope

door kardan *n* دورکردن kickoff

dournama *n* دورنما landscape

doreh *n* دوره course

doureh *n* دوره period

dourehye seh mahe *n* دوره‌سه‌ماهه trimester

douri kardan *v* دوری‌کردن‌از avoid

do-zabani *adj* دوزبانی bilingual

dozakh *n* دوزخ hell

dozakh *n* دوزخ inferno

dozakhi دوزخی damned

doost *n* دوست friend

douste pesar *n* دوست‌پسر boyfriend

doust dashtan *v* دوست‌داشتن like

ashegh shodan *v* دوست‌داشتن love

doust dashtani *adj* دوست‌داشتنی likable

doustdashtani *adj* دوست‌داشتنی lovable

doust dashtan *adj* دوست‌داشتنی lovely

dost dokhtar *n* دوست‌دختر girlfriend

doust nadashtan *v* دوست‌نداشتن dislike

dostaneh *adj* دوستانه fraternal

doostaneh raftar kardan *v* دوستانه‌رفتارکردن befriend

doosti *n* دوستی friendship

doush *n* دوش shower

do shakheh *n* دوشاخه plug

doshes *n* دوشس duchess

doshanbeh *n* دوشنبه Monday

doushizeh *n* دوشیزه miss

doushizeh *n* دوشیزه maiden

do-tarafeh *adj* دوطرفه bilateral

do gholoo *n* دوقلو twin

dook *n* دوک duke

dola shodan *v* دولاشدن crouch

dolat *n* دولت government

dibacheh *n* دیباچه preamble

dibacheh *n* دیباچه preface

diplomasi *n* دیپلماسی diplomacy

did *n* دید perspective

did *n* دید vision

did *n* دید eyesight

didar *n* دیدار visit

didar *n* دیدار(برای‌گفتگو)
interview

didari-shenidari *adj* - دیداری
شنیداری audiovisual

didani *adj* دیداري visual

didgah *n* دیدگاه viewpoint

didan *iv* دیدن behold

didan *iv* دیدن see

deir *n* دیر abbey

dir *adv* دیر late

dir *adj* دیر latest

dirpay *adj* دیرپای lasting

dirtar *adv* دیرتر later

dir shodeh *adj* دیرشده belated

dir kard *n* دیرکرد tardiness

dirouz *adv* دیروز yesterday

dirineh *adj* دیرینه chronic

dirineh *adj* دیرینه ingrained

diktator *n* دیکتاتور dictator

dikteh kardan *v* دیکته‌کردن dictate

dig *n* دیگ pot

digg-e bokhar *n* دیگ‌بخار boiler

digar *adj* دیگر another

digar *adv* دیگر else

digari *adj* دیگري other

dinyar *n* دین یار chaplain

dinamit *n* دینامیت dynamite

dindar *adj* دیندار devout

divar *n* دیوار wall

divanegi *n* دیوانگی craziness

divanegi *n* دیوانگی madness

divanegi *n* دیوانگی furor

divanegi *n* دیوانگی insanity

divanegi *n* دیوانگی lunacy

divanegiye ani *n* دیوانگی‌آني
frenzy

divaneh *adj* دیوانه berserk

divaneh *adj* دیوانه crazy

divaneh *adj* دیوانه demented

divaneh *adj* دیوانه insane

divaneh *adj* دیوانه lunatic

divaneh *adj* دیوانه mad

divaneh shodan *v* دیوانه‌شدن rave

divanehvar *adv* دیوانه‌وار madly

dion *n* دیون dues

ذ

za't *n* ذات matter

zati *adj* ذاتي intrinsic

zebh kardan *iv* ذبح کردن slay

zakhireh *n* ذخیره reservation

zorate boo dadeh *n* ذرت‌بوداده
popcorn

zarreh *n* ذره bit

zarreh *n* ذره vestige

zare-bin *n* ذره‌بین microscope

zoghali *adj* ذغالی charcoaled

zekr kardan *v* ذکر کردن mention

zob *n* ذوب fusion

zogh *n* ذوق gusto

ر

reyis *n* رئیس regent

re'eis *n* رئیس boss

re'eis *n* رئیس chief

rais *n* رئیس dean

reies *n* رئیس president

rabeteh *n* رابطه respect

rabetehe' na-mashro'e *n* رابطه نامشروع liaison

rahat *n* راحت relax

rahat *adj* راحت comfortable

rahat *adv* راحت convenient

rahat *adj* راحت cozy

rahat kardan *v* راحت کردن ease

rahati *n* راحتی relief

rahati *n* راحتی comfort

rad *adj* راد upright

radiyator *n* رادیاتور radiator

radiyo *n* رادیو radio

raz *n* راز secret

raz dar *n* رازدار secretary

raz dar *adj* رازدار confidant

rast *adj* راست right

rast *adj* راست straight

rast kardan *v* راست کردن erect

rast kardan *v* راست کردن straighten

rastgoo *adj* راستگو truthful

rasti *n* راستی truth

razi shodan *v* راضی شدن consent

razi kardan *v* راضی کردن satisfy

raket *n* راکت racket

raked shodan *v* راکدشدن stagnate

rakoun *n* راکون raccoon

ram *adj* رام subdued

ram *adj* رام docile

ram *adj* رام tame

ram shodani *adj* رام شدنی amenable

ram kardan *v* رام کردن subdue

ram kardan *v* رام کردن daunt

ram kardan *adj* رام کردن daunting

ram nashodeh *adj* رام نشده unbroken

ran *n* ران thigh

randan *iv* راندن run

randan *iv* راندن drive

randeh shodan *v* رانده شدن chase away

ranandeh kamiyoun *n* راننده کامیون trucker

rah andakhtan *v* راه انداختن initiate

rah ahan *n* راه آهن railroad

rah bandan *n* راه بندان blockade

rah pelleh *n* راه پله staircase

rahpeyma'ei kardan *v* راهپیمایی کردن march

rah raftan *v* راه رفتن walk

rah raftan *iv* راه رفتن tread

rah gozidan *v* راه گزیدن switch

raheb *n* راهب monk

raheb some'eh *n* راهب صومعه friar

rahbord *n* راهبرد guidelines

rahebeh *n* راهبه deaconess

rahebeh *n* راهبه nun

rahrow *n* راهرو aisle

rahrow *n* راهرو cloister

rahro *n* راهرو corridor

rahroo *n* راهرو doorway

rahroo *n* راهرو lobby

rahzani *n* راهزنی holdup

rahnama *n* راهنما adviser

rahnamaee kardan *n* راهنما guide

rahnama *n* راهنما index

rahnama *n* راهنما usher

rahnamaee kardan *v* راهنمایی کردن guide

rahnamaei *n* راهنمایی advise	**rad kardan** *v* ردکردن deny
rahnamaei kardan *v* راهنمایی کردن advice	**rad kardan** *v* ردکردن disclaim
	rad kardan *v* ردکردن disprove
rahi shodan *v* راهی‌شدن depart	**rad kardan** *v* ردکردن rebuff
ra'ey *n* راي poll	**rada** *n* ردا cloak
ra'ei *n* راي vote	**radyab** *n* ردیاب detector
ra'y dadan *v* راي‌دادن vote	**radif** *v* ردیف row
rayaneh *n* رایانه computer	**radif** *n* ردیف class
rayej *adj* رایج current	**radif** *n* ردیف series
rayej *adj* رایج prevalent	**radif kardan** *v* ردیف کردن align
rayeheh *n* رایحه aura	**razm** *n* رزم battle
robaiesh *n* ربایش abduction	**razmandeh** *n* رزمنده fighter
rabt *n* ربط concern	**rezheh** *n* رژه parade
roboodan *v* ربودن abduct	**rezhim** *n* رژیم regime
robodan *v* ربودن grab	**rezhime saltanati** *n* رژیم‌سلطنتي monarchy
robudan *v* ربودن snatch	
roboudan-e havapeyma *n* ربودن هواپیما hijack	**resalat** *n* رسالت apostrophe
	resalati *adj* رسالتي apostolic
rotbeh *n* رتبه rank	**resandan** *v* رساندن supply
rahm *n* رحم mercy	**rastakhiz** *n* رستاخیز resurrection
rahem *n* رحم uterus	**rastgari** *n* رستگاری salvation
rokh dadan *v* رخ‌دادن occur	**rastan** *v* رستن escape
rakhtshoy khaneh *n* رختشوي‌خانه laundry	**rostan** *iv* رستن grow
	restouran *n* رستوران restaurant
rokhsat *n* رخصت reprieve	**rasm** *n* رسم tradition
rokhsat dadan *v* رخصت‌دادن allow	**rasm** *n* رسم custom
	rasm *n* رسم mode
rekhneh *n* رخنه crack	**rasmi kardan** *v* رسمی کردن formalize
rakhneh *n* رخنه leak	
rakhneh kardan *v* رخنه‌کردن penetrate	**rasmi** *adj* رسمي solemn
	rasmi *adj* رسمي formal
rad *n* رد denial	**rasmi** *adj* رسمي starchy
rad *n* رد repulse	**rasmiat** *n* رسمیت formality
radshodan-az *v* ردشدن‌از overtake	**rasmi** *adj* رسمي official
rad kardan *v* ردکردن withdraw	**rosva** *adj* رسوا infamous
rad kardan *v* ردکردن contradict	

rosva kardan v رسواکردن scandalize

rosva'ei n رسوایی disgrace

rosva'ei avar adj رسوایی‌آور disgraceful

rosoukh kardan v رسوخ‌کردن perforate

rasoul n رسول apostle

rasidegi kardan v رسیدگی‌کردن look into

residegi n رسیدگی puberty

residegi n رسیدگی verification

residegi kardan v رسیدگی‌کردن investigate

residegi kardan v رسیدگی‌کردن supervise

rasidegi kardan v رسیدگی‌کردن (به) consider

residan be v رسیدن‌به reach

resideh adj رسیده mellow

resideh adj رسیده ripe

resideh kardan ya shodan v رسیده‌کردن‌یاشدن ripen

reshteh n رشته fiber

reshteh-farangi n رشته‌فرنگی noodle

roushd n رشد growth

roushd kardan v رشدکردن flourish

rashk n رشک envy

rashk n رشک jealousy

roshveh n رشوه bribery

roshveh dadan v رشوه‌دادن bribe

rasadkhaneh n رصدخانه observatory

rezamandi n رضامندی euphoria

rezayat n رضایت willingness

rezayat bakhsh adj رضایت‌بخش satisfactory

rotoubat n رطوبت humidity

rotoubat n رطوبت ، نم moisture

rotobat peida kardan v رطوبت پیداکردن dampen

ratil n رطیل tarantula

ra'ad n رعد thunder

reghbat n رغبت propensity

refaghat n رفاقت fellowship

raftar n رفتار demeanor

raftar n رفتار treatment

raftar n رفتار behavior

raftar n رفتار conduct

raftar n رفتار exploit

raftar kardan v رفتارکردن behave

raftar kardan v رفتارکردن treat

rafteh rafteh kochak shodan v رفته‌رفته‌کوچک‌شدن dwindle

rofo kardan v رفوکردن darn

rafigh n رفیق comrade

reghabat n رقابت rivalry

reghabat kardan v رقابت‌کردن compete

raghas n رقاص dancer

raghaseh n رقاصه ballerina

reghat n رقت pity

reghat angiz adj رقت‌انگیز pitiful

raghs n رقص dance

raghib n رقیب competitor

raghigh kardan v رقیق‌کردن dilute

raghib n رقیب rival

rouk go adj رک‌گو frank

rouk adj رک forthright

rokk adj رک outspoken

rouk goee n رک‌گویی frankness

rouk va post kandeh *adv* رکو پوست کنده frankly

rekab *n* رکاب pedal

ram *n* رم stampede

roma'n *n* رمان novel

roma'n-nevis *n* رمان‌نویس novelist

ramz *n* رمز mystery

ramzi *adj* رمزي mystic

ramzi kardan *v* رمزي‌کردن mystify

ranj *n* رنج affliction

ranj *n* رنج suffering

ranjandan *v* رنجاندن mortify

ranjesh *n* رنجش displeasure

ranj avar *adj* رنجش‌آور annoying

ranjidan az *v* رنجیدن‌از resent

rang *n* رنگ color

rang *n* رنگ dye

rang *n* رنگ paint

range' chehreh *n* رنگ‌چهره complexion

range sabze shabdari *n* رنگ‌سبز شبدري shamrock

rang kardan *v* رنگ‌کردن dye

rang kardan *v* رنگ‌کردن paint

rangarang *adj* رنگارنگ colorful

rangin kaman *n* رنگین‌کمان rainbow

raha kardan *v* رها‌کردن trigger

raha kardan *v* رها‌کردن let go

raha kardan *v* رها‌کردن loose

raha kardan *v* رها‌کردن release

raha kardan *v* رها‌کردن unleash

rahanidan *v* رهانیدن rescue

raha'ei az shiftegi *n* رهایي‌از شیفتگي disillusion

rahaee dadan *v* رهایي‌دادن redeem

rahbani *adj* رهباني monastic

rahbar *n* رهبر pilot

rahbari *n* رهبري leadership

rahn *n* رهن mortgage

ro be enhetat gozashtan *v* روبه انحطاط گذاردن degenerate

roo be bala *adv* روبه‌بالا upwards

roo sefidy *n* روسفیدي acquittal

ravabete jensi *n* روابط‌جنسي sex

ravaj *n* رواج vogue

ravagh *n* رواق portico

ravan *adv* روان fluently

ravan *n* روان fluid

ravan shenas *n* روان‌شناسي psychology

ravan pezeshk *n* روانپزشك psychiatrist

ravan pezeshki *n* روانپزشكي psychiatry

ravaneh kardan *v* روانه‌کردن dismiss

ravani *adj* رواني psychic

Roo-baleshi *n* روبالشي pillowcase

robah *n* روباه fox

robero shodan *v* روبروشدن cross

robero shodan *v* روبروشدن encounter

robero shodan *v* روبروشدن envisage

rooberooshodan ba *v* روبروشدن‌با confront

ro beh khavar *adv* روبه‌خاور eastward

rouh *n* روح soul

rouhan *adv* روحا "mentally

rouhani *adj* روحاني spiritual

rohiyeh *n* روحیه mentality
rood khaneh *n* رودخانه river
roudeh *n* روده bowels
rodeh *n* روده garbage
rodeh *n* روده gut
rowrowak *n* روروک scooter
rooz *n* روز day
rozaneh *adv* روزانه daily
rooznemeh *n* روزنامه journal
rooznameh *n* روزنامه newspaper
rooznameh forooshi *n* روزنامه
فروشي newsstand
rooznemehnegar *n* روزنامه‌نگار
journalist
rowzaneh *n* روزنه peephole
rouzi *adv* روزي someday
roostaee *adj* روستایی rustic
ravesh *n* روش manner
ravesh *n* روش procedure
rowshan *adj* روشن clean-cut
rowshan *adj* روشن clear-cut
roshan sakhtan *v* روشن‌ساختن
illuminate
rowshan shodan *v* روشن‌شدن
kindle
roshan fekr kardan *v* روشن‌فکر
کردن enlighten
roushan kardan *v* روشن‌کردنturn
on
rowshan kardan *v* روشن‌کردن
brighten
rowshan kardan *v* روشن‌کردن
clarify
rowshan kardan *v* روشن‌کردن
refresh
rowshan va tazeh kardan *v*
روشن‌وتازه‌کردن refurbish

roshana'eye khireh konanadeh
n روشنایي‌خیره‌کننده flare
rowshanfekr *adj* روشنفکر
broadminded
rowshanfekr *adj* روشنفکر
open-minded
rowshani *n* روشني brightness
rowshani *n* روشني clarification
roghan otomobil *n* روغن‌اتومبیل
grease
roghan zadan *v* روغن‌زدن grease
rowghanzadan *v* روغن‌زدن
lubricate
rowghanzani *n* روغن‌زني
lubrication
roghan mali kardan *v* روغن‌مالي
کردن anoint
roghani *adj* روغني greasy
roukesh *n* روکش clothing
rookesh zadan *v* روکش‌زدنrecap
roukesh kardan *v* روکش‌کردن
resurface
rownagh yaftan *v* رونق‌یافتنthrive
ronevesht *n* رونوشت copy
ronevis konandeh *n* copier
rou nevisi kardan *v* رونویسي‌کردن
transcribe
rouye' ore *n* روی over
rooye *adv* روي aboard
rouy *n* روي zinc
rouye kashti *adv* روي‌کشتي
overboard
rooie ham rafte *adj* روي‌همرفته
altogether
rooye'ham rikhtan *v* روي‌همریختن
huddle

roye yakh eski kardan *v* روي‌يخ اسكي‌كردن ice skate	**zanoo** *n* زانو knee
royaroe'e *n* رويارويي encounter	**zanoo kham kardan** *v* زانوخم كردن genuflect
rouyeh *n* رويه tenor	**zanoo zadan** *iv* زانوزدن kneel
raviyeh *n* رويه tack	**zahed** *adj* زاهد ascetic
riya *n* ريا hypocrisy	**zahed** *n* زاهد recluse
riyasat *n* رياست presidency	**zahed-e gosheh neshin** *n* زاهد گوشه‌نشين hermit
rikhtan *iv* ريختن spill	**zavieh dar** *adj* زاويه‌دار angular
riz *adj* ريز tiny	**zayesh** *n* زايش birth
riz-andam *n* ريزاندام midget	**zayeshgah** *n* زايشگاه maternity
riz baridan *v* ريزباريدن drizzle	**za'eideh shodan** *v* زاييده‌شدن be born
rizriz kardan *v* ريزريز كردن chop	**zobaleh** n زباله dump
rizriz kardan *v* ريزريز كردن mince	**zaban** *n* زبان language
rizesh atomi *n* ريزش‌اتمي fallout	**zaban** *n* زبان tongue
rizeh andam *adj* ريزه‌اندام petite	**zaban basteh** *adj* زبان‌بسته dumb
rish *n* ريش beard	**zebr** *adj* زبر coarse
rish *n* ريش whiskers	**zaboon** *adj* زبون humble
rish khand *n* ريشخند sarcasm	**zajr** *n* زجر torment
rishkhand *n* ريشخند ridicule	**zajrkosh kardan** *v* زجركش كردن lynch
risheh *n* ريشه root	**zahmat keshidan** *v* زحمت‌كشيدن toil
risheh kan kardan *v* ريشه‌كن‌كردن root	**zakhm** *n* زخم sore
rishoo *adj* ريشو bearded	**zakhm** *n* زخم ulcer
rige ravan *n* ريگ‌روان quicksand	**zakhme chaghoo** *n* زخم‌چاقو stab
rimel *n* ريمل mascara	**zadan** *v* زدن throb
	zadan *iv* زدن hit
	zododan *v* زدودن eliminate
	zera'at *n* زراعت agriculture
	zarafeh *n* زرافه giraffe
za'eideh shodeh *adj* زائيده‌شده born	**zard** adj زرد yellow
zad-rooz *n* زادروز birthday	**zard'aloo** *n* زردآلو apricot
zari *n* زاري moan	**zardehye tokhme morgh** *n* زرده تخم‌مرغ yolk
zari kardan *v* زاري‌كردن moan	
zaloo *n* زالو leech	

zereshki *adj* زرشکی purple

zargh va bargh *n* زرق‌وبرق splendor

zereh *n* زره armor

zesht *adj* زشت awkward

zesht *adj* زشت heinous

zesht *adj* زشت ugly

zesht kardan *v* زشت‌کردن deform

zeshti *n* زشتی clumsiness

zeshti *n* زشتی ugliness

zoghale' choub *n* زغال‌چوب charcoal

zoghalsang *n* زغال‌سنگ coal

zoghale' nimsouz *n* زغال‌نیم‌سوز cinder

zokam *n* زکام grip

zaman *n* زمان time

zomokht *adj* زمخت rude

zomokht *adj* زمخت crass

zemorod sabz *n* سبز زمرد emerald

zamzameh *n* زمزمه murmur

zamzameh kardan *v* زمزمه‌کردن murmur

zemestan *n* زمستان winter

zamin *n* زمین soil

zamin *n* زمین ground

zamin *n* زمین land

zamine bazi *n* بازی زمین playground

zamin shenasi *n* زمین‌شناسی geology

zamin larzeh *n* زمین‌لرزه earthquake

zamineh *n* زمینه background

zamineh *n* زمینه context

zamineh *n* زمینه groundwork

zamineh *n* زمینه terrain

zan *n* زن wife

zan *n* زن woman

zane' mehmankhanehdar *n* زن مهمانخانه‌دار landlady

zan-e mizban *n* زن‌میزبان hostess

zane harzeh *n* زن‌هرزه tart

zena *n* زنا adultery

zanashoo'ei *n* زناشویی matrimony

zanan *n* زنان women

zanbour *n* زنبور wasp

zanbour-e sorkh *n* زنبورسرخ hornet

zanboore' asal *n* زنبورعسل bee

zanbil *n* زنبیل basket

zanjebil *n* زنجبیل ginger

zanjir *n* زنجیر chain

zanjir kardan *v* زنجیرکردن chain

zendanban *n* زندان jail

zendan *n* زندان prison

zendanban *n* زندانبان jailer

zendani *n* زندانی prisoner

zendani kardan *v* زندانی‌کردن incarcerate

zendegi bakhshidan *v* زندگی بخشیدن animate

zendegi kardan *v* زندگی‌کردن live

zendegiye giyahi *n* زندگی گیاهی vegetation

zendegiye dobareh yaftan *v* زندگی‌دوباره‌یافتن relive

zende *adj* زنده alive

zendeh shodan *v* زنده‌شدن revive

zendeh kardan *v* زنده‌کردن quicken

zendeh mandan *v* زنده‌ماندن survive

zang *n* زنگ rust

zang-e' akhbar *n* زنگ‌اخبار buzzer

zange' darb *n* زنگ‌درب doorbell

zang zadan *iv* زنگ‌زدن ring

zang zadan *v* زنگ‌زدن rust

zang zadeh *adj* زنگ‌زده rusty

zang-e zangoleh *n* زنگ‌زنگوله bell

zanandeh *adj* زننده poignant

zanandeh *adj* زننده repugnant

zanandeh *adj* زننده nasty

zenhar dadan *v* زنهاردادن beware

zahr *n* زهر poison

zahr agin *adj* زهرآگین virulent

zaval *n* زوال decadence

zaval *n* زوال decline

zoj *n* زوج couple

zood *adv* زود early

zood *adv* زود speedily

zood ras *adj* زودرس precocious

zood gozar *adj* زودگذر transient

zoor *n* زور force

zoor zadan *v* زورزدن strain

zourmand *adv* زورمند vigor

zouzeh *n* زوزه howl

zouzeh keshidan *v* زوزه‌کشیدن howl

ziyad *adv* زیاد widely

ziad *adj* زیاد intense

ziyad *adj* زیاد many

ziyad *adv* زیاد too

ziyad ba'r kardan *v* زیادبارکردن overload

ziyad baravard kardan *v* زیاد برآوردکردن overrate

ziad raft-o amad kardan *v* زیاد رفت‌وآمدکردن haunt

ziyadeh-joo'ei *n* زیاده‌جوئی avarice

ziadi *n* زیادی immensity

zeyadi *adj* زیادی superfluous

ziyarat *n* زیارت pilgrimage

ziyaratgah *n* زیارتگاه shrine

zian *n* زیان disadvantage

zian avar *adj* زیان‌آور detrimental

zibe lebas *n* زیب‌لباس zipper

ziba *adj* زیبا picturesque

ziba *adj* زیبا beautiful

ziba *adj* زیبا elegant

ziba kardan *v* زیباکردن adorn

ziba'ei *n* زیبایی beauty

zeytoon *n* زیتون olive

zir'e ab raftan *n* زیرآب‌رفتن duct

zir ab zani *n* زیرآب‌زنی drainage

zire chizi khat keshidan *v* زیر چیزی‌خط‌کشیدن underline

zira *c* زیرا because

zirzamin *n* زیرزمین basement

zirzamin *n* زیرزمین cellar

zirak *adj* زیرک shrewd

zirak *adj* زیرک subtle

zirak *adj* زیرک astute

zirak *adj* زیرک cunning

zirin *pre* زیرین underneath

zistnameh *n* زیست‌نامه biography

zistan *v* زیستن exist

zivar *n* زیور ornament

zire' andazeh *v* زیراندازه downsize

zir nevis *n* زیرنویس subtitle

zirsigari *n* زیرسیگاری ashtray

zistshenasi n زیست‌شناسی biology

zhapon n ژاپن Japan

zhaponi adj ژاپني Japanese

zhaket n ژاکت jacket

zhakete' pashmi n ژاکت کش‌باف پشمي cardigan

zhaleh n ژاله frost

zhanviyeh n ژانویه January

zheton n ژتن chip

jarfa n ژرفا depth

zhen n ژن gene

zho'an n ژوئن June

zho'eiyeh n ژوئیه July

saeedan iv سائیدن grind

sabegheh n سابقه precedent

saher n ساحر sorcerer

sahereh n ساحره witch

sahel n ساحل beach

sahel n ساحل coast

sahel n ساحل shore

sahele darya n ساحل‌دریا seashore

saheli adj ساحلي coastal

sakhtegi adj ساختگي artificial

sakhtegi adj ساختگي bogus

sakhtegi adj ساختگي phony

sakhteman n ساختمان structure

sakhteman n ساختمان building

sakhtemane foughani adv ساختمان‌فوقاني upstairs

sakhtan iv ساختن build

sakhtan v ساختن construct

sakhtan v ساختن fabricate

sakhtan iv ساختن make

sakhtane' tadriji v ساختن‌تدریجی buildup

sadegi n سادگي simplicity

sadeh adj ساده simple

sadeh kardan v ساده‌کردن simplify

saregh n سارق thief

sareghe' mosalah n سارق‌مسلح bandit

saz-o-avaz n سازوآواز concert

saz-o-barg n سازوبرگ outfit

sazesh n سازش agreement

sazgar adj سازگار compatible

sazgar adj سازگار consistent

sazegar kardan v سازگارکردن adapt

sazegary n سازگاري accord

sazgari n سازگاري rapport

sazegary n س سازگاري adaptation

sazeman dadan v سازمان‌دادن organize

sazandeh n سازنده builder

sate'e kardan v ساطع‌کردن emit

satour n ساطور chopper

sa'at n ساعت clock

sa'at n ساعت watch

sa'at n ساعت hour

sa'at saz n ساعت‌ساز watchmaker

soat e shammatei n ساعت‌شماطه ای alarm clock

sa'ati *adv* ساعتی hourly

sagh *n* ساق stalk

saghdoosh-e damad *n* ساقدوش داماد best man

sagheh *n* ساقه stem

saket *adj* ساکت serene

saket kardan *v* ساکت کردن conciliate

saket kardan *v* ساکت کردنmuffle

saken *adj* ساکن stationary

saken *n* ساکن dwelling

saken bodan *iv* ساکن بودن dwell

saken shodan *v* ساکن شدن populate

saken shodan *v* ساکن شدن(در) inhabit

sal *n* سال year

sal be sal *adv* سال به سالannually

sal be sal *adv* سال به سالyearly

sal-e kabiseh *n* سال کبیسه leap year

salad *n* سالاد salad

salade' kalam *n* سالاد کلمcoleslaw

salkhordeh va fartot *adj* سالخورده و فرتوت decrepit

salem *adj* سالم healthy

salon *n* سالن amphitheater

salon *n* سالن saloon

salon *n* سالن nave

saloone raghs *n* سالن رقص ballroom

salname *n* سالنامه almanac

salnameh *n* سالنامه calendar

saliyaneh *adj* سالیانه annual

saman *n* سامان repose

saneheh *v* سانحه pileup

sandvich *n* ساندویچ sandwich

sansore' aghayed *n* سانسورعقاید censorship

sayt-haye interneti *n* سایتهای اینترنتی website

sayesh *n* سایش friction

sayeh *n* سایه shadow

sayeh ban *n* سایه بانshade

sayeh dar *adj* سایه دار shady

sabab *n* سبب cause

sabz *adj* سبز green

sabzeh *adj* سبزه brunette

sabzi kashtan *v* سبزی کاشتن vegetable

sabo'eiyat *n* سبعیت atrocity

sebghat jostan *v*]anticipate

sebghat jostan *v* سبقت جستن transcend

sabokbar *adj* سبکبار carefree

sabk *n* سبک style

sabk *n* سبک fashion

sabk raftar *adj* سبک رفتار frivolous

sabke shakhsi *n* سبک شخصی mannerism

sabok kardan *v* سبک کردن alleviate

sabok vazn *n* سبک وزن lightweight

saboos *n* سبوس bran

sibil *n* سبیل mustache

sepasgozar *adj* سپاسگزار grateful

sepas gozar *adj* سپاسگزار thankful

sepas gozari kardan *v* سپاسگزاری کردنthank

septambr *n* سپتامبر September

separe' automobil n سپراتومبیل bumper

separ shodan v سپرشدن shield

sepordan v سپردن commit

sopordan v سپردن confide

sepordan v سپردن entrust

sepordan v سپردن surrender

separi shodan v سپری‌شدن expire

separi shodan v سپری‌شدن lapse

sepas adv سپس then

setarak n ستارک asteroid

setareh n ستاره star

setareh donbalehdar n ستاره‌دنباله‌دار comet

setareh shenas n ستاره‌شناس astronomer

setayesh n ستایش adoration

setayesh n ستایش tribute

setayesh n ستایش praise

setorg adj سترگ huge

setam kardan v ستم‌کردن oppress

setamgar n ستمگر tyrant

setamgari n ستمگري tyranny

setvan n ستوان lieutenant

sotodan v ستودن commend

sotudani adj ستودني praiseworthy

payeh n ستون pillar

sotoun n ستون column

sotoun n ستون pier

sotune fagharat n ستون‌فقرات spine

sotoh n ستوه harassment

setiz n ستیز struggle

setizegar adj ستیزگر militant

setizeh n ستیزه strife

setizeh n ستیزه altercation

setizeh n ستیزه conflict

setizeh n ستیزه dispute

setizehjoo n ستیزه‌جو contestant

setizeh kardan v ستیزه‌کردن quarrel

setizeh kardan v ستیزه‌کردن contend

sehr n سحر spell

sakht adj سخت strict

sakht n سخت austere

sakht adv سخت gravely

sakht adj سخت hard

sakht adv سخت hardly

sakht adj سخت inflexible

sakht adj سخت rigid

sakht adj سخت stern

sakht afzar n سخت‌افزار hardware

sakht kardan v سخت‌کردن harden

sakht kardan v سخت‌کردن intensify

sakhtgir adj سختگیر stringent

sakhti n سختي aggravation

sakhti n سختي rigor

sakhti n سختي severity

sakhti n سختي austerity

sakhti n سختي difficulty

sakhti n سختي hardship

sakhti n سختي tenacity

sokhan n سخن saw

sokhan goftan iv سخن‌گفتن speak

sokhanrani n سخنراني lecture

sad n سد dam

sadd-bandi n سدبندي barrage

sedr n سدر cedar

saddeh n سده century

sar *n* سر head

sar *n* سر top

sarbaz zadan *v* سربازدن refuse

sar bar afrashtan *v* سربرافراشتن stick up

sar tisheh *n* سرتیشه wedge

sar khordan *v* سرخوردن glide

sar dasteh *n* سردسته ringleader

sar davandan *v* سردواندن put off

sarrasideh *adj* سررسیده overdue

sare keif *adj* سرکیف jolly

saro-seda *n* سروصدا noise

sarab *n* سراب mirage

sarazir *adj* سرازیر steep

saraziri *adv* سرازیری downhill

seramik *n* سرامیک ceramic

saranjam *adv* سرانجام eventually

seraydar *n* سرایدار custodian

sarayandeh *n* سراینده composer

sarastin *n* سرآستین cuff

sarashpaz *n* سرآشپز chef

sarbaz *n* سرباز soldier

sarbazkhaneh *n* سربازخانه barracks

sar boridan *v* سربریدن behead

sarparast *n* سرپرست caretaker

sarparast *n* سرپرست attendant

sarparast *n* سرپرست warden

sarpoush *n* سرپوش valve

sarpoosh *n* سرپوش lid

sarpichi *n* سرپیچی refusal

sarpichi *n* سرپیچی disobedience

sar-ta-sar *pre* سرتاسر across

sartakan dadan *v* سرتکان‌دادن nod

sare jaye khod gozardan *v* سرجای‌خودگذاردن relocate

sarcheshmeh *n* سرچشمه source

sar cheshmeh *n* سرچشمه principle

sarchashmeh gereftan *v* سرچشمه‌گرفتن originate

sar hal *adj* سرحال wholesome

sar hadd *n* سرحد border

sorkh shodan *v* سرخ‌شدن blush

sorkh kardan *v* سرخ‌کردن fry

sorkh kardan *v* سرخ‌کردن(روی آتش) broil

sorkh kardan *adj* سرخ‌کرده fried

sarakhs *n* سرخس fern

sorkhak *n* سرخک measles

sor khordan *v* سرخوردن skate

sorkhiye khejlat *n* سرخی‌خجلت blush

sard *adj* سرد chilly

sard kardan *v* سردکردن chill

sar davar *n* سرداور umpire

sardard *n* سردرد headache

sar-dasteh *n* سردسته leader

sar dasti *adj* سردستی sketchy

sardi *n* سردي coldness

sarzadeh amadan *v* سرزده‌آمدن intrude

sarzamin *n* سرزمین territory

sarzamin *n* سرزمین region

sarzendeh *adj* سرزنده brisk

sarzanesh *n* سرزنش rail

sarzanesh *n* سرزنش reproach

sarzanesh *n* سرزنش scolding

sarzanesh *n* سرزنش snub

sarzanesh e doostane *n* سرزنش دوستانه admonition

sarzanesh kartdan *v* سرزنش‌کردن censure

sarzanesh kardan *v* سرزنش کردن chide	**sargarm konandeh** *adj* سرگرم کننده amusing
sarzanesh kardan *v* سرزنش کردن scold	**sargarm konandeh** *adj* سرگرم کننده entertaining
sarzanesh kardan *v* سرزنش کردن snub	**sargarmy** *n* سرگرمی amusement
sarsepordegi *n* سرسپردگی commitment	**sargarmi** *n* سرگرمی pastime
sarsakht *adj* سرسخت obstinate	**sargarmi** *n* سرگرمی recreation
sar sakht *adj* سرسخت recalcitrant	**sarma** *n* سرما chill
sarsara *n* سرسرا hall	**sarma** *adj* سرما cold
sar-shomari *n* سرشماری census	**sarma zadegi** *n* سرمازدگی frostbite
sarshir *n* سرشیر cream	**sarmayeh dare ba nofooz** *n* سرمایه دار بانفوذ tycoon
saratan *n* سرطان cancer	**sarmaye'h dari** *n* سرمایه داری capitalism
saratan-e khoun *n* سرطان خون leukemia	**sarmaye gozari** *n* سرمایه گذاری investment
sorfeh *n* سرفه cough	**sarmaghaleh** *n* سرمقاله editorial
sorfeh kardan *v* سرفه کردن cough	**sorang** *n* سرنگ syringe
sare ghowl boudan *v* سرقول بودن stick to	**sarnevesht** *n* سرنوشت destiny
sar kargar *n* سرکارگر foreman	**sarnevesht** *n* سرنوشت fate
sarkesh *adj* سرکش rowdy	**sar neize** *n* سرنیزه bayonet
sarkeshi *n* سرکشی mutiny	**sarhang** *n* سرهنگ colonel
sarkeshi kardan *v* سرکشی کردن inspect	**sarvan** *n* سروان captain
sarkeshi kardan *v* سرکشی کردن oversee	**soroud** *n* سرود chant
serkeh *n* سرکه vinegar	**sorood** *n* سرود anthem
sar koubi *n* سرکوبی repression	**soroud** *n* سرود song
sargozasht *n* سرگذشت memoirs	**soroud-e rouhani** *n* سرودروحانی hymn
sargozasht *n* سرگذشت case	**soroudan** *v* سرودن compose
sargardan *adj* سرگردان disoriented	**soridan** *iv* سریدن slide
sargardan *n* سرگردان wanderer	**sari o seyr** *n* سریع السیر express
sargarm kardan *v* سرگرم کردن amuse	**sari'e tar** *adv* سریع تر rather
	sost *adj* سست flimsy
	sost shodan *v* سست شدن weaken
	sath *n* سطح surface

sat-h *n* سطح level

sathe shib dar *n* سطح‌شیب‌دار ramp

sathi *adj* سطحی shallow

zaheri *adj* سطحي skin-deep

satl *n* سطل bucket

satl *n* سطل pail

satle ashghal *n* سطل‌آشغال trash can

sefarat khaneh *n* سفارت‌خانه embassy

sefaresh kardan *v* سفارش‌کردن recommend

sefareshi *adj* سفارشي custom-made

saffak *adj* سفاک bloodthirsty

seft *adj* سفت stiff

seft *adj* سفت tight

seft shodan *v* سفت‌شدن toughen

seft kardan *v* سفت‌کردن tighten

safar *n* سفر journey

safare darya kardan *v* سفردریا کردن voyage

safar kardan *v* سفرکردن travel

sofreh *n* سفره tablecloth

safsateh *n* سفسطه fallacy

safid *adj* سفيد blank

sefid *adj* سفيد white

sefid kardan *v* سفيدکردن whiten

safid kardan *v* سفيدکردن bleach

safid konandeh *n* سفيد‌کننده bleach

safideh-e tokhmmorgh *n* سفيده تخم‌مرغ egg white

safidi *n* سفيدي candor

safir *n* سفير ambassador

seghte janin *n* سقط‌جنین abortion

seght kardan *v* سقط‌کردن abort

saghf *n* سقف roof

saghf *n* سقف ceiling

soghout *v* سقوط come down

soghot *n* سقوط crash

soghout kardan *v* سقوط‌کردن precipitate

sokan *n* سکان helm

sokkan *n* سکان rudder

seksekeh *n* سکسکه hiccup

sekkeh *n* سکه coin

sakkoo *n* سکو platform

sag *n* سگ dog

sagg-e abbi *n* سگ‌آبي beaver

sag-e shekari *n* سگ‌شکاري hound

sagak *n* سگک buckle

selah *n* سلاح armaments

selahe partabi *n* سلاح‌پرتابی projectile

salam *n* سلام hail

salam *e* سلام hello

salam kardan *v* سلام‌کردن hail

salamat *n* سلامت safety

salamate aghl *n* سلامت‌عقل sanity

salbe-salahiyyat kardan *v* سلب صلاحيت کردن disqualify

salb malekiat kardan *v* سلب مالکيت‌کردن expropriate

selseleh *n* سلسله dynasty

selseleh marateb *n* سلسله‌مراتب hierarchy

soltan *n* سلطان monarch

saltanat *n* سلطنت dominion

saltanati *adj* سلطنتي royal

solteh *n* سلطه sovereignty

solteh *n* سلطه yoke	**sangposht** *n* سنگ‌پشت tortoise
salmani *n* سلمانی barber	**sang-e khara** *n* سنگ‌خارا granite
salmani *n* سلمانی haircut	**sange ghabr** *n* سنگ‌قبر tombstone
salis *adj* سلیس versatile	**sang gosheh** *n* سنگ‌گوشه cornerstone
sam *n* سم hoof	**sange'ma'dan** *n* سنگ‌معدن ore
sam *n* سم toxin	**sangdel** *adj* سنگدل implacable
sam e mohlek *n* سم‌مهلک cyanide	**sangar** *n* سنگر fort
semajat kardan *v* سماجت‌کردن persist	**sang rizeh** *n* سنگ‌ریزه pebble
semate Papi *n* سمت‌پاپی papacy	**sang farsh** *n* سنگفرش pavement
semej *adj* سمج stubborn	**sanglakh** *adj* سنگلاخ rocky
samfouni *n* سمفونی symphony	**sangvareh** *n* سنگواره fossil
samoure darya'ei *n* سمور دریایی otter	**sangin** *adj* سنگین cumbersome
sammi *adj* سمی toxic	**sangini** *adj* سنگین heavy
sammi *adj* سمی poisonous	**sangin kardan** *v* سنگین‌کردن clog
sen *n* سن age	**sangini** *n* سنگینی gravity
senator *n* سناتور senator	**sangini** *n* سنگینی heaviness
sonbadeh *n* سنباده sandpaper	**she** *adj* سه three
sonbeh *n* سنبه piston	**se payeh** n سه‌پایه tripod
senj *n* سنج chime	**she payeh naghashi** *n* سه‌پایه‌نقاشی easel
sanjagh sineh *n* سنجاق‌سینه brooch	**she shanbeh** *n* سه‌شنبه Tuesday
sanjidan *v* سنجدین measure	**she ganeh** *adj* سه‌گانه triple
sanjesh *n* سنجش trials	**se mahe'** *adj* سه‌ماهه quarterly
sanjesh *n* سنجش measurement	**sahm bordan** *v* سهم‌بردن share
sanjesh bar hasb-e mill *n* سنجش برحسب‌میل mileage	**sahm dadan** *v* سهم‌دادن ration
sanjidan *v* سنجیدن ponder	**sahm dar** *n* سهم‌دار shareholder
sanjidane ba me'eyar *v* سنجیدن‌با معیار standardize	**sahv** *n* سهو oversight
sanad *n* سند voucher	**sahv kardan** *v* سهو‌کردن stumble
sendan *n* سندان anvil	**soo estefade kardan** *v* سو‌استفاده کردن abuse
sang *n* سنگ rock	**so'e'estefadeh** *n* سوءاستفاده misuse
sang *n* سنگ stone	**so'e' taghziyeh** *n* سوءتغذیه malnutrition
sang ahak *n* سنگ‌آهک limestone	**so'e hazemeh** *n* سوءهاضمه indigestion

sava kardan v سواکردنsort

savar shodan iv سوارشدن ride

savareh nezam n سواره‌نظام cavalry

savari n سواري ride

soup n سوپ soup

soot n سوت whistle

soot zadan v سوت‌زدنwhistle

soukht n سوخت combustion

sookht n سوخت fuel

soukht giri kardan(mojadad) v سوخت‌گيري(مجدد)کردنrefuel

soukhtani n سوختنی combustible

soukhteh adj سوخته charred

sood n سود gain

sowda n سودا bargain

soda n سودا soda

sowdagar adj سوداگر bourgeois

soodmand adj سودمند advantageous

soudmand adj سودمند beneficial

soudmand adj سودمند lucrative

soodmand boodan v سودمندبودن avail

soudmandi n سودمندي usefulness

sourakh n سوراخ hole

sourakh n سوراخ mesh

sourakh n سوراخ peck

sourakhe bini n سوراخ‌بينيnostril

sourakhe' zirzamini n سوراخ زيرزميني burrow

sourakhe sangar n سوراخ‌سنگر loophole

sourakh kardan v سوراخ‌کردن scuttle

sourakh kon n سوراخ‌کن punch

soozan adj سوزان ablaze

soozan adv سوزان alight

souzan adj سوزان torrid

souzandan iv سوزاندن burn

soozan n سوزن needle

souznak adj سوزناک pathetic

sozanak n سوزنک gonorrhea

sousk n سوسك cockroach

sousk n سوسک beetle

sousane' safid n سوسن‌سفيد lily

socialist adj سوسياليستsocialist

sosis n سوسيس sausage

sowgh dadan iv سوق‌دادنlead

sough dadan v سوق‌دادن propel

sogand n سوگند oath

sougvari n سوگواری mourning

sougvari kardan v سوگواري‌کردن mourn

sougvari n سوگواري lament

soogvary e saliane n سوگواري ساليانهanniversary

sevvomi adj سومي third

sohan n سوهان file

sowisi adj سويسي Swiss

si adj سي thirty

siahat kardan v سياحت‌کردن explore

siyasat n سياست policy

siyasatmadar n سياستمدار politician

siasatmadar n سياستمدار diplomat

siyah adj سياه black

siyahi n سياهی blackout

sib n سيب apple

sib zamini n سيب‌زميني potato

sikh *n* سیخ spur

sikh shabakehee *n* سیخ‌شبکه‌ای grill

sir *n* سیر garlic

sirk *n* سیرک circus

sizdah *adj* سیزده thirteen

siflis *n* سیفیلیس syphilis

sigar *n* سیگار cigar

sigar keshidan *v* سیگار کشیدن smoke

sigaret *n* سیگارت cigarette

sayl *n* سیل deluge

sayl *n* سیل flooding

seylab *n* سیل torrent

seile' bozorg *n* سیل‌بزرگ cataclysm

sayl zadeh kardan *v* سیل‌زده‌کردن inundate

sayl gir *n* سیل‌گیر floodgate

seylab *n* سیلاب tidal wave

sili *n* سیلی slap

sili zadan *v* سیلی‌زدن slap

sim *n* سیم wire

sim *n* سیم cord

sima *n* سیما countenance

siman *n* سیمان cement

sinema *n* سینما cinema

sinema *n* سینما movie

sini *n* سینی tray

sayareh *n* سیاره planet

sib zamini sorkh kardaeh *n* سیب زمینی‌سرخ‌کرده fries

sili *n* سیلی smack

sineh band *n* بند سینه brassiere

shakh beh shakh *n* شاخ horn

shakh beh shakh *adv* شاخ‌به‌شاخ head-on

shakhes *n* شاخص dial

shakhak *n* شاخک tentacle

shakheh *n* شاخه bough

shakheh *n* شاخه branch

shad *adj* شاد joyful

shad *adj* شاد merry

shadab *adj* شاداب succulent

shadi va soroure omoumi *n* شادی و سرور عمومی ovation

sha'er *n* شاعر poet

sha'gh *n* شاق ordeal

shagerd *n* شاگرد pupil

shagerd *n* شاگرد apprentice

shagerd *n* شاگرد disciple

shal *n* شال shawl

shalle' keshmiri *n* شال کشمیری cashmere

shal gardan *n* شال‌گردن scarf

sham *n* شام supper

sham *n* شام dinner

shanzdah *adj* شانزده sixteen

shans *n* شانس luck

shaneh *n* شانه comb

shaneh kardan *v* شانه‌کردن comb

shahbaloot *n* شاه‌بلوط chestnut

shahaneh *adj* شاهانه majestic

shahed *n* شاهد witness

shah dokht *n* شاهدخت princess

shahrah *n* شاهراه highway

shahrokh *n* شاهرخ condor

shah zadeh *n* شاهزاده prince

shahkar *n* شاهکار masterpiece

shahva'r *adj* شاهوار regal

shahi *n* شاهی penny

shayan taghlid *adj* شایان‌تقلید exemplary

shayad *adv* شاید maybe

shayad *adv* شاید perhaps

shayestegi *n* شایستگی merit

shayesteh *adj* شایسته proper

shayesteh *adj* شایسته worthy

shayeat bi asas *n* شایعات‌بی‌اساس gossip

shayeat bi asas dadan *v* شایعات‌بی اساس‌دادن gossip

shaye'eh *n* شایعه rumor

shye'eh *n* شایعه hearsay

shayesteh *adv* شایسته right

shab *n* شب night

shab zendeh dari *n* شب‌زنده‌داری vigil

shab zendeh dari kardan *iv* شب‌زنده‌داری‌کردن wake

shab eyd *n* شب‌عید eve

shabangah *n* شبانگاه nightfall

shabaneh *adj* شبانه nocturnal

shabaneh dozdidan *v* شبانه‌دزدیدن burglarize

shabani *adj* شبانی pastoral

shabahat *n* شباهت likeness

shabahat *n* شباهت semblance

shabahat dashtan *v* شباهت‌داشتن resemble

shabah *n* شبح ghost

shabah var *adj* شبح‌وار spooky

shabakeh *n* شبکه network

shabnam *n* شبنم dew

shebhe jazireh *n* شبه‌جزیره peninsula

shobheh *n* شبهه misgiving

shabih *pre* شبیه like

shepesh *n* شپش louse

shetab *n* شتاب velocity

shetab *n* شتاب expediency

shetab dahande *n* شتاب‌دهنده accelerator

shetab kardan *v* شتاب‌کردن hurry

shetabandan *v* شتاباندن hasten

shetabandan *v* شتاباندن hasten

shotor *n* شتر camel

shotormorgh *n* شترمرغ ostrich

shoja *adj* شجاع valiant

shoja'e *adj* شجاع bold

shajareh nameh *n* شجره‌نامه genealogy

shakhs *n* شخص person

shakhs *n* شخص guy

shakhse' shoma *pro* شخص‌شما yourself

shakhs'e moteaseb *adj* شخص متعصب fanatic

shakhse mohem va barjasteh *n* شخص‌مهم‌وبرجسته baron

shakhsi *adj* شخصی own

shakhsi *adj* شخصی personal

shakhsiyat *n* شخصیت personality

shakhsiyat dadan *v* شخصیت‌دادن personify

shokhm zadan *v* شخم‌زدن plow

shedat *n* شدت intensity

shodan *iv* شدن become

shadid *adj* شدید violent

sharab *n* شراب wine

sharabe espaniyoli *n* شراب اسپانیولی sherry

sharab-e sib *n* شراب‌سیب cider

sherarat *n* شرارت wickedness

sharayet *n* شرایط terms

sharbat *n* شربت syrup

sharh dadan *v* شرح‌دادن describe

shart *n* شرط bet

shart *n* شرط clause

shart *n* شرط condition

shart bastan *iv* شرط‌بستن bet

sharti *adj* شرطی conditional

sharghi *adj* شرقی eastern

sharghi *adj* شرقی oriental

sherkat *n* شرکت association

sherkat *n* شرکت company

sherkat *n* شرکت corporation

sharm *n* شرم shame

sharmsar *adj* شرمسار ashamed

shariyan *n* شریان artery

sharir *adj* شریر naughty

sharir *n* شریر viper

sharir *adj* شریر wicked

sharik *n* شریک partner

sharik shodan *v* شریک‌شدن participate

sharike' jorm *n* شریک‌جرم complicity

shast *n* شست thumb

shostoshoo *n* شستشو cleaning

shostoshoo *n* شستشو lotion

shodtoshoo kardan *v* شستشو کردن bathe

shostoshoye maghzi dadan *v* شستشوی‌مغزی‌دادن brainwash

shostan *v* شستن wash

shosteh-rofteh *adj* شسته‌ورفته neat

shesh *adj* شش six

sheshlool *v* ششلول revolver

shamshir bazi *n* ششمشیربازی fencing

sheshomin *adj* ششمین sixth

shast *adj* شصت sixty

shatranj *n* شطرنج chess

sho'badehbaz *n* شعبده‌باز juggler

she'er *n* شعر poetry

she'er *n* شعر verse

shere' afsaneh'ei *n* شعرافسانه‌ای ballad

sho'leh *n* شعله blaze

sho'eleh *n* شعله flame

sho'eleh dar *adj* شعله‌دار flamboyant

shoghal *n* شغال jackal

shoghl *n* شغل position

shafa dadan *v* شفادادن cure

shafa dadan *v* شفادادن heal

shafa dahandeh *n* شفادهنده healer

shafaf *adj* شفاف lucid

shafaf *adj* شفاف transparent

shafahan *adv* شفاها" orally

shafahan *adv* شفاها" verbally

shafahi *adj* شفاهی oral

shekar *n* شکار hunting

shekam *n* شکم womb

shak *n* شک doubt

shak dashtan *v* شک‌داشتن suspect

shak dashtan *v* شک‌داشتن doubt

shekar *n* شکار quarry

shekar *n* شکار prey

shekar kardan *v* شکارکردن hunt

shekarchi *n* شکارچی hunter

shekaf *n* شکاف chasm

shekaf *n* شکاف gap

shekaf *n* شکاف incision

shekaftan *n* شکافتن breakthrough

shekaftan *v* شکافتن pierce

shekaftan *iv* شکافتن split

shekayat *n* شکایت grievance

shekayat *n* شکایت rumble

shekayat *n* شکایت complaint

shekayat *n* شکایت gripe

shekayat kardan *v* شکایت کردن complain

shekar *n* شکر sugar

shekast *adj* شکست unsuccessful

shekast khordan *v* شکست خوردن (امتحانات در) flunk

shekast dadan *v* شکست دادن outdo

shekast dadan *v* شکست دادن defeat

shekast na-pazir *adj* شکست ناپذیر unbeatable

shekast napazir *adj* شکست ناپذیر invincible

shekastegi *n* شکستگی fracture

shekastan *v* شکستن shatter

shekastan *iv* شکستن break

shekastani *adj* شکستنی breakable

shekl *n* شکل figure

shekl dadan *v* شکل دادن shape

shekl hendesi *n* شکل هندسی diagram

shokolat *n* شکلات chocolate

shekam *n* شکم abdomen

shekam *n* شکم belly

shekam *n* شکم tummy

shekam parast *adj* شکم پرست glutton

shekami *adj* شکمی abdominal

shekanjeh *n* شکنجه torture

shekanandeh *adj* شکننده fragile

shekoufa *adj* شکوفا prosperous

shekoufaie *n* شکوفائی prosperity

shekoufeh-zar *n* شکوفه زار orchard

shekoofeh kardan *v* شکوفه کردن bloom

shokouh *n* شکوه magnitude

shokouh *n* شکوه pomp

shegarf *adj* شگرف tremendous

shegarf *adj* شگرف wonderful

shegarfi *n* شگرفی excellence

shegeft *n* شگفت marvel

shegeft *n* شگفت muse

shegeft *n* شگفت surprise

shegeft *n* شگفت wonder

shegeft avar *adj* شگفت آور astonishing

shegefti *n* شگفتی prodigy

shol *adj* شل loose

shol kardan *v* شل کردن loosen

shol kardan *v* شل کردن relax

shallagh *n* شلاق scourge

shalagh khordan *v* شلاق خوردن lash

shalagh zadan *v* شلاق زدن flog

shallagh zadan *v* شلاق زدن whip

shalgham *n* شلغم turnip

shalvar *n* شلوار trousers

shalvar koutah *n* شلوار کوتاه shorts

shalvare goshad *n* شلوارگشاد pajamas

sholoogh *adj* غ شلوغ tumultuous

sholough *adj* غ شلوغ messy

sholoogh *adj* غ شلوغ noisy

shalidan *v* شلیدن limp

shelik tir *n* تیر شلیک fire

shelik kardan *v* شلیک کردن fire

shalil *n* شلیل nectarine

shoma *pro* شما you

shomareshe mojadad *n* شمارش مجدد recount

shomareshgar *n* شمارشگر counter

shomareh *n* شماره number

shomareh gereftan *v* شماره گرفتن dial

shamas *n* شماس deacon

shomal *n* شمال north

shomal-e sharghi *n* شمال شرقی northeast

shomali *adj* شمالی northern

shamayel *n* شمایل icon

shemordan *v* شمردن count

shomordeh sokhan goftan *v* شمرده سخن گفتن articulate

shamshir *n* شمشیر sword

sham'e *n* شمع candle

sham'e *n* شمع spark plug

shamdaniye atri *n* شمعدانی عطری geranium

shena kardan *iv* شناکردن swim

shenakhtan *v* شناختن recognize

shenakhtan *v* شناختن identify

shena gar *n* شناگر swimmer

shenavar *adv* شناور afloat

shenavar *n* شناور buoy

shenavar shodan *v* شناورشدن float

shanbeh *n* شنبه Saturday

shenel *n* شنل cape

shenidan *iv* شنیدن hear

shanidan *v* شنیدن listen

shanidani *adj* شنیدنی audible

shahab *n* شهاب meteor

shahadat *n* شهادت martyrdom

shahr *n* شهر city

shahr *n* شهر parish

shohrat *n* شهرت publicity

shohrat *adj* شهرت celebrity

shohrat *n* شهرت fame

shohrat *n* شهرت reputation

shahrdar *n* شهردار mayor

shahrdari *n* شهرداری city hall

shahrak *n* شهرک town

shahrvandan *n* شهروندان citizenship

shahri *adj* شهري civic

shahri *adj* شهري urban

shahmat kardan *n* شهمات کردن checkmate

shahavani *adj* شهواني erotic

shahvat angiz *adj* شهوت انگیز sexy

shahvat dashtan *v* شهوت داشتن lust

shahid *n* شهید martyr

shokhi *n* شوخي fun

shoukhi *n* شوخي joke

shoukhiye farib-amiz *n* شوخي فریب آمیز hoax

shoukhi kardan *v* شوخي کردن joke

shor *n* شور excitement

shor o zogh *n* شوروذوق enthusiasm

showraye kelisaee *n* شوراي كليسايي synod

shouresh *n* شورش revolt

shouresh *n* شورش uprising

shouresh kardan *v* شورش كردن revolt

shoureshi *n* شورشي rebel

shoreh sar *n* شوره‌سر dandruff

shouridan *v* شوريدن rebel

shoufer *n* شوفر chauffeur

shoom *n* شوم sinister

shoom *adj* شوم ominous

showhar *n* شوهر husband

shiyar *n* شيار groove

shiyar *n* شيار rake

shib *n* شيب slope

shib peida kardan *v* شيب‌پيدا كردن decline

shibe' tonde roudkhaneh *n* شيب تندرودخانه chute

sheypour *n* شيپور trumpet

shir *n* شير lion

shir *n* شير milk

shir'e ab *n* شيرآب faucet

shire ab *n* شيرآب tap

shir bandi *n* شيربندي dairy

shirkhargah *n* شيرخوارگاه nursery

shirforoush *n* شيرفروش milkman

shir mahi *n* شيرماهي walrus

shirjeh raftan *v* شيرجه‌رفتن dive

shiri *adj* شيري milky

shirin *adj* شيرين amiable

shirin *adj* شيرين sweet

shirin kari *n* شيرين‌كاري gag

shirin kardan *v* شيرين‌كردن sweeten

shirini *n* شيريني pastry

shirini'e badami *n* شيريني‌بادامي marzipan

shisheh *n* شيشه glass

shisheh alat *n* شيشه‌آلات glassware

shishehye jelowye otomobil *n* شيشه‌جلو اتومبيل windshield

sheytan *n* شيطان devil

sheytani *adj* شيطاني satanic

sheytanat *n* شيطنت mischief

shiftan *v* شيفتن allure

shiftan *v* شيفتن captivate

shik *adj* شيك chic

shik *adj* شيك fashionable

shimi *n* شيمي chemistry

shimiya'ei *adj* شيميايي chemical

shivaee *n* شيوايي eloquence

shiyo'e *n* شيوع outbreak

shiveh *n* شيوه method

shirin *adj* شيرين smart

shirini *n* شيريني candies

saheb *v* صاحب owner

saheb *n* صاحب lord

sader shavandeh *adj* صادرشونده outgoing

sader kardan *v* صادركردن export

sadegh *adj* صادق sincere

sadegh *adj* صادق honest

saf *adj* صاف smooth

saf kardan-e sineh *n* صاف کردن سینه hem

saf kardeh *adj* صاف کرده strained

safi *n* صافي filter

safi *n* صافي strainer

sobh *n* صبح morning

sobhaneh *n* صبحانه breakfast

sabr kardan *v* صبر کردن wait

sohbat kardan *v* صحبت کردن converse

sahneh sazi *n* صحنه‌سازي scenery

sahih *adv* صحیح all right

sahih *adj* صحیح authentic

sahih kardan *v* صحیح کردن correct

sad *adj* صد hundred

seda *n* صدا sound

seda'khafehkon *n* صداخفه‌کن muffler

seda kardan *v* صداکردن sound

sedaye beine bam va zir *adj* صداي‌بین‌بم‌وزیر baritone

sedaye telep *n* صداي‌تلپ flop

sedaye' khandeh *n* صداي‌خنده laugh

sedaye senj eijad kardan *v* صداي‌سنج‌ایجاد کردن chime

sedaye sheypour *n* صداي‌شیپور trump

sedaye ghok daravardan *v* صداي غوک‌درآوردن creak

sadre' a'azam *n* صدراعظم chancellor

sad-saleh *n* صدساله centenary

sadaf *n* صدف clam

sadaf *n* صدف oyster خوراکي صدف

sadaghe *n* صدقه alms

sadameh *n* صدمه shock

sadameh zadan *v* صدمه‌زدن offend

sodor *n* صدور emission

sadi chand *n* صدي‌چند percentage

sarf kardan *v* صرف کردن conjugate

sarf kardan *iv* صرف کردن spend

sarfeh jo *adj* صرفه‌جو economical

sarfeh joo *adj* صرفه‌جو frugal

sarfeh joee *n* صرفه‌جویي frugality

sarfeh joe'e kardan *v* صرفه‌جویي کردن economize

sarih *adj* صریح explicit

sarihan *adv* صریحا expressly

sarihan *adv* صریحا plainly

so'oud *n* صعود climbing

so'oud kardan *v* صعودکردن mount

saghir *adj* صغیر minor

saff *n* صف array

sefat *n* صفت adjective

safheh *n* صفحه page

safheh kilid *n* صفحه‌کلید keyboard

sefr *n* صفر zero

salahiyyat *n* صلاحیت competence

salahiyat dashtan *v* صلاحیت داشتن qualify

solh *n* صلح peace

solh amiz *adj* صلح‌آمیز peaceful

solh dadan *v* صلح‌دادن reconcile

salib *n* صلیب cross

salib eisa *n* صلیب‌عیسي crucifix

salibion *n* صلیبیون crusader

samimy *adj* صمیمي intimate

samimiyat *n* صمیمیت intimacy

sandal *n* صندل sandal

sandali *n* صندلي chair

sandaliye charkh dar *n* صندلي چرخ‌دار wheelchair

sandaliye dastehdar *n* صندلی‌دسته‌دار armchair

sandoughdar *n* صندوق chest

sandoughe posti *n* صندوق‌پست mailbox

sandoughkhaneh *n* صندوق‌خانه closet

sandoughcheh *n* صندوقچه bin

sandoughdar *n* صندوق‌دار cashier

sandogh dar *n* صندوق‌دار treasurer

sanat *n* صنعت industry

san'atgar *n* صنعتگر artisan

sout *n* صوت voice

sowti *adj* صوتي acoustic

souti *n* صوتي vowel

sourat *n* صورت phase

sorat *n* صورت face

sourat pardakht *n* صورت‌پرداخت payroll

sourate hesab *n* صورت‌حساب bill

sorat hesab *n* صورت‌حساب invoice

sourat-e ghaza *n* صورت‌غذا menu

sourat foroosh *n* صورت‌فروش sales slip

sorat kochak *n* صورت‌کوچک facet

sourati *adj* صورتي pink

someeh *n* صومعه convent

soume'eh *n* صومعه monastery

siyam *n* صيام Lent

sighehye jam'e *n* صيغه‌جمع plural

seyghal *n* صيقل varnish

barragh *adj* صيقلي shiny

sayyad *n* صياد sailor

seyd *n* صيد sail

seyd kardan *v* صيدکردن sail

zabeteh *n* ضابطه criterion

zareb *n* ضارب attacker

zamen *n* ضامن sponsor

zaye' kardan *v* ضايع‌کردن spoil

zabte sout *n* ضبط‌صوت tape recorder

zabt kardan *v* ضبط‌کردن confiscate

zajeh va faryad zadan *v* ضجه‌و فرياد‌زدن cry out

zakhim *adj* ضخيم thick

zedd *adj* ضد opposite

zede zang *adj* ضدزنگ rustproof

zedde' ofouni kardan *v* ضدعفوني کردن disinfect

zeddiyat *n* ضديت opposition

zarb *n* ضرب beating

zarbol ajal *n* ضرب‌العجل deadline

zarbo-shatm *n* ضربوشتم mayhem

zaraban-e ghalb *n* ضربان‌قلب heartbeat

zarbat *n* ضربت impact

zarbat *n* ضربت lung

zarbat vared avardan *v* ضربت وارد‌آوردن inflict

zarbeh *n* ضربه pulse

zarbeh *n* ضربه stroke

zarbeh zadan *v* ضربه‌زدن click

zarbeh zadan *iv* ضربه‌زدن strike

zaroorat *n* ضرورت necessity

zarouri *adj* ضروري necessary

zarouri *adj* ضروري urgent

za'af *n* ضعف weakness

zaf kardan *v* ضعف‌کردن faint

zaif *n* ضعيف defective

zaif *adj* ضعيف faint

za'eif *adj* ضعيف light

za'eif *adj* ضعيف weak

zaif *adj* ضعيف feeble

zemanat kardan *n* ضمانت guaranty

zemanat-e ejra kardan *v* ضمانت اجراکردن sanction

zemanat kardan *v* ضمانت‌کردن guarantee

zemnan *adv* ضمنا meanwhile

zemnan *adv* ضمنا incidentally

zemni *adj* ضمني implicit

zamir *n* ضمير pronoun

zamimeh *n* ضميمه appendix

tas *adj* طاس bald

tas e takhteh nard *n* طاس‌تخته‌نرد dice

tagh *n* طاق cap

taghat farsa *adj* طاقت‌فرسا demanding

taghatfarsa' *adj* طاقت‌فرسا overbearing

taghcheh *n* طاقچه mantel

taghchehe balaye bokhari *n* طاقچه‌بالابخاري mantelpiece

tavous *n* طاووس peacock

tab'an *adv* طبعا "naturally"

tebghe akhbar *adv* طبق‌اخبار reportedly

tabagheh bandi kardan *v* طبقه‌بندي‌کردن staple

tabagheh bandi kardan *v* طبقه‌بندي‌کردن type

tabaghehe pa'ein *adv* طبقه‌پائين downstairs

tabi'ei *adj* طبيعي natural

tabi'ei kardan *v* طبيعي‌کردن normalize

tarahiye kolliyat *n* طراحي‌کليات sketch

taravat *n* طراوت freshness

tarh *n* طرح plan

tarh *n* طرح plot

tarh *n* طرح project

tarh bandi *n* طرح‌بندي layout

tarhe' da'vi kardan *v* طرح‌دعوي‌کردن litigate

tarhe' kolli *n* طرح‌کلي outline

tarhe mouzooei *n* طرح‌موضوعي ventilation

tarz-e zendegi *n* طرززندگي lifestyle

tarafdar *n* طرفدار partisan

tarafdare' estebdad *adj* طرفدار استبداد authoritarian

tarafdar-e berahnegi *n* طرفدار برهنگي nudist

tarafdari *n* طرفداري bias

tarigh *n* طريق way

tarigheh *n* طريقه system

ta'eneh *n* طعنه irony

toghyan *n* طغيان insurrection

toghyan *n* طغيان rebellion

toghyan kardan *v* طغيان کردن overflow

tafreh *n* طفره evasion

tafreh zadan az *v* طفره زدن از evade

tala *n* طلا gold

talagh *n* طلاق divorce

talaee *adj* طلايي golden

hagh talab *n* حق طلب challenge

talab kardan *iv* طلب کردن seek

tolou'e kardan *v* طلوع کردن sunrise

tanab *n* طناب rope

tanz *n* طنز satire

tanin *n* طنين echo

touti *n* طوطي parrot

toutiye kouchake sabz rang *n* طوطي کوچک سبز رنگ parakeet

tofan e mosemi *n* طوفان موسمي cyclone

tool *n* طول length

toumar *n* طومار roll

toumar *n* طومار scroll

tavil *adj* طويل lengthy

za'le'maneh *adj* ظالمانه outrageous

zaher *n* ظاهر appearance

zaher *n* ظاهر guise

zaher *n* ظاهر looks

zaher shodan *v* ظاهر شدن turn up

zaheran *adv* ظاهرا apparently

zaheran *adv* ظاهرآ allegedly

zahershodan *v* ظاهر شدن appear

zerafat *n* ظرافت delicacy

zerafat *n* ظرافت elegance

zarf *n* ظرف container

zarf *n* ظرف dish

zarfshoo *n* ظرفشو dishwasher

zorufe noghreh *n* ظروف نقره silverware

zohr *n* ظهر noon

zohour *n* ظهور advent

zohour *n* ظهور apparition

ع

aber *n* عابر passerby

ajez *adj* عاجز unable

ajez *adj* عاجز incapable

ajez kardan *v* عاجز کردن harass

adat *n* عادت habit

adat kardan *v* عادت کردن accustom

adat kardan *adj* عادت کردن used to

ade'l *adj* عادل just

ariyeh dadan *v* عاريه دادن loan

azem shodan *v* عازم شدن set out

ashegh *n* عاشق lover

asi *adj* عاصي sinful

aghel *adj* عاقل sane

alli *adv* عالي highly

a'li *adj* عالي supreme

ali *adj* عالي excellent

am *n* عام general

amel *n* عامل factor

a'yedat *n* عايدات proceeds

ebarat *n* عبارت phrase

obour *n* عبور transit

obour dadan *v* عبوردادن transmit

obour va morour *n* مرور و عبور
traffic

aboos *adj* عبوس moody

atigheh *n* عتيقه relic

ajaleh *n* عجله haste

ajol *adj* عجول hasty

ajib *adj* عجيب extravagant

ajib *adj* عجيب stupendous

ajjib-o-gharib *adj* عجيب وغريب
bizarre

ajib *n* عجيب rum

adavat *n* عداوت hostility

adad'e panj *adj* عددپنج five

adad' e zoj *adj* عددزوج even

yazdah *adj* عدديازده eleven

adad-e hasht *adj* عددهشت eight

adas *n* عدس lentil

adl *n* عدل bale

adam-e taadoul *n* عدمتعادل
imbalance

adam-e towfigh *n* عدمتوفيق
miscarriage

adam-e samimiyat *n* عدمصميميت
insincerity

adame' vefgh *adj* عدموفق
disparaging

azab dadan *v* عذاب دادن torment

azab dadan *v* عذاب دادن torture

azab dadan *v* عذاب دادن agonize

arsheh *n* عرشه deck

arz-e hall dadan *v* عرض حال دادن
plead

orf *n* عرف convention

aragh *n* عرق sweat

aragh rizi *n* عرق ريزي perspiration

aragh kardan *v* عرق كردن
perspire

aragh gir *n* عرق گير sweater

aragh gire varzeshi *n* عرق گير
ورزشي sweets

aroos *n* عروس bride

aroosak *n* عروسك puppet

arousak *n* عروسك doll

arousi kardan *iv* عروسي كردن wed

oryan *adj* عريان nude

ariz kardan *v* عريض كردن widen

azm *n* عزم decision

aziz *adj* عزيز dear

eshay-e rabbani *n* عشاي رباني
Mass

asa ya choobe saheb mansaban
n عصا ياچوب صاحب منصبان
baton

asaye sarkaj *n* عصاي سركج crook

asab *n* عصب nerve

asabani *adj* عصباني red-hot

asabani *adj* عصباني furious

asabani *adj* عصباني nervous

asabani kardan *v* عصباني كردن
irritate

asabi *adj* عصبي neurotic

asabi va hayajan zadeh *adj*
عصبي وهيجان زده tense

asr *n* عصر afternoon

ozv *n* عضو limb

ozv *n* عضو member

ozviyat *n* عضویت membership

attar *n* عطار groceries

otarod *n* عطارد mercury

atr *n* عطر perfume

atr *n* عطر scent

atseh kardan *v* عطسه کردن sneeze

atf *n* عطف conjunction

attiyeh elahi *n* عطیه الهی charisma

effat va esmat *n* عفت و عصمت chastity

oufoonat *n* عفونت infection

oghab *n* عقاب eagle

aghab *n* عقب rear

aghab oftadan *v* عقب افتادن fall behind

aghab oftadeh *adj* عقب افتاده backward

aghab andakhtan *v* عقب انداختن defer

aghab andakhtan *v* عقب انداختن hinder

aghab andakhtan *v* عقب انداختن postpone

aghab keshidan *v* عقب کشیدن move back

aghab keshidan *v* عقب کشیدن scratch

aghab mandeh *adj* عقب مانده retarded

aghab neshandan *v* عقب نشاندن retreat

aghab neshini *n* عقب نشینی retreat

aghabi *adj* عقبی posterior

aghrab *n* عقرب scorpion

aghli *adj* عقلی rational

aghideh *n* عقیده view

aghideh *n* عقیده doctrine

aghim *adj* عقیم sterile

aghim gozardan *v* عقیم گذاردن thwart

akkas *n* عکاس photographer

ax *n* عکس photo

axe fowri *n* عکس فوری snapshot

alaj *n* علاج cure

alaj pazir *adj* علاج پذیر curable

alaj napazir *adj* علاج ناپذیر incurable

alaghmand *adj* علاقمند fond

alagheh *n* علاقه fondness

alagheh *n* علاقه penchant

alamat *n* علامت mark

alamat *n* علامت signal

alamat *n* علامت stripe

alamat *n* علامت symptom

alamate estefham *adj* علامت استفهام what

alamate tejari *n* علامت تجارتی trademark

alamat gozardan *v* علامت گذاردن mark

alamatgozari *n* علامت گذاری marker

alaf *n* علف grass

alaf-e khoshk *n* علف خشک hay

alaf keshidan *v* علف کشیدن weed

alafzar *n* علفزار meadow

elm *n* علم science

elme' ahkam-e nojoum *n* علم احکام نجوم astrology

elm adab moasherat *n* علم آداب معاشرت etiquette

elm-e behdasht *n* علم بهداشت hygiene

elme siyasi *n* علم‌سیاسی politics

elm hendeseh *n* علم‌هندسه geometry

elmi *adj* علمی scientific

olum-e ensani *n* علوم‌انسانی humanities

alaiheh kasi ezhari kardan *v* علیه کسی اظهاری کردن denounce

emarat *n* عمارت edifice

emarat-e bozorg *n* عمارت‌بزرگ mansion

amdan *adv* عمدا purposely

omdeh *adj* عمده gross

omdeh *adj* عمده main

omdeh forush *n* عمده‌فروش wholesale

amdi *adj* عمدی deliberate

omr *adv* عمر lifetime

amal *n* عمل action

amal *n* عمل operation

amal avari *n* آوری عمل production

amal-e bedon-e fekr *adj* عمل بدون‌فکر impulsive

amal tahavor amiz *n* عمل‌تهورآمیز enterprise

amal kardan *v* عمل کردن act

amal kardan *v* عمل کردن exercise

amal kardan *v* عمل کردن operate

amali *adj* عملی practical

ammeh *n* عمه aunt

amodi *adj* عمودی erect

amigh *adj* عمیق profound

amighan *adv* عمیقا in depth

e'nad *n* عناد malice

onsor *n* عنصر element

onsori *adj* عنصری elemental

ankabut *n* عنکبوت spider

onvan *n* عنوان heading

anin *adj* عنین(ناتوان‌جنسی) impotent

ahd *n* عهد pact

ahd-e' atigh *n* عهدعتیق antiquity

ahd kardan *v* عهدکردن vow

ohde'dar kardan *v* عهده‌دار کردن charge

avarez n عوارض toll

avam *n* عوام vulgarity

avamaneh *adj* عوامانه vulgar

oud *n* عود guitar

avaz kardan *v* عوض کردن change

avaz kardan *v* عوض کردن remodel

avazi *adv* عوضی inside out

aya'r *n* عیار alloy

ayashi kardan *v* عیاشی کردن riot

eibjoo'ei *adj* عییجویی nagging

ayd'e pak *n* عیدپاک Easter

eide' milade' masih *n* عیدمیلاد مسیح Christmas

eynak fanari *n* عینک‌فنری eyeglasses

eynak *n* عینک glasses

eynake aftabi *n* عینک‌آفتابی sunglasses

einaksa'z *n* عینک‌ساز optician

ghar *n* غار grotto

gha'r *n* غار cave

gha'r *n* غار cavern

ghar *n* غار den

gharat kardan *v* غارت کردن loot

ghrat kardan *v* غارت کردن plunder

gharat kardan *v* غارت کردن pillage

gharat kardan *v* غارت کردن ransack

ghar *n* غاز goose

ghafel gir kardan *v* غافلگیر کردن surprise

ghaieb *adj* غایب absent

ghobar *n* غبار mist

ghodeh *n* غده gland

ghddeh *n* غده tumor

ghaza *n* غذا meal

ghaza dadan *v* غذادادن foster

ghazaye daryaye *n* غذاهای دریایی seafood

ghaza'ei az goosht va ard *n* غذای از گوشت و آرد casserole

gherabat *n* غرابت oddity

gharamat *n* غرامت ransom

gheramat *n* غرامت repayment

gharbi *adj* غربی western

ghorresh *n* غرش boom

ghorresh kardan *v* غرش کردن roar

ghor ghor kardan *v* غرغر کردن growl

ghor ghor kardan *v* غرغر کردن grumble

gher ghereh kardan *v* غرغره کردن gargle

ghorfeh-ye namayesh gah *n* غرفه نمایشگاه pavilion

ghargh *n* غرق shipwreck

ghargh kardan *v* غرق کردن drown

ghargh kardan *v* غرق کردن flood

ghorub *n* غروب sundown

ghorob *n* غروب evening

ghorob kardan *v* غروب کردن go down

gharib *adj* غریب grotesque

ghorridan *v* غریدن rumble

ghariv *n* غریو outcry

ghariv keshidan *v* غریو کشیدن clamor

ghazal *n* غزل sonnet

ghosl *n* غسل immersion

ghash *n* غش faint

ghazab *n* غضب fury

ghaflat *n* غفلت negligence

ghaflat kardan *v* غفلت کردن neglect

gholam *n* غلام slave

ghalabeh *n* غلبه conquest

ghalabeh yaftan *v* غلبه یافتن overcome

ghaltandan *v* غلتاندن turn over

ghalat *adj* غلط wrong

ghalate-chapi *n* غلط چاپی misprint

ghel ghelak dadan *v* غلغلک دادن tickle

ghel ghelaki *adj* غلغلکی ticklish

ghalleh *n* غله cereal

ghaleh *n* غله corn

gholov kardan *v* غلو کردن overcharge

gham *n* غم sadness

gham *n* غم grief

gham *n* غم sorrow

gham angiz *adj* غم انگیز tragic

gham khordan *v* غم خوردن care for

ghamfaza *adj* غمفزا distressing

ghamgin *adj* غمگین sorry

ghamgin kardan *v* غمگین کردن grieve

ghamgin *adj* غمگین sad

ghamgin kardan *v* غمگین کردن sadden

ghanaem *n* غنائم trophy

ghanayem *n* غنایم spoils

ghani kardan *v* غني کردن enrich

ghanimat *n* غنیمت booty

ghoutehvar *adv* غوطهور nosedive

ghoutehvar sa'khtan *v* غوطهور ساختن overwhelm

ghouteh var sakhtan *v* غوطهور ساختن submerge

ghoteh var sakhtan *v* غوطهور ساختن engulf

ghowgha *adj* غوغا turmoil

ghowgha *n* غوغا tumult

ghook *n* غوک toad

ghol peykar *adj* غولپیکر gigantic

ghoulpeykar *adj* غولپیکر monstrous

gheyre eradi *adj* غیرارادي automatic

ghayr-e daghigh *adj* غیردقیق imprecise

gheyre doostaneh *adj* غیردوستانه unfriendly

ghayr-e rasmi *n* غیررسميبودن informality

gheyr-e soori *adj* غیرصوري informal

gheyr-e zarouri *adj* غیرضروري unnecessary

gheyre adelaneh *adj* غیرعادلانه unjust

ghayr e adi *adj* غیرعادي eccentric

gheire addi *adj* غیرعادي uncommon

ghayr-e amali *adj* غیرعملي impractical

ghayr-e ghabel-e taghsim *adj* غیرقابلتقسیم indivisible

ghayr-e ghabel-e tozih *adj* غیرقابلتوضیح inexplicable

geyr-e ghabel-e moghavemat *adj* غیرقابلمقاومت irresistible

gheyre ghanooni *adj* غیرقانوني wrongful

gheyre mobham *adj* غیرمبهم unequivocal

gheyre moteahel *adj* غیرمتاهل unmarried

gheyre' motedavel *adj* غیرمتداول outmoded

gheyr-e mohtamel *adj* غیرمحتمل improbable

ghayr-e mostaghim *adj* غیرمستقیم indirect

gheire mosallah *adj* غیرمسلح unarmed

ghayr-e momken *adj* غیرممکن impossible

gheire monsefaneh *adv* غیرمنصفانه unfairly

ghayr-e manteghi *adj* غیرمنطقي illogical

gheyre' nezami *adj* غیرنظامي civil

gheyre vaghei *adj* غیرواقعي unrealistic

gheir e akhlaghy *adj* غیراخلاقي amoral

gheyr-e daghigh *adj* غیردقیق inaccurate

ghayr-e shakhsi *adj* غیرشخصی impersonal

gheyre addi *adj* غیرعادی unusual

gheyre ghabele fekr *adj* غیرقابل فکر unthinkable

gheibat *n* غیبت absence

gheyre rasmi *adv* غیررسمی unofficially

gheyre-sigari *n* غیرسیگاری nonsmoker

gheire addi *adj* غیرعادی abnormal

gheyre motehammel *adj* غیرمحتمل unlikely

gheyre montazereh *adj* غیرمنتظره unexpected

fateh *adj* فاتح victorious

fateh *n* فاتح conqueror

fahesheh *n* فاحشه prostitute

fahesheh khaneh *n* فاحشه‌خانه brothel

fakhteh *n* فاخته dove

faregh-ul-tahsil shodan *v* فارغ التحصیل‌شدن graduate

fased *adj* فاسد rotten

fased *adj* فاسد vicious

fased shodan *v* فاسدشدن decay

fased kardan *v* فاسدکردن corrupt

fash kardan *v* فاش کردن unfold

fash kardan *v* فاش کردن disclose

fash kardan *v* فاش کردن divulge

fash kardan *v* فاش کردن reveal

faseleh *n* فاصله distance

faseleh *n* فاصله interval

fazelab *n* فاضلاب sewage

faghed-e hes-e tashkhis *adj* فاقد حس تشخیص indiscreet

famili *n* فامیلی last name

fanous *n* فانوس lantern

fanouse' darya'ei *n* فانوس دریایی lighthouse

fa'ni *adj* فانی mortal

fayedeh *n* فایده advantage

fayedeh *n* فایده profit

fayegh amadan bar *v* فایق‌آمدن بر get over

fath *n* فتح victory

ghalabeh kardan *v* فتح کردن overpower

fath kardan *v* فتح کردن reduce

fatgh *n* فتق hernia

fotokopi *n* فتوکپی photocopy

fetileh mavad monfajereh *n* فتیله موادمنفجره fuse

fajr *n* فجر dawn

fahsha *n* فحشاء prostitution

fakhr *n* فخر pride

federal *adj* فدرال federal

fara khandan *v* فراخواندن call

fara gereftan *v* فراگرفتن surround

farakh *adj* فراخ ample

farakh *adj* فراخ spacious

fara khandan *v* فراخواندن summon

farari *n* فراری deserter

farari *n* فراری fugitive

faraze' badan *n* فراز ascendancy

farazidan v فرازیدن ascend	**farz** n فرض hypothesis
faragiry n فراگیری acquisition	**farz** n فرض presumption
faramoosh kardan v فراموش کردن forget	**farz kardan** v فرض کردن presume
faramooshy n فراموشی amnesia	**farz kardan** v فرض کردن assume
faransavi adj فرانسوی French	**farziyeh** n فرضیه premise
faraham avardan v فراهم‌آوردن get together	**faree** adj فرعی petty
faravan adj فراوان affluent	**fargh** n فرق odds
faravan adj فراوان lavish	**farghe joz'ei** n فرق‌جزیی nuance
faravan adj فراوان plentiful	**fargh dashtan** v فرق‌داشتن differ
faravan adj فراوان rampant	**ferghet** n فرقت frigate
faravan boodan v فراوان‌بودن abound	**fergheh** n فرقه sect
faravani n فراوانی abundance	**ferekans** n فرکانس frequency
faravany n فراوانی affluence	**form** n فرم profile
faravani n فراوانی plenty	**formalitehye edari** n فرمالیته‌اداری red tape
faravardeh-e far'ee n فرآورده فرعی by-product	**farman** n فرمان charter
farbeh adj فربه plump	**farman** n فرمان sanction
farbeh adj فربه corpulent	**farman bordan** v فرمان‌بردن abide by
farbeh adj فربه fat	**farman dadan** v دادن فرمان command
farjam v فرجام end up	**farmandar** n فرماندار governor
fard adj فرد odd	**farmandeh** n فرمانده commander
farda adv فردا tomorrow	**formol** n فرمول formula
farzaneh n فرزانه wise	**far neshin** n فرنشین chairman
farzand n فرزند breed	**fereni** n فرنی custard
farsayesh n فرسایش wear	**farhang** n فرهنگ culture
ferestadan v فرستادن refer	**farhang** n فرهنگ dictionary
ferestadan iv فرستادن send	**farhangestan** n فرهنگستان academy
ferestadeh n فرستاده envoy	**foro bordan** v فروبردن depress
farsh n فرش carpet	**foro bordan** v فروبردن immerse
fereshteh n فرشته angel	**forou bordan** v فروبردن plunge
fereshtei adj فرشته‌ای angelic	**forou bordan** iv فروبردن sink
forsat n فرصت opportunity	**forou-rikhtan** v فروریختن break down
farz n فرض assumption	

forourikhtan *v* فروریختنcollapse

foroo kardan *iv* فروکردن thrust

foroutani *adj* فروتن modest

foroutananeh *adv* فروتنانه humbly

foroutani *n* فروتني humility

foroutani *n* فروتني meekness

foroutani *n* فروتني modesty

foroukhtan *iv* فروختن sell

foroodgah *n* فرودگاه airport

forush *n* فروش sellout

forooshandeh *n* فروشنده salesclerk

forushandeh *n* فروشنده seller

foroushandeh *n* فروشنده supplier

forooshandehye agha *n* فروشنده آقا salesman

forough *n* فروغ light

forokesh kardan *v* فروکش کردن ebb

faryad *n* فریاد calling

faryad zadan *v* فریادزدنshout

faryad zadan *v* فریادزدن cry

farib *n* فریب deceit

farib *n* فریب delusion

farib n فریب fraud

farib *n* فریب illusion

farib *n* فریب swindle

faribamiz *adj* فریب آمیز deceitful

farib dadan *v* فریب دادن cheat

fariba *adj* فریا charming

faribande *adj* فریبنده alluring

faribandeh *adj* فریبنده deceptive

faribandeh *adj* فریبنده glamorous

fariftan *v* فریفتن deceive

fariftan *v* فریفتن entice

fozoni *n* فزوني excess

fesad *n* فساد corruption

fesad *n* فساد pus

faskh *n* فسخ annulment

faskh *n* فسخ cancellation

faskh *n* فسخ repeal

faskh *n* فسخ waiver

faskh kardan *v* فسخ کردن cancel

fosfor *n* فسفر phosphorus

feshar *n* فشار stress

feshar *n* فشار pressure

feshordan *v* فشردن pressure

feshordan *v* فشردن squeeze

feshordan *iv* فشردن wring

fasl *n* فصل season

fasl *n* فصل(کتاب) chapter

fasli *adj* فصلي seasonal

faza *n* فضا space

fazanavard *n* فضانورد astronaut

fazaie havaei *n* فضاي هوايي airspace

fazl foroushi *adj* فضل فروشي pedantic

fozool *adj* فضول nosy

fozouli-kardan *v* فضولي کردن meddle

fa'al *adj* فعال active

fa'al sazy *n* فعال سازي activation

fa'al kardan *v* فعال کردن activate

fa'aliat *n* فعاليت activity

fe'el *n* فعل verb

faghr *n* فقر poverty

faghareh *n* فقره item

faghat *adv* فقط solely

faghat *adv* فقط merely

faghat *adv* فقط only

faghir *n* فقیر poor

fak *n* فک jaw

fokahi *adj* فکاهی humorous

fekr *n* فکر mind

fekr kardan *iv* فکر کردن think

falat *n* فلات plateau

falaj *n* فلج paralysis

falaje atfal *n* فلج اطفال polio

falaj kardan *v* فلج کردن paralyze

felez *n* فلز metal

felezi *adj* فلزي metallic

falsafeh *n* فلسفه philosophy

felfel *n* فلفل pepper

foulot *n* فلوت flute

fann *n* فن technique

fane enteghad *n* فن انتقاد critique

fan shenasi *n* فن شناسی technology

fana kardan *v* فنا کردن ruin

fenjan *n* فنجان cup

fandogh *n* فندق hazelnut

fandak *n* فندک lighter

fonoon *n* فنون tactics

fanni *adj* فني technical

fehrest *n* فهرست catalog

fehrest *n* فهرست list

fehrest kardan *v* فهرست کردن list

fahmandan *v* فهماندن represent

fahmidan *v* فهمیدن understand

fot *n* فوت demise

foot-o-fan *n* فوت و فن know-how

fowj *n* فوج regiment

foran *adv* فورا instantly

favaran *n* فوران outburst

favaran konandeh *adj* فوران کننده effusive

ghoort dadan *v* فورت دادن swallow

fevriyeh *n* فوریه February

fogh-oladeh sard *adj* فوق العاده سرد ice-cold

fowghani *adj* فوقانی upper

foulad *n* فولاد steel

fi ma beyn *adv* فی مابین interim

feedbak *n* فیدبک feedback

fizik *n* فیزیک physics

fiziki *adj* فیزیکی physical

feysaleh dadan *v* فیصله دادن evict

fayz *n* فیض grace

fil *n* فیل elephant

filsouf *n* فیلسوف philosopher

film *n* فیلم film

fel bedaheh sakhtan *v* فی البداهه ساختن improvise

ق

gha'em magham *n* قائم مقام substitute

ghab *n* قاب frame

ghabele ejra *adj* قابل اجراء applicable

ghabel erteja'e *adj* قابل ارتجاع elastic

ghabel eshteal *adj* قابل اشتعال flammable

ghabele etminan *adj* قابل اطمینان reliable

ghabel-e' enetaf *adj* قابل انعطاف pliable

ghabele bahs *adj* قابل بحث debatable

ghabel'e bakhshayesh *adj* قابل بخشایش forgivable

ghabele pardakht *adj* قابل‌پرداخت
payable

ghabel e parastesh *adj* قابل‌پرستش
adorable

ghabele ta'assof *adj* قابل‌تاسف
regrettable

ghabele tahammol *adj* قابل‌تحمل
tolerable

ghebel e tanzim *adj* قابل‌تنظیم
adjustable

ghabel e tavafogh *adj* قابل‌توافق
adaptable

ghabele tavajjoh *adj* قابل‌توجه
remarkable

ghabele hall *adj* قابل‌حل soluble

ghabele haml *adj* قابل‌حمل
portable

ghabele ghabool *adj* قابل‌قبول
acceptable

ghabel e ghias *adj* قابل‌قیاس
analogous

ghabele keshtkari *adj* قابل
کشتکاری arable

ghabele kontrol *adj* قابل‌کنترل
manageable

ghabele lams *adj* قابل‌لمس
palpable

ghabele mojazat *adj* قابل‌مجازات
punishable

ghabele mohasebe *adj* قابل‌محاسبه
accountable

ghabele' moghayeseh *adj* قابل
مقایسه comparable

ghabele molahezeh *adj* قابل
ملاحظه noticeable

ghabele naghz *adj* قابل‌نقض
reversible

ghabel e hedaiat *adj* قابل‌هدایت
advisable

ghabeleh *n* قابله midwife

ghabeliyat *n* قابلیت capability

ghabeliyate' estefadeh *n* قابلیت
استفاده availability

ghabeliat mojazat *n* قابلیت
مجازات culpability

ghapidan *v* قاپیدن seize

ghatel *n* قاتل murderer

ghach kardan *v* قاچ کردن slice

ghachghi *n* قاچاقچی smuggler

ghader be pardakhte ghorouz
adj قادربه‌پرداخت‌قروض solvent

ghader e motlagh *adj* قادرمطلق
almighty

ghader boudan *iv* قادربودن can

gharch *n* قارچ mushroom

gharreh *n* قاره mainland

ghari *n* قاري reader

ghshogh *n* قاشق spoon

ghashoghe chai khori *n* قاشق‌چاي
خوري teaspoon

ghashoghe soup khori *n* قاشق
سوپ‌خوري tablespoon

ghazi *n* قاضي judge

ghatir *n* قاطر mule

gha'edegi *n* قاعدگي menstruation

gha'edeh *n* قاعده rule

ghafeleh *n* قافله convoy

ghafiyeh *n* قافیه rhyme

ghaleb zadan *v* قالب‌زدن mold

ghaleb giri *iv* قالب‌گیری cast

ghalebe yakh *n* قالب‌یخ ice cube

ghalicheh *n* قالیچه rug

ghlicheh nama *n* قالیچه‌نما tapestry

ghangharia *n* قانقاریا gangrene

ghanoon *n* قانون statute

ghanoon *n* قانون law

ghanoone' asasi *n* قانون اساسی constitution

ghanoon gozar *n* قانون گزار lawmaker

ghanoon vaz'e kardan *v* قانون وضع کردن legislate

ghanooni *adj* قانونی lawful

ghanooni *adj* قانونی legal

ghanouni kardan *v* قانونی کردن validate

ghanooni kardan *v* قانونی کردن legalize

ghayegh *n* قایق gondola

ghayeghe' barik *n* قایق باریک canoe

ghayeghe sayyadi *n* قایق صیادی sailboat

ghabrestan *n* قبرستان graveyard

ghabz kardan *adj* قبض کردن constipated

ghablan tahiyeh didan *iv* قبلاتهیه دیدن foresee

ghablan fekre chizi ra kardan *v* قبلافکر چیزی را کردن premeditate

ghabli *adj* قبلی previous

ghabool *n* قبول admittance

ghaboul *n* قبول compliance

ghabool kardan *v* قبول کردن adopt

ghabool kardan *v* قبول کردن ratify

ghatl *n* قتل murder

ghatl *n* قتل killing

ghatl-e 'am *n* قتل عام holocaust

ghatle am *n* قتل عام slaughter

ghatl-e nafs *n* قتل نفس manslaughter

ghahti *n* قحطی famine

ghdrdani *n* قدر دانی gratitude

ghodrat *n* قدرت authority

ghodrat *n* قدرت power

ghodrate ebdae *n* قدرت ابداع creativity

ghodrate hayati *n* قدرت حیاتی vitality

ghadrdani kardan *n* قدردانی کردن appreciate

ghadrdani *n* قدردانی appreciation

ghadrdany kardan *v* قدردانی کردن acknowledge

ghadri *adv* قدری somewhat

ghadghan *v* قدغن کردن ban

ghadeghan kardan *iv* قدغن کردن forbid

ghadam zadan *v* قدم زدن pace

ghadam zadan *iv* قدم زدن stride

ghadam zadan *n* قدم زدن stroll

gheddis kardan *v* قدیس کردن bless

ghadimi *adj* قدیمی ancient

ghara'at *n* قرائت reading

gharar dadan *v* قرار دادن park

gharardad *n* قرارداد contract

ghorazeh *n* قراضه scrap

ghorbangah *n* قربانگاه altar

ghorbani *n* قربانی victim

ghorbani *n* نذر ، قربانی sacrifice

ghors *n* قرص wafer

ghors-e nan *n* قرص نان loaf

gharz dadan *iv* قرض دادن lend

gharz gereftan *v* قرض گرفتن borrow

ghore'keshi *n* قرعه کشی draw

ghor'eh keshi *n* قرعه کشی lottery

gher ghereh *n* قرقره pulley

ghermez *adj* قرمز red

ghermez shodan *v* قرمزشدن redden

ghare'ney *n* قرهنی clarinet

ghoroone vosta *adj* قرونوسطی medieval

gharib-olvogho *adj* قریبالوقوع impending

gharib-olvogho *adj* قریبالوقوع imminent

ghezel ala *n* قزلآلا trout

ghest *n* قسط payment

ghest *n* قسط installment

ghesm *n* قسم species

ghasam dadan *iv* قسمدادن swear

ghesmat *n* قسمت ratio

ghesmat *n* قسمت share

ghesmat e pahn *n* قسمتپهن flat

ghesmati *adj* قسمتی partial

gheshr *n* قشر shell

ghashang *adj* قشنگ pretty

ghasab *n* قصاب butcher

ghasabi *n* قصابی butchery

ghasd *n* قصد intention

ghasd dashtan *iv* قصدداشتن mean

ghasd dashtan *v* قصدداشتن intend

ghezavat *n* قضاوت verdict

ghaziyeh *n* قضیه proposition

ghatar *n* قطار train

ghatare zir zamini *adj* قطارزیرزمینی underground

ghotb *n* قطب pole

ghotbe' shomali *adj* قطبشمالی arctic

ghotbi *adj* قطبی polar

ghotr e dayereh *n* قطردایره diameter

ghotr-e' golooleh *n* قطرگلوله caliber

ghotri *adj* قطری diagonal

ghate' *adv* قطع off

ghate' *n* قطع disruption

ghat'e *n* قطع format

ghate'e ozvi az badan *n* قطع عضویازبدن amputation

ghate' nazar az *adv* قطعنظراز aside from

ghateh *n* قطعه piece

ghat'eh *n* قطعه block

ghate'he manzoome razmi *n* قطعهمنظومرزمی odyssey

ghet'eh mousighiye asheghaneh *n* قطعهموسیقیعاشقانه serenade

ghatehe yadaki *n* قطعهیدکی spare part

ghet'eye montakhab *n* قطعهء منتخب excerpt

ghatee *adj* قطعی decisive

ghafaseh *n* قفس cage

ghafaseh *n* قفسه cabinet

ghafasehe ketab *n* قفسهکتاب bookcase

ghafasehha *n* قفسهها shelves

ghofl *n* قفل lock

ghoflsaz *n* قفلساز locksmith

ghofl kardan *v* قفلکردن lock

ghollab *n* قلاب bracket

ghollab *n* قلاب hook

gholab dozi kardan *v* قلابدوزی کردن embroider

ghalb *n* قلب heart

ghalbshenasi *n* قلب‌شناسی cardiology

ghalbi *adj* قلبي cordial

ghalbi *adj* قلبي hearty

gholdor *adj* قلدر bully

ghal'e *n* قلع tin

ghal'eh *n* قلعه chateau

ghalam *n* قلم pen

ghalam zadan *v* قلم‌زدن cross out

ghalam zadan *v* قلم‌زدن engrave

ghalammoo *n* قلم‌مو paintbrush

ghalamroe osghof *n* قلمرواسقف diocese

gholonbeh *n* قلنبه lump

gholleh *n* قله peak

gholleh *n* قله summit

gholvehsang *n* قلوه‌سنگ cobblestone

ghomar *n* قمار hazard

ghomar kardan *v* قمارکردن gamble

ghomghomeh *n* قمقمه canteen

ghomghomeh *n* قمقمه flask

ghanari *n* قناري canary

ghande' soukhteh *n* قندسوخته caramel

ghahr *adj* قهر estranged

ghahraman *n* قهرمان victor

ghahraman *n* قهرمان hero

ghahreman var *adj* قهرمان‌وار heroic

ghahveh *n* قهوه coffee

ghahve'ei *adj* قهوه‌اي brown

ghahveiye soukhteh *adj* قهوه‌اي‌سوخته tan

ghavas *n* قواص diver

ghooch *n* قوچ ram

ghourkhaneh *n* قورخانه arsenal

ghooriye chai *n* قوري‌چاي teapot

ghooz *n* قوز hump

ghooz *n* قوز hunch

ghoozak *n* قوزک ankle

ghoozi *adj* قوزى hunched

ghows *n* قوس arc

ghouti halabi *n* قوطي‌حلبى can

ghoulanj *n* قولنج colic

ghom o khish *n* قوم‌وخويش folks

ghoveh mokhayaleh *n* قوه‌مخيله fantasy

ghavi *adj* قوي strong

ghavi *adj* قوي forceful

ghavi heykal *adj* قوي‌هيکل robust

ghavi heykal *adj* قوي‌هيکل sturdy

ghias *n* قياس analogy

ghiyas *n* قياس parable

ghiyam *n* قيام insurgency

gheychi *n* قيچي scissors

gheyd *n* قيد bond

gheyd *n* قيد constraint

gheyd *n* قيد provision

ghir *n* قير tar

ghir *n* قير asphalt

ghirat *n* قيراط carat

ghaysar *n* قيصر czar

gheytan *n* قيطان braid

gheymat *n* قيمت price

gheymat *n* قيمت value

ghaymat dashtan *iv* قيمت‌داشتن cost

gheid *n* قيد adverb

gheymati *adj* قيمتى pricey

<table>
<tr><td>

kart postal *n* كارت‌پستال postcard

kar kon *adv* كاركن drastic

kafer *n* كافر heathen

kala *n* كالا goods

kesafat *adj* كثافت dirt-poor

kerayeh *n* كرايه rent

kari *n* كري deafness

**kasi ke ghorbaniye digaran
shavad** *n* كسيكه‌قرباني‌ديگران
شود scapegoat

koshtan *v* كشتن deaden

keshidan *v* كشيدن pull

kafal *n* كفل hip

kolah gis *n* كلاه‌گيس wig

kolbeh *n* كلبه hut

kam khoon *adj* كم‌خون anemic

kam khoony *n* كم‌خوني anemia

kamrouee *n* كمرويي shyness

kamyab *adj* كمياب scarce

kamyabi *n* كميابي scarcity

kamin kardan *v* كمين‌كردن lurk

kenar *n* كنار edge

kenareh giri *n* كناره‌گيري
withdrawal

konjkav *n* كنجكاو prowler

kandoo *n* كندو hive

kouzeh dahan-goshad *n* كوزه
دهن‌گشاد jar

komeh alaf-e khoshk *n* كومه‌علف
خشك haystack

kooh *n* كوه mount

kabl *n* كابل cable

</td><td>

karbourator *n* كاربوراتور
carburetor

kaboos *n* كابوس nightmare

katoulik *adj* كاتوليك catholic

kaj *n* كاج pine

kakh *n* كاخ palace

kar *n* كار affair

kar *n* كار job

kar *n* كار work

kar amouz *n* كارآموز trainee

kar barjasteh *n* كاربرجسته feat

kar-e khareghol'adeh *v* كارخارق
العاده outperform

kar gozashtan *v* كارگذاشتن install

kare' na-tamam *n* كارناتمام
backlog

karateh *n* كاراته karate

karbord *n* كاربرد application

karbord *n* كاربرد usage

kart *n* كارت card

kartrij *n* كارتريج cartridge

karkhaneh *n* كارخانه factory

karkhaneh labaniat sazi *n*
كارخانه‌لبنيات‌سازي dairy farm

kard va changal *n* كاردوچنگال
cutlery

karfarma *n* كارفرما employer

karkonan *n* كاركنان personnel

kargah *n* كارگاه detective

kargah *n* كارگاه workshop

karegar *n* كارگر worker

kargar *n* كارگر laborer

kar gosha *n* كارگشا entrepreneur

karmayeh *n* كارمايه energy

karmand *n* كارمند employee

</td></tr>
</table>

karmande tazeh *n* کارمندتازه recruit

karmandan *n* کارمندان staff

kar nameh *n* کارنامه workbook

karhay-e khaneh *n* کارهای‌خانه housework

karavan *n* کاروان caravan

karikatoor *n* کاریکاتور caricature

karikator *n* کاریکاتور cartoon

kazino *n* کازینو casino

kastan *v* کاستن subtract

kasti *n* کاستی defect

kasti *n* کاستی fault

kaseh *n* کاسه bowl

kasehe' zanoo *n* کاسه‌زانو kneecap

kashtan *v* کاشتن plant

kashtan *iv* کاشتن sow

kashi *n* کاشی tile

kaghaz *n* کاغذ paper

kaghaz bazi *n* بازی کاغذ paperwork

kaghaze poust *n* کاغذپوست parchment

kafe'ein *n* کافئین caffeine

kafe' *n* کافه cafe

kafi *adj* کافی sufficient

kafi *adv* کافی enough

kaka'ou *n* کاکائو cocoa

kakol ya mooye masnoui *n* کاکل یاموی‌مصنوعی toupee

kala *n* کالا article

kala *n* کالا merchandise

kalaye ghachagh *n* کالای‌قاچاق contraband

kalaye vizheh *n* کالای‌ویژه specialty

kalbod *n* کالبد skeleton

kalbad-shekafi *n* کالبدشکافی autopsy

kalej *n* کالج college

karori *n* کالری calorie

kaleskeh *n* کالسکه carriage

kaleskeh *n* کالسکه coach

ka'mkar shodan *v* کامکارشدن prosper

kamel *adj* کامل perfect

kamel *adj* کامل complete

kamel kardan *v* کامل‌کردن complete

kamel kardan *v* کامل‌کردن finish

kamelan *adv* کاملا entirely

kamelan *adv* کاملا quite

kamelan foroush rafteh *adj* کاملا فروش‌رفته sold-out

kamelan now *adj* کاملانو brand-new

kamyab *adj* کامیاب successful

kamyab budan *iv* کامیاب‌بودن speed

kamiyoun *n* کامیون truck

kanal *n* کانال channel

kandid kardan *v* کاندیدکردن nominate

kangoro *n* کانگورو kangaroo

kanoon *n* کانون focus

kah *n* کاه straw

kahesh *n* کاهش subtraction

kahoo *n* کاهو lettuce

kavosh *n* کاوش probing

kavosh kardan *iv* کاوش‌کردن dig

kavosh kardan *v* کاوش‌کردن probe

kavidan *v* کاویدن excavate

kabab kardan *v* کباب کردن roast

kebreh *n* کبره crust

kebrit *n* کبریت match

kabk *n* کبک partridge

kaboutar *n* کبوتر pigeon

kabood *adj* کبود livid

kaboudshodegi *n* کبودشدگي bruise

kopi kardan *v* کپي کردن copy

kot *n* کت coat

ketab *n* کتاب book

ketabe darsi *n* کتاب درسي textbook

ketab dasti *n* کتاب دستي handbook

ketab-e kouchak *n* کتاب کوچک booklet

ketabe moghadas *n* کتاب مقدس bible

ktebkhabeh *n* کتابخانه library

ketabdar *n* کتابدار librarian

ketabdar *n* کتابدار curator

ketabforoosh *n* کتابفروش bookseller

ketabforooshi *n* کتابفروشي bookstore

katan *n* کتان linen

ketri n کتري kettle

ketf *n* کتف shoulder

kotak zadan *v* کتک زدن mug

kesafat *n* کثافت pollution

kasif *adj* کثيف lousy

kasif *adj* کثيف sloppy

kasif *adj* کثيف squalid

kasif kardan *v* کثيف کردن soil

kaj kholgh *adj* کج خلق sullen

kaj kardan *v* کج کردن distort

kaj kardan *v* کج کردن tilt

kode posti *n* کدپستي zip code

kodam *adj* کدام which

kadbanoo n کدبانو housewife

keder kardan *v* کدر کردن tarnish

kadou tanbal *n* تنبل کدو pumpkin

kadoo sabz *n* کدوسبز zucchini

kezb *n* کذب falsehood

kar *adj* کر deaf

kar kardan *v* کر کردن deafen

keravat *n* کراوات necktie

keravat *n* کراوات tie

kerayeh *n* کرايه fare

kerayeh *n* کرايه freight

kerayeh kardan *v* کرايه کردن hire

karbas *n* کرباس canvas

karji *n* کرجي barge

karji *n* کرجي yacht

karakht *adj* کرخت numb

kerdar *n* کردار deed

kardan *v* کردن conceal

kardan iv کردن do

korsi *n* کرسي stool

karafs *n* کرفس celery

kork *n* کرک pile

karkas *n* کرکس vulture

korki *adj* کرکي fuzzy

kargadan *n* کرگردن rhinoceros

kerm *n* کرم worm

kerme' sad-pa *n* کرم صدپا caterpillar

koreh *n* کره sphere

kareh *n* کره butter

koreh *n* کره globe

koreh-asb *n* کره‌اسب colt	**koshtan** *v* کشتن kill
karim *adj* کریم benevolent	**keshti** *n* کشتي ship
kerismas *n* کریسمس X-mas	**koshti** *n* کشتي wrestling
kesadi *n* کسادي recession	**keshtiye jangi** *n* کشتي‌جنگي warship
kesadi *n* کسادي stagnation	
kasr *n* کسر deduction	**keshti hamel'e parcham** *n* کشتي حامل‌پرچم flagship
kasr *n* کسر fraction	
kasr pazir *adj* کسرپذیر deductible	**kashtiye kouchak** *n* کشتي‌کوچک boat
kasri *n* کسري shortage	**koshti gereftan** *v* کشتي‌گرفتن wrestle
kesel *adj* کسل weary	
kasi ra paeen bordan *v* کسي‌را پائین‌بردن debase	**koshti gir** *n* کشتي‌گیر wrestler
	kashtie tafrihi *n* کشتي‌تفریحی cruise ship
kasi ra kouchek kardan *v* کسي‌را کوچک‌کردن belittle	**keshesh** *n* کشش attraction
kasi ke eijad-e harigh konad *n* کسي‌که‌ایجادحریق‌کند arsonist	**keshesh** *n* کشش magnetism
	keshesh *n* کشش reach
kasi ke sham mikhorad *n* کسي که‌شام‌می‌خورد diner	**keshesh** *n* کشش strain
	keshesh *n* کشش tension
kasi *pro* کسي someone	**keshesh** *n* کشش traction
kesh dar *adj* کش‌دار supple	**kashf** *n* کشف discovery
kesh raftan *v* کش‌رفتن snitch	**kashf ramz nemodan** *v* کشف‌رمز نمودن decipher
kesh raftan *v* کش‌رفتن pilfer	
keshandan *v* کشاندن drag	**kashf kardan** *v* کشف‌کردن figure out
keshavarz *n* کشاورز farmer	
keshbaf *n* کشباف jersey	**keshmesh** *n* کشمش raisin
kesht kardan *v* کشت‌کردن till	**keshmakesh** *n* کشمکش skirmish
kesht kardan *adj* کشت‌کردن cultivate	**keshmakesh kardan** *v* کشمکش کردن scuffle
koshtar *n* کشتار massacre	**koshandeh** *adj* کشنده pernicious
koshtar *n* کشتار carnage	**keshandeh** *adj* کشنده attractive
koshtar dasteh jamee *n* کشتار دسته‌جمعي genocide	**koshandeh** *adj* کشنده enticing
	koshandeh *adj* کشنده fatal
koshtar kardan *v* کشتارکردن slaughter	**koshandeh** *adj* کشنده lethal
	kesho *n* کشو drawer
koshtargah *n* کشتارگاه shambles	**keshvar** *n* کشور country
koshtan *v* کشتن assassinate	

keshidan *iv* كشيدن draw

keshidan *v* كشيدن haul

keshidan *v* كشيدن stretch

keshideh *adj* كشيده oblong

keshish *n* كشيش cleric

keshish *n* كشيش priest

keshisheh *n* كشيشه priestess

keshishi *n* كشيشي priesthood

keshidan periz az bargh *v*
برق از پريز كشيدن unplug

kaf *n* كف foam

kaf *v* كف skim

kafe pa *n* كفِ پا sole

kafzadan *v* كف‌زدن clap

kaf'e zamin *n* كفِ زمين floor

kaf saboon *n* كفِ صابون lather

kaffareh *n* كفاره atonement

kaffareh dadan *v* كفاره‌دادن
atonement

kaftar *n* كفتار hyena

kofr *n* كفر blasphemy

kofr *n* كفر heresy

koufr *n* كفر infidelity

kofr amiz *adj* كفرآميز profane

kofr-goo'ei kardan *v* كفرگويي
كردن blaspheme

kafsh *n* كفش footwear

kafsh *n* كفش shoe

kafshe charkhdar *n* كفش چرخدار
skate

kafan *n* كفن shroud

kak *n* كك flea

kelaj *n* كلاج clutch

kelas *n* كلاس classroom

kalaghe siyah *n* كلاغ سياه raven

kalan *adj* كلان massive

kalanshahr *n* شهر كلان
metropolis

kolah gis *n* كلاه hat

kolah bardar *adj* كلاه‌بردار
fraudulent

kolah bardar *n* كلاه‌بردار swindler

kollahe bere *n* كلاه‌بره beret

kolah gis *n* كلاه گيس hairpiece

kolbeh *n* كلبه cottage

kolbeh *n* كلبه shack

kolbehe' ye'laqi *n* كلبه‌ييلاقي chalet

kolestrol *n* كلسترول cholesterol

koloft kardan *v* كلفت كردن
thicken

kolofti *n* كلفتى thickness

kalam *n* كلم cabbage

kalameh *n* كلمه word

kolon *n* كلن cologne

kolocheh *n* كلوچه cookie

kolouchehe khoshk *n* كلوچه
خشك biscuit

kolliyat *n* كليت totality

kilid *n* كليد key

kelissa *n* كليسا church

kelisaye' jame'e *n* كليساي‌جامع
cathedral

kelisay-e kouchak *n* كليساي
كوچك chapel

kam *adj* كم infrequent

kam *adj* كم little

kam bazdeh *adj* كم‌بازده
inefficient

kamroo *adj* كمرو bashful

kam shodan *v* كم‌شدن wane

kam shodan *v* كم‌شدن diminish

kam kardan *v* كم كردن deduct

kamal *n* كمال perfection

kaman *n* كمان arch

komando *n* كماندو commando

kambod *n* كمبد deficit

kamboud *n* كمبود shortcoming

kamtar kardan *v* كمتر كردن lessen

komedi *n* كمدى comedy

komedian *n* كمدين comedian

kamar *n* كمر loin

kamarband *n* كمربند belt

kamarband *n* كمربند cordon

kamrang *adj* كمرنگ pale

kam rou *adj* كمرو timid

kam roui *n* كمرويى timidity

komak *n* كمك aid

komak *n* كمك help

komak kharj dadan *v* كمك خرج دادن subsidize

komak kardan *v* كمك كردن help

komak kardan *v* كمك كردن relieve

komake mali *n* كمك مالى subsidy

komakhaye avaliyeh *n* كمكهاى اوليه first aid

komaki *adj* كمكى secondary

komonist *adj* كمونيست communist

kami *adv* كمى slightly

kamin kardan *v* كمين كردن ambush

kenar keshidan *v* كنار كشيدن recede

kenar gozardan *v* كنار گذاردن put away

kenargozashtan *v* كنار گذاشتن brush aside

kenar gozashtan *v* كنار گذاشتن put aside

kenar gozashtan *v* كنار گذاشتن overrule

kenar gozashtan *v* كنار گذاشتن reserve

kenareh gereftan *v* كناره گرفتن resign

kenareh giri kardan *v* كناره گيرى كردن secede

kenayeh *n* كنايه metaphor

kontorol *n* كنترل control

kontrol-e dobareh *v* كنترل دوباره double-check

kontes *n* كنتس countess

konjkav *adj* كنجكاو curious

kond *adj* كند blunt

kond *adj* كند dull

kandan *v* كندن pluck

kondeh *n* كنده chunk

kondeh *n* كنده log

kandoo *n* كندو beehive

kondi *n* كندى bluntness

konsersiyom *n* كنسرسيوم consortium

konserv shodeh *adj* كنسرو شده canned

konsoolgari *n* كنسولگرى consulate

koniak *n* كنياك cognac

kaniseh *n* كنيسه synagogue

kehtar *adj* كهتر less

kahkeshan *n* كهكشان galaxy

kohneh *adj* كهنه antique

kohneh *adj* كهنه archaic

kohneh *n* كهنه rag

kohneh kar *n* كهنه كار veteran

kahir *n* کهیر bay

koubidan *v* کوبیدن knock

koobide *adj* کوبیده beaten

kopen *n* کوپن coupon

koutah *adj* کوتاه brief

koutah *adj* کوتاه short

koutah *n* کوتاه pygmy

koutah-bin *adj* کوتاه‌بین shortsighted

kootah kardan *v* کوتاه کردن abridge

koutah kardan *v* کوتاه کردن clip

kotah kardan *v* کوتاه کردن curtail

koutahi *n* کوتاهی brevity

kotoleh *n* کوتوله dwarf

kouchek *adj* کوچک small

kouchektarin *adj* کوچکترین least

kooche *n* کوچه alley

koucheh *n* کوچه lane

kod *n* کود dung

koud *n* کود manure

koodak *n* کودک infant

koudake nou pa *n* کودک‌نوپا toddler

koodaki *n* کودکی infancy

kowdan *adj* کودن moron

kodan *n* کودن goof

koor *adj* کور blind

koor kardan *v* کور کردن blind

koorkooraneh *adv* کورکورانه blindly

koreh *n* کوره furnace

koreh sozandane ashghal *n* کوره سوزاندن‌آشغال crematorium

koori *n* کوری blindness

koozeh *n* کوزه jug

kouzeh *n* کوزه urn

kouseh *n* کوسه piranha

kooseh *n* کوسه swordfish

kouseh mahi *n* کوسه‌ماهی shark

koshesh e peyvasteh *n* کوشش پیوسته diligence

kooshesh kardan *v* کوشش کردن try

kooshesh kardan *v* کوشش کردن attempt

koushidan *iv* کوشیدن strive

koufteh *n* کوفته meatball

kook *n* کوک stitch

kook kardan *iv* کوک کردن wind

koka'ein *n* کوکائین cocaine

koktel *n* کوکتل cocktail

koulak *n* کولاک storm

koulak *n* کولاک blizzard

kooleh poshti *n* کوله‌پشتی backpack

koli *n* کولی gypsy

koohestan *n* کوهستان mountain

koohestani *adj* کوهستانی mountainous

kip *adj* کیپ watertight

kisseh *n* کیسه bag

kiseh *n* کیسه bladder

kiseh *n* کیسه cod

kiseh *n* کیسه purse

kiseh safra *n* کیسه‌صفرا gall bladder

kish *n* کیش creed

kiffe asnad *n* کیف‌اسناد briefcase

kife poul *n* کیف‌پول wallet

keyf kardan *v* کیف کردن please

keyfar *n* کیفر penalty

keyfari *adj* كيفري penal
keyfiyat *n* كيفيت quality
keyk *n* كيك cake
kiloogeram *n* كيلوگرم kilogram
kiloovat *n* كيلووات kilowatt
kiloometr *n* كيلومتر kilometer
kiloometrshomar *n* كيلومترشمار odometer
kineh *n* كينه venom
kineh touz *adj* كينهتوز spiteful
kineh joo *adj* كينهجو vindictive
kine' jo'ei kardan *v* كينهجويي كردن avenge
keihan navard *n* كيهاننورد cosmonaut
kiseh *n* كيسه sack
kif-e jibiye eskenas *n* كيفجيبي اسكناس billfold
kif dasti *n* كيفدستى handbag

garaj *n* گاراژ garage
gard-e makhsous *n* گاردمخصوص bodyguard
garson *n* گارسون barmaid
gari *n* گاري trolley
gaz *n* گاز bite
gaz *n* گاز gas
gaz anbor *n* انبر گاز pincers
ga'z gereftan *v* گازگرفتن nip
gaz gereftan *iv* گازگرفتن bite
galeri *n* گالري gallery
galon *n* گالن gallon
ga'm *n* گام pace

gam *n* گام step
gam be gam *adv* گامبهگام step-by-step
gahi *adv* گاهي sometimes
gave madeh *n* گاوماده cow
gave' nar *n* نر گاو bull
gav-e nar *n* نر گاو ox
gave' vahshi *n* گاووحشي buffalo
gav baz *n* گاوباز bullfighter
gav bazi *n* گاوبازى bullfight
gavcheran *n* گاوچران cowboy
gavmishe kowhandar *n* گاوميش كوهاندار bison
gap zadan *v* گپزدن chat
gach *n* گچ plaster
gach *n* گچ chalk
gada *n* گدا beggar
godakhtan *v* گداختن thaw
godazesh *n* گدازش, گرمى thaw
gozardan *v* گذاردن pose
gozardan *iv* گذاردن put
gozardan *v* گذاردن invest
gozashtan *iv* گذاشتن let
gozashtan-e dastgireh *v* گذاشتن دستگيره handle
gozaran kardan *v* گذران كردن get along
gozargah *n* گذرگاه bypass
gozargah *n* گذرگاه ferry
gozar nameh *n* گذرنامه pass
gozar nameh *n* گذرنامه passport
gozasht *n* گذشت amnesty
gozashtan *v* گذشتن elapse
gozashtan *v* گذشتن pass
gozashteh *adj* گذشته past
gozashteh az in *pre* گذشتهازاين besides

goraz *n* گراز pig

goraz-e nar *n* گرازنر boar

gerami dashtan *v* گرامی‌داشتن cherish

geran *adj* گران costly

geran *adj* گران expensive

geranbar *adj* گرانبار burdensome

geran baha *adj* گرانبها precious

gerayesh *n* گرایش attitude

gera'yesh *n* گرایش orientation

gerayesh *n* گرایش tendency

gerayesh *n* گرایش trend

gorbeh *n* گربه cat

gorbehe vahshi *n* گربه‌وحشی bobcat

gerd *adj* گرد round

gard *n* گرد compass

gerd amadan *v* گردآمدن convene

gerd avardan *v* گردآوردن amass

gerd avardan *n* گردآوردن roundup

gerd avari *n* گردآوری gathering

gerd avari kardan *v* گردآوري کردن gather

gard'o khaki *adj* گردوخاکي dusty

gerdagerd *pro* گرداگرد around

gordan *n* گردان battalion

gerd avardan *v* گردآوردن compile

gerd bad *adj* گردباد twisted

gardesh *v* گردش stroll

gardesh *n* گردش trip

gardesh *n* گردش circulation

gardesh *n* گردش excursion

gardesh *n* گردش flow

gardesh *n* گردش promenade

gardeshgah *n* گردشگاه park

gardan *n* گردن neck

gardanband *n* گردنبند necklace

gardan zadan *v* گردنزدن decapitate

gardanfaraz *adj* گردنفراز arrogant

gardanfarazi *n* گردنفرازي arrogance

gardaneh *n* گردنه saddle

gordeh *n* گرده disk

gardeh *n* گرده kidney

gardeh *n* گرده pollen

gerdoo *n* گردو walnut

gardi *n* گردي heroism

gorosnegi *n* گرسنگي hunger

gorosnegi dadan *v* گرسنگي‌دادن starve

gorosneh *adj* گرسنه hungry

gereftar shodan *v* گرفتارشدن run into

gereftar kardan *v* گرفتارکردن entangle

gereftar kardan *v* گرفتارکردن involve

gereftegi *n* گرفتگي eclipse

gereftan *iv* گرفتن catch

gereftan *iv* گرفتن hold

gereftan *v* گرفتن obtain

gereftan *iv* گرفتن take

gorg *n* گرگ wolf

garm *adj* گرم warm

garm *adj* گرم ardent

garm *adj* گرم hot

garm kardan *v* گرم کردن heat

garma *n* گرما heat

garmabe *n* گرمابه bath

garm khaneh *n* گرمخانه greenhouse

garmak *n* گرمک cantaloupe

garmi *n* گرمی ardor

gereh *n* گره knot

gereh zadan *v* گره‌زدن tie

geroo *n* گرو hostage

gerou *n* گرو pledge

gerou gozashtan *v* گروگذاشتن pledge

gorouh *n* گروه troop

gorrouh *n* گروه concourse

goroh *n* گروه group

gorouh *n* گروه team

gorouhban *n* گروهبان sergeant

gheravidan *v* گرویدن gravitate

geryan *adj* گریان tearful

grapeforout *n* گریپ‌فروت grapefruit

gorikhtan *v* گریختن run away

gorikhtan *v* گریختن shun

gorikhtan *iv* گریختن flee

goriz *n* گریز allusion

goriz *n* گریز flight

gorizan *adj* گریزان evasive

geristan *iv* گریستن weep

gerye *n* گریه bawl

geryeh *n* گریه tear

geryeh kardan *v* گریه‌کردن sob

enteshar *n* گزارش report

gozaresh dadan *v* گزارش‌دادن report

gazaf *adj* گزاف exorbitant

gazand *n* گزند detriment

gazandeh *n* گزنده biting

gazidan *v* گزیدن select

gazidan *iv* گزیدن sting

gazidan *iv* گزیدن choose

gozinesh *n* گزینش selection

gozingar *adj* گزینگر choosy

gozineh n گزینه switch

gostakh *adj* گستاخ brash

gostakh *adj* گستاخ impertinent

gostakh *adj* گستاخ insolent

gostardan *v* گستردن propagate

gostardan *iv* گستردن spread

gostardeh *adj* گسترده widespread

gostaresh yaftan *v* گسترش‌یافتن deploy

gosikhtan *v* گسیختن interrupt

goshad neshastan *v* گشادنشستن sprawl

gasht *n* گشت patrol

gasht *n* گشت tour

gasht zadan *v* گشت‌زدن cruise

gashtan *v* گشتن search

gashtan *iv* گشتن go

goshodan *v* گشودن inaugurate

goshoudan *v* گشودن open

goshoudan(ghofl) *v* گشودن(قفل) unlock

goshoodane dokmeh *v* گشودن دکمه unbutton

goftar *n* گفتار speech

goftego *n* گفتگو conversation

goftego *n* گفتگو dialogue

goft-o-goo kardan *v* گفتگو کردن communicate

goftan *iv* گفتن say

goftan *iv* گفتن tell

gofteh *n* گفته saying

gol *n* گل flower	**gomrah** *adj* گمراه astray
gela'lood *adj* گل‌آلود muddy	**gool zani** *n* گمراه‌سازي seduction
gol dadan *v* گل دادن blossom	**gomrah shodan** *v* گمراه‌شدن pervert
gole sorkh *n* گل‌سرخ rose	**gomrah kardan** *v* گمراه‌کردن seduce
gol kalam *n* گل‌کلم cauliflower	**gomrah kardan** *v* گمراه‌کردن baffle
gol e morvarid *n* گل‌مروارید daisy	**gomrahi** *n* گمراهي slip
golabi *n* گلابي pear	**gomnamy** *n* گمنامي anonymity
geladiator *n* گلادیاتور gladiator	**gonah** *n* گناه vice
galaviz shodan *v* گلاویزشدن tackle	**gonah** *n* گناه sin
golbarg *n* گلبرگ petal	**gonahkar** *adj* گناهکار felon
golchin adabi *n* گلچین‌ادبي garland	**gonahkar** *adj* گناهکار guilty
goldar *adj* گلدار floral	**gonah-kar** *n* گناهکار sinner
goldan *n* گلدان vase	**gonbad** *n* گنبد dome
goldan kozehee *n* گلدان‌کوزه‌ای flowerpot	**ganj** *n* گنج treasure
goldozi *adj* گلدوزي embroidery	**gonjayesh** *n* گنجایش capacity
golf *n* گلف golf	**gonjeshk** *n* گنجشگ sparrow
golf baz *n* گلف‌باز golfer	**ganjeh** *n* گنجه cupboard
golgoon *adj* گلگون rosy	**gand** *n* گند stink
galeh *n* گله flock	**gandab** *n* گنداب sewer
gallehe gav *n* گله‌گاو cattle	**gandom** *n* گندم wheat
galoo *n* گلو throat	**gandome siah** *n* گندم‌سیاه crap
galo *n* گلو gorge	**gong** *adj* گنگ mute
golokoz *n* گلوکز glucose	**gahvareh** *n* گهواره cradle
golooleh *n* گلوله ball	**govaridan** *v* گواریدن digest
golouleh *n* گلوله bullet	**govah** *n* گواه proof
golouleh *n* گلوله pellet	**govah** *n* گواه evidence
goloolehye narenjaki *n* گلوله نارنجکی shrapnel	**govahi** *n* گواهي testimony
goloulehe nakh *n* گلوله‌نخ clue	**govahi dadan** *v* گواهي‌دادن testify
gom kardan *iv* گم‌کردن lose	**govahiye dorough** *n* گواهي‌دروغ perjury
gomkardan *v* گم‌کردن misplace	**govahinameh** *n* گواهینامه certificate
gomaresh *n* گمارش assignment	**gouje farangi** *n* گوجه‌فرنگي tomato
goman *n* گمان conjecture	

gowd *adj* گود deep

gowd kardan *v* گودکردن deepen

gowdal *n* گودال cavity

goudale amigh *n* گودال‌عمیق plunge

goure khar *n* گورخر zebra

gourestan *n* گورستان cemetery

gavazn shomali *n* گوزن‌شمالی elk

gavazne shomali *n* گوزن‌شمالی reindeer

goosaleh *n* گوساله calf

goosfand *n* گوسفند sheep

gosh *n* گوش ear

goosh be zang *n* گوش‌بزنگ alert

gousht *n* گوشت meat

gosht *n* گوشت flesh

gooshte' khook *n* گوشت‌خوک bacon

gosht-e ran *n* گوشت‌ران ham

gousht-e ghimeh shodeh *n* گوشت‌قیمه‌شده mincemeat

goosht-e gav *n* گوشت‌گاو beef

goushte gousaleh *n* گوشت‌گوساله veal

goosh mali *n* گوش‌مالی punishment

gooshmali *n* گوش‌مالی rebuke

gooshe *n* گوشه angle

gosheh *n* گوشه corner

goushehgir *adj* گوشه‌گیر loner

goshvareh *n* گوشواره earring

goshi *n* گوشی earphones

goshi-e hedfon *n* گوشی‌هدفون headphones

gool zadan *v* گول‌زدن defraud

gol zadan *v* گول‌زدن dupe

gol zadan *v* گول‌زدن fool

gool zadan *v* گول‌زدن swindle

goul zanandeh *n* گول‌زننده cheater

gounagoun *adj* گوناگون various

gounagoun *adj* گوناگون diverse

gounagoun sakhtan *v* گوناگون ساختن diversify

gooneh *n* گونه cheek

gohar *n* گوهر gem

gowhar *n* گوهر jewel

gooiande *n* گوینده announcer

gooyandeh *n* گوینده(رادیو تلویزیون) broadcaster

giyah *n* گیاه herb

giah e bedoon e saghe va barg *n* گیاه‌بدون‌ساقه‌وبرگ algae

giyah gharchi *n* گیاه‌قارچی fungus

giyah-khari *v* گیاه‌خواری vegetarian

gij *adj* گیج astounding

gij *adj* گیج dizzy

gij khordan *v* گیج‌خوردن stagger

gij shodeh *adj* گیج‌شده bewildered

gij kardan *v* گیج‌کردن astound

gij kardan *v* گیج‌کردن stun

gij kardan *v* گیج‌کردن confuse

gij kardan *v* گیج‌کردن daze

gij konandeh *adj* گیج‌کننده stunning

giji *n* گیجی confusion

giji *n* گیجی distraction

giji *n* گیجی dizziness

gir-avardan *v* گیرآوردن grasp

gir kardan *v* گیرکردن stick

gir kardan *v* گیرکردن falter

girandeh *n* گیرنده payee

gireh *n* گیره tongs
gireh *n* گیره clamp
gilas *n* گیلاس cherry
giyotin *n* گیوتین guillotine
giyah *n* گیاه plant
gij konandeh *adj* گیج‌کننده
  puzzling

lat *n* لات scoundrel
latari n لاتاري raffle
lazem boudan *v* لازم‌بودن require
las zadan *v* لاس‌زدن mash
las zadan *v* لاس‌زدن flirt
lastik *n* لاستیک rubber
lasheh *n* لاشه cadaver
laghar *adj* لاغر emaciated
laghar *adj* لاغر skinny
laghar *adv* لاغر thinly
laghar *adj* لاغر lean
laghar *adj* لاغر meager
laghar shodan *v* لاغرشدن slim
lafzan *v* لاف‌زدن brag
lak posht *n* لاک‌پشت turtle
lal *adj* لال speechless
laleh *n* لاله tulip
lamp *n* لامپ bulb
lamp *n* لامپ lamp
lanehe sag *n* لانه‌سگ kennel
layegh *adj* لایق competent
layegh danestan *v* لایق‌دانستن
  esteem
la yanghat'e *adj* لاینقطع incessant

lab *n* لب brink
lab *n* لب lip
lebas *n* لباس clothes
lebas *n* لباس costume
lebas *n* لباس suit
lebas *n* لباس dress
lebas poshidan *v* لباس‌پوشیدن
  dress
lebase' zir *n* لباس‌زیر lingerie
lebase zir *n* لباس‌زیر underwear
lebas-e shab *n* لباس شب
  nightgown
lebase shenaye zananeh do-tikeh
  n لباس‌شناي‌زنانه‌دوتکه bikini
lebase mondares *n* لباس‌مندرس
  rags
labkhand zadan *v* لبخندزدن smile
labriz shodan *v* لبریزشدن run over
labeh dar *adj* لبه‌دار edgy
laseh dandan *n* لثه‌دندان gum
laj *n* لج spite
lajan *n* لجن mud
lahzeh *n* لحظه instance
lahn *n* لحن tone
lahim kardan *v* لحیم‌کردن solder
lokht *adj* لخت bare
lokht *adj* لخت lax
lezzat *n* لذت pleasure
lazat *n* لذت enjoyment
lazat bakhshidan *adj* لذت‌بخش
  delightful
lazat bakhsh *adj* لذت‌بخش
  enjoyable
lazat bordan *v* لذت‌بردن enjoy
lezzat bordan az *v* لذت‌بردن‌از
  relish

laziz *adj* لذیذ delicious

larzan *adj* لرزان shaky

larzan *adj* لرزان unsteady

larzesh *n* لرزش tremor

larzeh *n* لرزه shiver

larzidan *v* لرزیدن tremble

larzidan *v* لرزیدن vibrate

larzidan *v* لرزیدن quake

larzidan *v* لرزیدن shiver

larzidan *v* لرزیدن shudder

lezhiyon *n* لژیون legion

lotfan paziroftan *v* لطفاپذیرفتن deign

latifeh goo *adj* لطیفه گو witty

la'n *n* لعن ban

lanat kardan *v* لعنت کردن damn

laghzesh *n* لغزش stumble

laghzesh *n* لغزش error

laghzesh napazir *adj* لغزش ناپذیر infallible

laghv tabiz nejadi *v* لغوتبعیض نژادی desegregate

laghv kardan *v* لغوکردن annul

laghv kardan *v* لغوکردن nullify

laghv kardan *v* لغوکردن repeal

laghv kardan *v* لغوکردن revoke

lafaf *n* لفاف padding

lafaf *n* لفاف wrapping

lafz be lafz *adv* لفظ به لفظ literally

laghab *n* لقب nickname

laghab *n* لقب surname

loghmeh *n* لقمه morsel

lakkeh *adj* لکه blurred

lakkeh dar kardan *adj* لکه دار کردن tainted

lak *n* لک blot

lak kardan *v* لک کردن blur

lak lak *n* لک لک stork

loknat dashtan *v* لکنت داشتن stutter

lakeh *n* لکه freckle

lakkeh *n* لکه stain

lakkeh dar shodan *v* لکه دارشدن spot

lakeh dar kardan *v* لکه دار کردن denigrate

lagad zadan *v* لگدزدن kick

lagadmal shodeh *adj* لگدمال شده downtrodden

lagane khasereh *n* لگن خاصره pelvis

lams *n* لمس touch

lams kardan *v* لمس کردن touch

long *adj* لنگ cripple

lang *adj* لنگ lame

langar *n* لنگر anchor

langar andakhtan *v* لنگرانداختن moor

langar gah *n* لنگرگاه harbor

leh kardan *v* له کردن mangle

leh kardan *v* له کردن maul

leh kardan *v* له کردن squash

lahjeh *n* لهجه dialect

lahjeh *n* لهجه idiom

lahestani *adj* لهستانی Polish

lavazeme ashpaz khaneh *n* لوازم آشپزخانه utensil

lavazem yadaki *n* لوازم یدکی accessory

loobiya ghermez *n* لوبیاقرمز kidney bean

lobia sabz *n* لوبیای سبز green bean

looch *adj* لوچ cross-eyed

louh *n* لوح tablet
lowdeh *n* لوده buffoon
lowdeh *n* لوده clown.
louz-al me'deh *n* لوزالمعده pancreas
louzeh *n* لوزه tonsil
lowla *n* لولا hinge
lowla zadan *v* لولازدن hinge
looleh *n* لوله pipeline
looleh kesh *n* لوله‌کش plumber
looleh keshi *n* لوله‌کشی plumbing
leyley kardan *v* لی‌لی کردن hop
litr *n* لیتر liter
lireh *n* لیره pound
leyzer *n* لیزر laser
lisidan *v* لیسیدن lick
lif *n* لیف brush
likour *n* لیکور liqueur
limoo *n* لیمو lemon
limoo-torsh *n* لیموترش lime
limoonad *n* لیموناد lemonade
livan *n* لیوان mug

ma *pro* ما we
ma'at *adj* مات opaque
majara joo *n* ماجراجو adventurer
madar *n* مادر mom
ma'dar *n* مادر mother
madar bozorg *n* مادربزرگ grandmother
ma'dar-zan *n* مادرزن mother-in-law

madaraneh *adj* مادرانه maternal
ma'dari *n* مادري motherhood
madeh *n* ماده stuff
madeh-parasti *n* مادهپرستي materialism
padehe' tamiz-konandeh *n* ماده تمیزکننده cleanser
maddeh sag *n* مادهسگ bitch
maddehye zede afat *n* مادهضد آفت pesticide
madeh ghazaee *n* مادهغذایي foodstuff
madeye atri *n* مادهعطري aroma
madiyan *n* مادیان mare
mar *n* مار snake
mare bozorg *n* ماربزرگ serpent
marchoubeh *n* مارچوبه asparagus
mars *n* مارس March
mark *n* مارک brand
marmoulak *n* مارمولک lizard
mazad *n* مازاد surplus
mazoo *n* مازو acorn
mazokhism *n* مازوخیسم masochism
masazh *n* ماساژ massage
masazh-dahandeh *n* ماساژدهنده masseur
maseh *n* ماسه sand
mashin *n* ماشین engine
mashin *n* ماشین machine
mashin panbeh pak koni *n* ماشین پنبهپاک کني gin
mashin khoshk koni *n* ماشین خشک کني dryer
mashin-savar *n* ماشین‌سوار motorist

mashine adl bandi *n* ماشین‌عدل بندی stapler

mashine makhloot-kon *n* ماشین مخلوط‌کن blender

mashini kardan *v* ماشینی کردن mechanize

ma ghable tarikhi *adj* ماقبل‌تاریخی prehistoric

mal-e an zan *adj* مال‌آن‌زن her

male an zan *pro* مال‌آن‌زن hers

mal-e an mard *adj* مال‌آن‌مرد his

ma'le' khodeman *pro* مال‌خودمان ours

male shoma *adj* مال‌شما your

male shoma *pro* مال‌شما yours

ma'le' ma' *adj* مال‌ما our

ma'le'man *pro* مال‌من mine

malariya *n* مالاریا malaria

malek *n* مالک landlord

ma'lekiyat *n* مالکیت ownership

maliyat *n* مالیات tax

malikhouliya *n* مالیخولیا melancholy

malidan *v* مالیدن rub

malidan *v* مالیدن scrub

ma'mour *n* مامور officer

ma'moure' edari *n* ماموراداری bureaucrat

ma'emor atash neshani *n* مامور آتش‌نشانی fireman

ma'moure polis *n* مامورپلیس policeman

ma'mouriat *n* ماموریت mission

ma'mouriat *n* ماموریت commission

mandan *v* ماندن settle

mandan *v* ماندن stay

mandan *v* ماندن subsist

mane' *n* مانع barricade

man'e *n* مانع hurdle

man'e *n* مانع impediment

mane'e *n* مانع setback

mane' shodan *v* مانع‌شدن bar

manand kardan *v* مانندکردن liken

manand e ham *adj* مانندهم alike

mah *n* ماه month

mah *n* ماه moon

oktobr *n* ماه‌اکتبر October

mah-e asal *n* ماه‌عسل honeymoon

mahaneh *adv* ماهانه monthly

maher *adj* ماهر proficient

maher *adj* ماهر skillful

maher *adj* ماهر expert

maher *adj* ماهر industrious

maheraneh *adj* ماهرانه tactical

mahvareh *n* ماهواره satellite

mahi-kouli *n* ماهی‌کولی anchovy

mahi gir *n* ماهی‌گیر fisherman

mahi *n* ماهی fish

mahi tabeh *n* ماهی‌تابه pan

mahi tabeh *n* ماهی‌تابه saucepan

mahitabeh *n* ماهی‌تابه frying pan

mahiye ton *n* ماهی‌تون tuna

mahiyane riz *n* ماهیان‌ریز sardine

ma'hicheh *n* ماهیچه muscle

mahiye azad *n* ماهی‌آزاد salmon

ma'vara'e' bahar *adv* ماوراءدریا overseas

maye' *n* مایع liquid

mayamlak *n* مایملک property

mayos kardan *v* مایوس کردن disappoint

mayonez *n* مایونز mayonnaise

mobaheseh *n* مباحثه discourse

mobahesee *adj* اي مباحثه controversial

mobadeleh kardan *v* مبادله کردن swap

mobadeleh kardan *v* مبادله کردن exchange

mobadeleh kardan *v* مبادله کردن interchange

mobadeleh kardan *v* مبادله کردن trade

mobadiye adab *adj* مبادي آداب tactful

mobarezeh talabi *n* مبارزه طلبي defiance

mobarezeh kardan *v* مبارزه کردن combat

mobarak *adj* مبارک blessed

mobtadi *n* مبتدي beginner

mobtazal *adj* مبتذل trivial

mobtazal kardan *v* مبتذل کردن trivialize

motala be maraz ghand *adj* مبتلا به مرض قند diabetic

mabda'e *v* مبدا embark

mabd'a *n* مبدا offspring

mabda'e *n* مبدا era

mabda'e tarikh *n* مبدا تاريخ epoch

mabsout *adj* مبسوط outstretched

mablagh *n* مبلغ amount

mablagh ra bala bordan *v* مبلغ را بالا بردن hike

mobaleghe maz-habi *n* مبلغ مذهبي missionary

mobleh kardan *v* مبله کردن furnish

mobham *adj* مبهم obscure

mobham *adj* مبهم vague

mobham *adj* مبهم ambiguous

mobham *adj* مبهم misty

mabhoot *adj* مبهوت aghast

motarekeh *n* متارکه separation

motarekehe jang *n* متارکه جنگ armistice

mote'ahel *adj* متاهل married

motejavez *adj* متجاوز offensive

motejavez *n* متجاوز aggressor

motehareb *adj* متحارب belligerent

motahed kardan *v* متحد کردن unify

motahed kardan *v* متحد کردن unite

moteharek *adj* متحرک mobile

motehamel shodan *v* متحمل شدن incur

motehaiier sakhtan *v* متحير ساختن amaze

motehayyer kardan *v* متحير کردن astonish

motehaiier konande *adj* متحير کننده amazing

motekhassese elahiyat *n* متخصص الهيات theologian

motekhases bargh *n* متخصص برق electrician

motekhalef *n* متخلف delinquent

motekhalkhel *adj* متخلل porous

metr *n* متر meter

motarakem *adj* متراکم dense

moterakem kardan *v* متراکم کردن compress

moterakem kardan *v* متراکم کردن condense

motarjem *n* مترجم translator

metrow *n* مترو subway
matrok *adj* متروك derelict
matrouk *adj* متروك antiquated
matrook *adj* متروك obsolete
metri *adj* متري metric
moteza'her *adj* متظاهر ostentatious
mote'aseb *adj* متعصب bigot
mote'afen *adj* متعفن putrid
mote'alegh be man *adj* متعلق به من my
mote'ahed kardan *v* متعهد کردن obligate
motefaker *adj* متفكر mindful
moteghabelan *adv* متقابلا mutually
moteghate *adj* متقاطع cross
moteghaed kardan *v* متقاعد کردن convince
moteghaed konandeh *adj* متقاعد کننده convincing
motegha'ed konnandeh *adj* متقاعد کننده cogent
motaka *n* متكا cushion
motaka *n* متكا pillow
motekaberaneh *adv* متكبرانه proudly
motelatem shodan *v* متلاطم شدن (دريا) loom
motemayel *adj* متمايل prone
motemayel-be *adj* متمايل به oriented
motemayel beh khakestari *adj* خاکستري به متمايل grayish
motemaden kardan *v* متمدن کردن civilize

motemarkez kardan *v* متمرکز کردن concentrate
motamem *n* متمم complement
matn *n* متن text
matn-e sinama'ei *n* متن سينمايي scenario
motenaghez *adj* متناقض incoherent
motenaghez *adj* متناقض inconsistent
motenaveb kardan *v* متناوب کردن alternate
mateh zadan *v* مته زدن drill
motaham *n* متهم culprit
mottaham kardan *v* متهم کردن accuse
motevahesh *adj* متوحش startled
motevaset *n* متوسط average
motevaset *adj* متوسط medium
motevasel shodan *v* متوسل شدن resort
motevasel shodan be *v* متوسل شدن به recourse
motevaghef sakhtan *v* متوقف ساختن lay off
matin *adj* متين placid
mesal *adv* مثال as
mosbat *adj* مثبت affirmative
mosbat *adj* مثبت positive
masal *n* مثل proverb
mesl'e mahi *adj* مثل ماهي fishy
mosallas *n* مثلث triangle
mojahed *adj* مجاهد zealous
mojaver *adj* مجاور adjacent
mojaverat *n* مجاورت proximity
mojaverat *n* مجاورت vicinity

majbor bodan *v* مجبوربودن have to

majbour kardan *v* مجبور کردن compel

majzob *adj* مجذوب enchanted

majzoob kardan *v* مجذوب کردن fascinate

majra' *n* مجرا runway

mojarad *n* مجرد single

majrooh *adj* مجروح hurt

majrouh *adj* مجروح sore

majruh kardan *v* مجروح کردن wound

mojri *n* مجري executive

mojaza kardan *v* مجزاکردن isolate

mojasam kardan *v* مجسم کردن portray

mojasam kardan *v* مجسم کردن embody

mojasameh *n* مجسمه image

mojasameh sazi *n* مجسمه‌سازي sculpture

mojaad *adj* مجعد curly

majles *n* مجلس parliament

majlese sena *n* مجلس سنا senate

mojalal *adj* مجلل sumptuous

mojalal *adj* مجلل glorious

mojallal *adj* مجلل grand

majalleh *n* مجله magazine

majnoon *adj* مجنون amok

majnoon *adj* مجنون maniac

mojahaz kardan *v* مجهز کردن equip

moch *n* مچ wrist

mohasebeh *n* محاسبه calculation

mohasereh *n* محاصره siege

mohasereh *n* محاصره blockage

mohasereh kardan *v* محاصره کردن siege

mohasereh kardan *iv* محاصره کردن besiege

mahat dar khoshki *adj* محاط در خشکي landlocked

mohafezat nashodeh *adj* محافظت نشده unprotected

mohafezeh kar *adj* محافظه کار conservative

mohakemeh *n* محاکمه trial

mahbas *n* محبس dungeon

mahboub *adj* محبوب popular

mahboob *v* محبوب beloved

mahbob *adj* محبوب darling

mohtat *adj* محتاط prudent

mohtat *adj* محتاط scrupulous

mohtaregh shodan *v* محترق شدن explode

mohtaram *adj* محترم venerable

mohtamal *adv* محتمل likely

mohtavi *adj* محتوي content

mohtavi boodan *v* محتوي بودن contain

mohtaviat *n* محتويات contents

mohadab *n* محدب crowning

mahdoud kardan *v* محدود کردن confine

mahdod kardan *v* محدود کردن curb

mahdood kardan *v* محدود کردن restrict

mahdoudeh *n* محدوده range

mahdoudiyat *n* محدوديت limitation

moharek *n* محرک driver

moharrek *n* محرک stimulus

mahramaneh *adj* محرمانه confidential

mahramaneh *adj* محرمانه private

mahrom kardan *v* محروم کردن exclude

mahroomiyat *n* محرومیت bereavement

mahzoun *adj* محزون sorrowful

maghzon *adj* محزون despondent

mahsous *adj* محسوس tangible

mashhoud *adj* محسوس sensible

mahsour *adj* محصور closed

mahsol *n* محصول fabric

mahsoul *n* محصول produce

mahsol *n* محصول crop

mahzour *n* محظور obstacle

mahfouz *adj* محفوظ safe

mahfooz az hava *adj* محفوظ از هوا airtight

adj محکم uptight

mohkam *adj* محکم firm

mohkam *adj* محکم secure

mohkam *adj* محکم stable

mohkam *adj* محکم steady

mohkam *adj* محکم tough

mohkam kardan *v* محکم کردن consolidate

mahkoum be fana *adj* محکوم به فنا doomed

mahkoom kardan *v* محکوم کردن condemn

mahkom kardan *v* محکوم کردن convict

mahkoom kardan *v* محکوم کردن sentence

mahalle' etesal *n* محل اتصال joint

mahale' ordou *n* محل اردو campsite

mahalle esterahat *n* محل استراحت lounge

mahale keshti sazi *n* محل کشتی سازی shipyard

mahlool ya bokhar e amoniak *n* محلول یا بخار آمونیاک ammonia

mahmouleh *n* محموله shipment

mahmouleh *n* محموله cargo

mehnat *n* محنت tribulation

mahv *adv* محو blurry

mahv kardan *v* محو کردن fade

mehvar *n* محور axis

mehvar *n* محور axle

mohavateh *n* محوطه compound

mohavateh *n* محوطه yard

mohavatehe' tir foroushi *n* محوطه تیر فروشی lumberyard

mohit *n* محیط surroundings

mohit *n* محیط environment

mohit *n* محیط perimeter

mohite maree *n* محیط مریی contour

makharej *n* مخارج spending

mokhatab *n* مخاطب addressee

mokhalef *adj* مخالف adverse

mokhalef *adj* مخالف contrary

mokhalefat kardan *v* مخالف کردن antagonize

mokhalef *n* مخالفت disagreement

mokhalefat *n* مخالفت objection

mokhalefat nakardan *v* مخالفت نکردن indulge

mokhtasar *n* مختصر briefs

mokhtasar *adj* مختصر concise

mokhtasar kardan *v* مختصرکردن shorten

mokhtal kardan *v* مختل کردن disturb

mokhader *n* مخدر narcotic

mokhreb *n* مخرب destroyer

makhraj *n* مخرج exit

makhrobeh *adj* مخروبه dilapidated

makhroot *n* مخروط cone

makhzan *n* مخزن reservoir

makhzan *n* مخزن bunker

makhzan *n* مخزن tank

makhzan *n* مخزن warehouse

makhsous *adj* مخصوص particular

makhsus *adj* مخصوص special

makhsousan *adv* مخصوصا chiefly

mokhafaf *n* مخفف initials

makhfi *adj* مخفي clandestine

makhfi *adj* مخفي invisible

makhfi kardan *v* مخفی کردن camouflage

makhloot *n* مخلوط mix

mokhammer *n* مخمر yeast

makhof *adj* مخوف gruesome

makhoof *adj* مخوف horrible

mokhi *adj* مخي cerebral

mode rouz *adj* مدروز trendy

mod zodgozar *n* مدزودگذر fad

medad *n* مداد pencil

medad pak kon *n* مدادپاک کن eraser

medadtarash *n* مدادتراش sharpener

medad rangiye momi *n* مدادرنگي مومي crayon

madar *n* مدار circuit

mada'r *n* مدار orbit

modafe *n* مدافع defender

modafe *n* مدافع defendant

medal-e bozorg *n* مدال بزرگ medallion

modavem *adj* مداوم ongoing

modat *n* مدت duration

moddat *n* مدت term

madkhal *n* مدخل entrance

madreseh *n* مدرسه school

madresehye oloome dini *n* مدرسه علوم ديني seminary

madrak *n* مدرک document

modaee *n* مدعي plaintiff

modir *n* مدير manager

modir *n* مدير director

madinehye fazeleh *n* مدينه فاضله utopia

madion *n* مديون debtor

madyoun boudan *v* مديون بودن owe

mozakerat parlemani *n* مذاکرات پارلماني debate

mozakereh kardan *v* مذاکره کردن negotiate

mozakar *n* مذکر male

mozakar *adj* مذکر masculine

mazhab *n* مذهب religion

mazhabi *adj* مذهبي religious

moraje'at kardan *v* مراجعت کردن return

moraje'eh *n* مراجعه recourse

marasem *n* مراسم rite

maraseme' ta'mid n مراسم‌تعميد christening

marasem dafn n مراسم‌دفن funeral

morafeh n مرافعه lawsuit

moragheb n مراقب onlooker

moragheb boudan v مراقب‌بودن mind

moragheb boudan v مراقب‌بودن look after

moraghebat kardan v مراقبت کردن watch

morabba n مربا marmalade

moraba n مربا jam

moraba'e adj مربع square

marbout boodan be v مربوط‌بودن به concern

marbouteh adj مربوطه respective

morabi n مربی trainer

moratab adj مرتب tidy

moratab kardan v مرتب کردن dispose

moratab kardan iv مرتب کردن set

morataban adv مرتبا "regularly

mortaesh adj مرتعش vibrant

mortakebe zanaye be onf n مرتکب‌زنای‌به‌عنف rapist

mortakeb shodan v مرتکب‌شدن perpetrate

marhaleh n مرحله stage

marhaleh n مرحله process

morakhasi gereftan n مرخصی گرفتن vacation

mard n مرد fellow

marde' bi-zan n مردبی‌زن bachelor

marde chand zaneh adj مردچند زنه polygamist

mard-e divaneh n مردديوانه madman

marde' roohani n مردروحانی clergy

marde zan mordeh n مردزن‌مرده widower

mordab n مرداب lagoon

mordab n مرداب swamp

mordab n مرداب quagmire

mardan n مردان men

mardanegi n مردانگی manliness

mardaneh pro مردانه his

mardaneh adj مردانه virile

moradad adj مردد undecided

mardom n مردم people

mardom n مردم folk

mardom n مردم population

mordan v مردن die

mordan v مردن pass out

mordan v مردن perish

mordani adj مردنی dying

mordeh adj مرده deceased

mordeh adj مرده dead

mordeh adj مرده lifeless

morde'shoye-khaneh n مرده‌شوي‌خانه mortuary

mardood n مردود castaway

mardood sazi n مردودسازي rejection

mardi n مردي virility

mardi ke poshte bar kar mikonad n مردي که‌پشت‌بار کار کند مي barman

marz n مرز confines

marz n مرز boundary

marz n مرز frontier

maraz *n* مرض illness

maraze romatism *n* مرض رماتیسم rheumatism

maraze sel *n* مرض سل tuberculosis

martoub *n* مرطوب humid

martoub *adj* مرطوب wet

martoub shodan *v* مرطوب شدن moisten

morgh *n* مرغ hen

morghe daryaye *n* مرغ دریایی sea gull

morghe mahi khar *n* مرغ ماهیخوار pelican

morgh va khorus *n* مرغ و خروس poultry

morfin *n* مرفین morphine

morakab *n* مرکب ink

morakkab boudan az *v* مرکب بودن از consist

markaz *n* مرکز center

markaze bazarganiye omdeh *n* مرکز بازرگانی عمده staple

markaze shahr *n* مرکز شهر downtown

markaz-e farmandehi *n* مرکز فرماندهی headquarters

markazi *adj* مرکزی central

marg *n* مرگ death

marg-o-mir *n* مرگ و میر mortality

marg o mir *n* مرگ و میر death toll

maramat kardan *v* مرمت کردن reclaim

marmar *n* مرمر marble

marmooz *adj* مرموز mysterious

marham *n* مرهم balm

marhoon *adj* مرهون obliged

marhoon sakhtan *v* مرهون ساختن oblige

morvarid *n* مروارید pearl

moror kardan *v* مرور کردن go through

morourgar *n* مرورگر browser

meri *n* مری esophagus

merrikh *n* مریخ Mars

mariz shodan *v* مریض شدن sicken

mazaj *n* مزاج temper

mezah *n* مزاح prank

mezah *n* مزاح wit

mozahem *adj* مزاحم infested

mozayedeh *n* مزایده bid

mozakhraf *n* مزخرف nonsense

mozd *n* مزد pension

mozd *n* مزد wage

mozd *n* مزد fee

mozd *n* مزد reward

mazraeh *n* مزرعه farm

mazra'eh *n* مزرعه ranch

mazraeh shokhm zadeh *n* مزرعه شخم زده furrow

maz mazeh *n* مزمزه sip

mazeh *n* مزه taste

mazeh *n* مزه zest

mazeh kardan *v* مزه کردن savor

mazeh va boo *n* مزه و بو flavor

mozayan *v* مزین ornate

mozheh *n* مژه eyelash

mes *n* مس copper

masaleh ghamez *n* مسئله غامض dilemma

mas'oul *adj* مسئول liable

mas'oul *adj* مسئول responsible

mas'ouliyat *n* مسئولیت liability

mosabegheh *n* مسابقه competition

mosabegheh *n* مسابقه race

mosabegheh *n* مسابقه tournament

mosabeghe'ei *adj* مسابقه‌ای competitive

mosabegheh dadan *v* مسابقه‌دادن race

masahat *n* مساحت area

mosaed *adj* مساعد favorable

mosafer *n* مسافر pilgrim

mosafer *n* مسافر traveler

mosaferati *n* مسافر passenger

mosafer *n* مسافر voyager

mosafere maghreb *adv* مسافر مغرب westbound

mosafer khaneh *n* مسافرخانه inn

mosavat *n* مساوات equality

mast adl مست drunk

mast *adj* مست intoxicated

mast *adj* مست loaded

mostajer *n* مستاجر tenant

mostahagh *adj* مستحق deserving

mostahkam *adj* مستحکم entrenched

mostahkam kardan *v* مستحکم کردن fortify

mostarah *n* مستراح rest room

mostarah *n* مستراح toilet

mostatil *adj* مستطیل rectangular

mosta'ed *adj* مستعد predisposed

mosta'merati *adj* مستعمراتي colonial

mosta'mereh *n* مستعمره colony

mosta'mereh kardan *v* مستعمره کردن colonize

mostaghim *adj* مستقیم direct

mostalzem bodan *v* مستلزم‌بودن entail

mostame' *n* مستمع listener

mostanad *n* مستند documentary

masti *n* مستي drunkenness

masjed *n* مسجد mosque

maskh shodeh *adj* مسخ‌شده petrified

masdoud kardan *v* مسدودکردن obstruct

masroor *adj* مسرور vivacious

maskan *n* مسکن quarters

maskoni *adj* مسکوني habitable

mosallah kardan *adj* مسلح armed

mosallah kardan *v* مسلح کردن arm

mosalsal *n* مسلسل machine gun

mosalat boudan *v* مسلط‌بودن predominate

mosalma'n *n* مسلمان Muslim

masmoum kardan *v* مسموم‌کردن poison

masmoumiyat *n* مسمومیت poisoning

mesvak zadan *v* مسواک‌زدن brush

masih-e mowoud *n* مسیح‌موعود Messiah

masihi *adj* مسیحي Christian

masihiyat *n* مسیحیت Christianity

masir *n* مسیر path

masir *n* مسیر route

moshajereh *n* مشاجره contest

mosharekat *n* مشارکت partnership

mosharekat *n* مشارکت communion

moshahedeh kardan *v* مشاهده کردن observe

moshaver *n* مشاور counselor

moshavereh *n* مشاوره conference

moshavereh *n* مشاوره consultation

mosht *n* مشت fist

mosht *n* مشت knock

mosht zadan bar *v* مشت زدن بر punch

moshtzan *n* مشت زن boxer

moshtzani *n* مشت زنی boxing

moshtagh *adj* مشتاق eager

moshtagh *adv* مشتاق willfully

moshtarak *adj* مشترک common

moshtari *n* مشتری customer

moshakhas *adj* مشخص distinctive

moshakhas kardan *v* مشخص کردن specify

moshref boudan *v* مشرف بودن overlook

moshrek *adj* مشرک pagan

mashroob *n* مشروب beverage

mashroob *n* مشروب liquor

mashroob-e alkoli *n* مشروب الکلی booze

mash'al *n* مشعل torch

mashghoul *adj* مشغول busy

mashgh *n* مشق homework

masheghat bar *adj* مشقت بار excruciating

moshkel *n* مشکل difficult

moshkel *n* مشکل problem

mashkouk *adl* مشکوک doubtful

mashkouk *adj* مشکوک questionable

mashkook *adj* مشکوک skeptic

mashhor *adj* مشهور famous

mashverat kardan *v* مشورت کردن confer

masa'f dadan *v* مصاف دادن oppose

mosaleheh *adj* مصالحه conciliatory

mosaleheh *n* مصالحه compromise

mosaleheh kardan *v* مصالحه کردن compromise

masraf *n* مصرف consumption

masraf kardan *v* مصرف کردن consume

masraf kardan *v* مصرف کردن use

masraf konandeh *n* مصرف کننده consumer

maslehat gerai *adj* مصلحت گرای pragmatist

masnoo' *n* مصنوع artifact

masno-e dast *adj* مصنوع دست handmade

masoon *adj* مصون immune

masoniat *n* مصونیت immunity

masoniat dar kardan *v* مصونیت دار کردن immunize

mosibat *n* مصیبت tragedy

mosibat amiz *adj* مصیبت آمیز disastrous

moza'af *adj* مضاعف multiple

mozhek *adj* مضحک ridiculous

mozer *adj* مضر obnoxious

mozer *adj* مضر harmful

moztareb kardan *v* مضطرب کردن distress

motabeghe *pre* مطابق according to

motabeghe ketabe moghadas adj مطابق کتاب مقدس biblical

motabeghe marsoom adj مطابق مرسوم orthodox

motalebeh kardan v مطالبه کردن demand

motale'eh kardan v مطالعه کردن study

matbo'at n مطبوعات press

matbou'eiyat n مطبوعیت amenities

matrood adj مطرود outcast

matlabi ra hazf kardan v مطلبی را حذف کردن slur

motlagh adj مطلق absolute

motlagh adj مطلق sovereign

matlob adj مطلوب favorite

motma'en adj مطمئن confident

motmaen sakhtan v مطمئن ساختن ensure

moti'e adj مطیع submissive

moti'e kardan v مطیع کردن subject

maznoon adj مظنون suspect

moadeleh n معادله equation

moarefi adj معارفی educational

mo'af adj معاف exempt

moameleh kardan iv معامله کردن deal

moavezeh n معاوضه swap

mo'tad adj معتاد addict

mo'etad adj معتاد habitual

mo'tabar adj معتبر valid

moetabar adj معتبر credible

mo'tarez shodan v معترض شدن molest

mo'ejezeh n معجزه miracle

mo'ejeze asa adj معجزه آسا miraculous

ma'dan n معدن mine

me'edeh n معده stomach

ma'edod adj معدود few

ma'edom adj معدوم extinct

ma'doom kardan v معدوم کردن obliterate

me'edi adj معدی gastric

moazzab kardan v معذب کردن traumatize

m'azor dashtan v معذور داشتن excuse

moarefi kardan v معرفی کردن introduce

ma'shougheh n معشوقه mistress

ma'esom adj معصوم immaculate

mo'attel adj معطل stranded

ma'atouf be gozashteh adj معطوف به گذشته retroactive

ma'aghoul adj معقول reasonable

mo'allagh n معلق midair

mo'alagh adj معلق pending

moallagh n معلق suspense

moallem n معلم teacher

mo'alemi kardan v معلمی کردن coach

ma'eloom kardan v معلوم کردن manifest

ma'loom kardan v معلوم کردن ascertain

me'mar n معمار architect

me'mari n معماری architecture

ma'moulan adv معمولا normally

ma'moulan adv "معمولا" ordinarily

ma'mouli adj معمولی normal

ma'mouli adj معمولی ordinary

ma'eni *n* معنى innuendo
ma'ni *n* معنى meaning
moein *adj* معين certain
moayan *adj* معين definite
moein *n* معين ledger
moayan kardan *v* معين کردن define
ma'eyob *adj* معيوب faulty
ma'youb kardan *v* معيوب کردن maim
maghazeh *n* مغازه shop
maghazeh *n* مغازه store
moghazi *adj* مغذي nutritious
maghreb *n* مغرب sunset
maghreb *n* مغرب west
maghrour *adj* مغرور proud
maghror *adj* مغرور haughty
maghz *n* مغز marrow
maghz *n* مغز brain
maghz va darone har chizi *n* مغز و درون هرچيزي core
maghzi *adj* مغزي mental
maghshoush *adj* مغشوش mixed-up
maghshoosh *adj* مغشوش شدن confusing
maghloub sakhtan *v* مغلوب ساختن vanquish
moft-khor *n* مفت خور bum
mofrat *adj* مفرط excessive
mefragh *n* مفرغ bronze
mafrozat *n* مفروضات data
mafghoud *adj* مفقود missing
mofhoum *n* مفهوم concept
mofid *adj* مفيد profitable
mofid *adj* مفيد helpful

mofid *adj* مفيد useful
moghabeleh *n* مقابله check
moghabeleh kardan *v* مقابله کردن check
maghaleh *n* مقاله essay
maghaleh-nevis *n* مقاله نويس columnist
magham *n* مقام pew
moghavemat *n* مقاومت resistance
moghavemat kardan ba *v* مقاومت کردن با withstand
moghayeseh *n* مقايسه comparison
moghayeseh kardan *v* مقايسه کردن compare
moghtader *adj* مقتدر mighty
moghtader *adj* مقتدر powerful
moghtazi *adj* مقتضي expedient
meghdar *n* مقدار quantity
meghdar *n* مقدار deal
meghdare' tajviz-shodeh daroo *n* مقدار تجويز شده دارو dosage
moghaddas *adj* مقدس sacred
moghadas *adj* مقدس holy
moghadam *adj* مقدم first
moghadam *adj* مقدم premier
moghadam boudan *v* مقدم بودن precede
moghadamat *n* مقدمات premises
moghadamati *adj* مقدماتي preliminary
moghadameh *n* مقدمه prelude
moghadameh *adv* مقدمه primarily
mogharar da'shtan *v* مقرر داشتن award
mogharar dashtan *v* مقرر داشتن resolve

maghsad *n* مقصد destination

maghsad *n* مقصد goal

moghaser danestan *v* مقصردانستن blame

maghta'e *n* مقطع segment

megh'ad *n* مقعد colon

megh'ad *n* مقعد rectum

moghananeh *n* مقننه legislature

moghava *n* مقوا cardboard

moghavvi *n* مقوى tonic

meghyas *n* مقياس scale

meghyas gozashtan *v* مقياس گذاشتن scale

moghim *n* مقيم settler

moghim *n* مقيم inmate

mokashefeh *n* مكاشفه apocalypse

makan *n* مكان place

makan *n* مكان site

makanyabi kardan *v* مكان‌يابي كردن locate

mekanik *n* مكانيك mechanic

mekaniki *n* مكانيكي mechanism

maktab e kalbion *n* مكتب كلبيون cynicism

maks kardan *v* مكث كردن halt

makrooh *adj* مكروه abominable

mokaab *n* مكعب cube

makandeh *adj* مكنده sucker

makidan *v* مكيدن suck

magar *c* مگر unless

malahat *n* ملاحت sweetness

molahezeh kardan *v* ملاحظه كردن notice

molahezeh kardan *v* ملاحظه كردن regard

molaghat-e rasmi *n* ملاقات‌رسمي audience

malalat *n* ملالت boredom

malalat avar *adj* ملالت‌آور tedious

malamat kardan *v* ملامت كردن rebuke

molayem *adj* ملايم bland

molayem *adj* ملايم mild

molayemat *n* ملايمت gentleness

molayemat *n* ملايمت softness

mellat *n* ملت nation

molhagh kardan *v* ملحق كردن join

malakh *n* ملخ grasshopper

melk *n* ملك estate

malakeh *n* ملكه queen

melli *adj* ملي national

melli kardan *v* ملي كردن nationalize

melliyat *n* مليت nationality

momas *n* مماس tangent

momane'at *n* ممانعت prevention

moman'eat kardan *v* ممانعت كردن stall

momtad *adj* ممتد protracted

momken *adj* ممكن possible

mamlekat *n* مملكت realm

mamno'e *adj* ممنوع illicit

mamnoo'e kardan *v* ممنوع كردن outlaw

menmenkardan *v* من‌من كردن mumble

men men kardan *v* من‌من كردن stammer

monadi *n* منادي precursor

monaseb *adj* مناسب relevant

monaseb *adj* مناسب suitable

monaseb *adj* مناسب adequate

monaseb *adj* مناسب fitting

monasebat *n* مناسبت fitness

monazereh kardan *v* مناظره کردن debate

manba *n* منبع fountain

montaj kardan *v* منتج کردنderive

montasher kardan *v* منتشر کردن broadcast

montazer *n* منتظر waiter

montazer boudan *v* منتظر بودن await

monajjem *n* منجم astrologer

monharef *adj* منحرف perverse

monharef *adj* منحرف pervert

monharef kardan *v* منحرف کردن call off

monzajer konandeh *adj* منزجر کننده disgusting

manzel *n* منزل lodging

monzavi *adj* منزوی secluded

monsajem *adj* منسجم coherent

mansoukh *adj* منسوخ outdated

manesh *n* منش character

mansha'e *n* منشا origin

manshour *n* منشور prism

monshi *n* منشی clerk

monsaref kardan *v* منصرف کردن dissuade

monsef *n* منصف author

mantegh *n* منطق logic

manteghan *adv* منطقا" logically

mantaghehee *adj* منطقهای regional

mantaghehe naftkhiz *n* منطقه نفتخیز oilfield

manteghi *adj* منطقی logical

manteghi kardan *v* منطقی کردن rationalize

manzareh *n* منظره panorama

manzareh *n* منظره scene

manzour *n* منظور purpose

manzoomeh *n* منظومه poem

man'e *n* منع rebuff

man'e kardan *v* منع کردن inhibit

mon'akes shodani *adj* منعکس شدنی resounding

monfajer shavandeh *adj* منفجر شونده explosive

monfajer kardan *iv* منفجر کردن blow up

manfaz *n* منفذ pore

monfared *adj* منفرد singular

monfasel kardan *v* منفصل کردن disconnect

manfa'at *n* منفعت benefit

manfeat bordan *v* منفعت بردن profit

manfoor *adj* منفور hateful

manfi *adj* منفی negative

menghar *n* منقار beak

monghate' kardan *v* منقطع کردن disrupt

monkere' khoda *n* منکر خدا atheist

monker shodan *v* منکر شدن repudiate

manganeh *n* منگنه paper clip

menenzhit *n* مننژیت meningitis

menha *adj* منها minus

mei *n* مه May

meh *n* مه fog

meh alood *adj* مهآلود foggy

meh dar *adj* مهدار hazy

meh-e kam *n* مهکم haze

mohajer *n* مهاجر migrant

mohajer *n* مهاجر refugee

mohajer *n* مهاجر emigrant

mohajer *n* مهاجر immigrant

mohajerat *n* مهاجرت immigration

mohajerat kardan *v* مهاجرت کردن emigrate

mohajerat kardan *v* مهاجرت کردن migrate

mohajerat kardan *v* مهاجرت کردن(به کشور دیگر) immigrate

mahar kardan *v* مهار کردن restrain

maharat *n* مهارت skill

mohr *n* مهر seal

mehr *n* مهر love

mohr *n* مهر stamp

mohre batelehye tamre *n* مهر باطله تمبر postmark

mohr zadan *v* مهر زدن stamp

mohromoum kardan *v* مهر و موم کردن seal off

mehraban *adj* مهربان affable

mehraban *adj* مهربان affectionate

mehraban *adj* مهربان benign

mehrabani *adj* مهربان kind

mehrabany *n* مهربانی affection

mehrabani *n* مهربانی kindness

mohreh *n* مهره vertebra

mohlat *n* مهلت respite

mohlek *adj* مهلک deadly

mohem *adj* مهم fateful

mohemat *n* مهمات exploitation

mohemmat *n* مهمات ammunition

mohemma't *n* مهمات munitions

mehman *n* مهمان visitor

mehman *n* مهمان guest

mehman-navazi *n* مهمان نوازی hospitality

mehmankhaneh *n* مهمانخانه motel

mehmandare havapeyma *n* مهماندار هواپیما stewardess

mehmani *n* مهمانی banquet

mehmani *n* مهمانی feast

mehmani *n* مهمانی party

mohemtar boudan-az *v* مهمتر بودن از outweigh

mahmel *n* مهمل rot

mohmal *adj* مهمل trashy

mahmiz zadan *v* مهمیز زدن spur

mohandes *n* مهندس engineer

mahib *adj* مهیب grisly

mohayyej *adj* مهیج breathtaking

mohayej *adj* مهیج exciting

moo *n* مو hair

movajeh shodan *iv* مواجه شدن meet

movazeneh *n* موازنه equilibrium

movazi *n* موازی parallel

movazeb *adj* مواظب attentive

movazeb boudan *v* مواظب بودن look out

movafegh *adj* موافق amicable

movafeghat kardan *v* موافقت کردن comply

movafeghat kardan *v* موافقت کردن concur

motor *n* موتور motor

motorsiklet *n* موتورسیکلت motorcycle

mo'aser *adj* موثر effective

moasser *adj* موثر impressive

mowj *n* موج wave

mouj bazi kardan *v* موج‌بازی کردن surf

mowjebshavandeh *adj* موجب شونده conducive

mojez *adj* موجز terse

mojod dar siyah rag *adj* موجود در سیاهرگ intravenous

moo chin *n* موچین tweezers

mouhesh *adj* موحش shocking

mor mor konandeh *adj* مورمور کننده creepy

movarab *adj* مورب oblique

moorche *n* مورچه ant

movarekh *adj* مورخ dated

mourede pasande ammeh *v* مورد پسندعامه popularize

morede shak *adj* موردشک dubious

mourede tavajoh gharar nagerefteh *adj* موردتوجه قرارنگرفته unnoticed

mooriyaneh *n* موریانه termite

mowz *n* موز banana

mouzaeik *n* موزائیک mosaic

moozeh *n* موزه museum

moozik *n* موزیک music

moosikal *adj* موزیکال musical

moases *n* موسس founder

moosh *n* موش mouse

moushe sahraee *n* موش‌صحرایی rat

moushak *n* موشک missile

moushak *n* موشک rocket

moushha *n* موشها mice

mowzou *n* موضوع subject

mowzoo *n* موضوع theme

mowzoo *n* موضوع topic

mowezeh kardan *v* موعظه کردن preach

movafagh shodan *v* موفق‌شدن succeed

movafaghiyat *n* موفقیت success

movaghati *adj* موقتی temporary

movaghar budan *v* موقربودن sedate

mowghe'eiyat *n* موقعیت occasion

movakel *n* موکل client

moukool kardan *v* موکول‌کردن relegate

movaled *n* مولد generator

moulkool *n* مولکول molecule

moom *n* موم wax

moumiya *n* مومیا mummy

momiyae'e kardan *v* مومیایی‌کردن embalm

mohen *adj* موهن derogatory

moohen *adj* موهن obscene

miyanji *n* میانجي intermediary

miyanji *n* میانجي mediator

miyanhaal *adj* میانحال mediocre

miyangin *n* میانگین mediocrity

mey khaneh *n* میخانه tavern

mikhak-e sad-par *n* میخک‌صدپر carnation

meikharegi *n* میخوارگي alcoholism

meydan *n* میدان field

meydane min *n* میدان‌مین minefield

miras *n* میراث heritage

miras *n* میراث patrimony

miz *n* میز table

miz tahrir *n* ميزتحرير desk

mize farman *n* ميزفرمان pulpit

mizan kardan *v* ميزان‌کردن regulate

mizan kardan *v* ميزان‌کردن tune

mizbani *n* ميزبانی host

mikrob *n* ميکرب microbe

mikrobi *adj* ميکربی biological

mikrob *n* ميکروب germ

mikrofon *n* ميکروفن microphone

mikeowave *n* ميکروويو microwave

migren *n* ميگرن migraine

meygoo *n* ميگو shrimp

meygoo *n* ميگو prawn

meyl *n* ميل urgency

mill *n* ميل(متر) mile

meyl be tamalok e chizi kardan *v* ميل‌به‌تملک‌چيزی‌کردن covet

mail dashtan *v* ميل‌داشتن desire

milleh *n* ميله bar

mileh *n* ميله rod

million *n* ميليون million

millioner *adj* ميليونر millionaire

meymoun *n* ميمون chimpanzee

meymoon *n* ميمون ape

meymoon *n* ميمون monkey

min-gozar *n* مين‌گذار miner

mihan parast *n* ميهن‌پرست patriot

mihan parastaneh *adj* ميهن‌پرستانه patriotic

miveh *n* ميوه fruit

miveh dar *adj* ميوه‌دار fruitful

miyan bor *n* ميانبر shortcut

meykhareh *adj* ميخواره alcoholic

meydan *n* ميدان square

miliyarder *n* ميلياردر billionaire

miniyator *n* مينياتور miniature

na ashena *adj* ناآشنا unfamiliar

na mahboub *adj* نامحبوب unpopular

na'el shodani *adj* نائل‌شدني attainable

na amn *adj* ناامن unsafe

na amni *n* ناامني insecurity

na arami *n* ناآرامي unrest

nabalegh *adj* نابالغ immature

na bekhrad *adj* نابخرد unreasonable

nabekhradi *n* نابخردي folly

na barabar *adj* نابرابر unequal

na barabari *n* نابرابري inequality

nabaradari *n* نابرادري stepbrother

na bordbari *n* نابردباري intolerance

nabegheh *n* نابغه genius

nabegheh *n* نابغه wizard

na be hanjari *n* نابه‌هنجاري abnormality

na be hengam *adj* نابهنگام untimely

nabood shodani *adj* نابودشدني perishable

nabood kardan *v* نابودکردن annihilate

naboodi *n* نابودي annihilation

na pak *adj* ناپاک foul

na paydar *adj* ناپايدار precarious

na pedari *n* ناپدري stepfather

napadid shodan *v* ناپدیدشدن disappear

na padid shodan *v* ناپدیدشدن vanish

na parhizkari *n* ناپرهیزکاري incontinence

na pesari *n* ناپسري stepson

napasand shemordan *v* ناپسند شمردن disapprove

natamam *adj* ناتمام incomplete

natavani *adj* ناتوان disable

natavani *n* ناتواني disability

na tavani *n* ناتواني inability

najour *adj* ناجور misfit

naji *n* ناجي savior

na char *adj* ناچار inevitable

nachiz *adj* ناچیز insignificant

na chiz *n* ناچیز trivia

na hagh *adj* ناحق unjustified

nahiyehee *adj* ناحیه‌اي parochial

na khales *adj* ناخالص impure

nakhon *n* ناخن fingernail

nakhon *n* ناخن nail

nakhone angoshte pa *n* ناخن انگشت پا toenail

na khana *adj* ناخوانا illegible

na khahari *n* ناخواهري stepsister

na khosh *adj* ناخوش ailing

na khoush *adj* ناخوش ill

nakhoshnood *adj* ناخوشنود disgruntled

nakhoshi *n* ناخوشي disease

nadan *adj* نادان unwise

nadan *adj* نادان fool

nadan *adj* نادان silly

nadani *n* ناداني foolishness

na dokhtari *n* نادختري stepdaughter

nader *adj* نادر rare

nadorost *adj* نادرست dishonest

nadorost *adj* نادرست erroneous

na dourost *adj* نادرست incorrect

nadem *adj* نادم remorseful

nadideh gereftan *v* نادیده گرفتن disregard

narahati *n* ناراحتى uneasiness

narahati *n* ناراحتي discomfort

narast *adj* ناراست crooked

narazi *adj* ناراضي dissatisfied

narasa *adj* نارسا insufficient

narasi *n* نارسي immaturity

nargil *n* نارگیل coconut

narenjak *n* نارنجک grenade

narengi *n* نارنگي tangerine

naro zadan *v* نارو زدن double-cross

na rava *adj* ناروا inadmissible

narvan ghermez *n* ناروون قرمز elm

naza *adj* نازا barren

naza kardan *v* نازا کردن sterilize

nazok *adj* نازک thin

nazouk *adj* نازک fine

nazouk *adj* نازک frail

nazok *adj* نازک slim

nazok *adj* نازک tenuous

nazok narenji *adj* نازک نارنجي touchy

na'zanin *adj* نازنین nice

nasazegari *n* ناسازگاري discord

na salem *adj* ناسالم unhealthy

nasepas *adj* ناسپاس disloyal

na sepas *adj* ناسپاس ungrateful

nasepasi *n* ناسپاسي ingratitude

na sezavar *adj* ناسزاوار abusive

nashayesteh *adj* ناشايسته improper

na shayesteh *adj* ناشايسته unfit

nashta va nahar ba ham *n* ناشتاو ناهارباهم brunch

nasher *n* ناشر publisher

nashenas *adj* ناشناس strange

na shenas *adj* ناشناس unknown

nashi shodan *v* ناشي‌شدن emanate

na'zer *n* ناظر onlooker

nazer *n* ناظر bailiff

nazer *n* ناظر butler

nazer *n* ناظر spectator

na'f *n* ناف navel

nafarman *adj* نافرمان disobedient

nafarmani kardan *v* نافرماني‌كردن disobey

naghabel sakhtan *v* ناقابل‌ساختن incapacitate

naghes *adj* ناقص rudimentary

naghola *adj* ناقلا sly

naghola *adj* ناقلا clever

na kafi *adj* ناكافي inadequate

na kam *adj* ناكام unhappy

na goftani *adj* ناگفتني unspeakable

nagah *adv* ناگهان suddenly

nagahani *n* ناگهاني spontaneity

nagahani *adj* ناگهاني sudden

nagoya *adj* ناگويا irrational

naleh *n* ناله groan

naleh kardan *v* ناله‌كردن groan

nalidan *v* ناليدن whine

namgozari kardan *v* نام‌گذاري كردن(هنگام‌تعميد) christen

nam nevisi *n* نام‌نويسي enrollment

nam nevisi kardan *v* نام‌نويسي كردن enlist

nam nevisi kardan *v* نام‌نويسي كردن enroll

na'mnevisi kardan *v* نام‌نويسي كردن matriculate

na madari *n* نامادري stepmother

na mahdood *adj* نامحدود unlimited

na mahdood *adv* نامحدود indefinite

namdar *adj* نامدار renowned

namarbot *adj* نامربوط irrelevant

namard *adj* نامرد coward

namzad *n* نامزد(مرد) fiancé

namzad kardan *v* نامزدكردن designate

namzadi *n* نامزدي engagement

na mosaed *adj* نامساعد unfavorable

na mashro'e *adj* نامشروع illegal

na mashrou *adj* نامشروع unlawful

na matbou *adj* نامطبوع unpleasant

na matloob *adj* نامطلوب undesirable

na motmaen *adj* نامطمئن unreliable

na ma'aloom *adj* نامعلوم uncertain

na monaseb *adj* نامناسب timeless

na monaseb *adj* نامناسب unsuitable

nameh *n* نامه epistle

namehrasan *n* نامه‌رسان mailman

nameh resan *n* نامه‌رسان postman

nan *n* نان bread

nan bereshteh kon *n* نان‌برشته‌کن toaster

nanva *n* نانوا baker

nanva'ei *n* نانوايي bakery

nahar *adj* ناهار lunch

nahar khordan *v* ناهارخوردن dine

naham ray bodan *v* ناهم‌رای‌بودن disagree

na-hamvar *adj* ناهموار bumpy

nahamvar *adj* ناهموار ragged

na hamvar *adj* ناهموار uneven

na vabasteh *adj* ناوابسته unattached

navgan *n* ناوگان fleet

nay *n* ناي windpipe

naylon *n* نايلون nylon

nabarde nav *n* نبردناو battleship

naboudan *v* نبودن lack

nobogh *n* نبوغ genuine

napaziroftan *v* نپذيرفتن repel

napaziroftan *v* نپذيرفتن reject

natijeh *n* نتيجه outcome

natijeh *n* نتيجه result

natijeh bakhsh *adj* بخش نتيجه consequent

natijehe ma'koos *v* نتيجه‌معکوس backfire

nasr *n* نثر prose

nejat *n* نجات liberation

nejat dadan *v* نجات‌دادن save

najes *adj* نجس untouchable

najva *n* نجوا whisper

najva kardan *v* نجواکردن whisper

nojoumi *adj* نجومي astronomical

najib *adj* نجيب gentle

najibzadeh *adj* نجيب‌زاده aristocrat

nakh *n* نخ string

nakh *n* نخ thread

nokhostin *adj* نخستين prior

nakhostin *adj* نخستين initial

nakhl *n* نخل palm

nokhod *n* نخود gram

nokhod farangi *n* نخودفرنگي pea

nadashtan *v* نداشتن miss

nedamat *n* ندامت repentance

nadimehe aroos *n* نديمه‌عروس bridesmaid

nerkh *n* نرخ rate

nardeban *n* نردبان ladder

nardebane moteharek *n* نردبان متحرک stepladder

narm *adj* نرم tender

narm *adj* نرم soft

narm kardan *v* نرم‌کردن pulverize

narm kardan *v* نرم‌کردن mellow

narm kardan *v* نرم‌کردن soften

narmi *n* نرمي leniency

narreh-khar *n* نره‌خر oxen

neza'e *n* نزاع scuffle

nezakat *n* نزاکت tact

nazdik *adj* نزديک adjoining

nazdik *adj* نزديک forthcoming

nazdikbin *adj* نزديک‌بين myopic

nazdikbin *adj* نزديک‌بين nearsighted

nazdik shodan *v* نزديک‌شدن approach

nazdik shodani adj نزدیک‌شدني
approachable

nazdiki n نزدیکي affinity

nazdik pre نزدیک near

nazdik be pre نزدیک‌به close to

nezhad parast adj نژادپرست racist

nezhad parasti n نژادپرستي racism

nasab n نسب descent

nesbat n نسبت proportion

nesbat dadan v نسبت‌دادن
attribute

nesbi adj نسبی relative

noskheh bardari n نسخه‌برداري
duplication

nasl n نسل descendant

nasnas n نسناس gorilla

nesyan n نسیان lapse

nesyan n نسیان oblivion

nasheh n نشئه trance

nash'e shodeh adj نشئه‌شده
ecstatic

nesh kardan v نشاکردن transplant

neshan n نشان medal

neshan n نشان score

neshan n نشان sign

neshan n نشان badge

neshan n نشان emblem

neshan dadan v نشان‌دادن indicate

neshan dadan iv نشان‌دادن show

neshan-e setareh n نشان‌ستاره
asterisk

neshan kardan v نشان‌کردن
earmark

neshane naghle ghowl n نشان‌نقل
قول quote

neshaneh n نشانه token

neshaneh gereftan v نشانه‌گرفتن
aim

neshanehgir n نشانه‌گیر
marksman

neshanvand n نشانوند argument

neshani n نشانی address

nashr n نشر publication

neshastan iv نشستن sit

nasb kardan v نصب‌کردن set up

nasihat kardan v نصیحت‌کردن
admonish

nasihat kardan v نصیحت‌کردن
exhort

notfeh n نطفه sperm

nezarat n نظارت surveillance

nezamnameh n نظامنامه code

nezamnameh n نظامنامه manual

nazar n نظر opinion

nazariyeh n نظریه theory

na'esh n نعش corpse

na'albeki n نعلبکي saucer

na'na n نعناع mint

naft n نفت petroleum

naft n نفت oil

naft kesh n نفت‌کش tanker

nafratangiz adj نفرت‌انگیز odious

nefrat avar adj نفرت‌آور stinking

nefrat dashtan az v نفرت‌داشتن‌از
hate

nafrat dashtan az v نفرت‌داشتن‌از
loathe

nefrat kardan v نفرت‌کردن detest

nefrin kardan v نفرین‌کردن curse

nafas nafas zadan v نفس‌نفس‌زدن
gasp

noufoz n نفوذ influence

nofoz *n* نفوذ influx

nafis *adj* نفيس exquisite

negh zadan *v* نق‌زدن nag

neghab *n* نقاب mask

neghab *n* نقاب veil

neghab bardashtan *v* نقاب برداشتن unmask

naghash *n* نقاش painter

naghashi *n* نقاشي painting

naghashiye shahvat angiz *n* نقاشي‌شهوت‌انگيز pornography

naghali kardan *v* نقالي‌كردن narrate

naghd *n* نقد cash

naghd adabi kardan *v* نقدادبي كردن criticize

naghdgar *n* نقدگر critic

neghres *n* نقرس gout

noghreh *n* نقره silver

noghreh saz *n* نقره‌ساز silversmith

naghsh *n* نقش infraction

naghsheh *n* نقشه scam

naghsheh *n* نقشه design

naghsheh *n* نقشه map

naghshehe pish-sakhteh *adj* نقشه پيش‌ساخته blueprint

naghsheh kargahi *n* نقشه‌كارگاهى drawing

naghsheh keshidan *v* نقشه‌كشيدن plot

naghsheh keshidan *v* نقشه‌كشيدن project

naghs *n* نقص blemish

naghs *n* نقص deficiency

naghs *n* نقص imperfection

naghz-e ahd *n* نقض‌عهد breach

noghteh *n* نقطه point

noghteh *n* نقطه dot

noghteh moghabel *n* نقطه‌مقابل counterpart

noghteh nazar *n* نقطه‌نظر standpoint

naghle ghowl *n* نقل‌قول quotation

naghle ghowl kardan *v* نقل‌قول كردن quote

nokat-e riz *n* نكات‌ريز fine print

nekahi *adj* نكاحي conjugal

negarandeh *n* نگارنده recorder

negashtan *v* نگاشتن register

negah *n* نگاه look

negah dashtan *iv* نگاه‌داشتن keep

negah dashtan *v* نگاه‌داشتن preserve

negah kardan *v* نگاه‌كردن look

negah kardan *v* نگاه‌كردن look at

negaran boudan *v* نگران‌بودن worry

negaran boudan *v* نگران‌بودن look for

negarani *n* نگراني stew

negah dari kardan *v* نگه‌داري كردن get by

negahban *n* نگهبان concierge

negahban *n* نگهبان sentry

negahban *n* نگهبان guard

negahban *n* نگهبان guardian

negahban *n* نگهبان lifeguard

negahban *n* نگهبان ward

negahdari *n* نگهداري conservation

negahdari *n* نگهداري restraint

negahdari *n* نگهداري upkeep

negahdari kardan *v* نگهداري کردن maintain

negahdari kardan *v* نگهداري کردن conserve

nam *adj* نم damp

nemad *n* نماد symbol

namaz *n* نماز prayer

namaz khandan *v* نمازخواندن pray

namayan *adj* نمايان rousing

namayan *adj* نمايان visible

namayesh *n* نمايش display

namayesh *n* نمايش exhibition

namayesh *n* نمايش performance

namayesh *n* نمايش presentation

namayeshe khandeh avar *n* نمايش خنده آور farce

namayesh dadan *v* نمايش دادن depict

namayesh dadan *v* نمايش دادن display

namayesh dadan *v* نمايش دادن exhibit

namayesh dar *adj* نمايش دار gorgeous

nemayeshi *adj* نمايشي dramatic

namayandegi *n* نمايندگي agency

namayandegi dadan *v* نمايندگي دادن delegate

namayandeh *n* نماينده deputy

namak *n* نمک salt

namaki *adj* نمکي salty

nemov *n* نمو increment

nemoud *n* نمود prospect

aspect *n* نمود aspect

nemoudar *n* نمودار chart

nemouneh *n* نمونه model

nemooneh *n* نمونه sample

nemoneh *n* نمونه example

nemuneh *n* نمونه specimen

nang *n* ننگ dishonor

nangin *adj* ننگين shameful

nano *n* ننو hammock

noh *adj* نه nine

na-in-o-na-'an *c* نه اين و نه آن nor

na-kheyr *adv* نه خير not

nahan *adj* نهان covert

nahai *adj* نهايي ultimate

nahr *n* نهر stream

nahr kandan *v* نهر کندن grip

nohomin *adj* نهمين ninth

nahang *n* نهنگ alligator

nahang *n* نهنگ whale

now kardan *v* نو کردن renew

navar *n* نوار ribbon

navar chasb *n* نوارچسب tape

navazesh *n* نوازش caress

navazesh *n* نوازش pat

navazesh kardan *v* نوازش کردن paddle

navazesh kardan *v* نوازش کردن fondle

navazesh kardan *v* نوازش کردن pat

navazandeh *n* نوازنده musician

navazandehe org *n* نوازنده ارگ organist

navazandeh-ye piyano *n* نوازنده پيانو pianist

novambre *n* نوامبر November

nowbat *n* نوبت turn

nobat-e bazi *n* نوبت بازي handout

noubate kar *n* نوبت کار shift

now javan *n* نوجوان juvenile

nowjavan *n* نوجوان (ازده‌تا19ساله) teenager

now javani *adj* نوجوانی juvenile

navad *adj* نود ninety

noor bargh asa va zood gozar *n* نوربرق‌آساوزودگذر flashlight

noor dadan *v* نوردادن gleam

noor zaif *n* نورضعیف gleam

noor kam *n* نورکم glimmer

nouri *adj* نوری optical

nowza'd *n* نوزاد newborn

noozdah *adj* نوزده nineteen

navasan *n* نوسان swing

navasan dashtan *v* نوسان‌داشتن fluctuate

nooshabeh *n* نوشابه refreshment

neveshtan *iv* نوشتن write

neveshteh *n* نوشته inscription

noshandeh *n* نوشنده drinker

no'e' ensan *n* نوع‌انسان humankind

now'e' bashar *n* نوع‌بشر mankind

noui *adj* نوعی typical

noee shaypor *n* نوعی‌شیپور cornet

no'ei moamma *n* نوعی‌معما charade

nok *n* نوک apex

nok angsht *n* نوک‌انگشت fingertip

nok-e pestan *n* نوک‌پستان nipple

noke panjeh *n* نوک‌پنجه tiptoe

nok zadan *v* نوک‌زدن peck

nowkar *n* نوکر servant

nowmid *adj* نومید hopeless

nomidi *n* نومیدی despair

naveh *n* نوه grandchild

naveh *n* نوه grandson

nevisandeh *n* نویسنده writer

ney *n* نی cane

ney *n* نی junk

ney *n* نی reed

niyaz *n* نیاز need

niyaz dashtan *v* نیازداشتن need

niyazmand *adj* نیازمند needy

niyam *n* نیام tunic

niyat *n* نیت sentiment

nitrozhen *n* نیتروژن nitrogen

neirang *n* نیرنگ deception

neyrang amiz *adj* نیرنگ‌آمیز tricky

niroo *n* نیرو strength

niroo dadan *v* نیرودادن pep

nirouye ensani *n* نیروی‌انسانی manpower

nirooye tazeh gereftan *v* نیروی‌تازه‌گرفتن recruit

niroye darya'ei *n* نیروی‌دریایی navy

nirooye havaei *n* نیروی‌هوایی air force

niz *adv* نیز also

neyzeh *n* نیزه dart

nayzeh *n* نیزه harpoon

neyzeh *n* نیزه spear

nish *n* نیش sting

nishdar *adj* نیشدار sarcastic

nishgoon *n* نیشگون nip

nishgoun gereftan *v* نیشگون‌گرفتن pinch

nik *adj* نیک good

nikotin *n* نیکوتین nicotine

nim *n* نیم half

nim baz *adj* نیم‌باز ajar

nim koreh *n* نیم‌کره hemisphere

nimrokh *n* نیم‌رخ silhouette

nimrooz *n* نیم‌روز midday

nimsal *n* نیم‌سال semester

nimkat *n* نیمکت bench

nimkat *n* نیمکت seat

nimkat *n* نیمکت sofa

nimeh-shab *n* نیمه‌شب midnight

niroo bakhsh *adj* نیروبخش
refreshing

و

va *c* و and

vohoush *n* وحوش wildlife

vabastegi *n* وابستگی affiliation

vabasteh *adj* وابسته dependent

vabasteh be dandansazi *adj*
وابسته‌به‌دندانسازی dental

vabaste be zibaei *adj* وابسته‌به
زیبایی aesthetic

vabasteh beh elm akhlagh *adj*
وابسته‌به‌علم‌اخلاق ethical

vabasteh be ghosle' ta'mid *adj*
وابسته‌به‌غسل‌تعمید baptismal

vabasteh be ghalb *adj* وابسته‌به
قلب cardiac

vabaste be kelisaye engelis *adj*
وابسته‌به‌کلیسای‌انگلیس Anglican

vabasteh be giti *adj* وابسته‌به‌گیتی
cosmic

vabasteh beh hermes-e mesri *adj*
وابسته‌به‌هرمس‌مصری hermetic

vabasteh boudan *v* وابسته‌بودن
pertain

vabasteh bodan *v* وابسته‌بودن
depend

vat *n* وات watt

vajed sharayet *adj*
واجدشرایط eligible

vahede hajm *n* واحدحجم pint

va khast *n* واخواست protest

vadar kardan *v* وادارکردن
persuade

vares *n* وارث heir

vareseh *n* وارثه heiress

varedshodan *v* واردشدن arrive

varedshodan *v* واردشدن check in

vared shavandeh *adj* واردشونده
incoming

vared kardan *v* واردکردن import

varouneh *adv* وارونه upside-down

variz *n* واریز settlement

vazhegan *n* واژگان terminology

vazhegan *n* واژگان vocabulary

vazhgoun kardan *v* واژگون‌کردن
overturn

vazhgoon kardan *v* واژگون‌کردن
topple

vazhgoon kardan *v* واژگون‌کردن
capsize

vazhgoun kardan *v* واژگون‌کردن
upset

vazhegooni *n* واژگونی reversal

vazheh *n* واژه term

vazeh *adj* واضح vivid

vaez *n* واعظ preacher

vaghe'bin *adj* واقع‌بین
down-to-earth

vaghe'e geraie *n* واقع‌گرایی realism

vaghe'an *adv* واقعا virtually

vaghe'eh *n* واقعه event

vaghe'eh *n* واقعه incident

vaghe'ei *adj* واقعی concrete

vaghei *adj* واقعی virtual

vagheiyat *n* واقعیت fact

vagheiat dadan *n* واقعیت‌دادن actualization

vaghe'ee *adj* واقعی real

vaghei *adj* واقعی actual

vaksan *n* واکسن vaccine

vaksan zadan *v* واکسن‌زدن vaccinate

vakonesh *n* واکنش response

vakonesh *n* واکنش reflex

vakonesh neshan dadan *v* واکنش نشان‌دادن react

vagozar kardan *v* واگذارکردن abdicate

vagozar kardan *v* واگذارکردن assign

vagozar kardan *v* واگذارکردن concede

vagozar kardan *iv* واگذارکردن give

vagon *n* واگن wagon

vagir *adj* واگیر contagious

vagir *adj* واگیر infectious

vala *adj* والا sublime

valedayn *n* والدین parents

vals *n* والس waltz

valiball *n* والیبال volleyball

vam *n* وام loan

van *n* وان tub

vane hammam *n* وان‌حمام bathtub

vanemood *n* وانمود pretension

vanemod kardan *v* وانمودکردن feign

vanemood kardan *v* وانمودکردن pretend

vaba *n* وبا cholera

vajab kardan *v* وجب‌کردن span

vajd *n* وجد ecstasy

vajd kardan *v* وجدکردن rejoice

vojdan *n* وجدان conscience

vajh *n* وجه fund

vajhe vasfi *n* وجه‌وصفی participle

vojood *n* وجود universe

vojood dashtan *iv* وجودداشتن be

voujoh *n* وجوه funds

vahdat *n* وحدت union

vahshat *n* وحشت panic

vahshat- avar *adj* وحشت‌آور awesome

vahshatnak *adj* وحشتناک dreadful

vahshat nak *adj* وحشتناک terrible

vahshi *adj* وحشی savage

vahshi *adj* وحشی barbaric

vahshi *adj* وحشی ferocious

vahshigari *n* وحشیگری rudeness

vahshigari *n* وحشیگری barbarism

vahshigari *n* وحشیگری savagery

vahshi gari *n* وحشیگری vandalism

vahshi *adj* وحشی wild

vakhim *adj* وخیم crucial

vakhim *adj* وخیم serious

verraj *adj* وراج talkative

verraji kardan *v* وراجی‌کردن rattle

varzesh *n* ورزش sport

varzeshkar *n* ورزشکار athlete

varzeshgah n ورزشگاه gymnasium

varzeshi adj ورزشی athletic

varzeshi n ورزشی sporty

varshekast kardan v ورشکست کردن bankrupt

varshekastegi n ورشکستگی bankruptcy

varshekasteh adj ورشکسته bankrupt

varshow n ورشو nickel

varagheh n ورقه form

varaghehe ra'ey n ورقه‌راي ballot

varam kardeh adj ورم‌کرده swollen

varame mafasel n ورم‌مفاصل arthritis

vorood n ورود arrival

vorod n ورود entree

vorod n ورود importation

voroud be khoshki n ورودبه خشکي landfill

voroude mojadad n ورودمجدد reentry

varid n ورید vein

vezaratkhaneh n وزارتخانه ministry

vazesh n وزش blast

vazagh n وزغ frog

vazn n وزن rhythm

vazn n وزن weight

vazn kardan v وزن‌کردن weigh

vezvez n وزوز buzz

vezvez kardan v وزوزکردن buzz

vezvez kardan v وزوزکردن hum

vazidan iv وزیدن blow

vazir n وزیر minister

vesatat kardan v وساطت‌کردن mediate

vasat n وسط middle

vasva's n وسواس obsession

vasvaseh n وسوسه temptation

vasvaseh kardan v وسوسه‌کردن tempt

vasi'e adj وسیع roomy

vasi'e adj وسیع large

vasileh n وسیله resource

vasileh arayesh n وسیله‌آرایش cosmetic

vasilehe' mo'ash n وسیله‌معاش livelihood

vasileh-e naghliyeh n وسیله‌نقلیه vehicle

vasleh n وصله patch

vasiyat n وصیت will

vasiyat nameh n وصیت‌نامه testament

vaz'e ghanoon n وضع‌قانون legislation

vaz'e kardan v وضع‌کردن ordain

vaz'e maliyat n وضع‌مالیات levy

vaziyat n وضعیت situation

vaz'eiyat n وضعیت status

vozouh n وضوح clarity

vazifeh v وظیفه duty

vagh vagh kardan v وغ‌وغ‌کردن bark

vafat nameh n وفات‌نامه epitaph

vafadari n وفاداري fidelity

vafadari n وفاداري loyalty

vefgh dahande n وفق‌دهنده adapter

veghahat n وقاحت obscenity

vaghar n وقار poise

vaghti keh *adv* وقتیکه when

vaghf *n* وقف devotion

vaghf shodeh *v* وقف‌شده consecrate

vaghf kardan *v* وقف کردن devote

vaghfeh *n* وقفه suspension

vakil *adv* وکیل proxy

vakil *n* وکیل attorney

vakil *n* وکیل lawyer

vagarne' *adv* وگرنه otherwise

vel kardan *iv* ول کردن forsake

vel kardan *iv* ول کردن quit

velayat *n* ولایت province

velayat *n* ولایت hometown

voltazh *n* ولتاژ voltage

velarm *adj* ولرم lukewarm

velarm *adj* ولرم tepid

velgard *n* ولگرد runner

vali *c* ولی yet

vali *c* ولی but

vitamin *n* ویتامین vitamin

virastan *v* ویراستن edit

viran *adj* ویران deserted

viran-sazi kardan *v* ویران‌سازی کردن vandalize

viran kardan *v* ویران کردن demolish

viran kardan *v* ویران کردن devastate

viran kardan *v* ویران کردن ravage

viran kardan *v* ویران کردن raze

virankonandeh *adj* ویران‌کننده devastating

virani *n* ویرانی desolation

virgool *n* ویرگول comma

virus *n* ویروس virus

vizhegi *n* ویژگی trait

vizheh *adj* ویژه peculiar

vizheh *adj* ویژه specific

violon *n* ویولن fiddle

viyolon zan *n* ویولن‌زن violinist

viyolon *n* ویلن violin

ه

hadi *n* هادي conductor

ha'van *n* هاون mortar

hay o hoy *n* هاي‌وهوي fuss

hatke namous kardan *v* هتک ناموس کردن rape

hotel *n* هتل hotel

heja *n* هجا syllable

hejdah *adj* هجده eighteen

hojoum *n* هجوم offense

hojoum avardan *v* هجوم‌آوردن raid

hojoom bordan *v* هجوم‌بردن rush

heji *n* هجی spelling

hedayat kardan *v* هدایت کردن (هواپیماوغیره) navigate

hadaf *n* هدف objective

hadaf *n* هدف target

hazyan *n* هذیان maze

hazian goftan *v* هذیان‌گفتن hallucinate

har *adj* هر any

har *adj* هر each

har *adj* هر every

har-chiz *adv* هرچیز apiece

har rooz *adj* هرروز everyday

har zaman keh *adv* هرزمان که
whenever

har koja *adv* هرکجا where

har kas *pro* هرکس everybody

harasan *adj* هراسان afraid

harj-o-marj *n* هرج‌ومرج chaos

harj o marj talab *n* هرج‌ومرج
طلب anarchist

har cheh *adj* هرچه whatever

har-do *adj* هردو both

harz dadan *v* هرزدادن waste

harzeh *n* هرزه harlot

harzeh *adj* هرزه lewd

har kasi keh *pro* هرکسی‌که
whoever

har kas *pro* هرکس anyone

har-kasi *pro* هرکسی anybody

hargez *adv* هرگز never

heram *n* هرم pyramid

heroin *n* هروئین heroin

hezar *adj* هزار thousand

hezareh *n* هزاره millennium

hazineh *n* هزینه cost

haste'ei *adj* هسته‌اي nuclear

hasti *n* هستي essence

hasti *n* هستي existence

hashtpa *n* پاهشت octopus

hashtad *adj* هشتاد eighty

hashtomin *adj* هشتمین eighth

hashti *n* هشتي porch

hoshdar *n* هشدار alarm

hoshdar dadan *v* هشداردادن warn

hoshyar *adj* هشیار wary

hazm *n* هضم digestion

haft *adj* هفت seven

haft tir *n* هفت‌تیر pistol

haftad *adj* هفتاد seventy

haftegi *adv* هفتگي weekly

haftom *adj* هفتم seventh

hafteh *n* هفته week

hefdah *adj* هفده seventeen

hegh hegh *n* هق هق sob

hol dadan *v* هل‌دادن shove

hol dadan *v* هل‌دادن push

helhelehe shadmaneh *adj* هلهله
شادمانه jubilant

holoo *n* هلو peach

helikopter *n* هلیکوپتر helicopter

helikopter *n* هلیکوپتر copter

ham arz *adj* هم‌ارز equivalent

ham-andazeh *v* هم‌اندازه
enumerate

ham andazeh *adj* هم‌اندازه equal

ham ahang *n* هم‌آهنگ consonant

ham peiman *n* هم‌پیمان ally

hamtaraz kardan *v* هم‌ترازکردن
justify

hamjavar *adj* هم‌جوار contiguous

ham setizi *n* هم‌ستیزي controversy

ham sanji *n* هم‌سنجي contrast

hamfekri kardan *v* هم‌فکري‌کردن
consult

hamkar *n* هم‌کار colleague

ham markaz *adj* هم مرکز
concentric

ham-mihan *n* هم‌میهن compatriot

ham mihan *n* هم‌میهن countryman

hamahang kardan *v* هماهنگ
کردن coordinate

hamahang konandeh *n* هماهنگ
کننده coordinator

hamayesh *n* همایش congress

hamayesh *n* همایش meeting

hamberger *n* همبرگر hamburger

hamjensbaz *adj* هم جنس باز homosexual

hamdardi *n* همدردي condolence

hamdast *n* همدست accomplice

hamdast *n* همدست collaborator

hamdasti kardan *v* همدستي کردن collaborate

hamdam *n* همدم companion

hamdami *n* همدمي sympathy

hamdigar *adj* همدیگر each other

hamrahi kardan *v* همراهي کردن accompany

hamzaman boudan *v* همزمان بودن coincide

hamzamani *n* همزماني simultaneous

hamsan *adj* همسان similar

hamsaye'gi *n* همسایگي neighborhood

hamsaye' *n* همسایه neighbor

hamsar *n* همسر spouse

ham gozardan *v* همگذاردن assemble

ham gozari *n* همگذاري assembly

hamgara bodan *v* همگرابودن converge

hamegi *adj* همگي all

ham nava *n* همنوا conformist

hamnava *adj* همنوا conformist

hamnava'ei kardan *v* همنوایي کردن conform

hameh *pro* (کس)همه everyone

hameh chiz *pro* همه چیز everything

hamvareh *adv* همواره always

hamvari *n* همواري smoothness

hamyari kardan *v* همیاري کردن cooperate

hamishegi *adj* همیشگي usual

hamisheh *adv* همیشه ever

hamin atra'f *adj* همین اطراف nearby

hanja'r *n* هنجار norm

hendel *n* هندل crank

hendevaneh *n* هندوانه watermelon

hendavaneh *n* هندوانه melon

honar *n* هنر art

honarmand *n* هنرمند craftsman

honarmandaneh *adj* هنرمندانه artistic

honarvar *n* هنرور artist

hangam *n* هنگام moment

hengameh *n* هنگامه uproar

hengami keh *c* هنگامي که while

hanuz *adv* هنوز still

hava *n* هوا weather

hava *n* هوا air

havapeyma *n* هواپیما aircraft

havapeima *n* هواپیما airplane

havapeyma roba *n* هواپیماربا hijacker

havapeyma roba'ei *v* هواپیماربایي hijack

havapeymaye fantom *n* هواپیمای فانتوم phantom

havapeimaie mosafer bary *n* هواپیمای مسافربري airliner

havapeyma'ei *n* هواپیمایي aviation

havapeyma *n* هواپیما plane

haza sanj *n* هواسنج barometer

havanavard *n* هوانورد aviator

haveye nafs *n* هوای‌نفس passion

hava'ei *adj* هوایی atmospheric

hormon *n* هورمون hormone

havas *v* هوس lust

havas *n* هوس whim

havas angiz *adj* هوس‌انگیز tempting

havas ran *adj* هوس ران sensual

houshyar *adj* هوشیار cautious

houshyar *adj* هوشیار conscious

hoshyar *adj* هوشیار sober

hoviyat *n* هویت identity

havij *n* هویج carrot

havije vahshi *n* هویج‌وحشی parsnip

hey'at *n* هیئت astronomy

heyat *n* هیئت committee

hey'at monsefeh *n* هیئت‌منصفه jury

heybat *n* هیبت awe

hipnotizm kardan *v* هیپنوتیزم کردن hypnotize

hipnotizm kardan *v* هیپنوتیزم کردن mesmerize

hayajan *v* هیجان flare-up

hayajan *n* هیجان thrill

hich *n* هیچ nothing

hich-ja *adv* هیچ جا nowhere

hich-kas *pro* هیچ‌کس nobody

hich-kas *pro* هیچکس no one

hichyek *adj* هیچیک neither

hidrojen *n* هیدروژن hydrogen

hizoum *n* هیزم firewood

hizom n هیزم woods

hiss kardan *v* هیس کردن hiss

hayoula *n* هیولا monster

ي

ya *c* یا or

ya'esegi *n* یائسگی menopause

yakhteh *n* یاخته cell

yad avardani *adj* یادآوردنی memorable

yadavari kardan *v* یادآوری کردن remind

yad dasht *n* یادداشت memo

yadegar *n* یادگار souvenir

yadgari *adj* یادگاری monumental

yadegari *n* یادگاری remembrance

yar *n* یار pal

yar *n* یار helper

yara bodan *v* یارابودن dare

yari kardan *v* یاری کردن assist

yazdahom *adj* یازدهم eleventh

yasaman *n* یاسمن jasmine

yaftan *iv* یافتن find

yaghoot *n* یاقوت ruby

komaj *n* یاکماج bun

youboosat *n* یبوست constipation

yatim *n* یتیم orphan

yakh *n* یخ ice

yakh bastan *iv* یخ بستن freeze

yakhe chizi ra ab kardan *v* یخ چیزی‌راآب کردن defrost

yakh e rood *n* یخرود glacier

yakhchal *n* یخچال icebox

yakhchal khayli sard *n* یخچال خیلی‌سرد freezer

yakhi *adj* یخی icy

yagheh *n* یقه collar

yaghinan *adv* یقینا surely

yek *art* يك an
yekdande *adj* يكدنده adamant
yeki *art* يكي a
yek *adj* يك one
yek charak *n* يک‌چارک quarter
yek shekl *n* يک شكل uniform
yek tarafeh *adj* يک‌طرفه unilateral
yek zarfe ghaza *n* يک‌ظرف‌غذا mess
yek kasi *pro* يک‌كسي somebody
yek martabeh *c* يک‌مرتبه once
yek-hezarome-geram *n* يک‌هزارم گرم milligram
yek-hezarome-litr *n* يک‌هزارم‌ليتر milliliter
yekan *n* يكان unit
yek parcheh *adj* يكپارچه seamless
yekdel *adj* يكدل wholehearted
yeksan kardan *v* يكسان‌كردن assimilate
yeksareh *adv* يكسره nonstop

yek shanbeh *n* يكشنبه Sunday
yeknavakht *adj* يكنواخت monotonous
yeknavakhti *n* يكنواختي monotony
yek navakhti *n* يكنواختي tedium
yekvaghti *adv* يكوقتى onetime
yeki *adj* يكي identical
yeganegi *n* يگانگى uniformity
yahoodiyat *adj* يهودي Jewish
yahoodiyat *n* يهوديت Judaism
yavashaki *adj* يواشكي stealthy
yoresh *n* يورش raid
youresh *n* يورش onslaught
yonani *adj* يوناني Greek
yonje *n* يونجه alfalfa
yeylagh *n* ييلاقات countryside
yaghin *adj* يقين sure
yek mosht *adj* يک‌مشت handful
yeksan *adj* يكسان same
yganeh *adj* يگانه unique
yavash *adj* يواش slow